FAMILIES OF THE SLUMS

SALVADOR MINUCHIN

BRAULIO MONTALVO

BERNARD G. GUERNEY, JR.

BERNICE L. ROSMAN

FLORENCE SCHUMER

An Exploratio

BASIC BOOKS, INC., *Publishers*

FAMILIES OF THE SLUMS

f Their Structure and Treatment

EW YORK   LONDON

SECOND PRINTING

© 1967 by Basic Books, Inc.
Library of Congress Catalog Card Number: 67–28507
Manufactured in the United States of America
Designed by Jacqueline Schuman

*To the children of the Wiltwyck School
for Boys and their families*

Those tears shining on Mama's face were falling for me. When the bus started down the street, I wanted to run back and say something to Mama. I didn't know what. I thought, maybe, I woulda said, "Mama, I didn't mean what I said, 'cause I really do care." No, I wouldn'a said that. I woulda said, "Mama, button up your coat. It's cold out here." Yeah, that's what I forgot to say to Mama.

—Claude Brown, *Manchild in the Promised Land*
(New York: Macmillan 1965; © 1965 by Claude Brown)

Preface

This book grew out of a research project in family therapy conducted at the Wiltwyck School for Boys. The project, directed by Salvador Minuchin, principal investigator, and Edgar Auerswald and Charles H. King, coinvestigators, was supported by a grant from the National Institute of Mental Health—#OM 745 (RI) MHPG (1). We wanted to study the structure and process of disorganized, low socioeconomic families that had each produced more than one acting-out (delinquent) child; and we hoped to experiment with and develop further therapeutic approaches designed for such families.

Seven therapists participated in the project. Three were psychiatrists—Salvador Minuchin, M.D., Edgar Auerswald, M.D., and Robert Stuckey, M.D. There were two social workers, Charles H. King, M.S.W., and Clara Rabinowitz, M.S.W., and two psychologists, Braulio Montalvo, M.A., and Saul Pavlin, M.A.

Two of the psychiatrists had had about ten years of experience working with children and adults, which included several years of work with underprivileged groups and substantial experience at Wiltwyck. They had both finished psychoanalytic training. One of the social workers, while primarily in administrative work at the time of the project, had previously specialized in group therapy, particularly with delinquent children and parents, for eleven years. He had also been a major participant in a study of fifty-two underprivileged and minority group children and their parents, designed to secure information pertinent to the drop-out problem at the junior and high school levels. The other social worker, in addition to having a master's degree in social work and additional training in clinical psychology, was a fully qualified analyst with hundreds of hours of experience. She had also worked over a period of years in a center which mainly served lower class Negro and Puerto Rican children and their parents. One psychologist had interned in a reformatory, had a year of work in a private clinic doing psychotherapy with a number of middle-class delinquent children, and had worked at Wiltwyck for two years. The other was an experienced psychotherapist and a certified school psychologist. One of the psychiatrists and one psychologist spoke Spanish fluently, having grown up in Spanish-speaking cultures. One of the social workers was a Negro born in New York City who had spent most of his childhood in North Carolina and then returned to New York. Thus, as a group, these therapists were in a better position to understand the cultural background of the families than are most psychotherapists.

The research team, headed by Salvador Minuchin, included Shirley Elbert, Ph.D., Bernice L. Rosman, Ph.D., and Bernard G. Guerney, Jr., Ph.D. Florence Schumer, Ph.D., joined us after the gathering of data had been completed. The administrative details of the project were handled by Louis Kerdman, M.S.W., who also interviewed and selected the families in the control group.

A great part of our current thinking on therapeutic interventions was developed after the completion of the clinical portion of the project. Reading the typed transcripts of the family sessions gave us new insights into the hows and whys of the interventions we had used with our project families and showed deficiencies in our armamentarium that we have tried to correct by developing new approaches. Most of these approaches were tested in work with nonproject families at Wiltwyck and later at the Philadelphia Child Guidance Clinic.

The structure of our book reflects this ongoing process. Part of it closely follows our thinking during the clinical phase of the project, and part discusses thinking which, though based on the initial concepts of the project, goes beyond them. Chapter 1, which discusses the methodology of our research, Chapters 3 and 4, which present transcripts of actual family sessions, and Chapter 7 and Appendixes B, C, and D, which describe the psychological instruments used and the analysis of the data, are all based largely on our initial conceptualizations. Chapters 5, 6, and 8 largely reflect our later thinking.

In general, the writing of the book followed this ongoing process. Though all the authors discussed all chapters and are responsible for the book as a whole, the main credit for the clinical chapters (3, 4, 5, 6, and 8) belongs to Salvador Minuchin and Braulio Montalvo. Chapters 1, 2, 7, and the appendixes are largely the work of Bernard G. Guerney, Jr.,

Bernice L. Rosman, and Florence Schumer. Dr. Schumer took the main responsibility for the final preparation of the entire manuscript.

We would like to express our appreciation to all the authors we have quoted in our book. We would particularly like to thank the following publications and companies, who have graciously given us permission to reproduce lengthy sections of their material: the American Ortho-psychiatric Association, the American Psychiatric Association, *Daedalus*, The Macmillan Company, and Teachers College Press.

We would also like to thank everyone connected with the project. The professional staffs of the Wiltwyck School for Boys and the Philadelphia Child Guidance Clinic were very helpful, especially the social workers at Wiltwyck, many of whom participated in the project. Jacob Cohen, Ph.D., Harriet L. Barr, Ph.D., and Patricia P. Minuchin, Ph.D., were called in as consultants to the research team. Terry Corrado was the project secretary at Wiltwyck and assisted in some of the coding of Family Task data. Frances C. Hitchcock, at the Philadelphia Child Guidance Clinic, assisted in the editing and preparation of the final manuscript. Special thanks go to the clerical staffs of both institutions and to Mrs. Louise Clempner of the Psychological Clinic of Rutgers—the State University.

Finally, for their unfailing support and encouragement, we would like to thank Louise F. Guerney, Patricia P. Minuchin, Margarita Montalvo, Abraham Rosman, and Leo Schumer.

SALVADOR MINUCHIN
BRAULIO MONTALVO
BERNARD G. GUERNEY, JR.
BERNICE L. ROSMAN
FLORENCE SCHUMER

September, 1967

Contents

Introduction   3

1   The Exploratory Research: Over-All Strategy   7

2   Overview   21

3   The Garcias and the Montgomerys: Excerpts from Transcripts of Family Treatment Sessions   42

4   The La Salles: Excerpts from Transcripts of Family Treatment Sessions   137

5   The Disorganized and Disadvantaged Family: Structure and Process   192

6   Therapeutic Intervention   244

7   Family Assessment: The Wiltwyck Family Task and Family Interaction Apperception Technique   298

8   Afterword   349

APPENDIX A   Twelve Families   381

APPENDIX B   Interaction in Selected Family Therapy Sessions: A Verbal Behavior Analysis—Findings and Coding System   391

APPENDIX C   Transcript from a Pre-Treatment Family Task
Session   421
Coding System for the Family Task   424

APPENDIX D   Wiltwyck Family Interaction Apperception
Technique (FIAT) Cards   437
Two Pre-Treatment FIAT Protocols   440
Coding System for the FIAT   443

Index   449

FAMILIES OF THE SLUMS

Introduction

On a beautiful spring afternoon two small ten- or eleven-year-old boys are playing near a brook at the Wiltwyck School for Boys. One of them, Peter, looking under some rocks, suddenly discovers a mother salamander with a litter of five. The other child, Jimmy, quickly grabs a rock and frantically attempts to crush the salamander. Peter screams, "Please don't, please don't!" Unable to stop his companion, he dashes over to the nearest counselor: "He's going to kill her, he's going to kill her!" Jimmy persists, but he is having quite a difficult time with the slippery animal. The counselor is startled and attentive; after an urgent "Where?" he runs over to the danger spot. He grabs Jimmy by the shoulders and pulls him out of the situation. He keeps his right arm on him until his fast panting diminishes; his left arm enfolds the crying Peter. "There, there, nothing is going to hurt her," he says reassuringly, and after a tense, motionless minute, the three of them walk to the dining room. Peter, pushing the counselor's arm away from him, mutters bitterly, "Man, you didn't do nothing." Surprised and let down, the counselor asks, "What do you mean you saw me do nothing?" Before Peter can answer, Jimmy begins kicking wildly at the counselor. "You mean bastard, you always pushing people around." He compels the counselor to tighten his hold again.

What was the underlying quality of this experience for Jimmy and Peter? Why did Peter, the panicky child, fail to perceive the forceful removal of Jimmy as protection, as some kind of answer to his concern? Why did Jimmy experience only an aggressive "pushing around"? What would have satisfied Peter? What would have satisfied Jimmy?

Peter continues, "Man, you didn't hit him or nothing." Nothing short of a fully violent move toward Jimmy would have satisfied Peter; yet Jimmy perceived little in the counselor's action beyond an extreme violence that was not there. Apparently their experiences were filtered only along a very narrow affective band—an "either/or" aggression dimension. What accounts for this way of experiencing in these children? Why do they relate to no components other than "aggression" in this adult? What happened to their main tasks—the rescuing or killing of the symbolic mother upon whom their attention was so focused at the beginning of the incident? Why did their tasks get lost in their intense involvement with the adult intervener?

Later, the counselor, realizing that both children had cooled down somewhat, tried to elicit from Jimmy and Peter something of their perception of this experience. "Why did you want to kill her, Jimmy?" Looking at his feet, Jimmy answers almost inaudibly, "I don't know." "Were you angry?" "No," says Jimmy. Different probings yield variations of the same response: "I don't know," or "Nothing." The child remains silent and angry at the counselor for his controlling action.

Turning toward Peter, the counselor asks, "Were you sort of frightened when you saw Jimmy wanting to kill the salamander?" Peter also answers, "I don't know." The same tried, stereotyped sequence of responses emerges regardless of the difference in questions.

Still trying to induce the children to learn something from the event and to explore possible lines of conflict resolution, the counselor suggests that they go back and see. Did the salamander protect its litter? Are they in the same place? What can be done? This is to no avail. The children are not interested. The relevance and excitement, vivid a few minutes ago, have disappeared; their concern with the salamander has vanished. Both children walk listlessly toward other directions of the field, ready to seize another situation that could give some meaning and vitality to this wonderful sunny afternoon. Two minutes from now another incident will surely occur, allowing them to find a sense of self and experience by a search for some way of establishing pre-eminence through aggression toward each other or some thing.

Impressive in this vignette, found again and again in children in many institutions as well as in the slums of the big cities, are: (1) the diffuseness of the experience—participation in a situation without sharply experiencing one's own participation; (2) the peaks of immediate reactivity to impinging stimuli and the equally fast de-fusing of affect; (3) the inability to recapture and explore an event when asked to do so; and (4) the predictable, projective nature of the forthcoming responses—"You are *doing* something to me," or "You are *not doing* anything to me."

What were the experiences of these children as they were growing up that induced this kind of stereotyped, either/or perception of the world and of their inner responses? Can we learn anything about the socialization process in their family environments, which eventually robs these children of the ability to experience and perceive the rich, subtle complexities of their surrounding life-field? Who are these children? What are their families like?

We began to be interested in the families of the delinquent children at the Wiltwyck School because we were confronted repeatedly with situations which yielded perplexities unanalyzable by the usual individualized approaches. We were faced with the irony and hopelessness of dramatic failures despite intensive, individualized treatment of these children and agonizing concern for their welfare.

At the same time, we found ourselves in an intellectual atmosphere in which the traditional views of the family's capacity to prepare the young for society were being seriously questioned. We felt surrounded by intervention programs designed to remake the family's influences without first carefully studying those influences. The emphasis in these programs was on the schools, the neighborhood, the community center, etc.—the systems outside the family. These programs seemed to have been designed with the implicit belief that the family as a social unit was too sluggish to cope in our fast-changing society.

We felt, however, that we needed more knowledge about the internal affairs of the family. Programs depending on extrafamilial agencies often were not working well, and we believed part of the reason for their failure could be found in the exploration of the culture of the family. Once we began to understand the family's basic influences, we might be able to suggest modifications of "external" programs in the light of this understanding. Consequently, our study and this book were largely limited to family interaction, though we are aware of the importance of extrafamilial factors.

Most of our work for this book was done at the Wiltwyck School for Boys, a private residential treatment center for 100 boys, eight to twelve years of age. Although originally designated for Protestant Negro delinquent boys, the school now is nondenominational, and it accepts children of any ethnic group. It educates, treats, and attends to the physical and religious needs of children who come from the most disadvantaged ghetto areas of New York City. These children, mostly from ethnic minority groups, are in trouble with the law and are seemingly destined for a life of crime, poverty, and mental and physical illness, aimed only for survival-no-matter-what; they are twisted, hurt, resentful, and hard to reach through the usual channels of psychotherapy, care, attention, and interest. They are products of the slum. They have rolled drunks and interchanged with pimps, prostitutes, and addicts in their hallways or on their crowded, smelly stoops. These children live in dire poverty; they have seen alcoholism, homosexuality, addiction, promiscuity, prostitution, and mental illness. Much is in their own families. Pathology and poverty have seeped into their lives with such a pervasive, dark insistence that many of them know of no other existence or reality. This *is* reality. You fend for yourself. If there's no food at home, you steal—from your neighbor, cousin, or local shopkeeper. If you're lucky enough to steal money, that's even better. You don't have to be home at any hour. Meal times are vague. And home may be some space in a bed with other kids. In the summer you pour out on the dirty streets and look for action and excitement. You keep moving and roaming and running. And you do things. Because when there's excitement and motion you can finally experience yourself as *somebody*.

These are the children who have challenged us. Their families are impoverished, disadvantaged, unstable, "hard-core" families. They are mostly from minority ethnic backgrounds (Negro and Puerto Rican), and they dwell in the congested, rat-infested ghettos and slums of New York City. Such children and their families can be found in the big cities throughout our nation. We do not know how "representative" the families we worked with are. But we do know that all such families have in common a difficult struggle for survival in our society. They are often "multi-agency" families. In varying degrees they are known to the police, courts, welfare facilities, shelter agencies, clinics, hospitals, social agencies, visiting nurse associations, truant officers, parole officers, and other private, city, and state institutions. And yet they are anonymous. For although they are in constant contact with the institutional representatives of society, they remain shadowy; they feel left out of the main stream, as indeed they are. Their joblessness, lack of productivity, antisocial behavior, and chronic dependency on various social institutions represent not only an enormous financial drain on the resources of the community-at-large, but also a threat to the feelings of well-being and complacency of the middle classes and the more stable elements of the working class that surround them.

CHAPTER *The Exploratory Research: Over-all Strategy*

We initiated our research program several years ago with many more questions than expectations. Our purposes were related more to exploration than to confirmation of hypotheses. We looked forward to constructing some systematic hypotheses at the *end* of the research.

In brief, the purpose of our research, which was conducted by a team of specialists in family therapy and in clinical psychology, was to shed light on the dynamics of disadvantaged, "hard-core" families which had produced more than one acting-out child (juvenile delinquent). An equally significant aspect of the research was to explore and to report on the efficacy of a specially developed technique of family treatment which employed a team of therapists working with family members as a group and in various subgroups. Concomitant with this exploration and an integral aspect of our investigation was a study of the performance of twelve delinquent-producing ("experimental") families and an equivalent control sample of ten families (which were matched to the experimental families on a number of variables but with no delinquent children) on a specially developed pictorial projective technique (The Wiltwyck Family Interaction Apperception Technique—FIAT) and in a specially developed behavioral situation (Family Task). The experimental families were tested with these instruments again after thirty family sessions. In addition, detailed analysis of the verbal interaction of family members and therapists during certain pre-selected family treatment sessions early and late in therapy has provided additional data. These data constitute the quantitative material which supplements the rich clinical and observational material our research yielded.

We should note again that our empirical investigations were not in the form of a controlled experiment. We did require, however, systematic ways of pulling together our thinking and observations so that we could begin to approach such questions as: How do our experimental and control families differ in terms of the initial measurements? Does family treatment appear to be an effective way of making inroads into the family system of our delinquent-producing families? After treatment, do the experimental families move in the direction of the control families?[1] Are there any changes in our families, even if tentative, that we can point to after treatment? What interventions in therapy seem most effective?

The field we were entering was largely uncharted. Before initiating our research, therefore, we were forced to formulate some early impressions of how these families functioned, how they saw the world, and how they behaved toward and experienced one another. These vaguely defined conceptualizations were derived not only from interviews with about thirty-five Wiltwyck families, many of whom had more than one delinquent child, but also from the therapists' experiences in family therapy of several months' duration with some of these families. Thus, we initiated our research with certain expectations, informal "hypotheses," as it were, which shaped the development of certain therapeutic techniques, the instruments we employed, and a number of quantitative variables in which we became interested. Some of these notions will be presented shortly, but we hasten to add that as our work with these families progressed, we found ourselves revising and modifying many of our a priori expectations. For we knew very little when we began, and what we thought we knew at times turned out to be erroneous.

The reader will note that ours is not a typical "clinical" study. We did

---

[1] Note that the control families could, in actuality, be compared to the experimental families only at the initiation of our research. Control families were not treated, nor were they tested at the end of the research.

not utilize traditional diagnostic categories or employ traditional tests such as intelligence tests; nor were we concerned with *individual* personality appraisals. Nosological unreliability and the questionable reliability and validity of traditional psychometric procedures when used with our present population are notorious. Traditional clinical procedures simply would not have been feasible, workable, or justifiable. What is more, even though some of our children are probably psychotic and others show primary behavior problems possibly associated with some degree of "organicity," we again were not devoting our major exploratory efforts to attempting to show correlations between delinquency patterns and such psychiatric or nosological considerations. We were concerned, rather, with the family subcultures which seem to be intrinsic to our population and with possible interventions into these subcultures in order to produce change.

Our book is more than a report of research findings. For in it we are attempting to convey not only the "hard" data—the quantitative facts—of our research, but also our thinking and experiences as we worked with these families. Although our research design pivoted around twelve families, in this book we are drawing on our entire backlog of experience with at least one hundred other Wiltwyck families as well as similar families in our day-to-day clinical work. We are not summarizing the point-by-point findings of our research, but instead we will use our findings to supplement and illustrate our discussion and as a jumping-off point with respect to a number of methodological and theoretical considerations. Our conceptualizations as presented in later chapters and intensive subsequent experiences with families similar to our research population have helped us go considerably beyond the crude, simple ideas with which we initiated our research. Without having gone through the earlier period of exploration, however, we would not have traveled the paths we find ourselves on now. With this in mind, we will briefly review our over-all research design, measurement procedures, and sample, so that we can set the stage for the chapters ahead.

General Conceptual Framework

We have already noted that when we initiated our investigation our purposes were twofold: we wanted to explore the structure and dynamics of delinquent-producing, disadvantaged, disorganized families, and we wanted to study the kinds of techniques and interventions in therapy which could best "reach" them. We began with a bias that a family therapy approach rather than an individual psychotherapeutic approach was the most appropriate treatment strategy. At the outset, we were forced to adopt several "working hypotheses" in order not only to begin to formulate therapeutic procedures, but also to devise the methods of assessment we would be developing. The next sections will describe these early "working" principles as well as the therapeutic strategy we developed in the research phase of our work with this population. These early thoughts were crucial in the development of our measurement procedures and in the kinds of variables we looked for in them. These variables were generally utilized as the framework in which the experimental and control families were compared in the initial phase of our project. They were also used to compare pre- and post-therapy responses of the experimental families. In addition, these variables and several others to be described later played a significant role in the development of the coding system employed in the Verbal Behavior Analysis of early and late sessions of therapy of the experimental families.

Working "Hypotheses"[2]

From the beginning we were impressed by the striking fact that more than three-fourths of the families to which we had been exposed had no father or stable father-figure. Moreover, even when he was in the home, the father appeared to delegate the rearing and education of the children completely to the mother, as if these areas of development were her exclusive province. For her part, the mother seemed able to respond to and interact with the children only when they were submissive or requesting that some infantile basic need be met. She seemed to conceive of her role as one of providing only for nurturing needs. Her maternal motto might have been, "I am available." But this availability did not include effective "*executive guidance*." She did not become anxious when she addressed herself to the *nurturance* needs of the child; but when she was called on to give *guidance* or to exercise *control* she did become anxious, and she communicated this to the children.

---

[2] Our major "working" variables appear in italics in this section. We were primarily concerned with *family* variables, interactions, and processes, and not individual psychological variables, despite the interconnections between the two levels of variables. Our instruments, measures, and therapeutic strategies all reflect this bias.

The mothers seemed to see themselves as powerless, helpless, and over-whelmed by the children's demands. Usually the mothers would finish by demanding protection and pity. They would gear punishment of the children to the immediate situation only. Punishment appeared inconsistent and often capricious—there was little possibility of the mother's providing controls for the children which would reflect the norms of society. She would express her impotence: "I am not able to do anything with him." When a child asked for parental guidance, the mother would respond with a counterdemand for the child's autonomy: "You should know"; or she would *relinquish authority* to a sibling: "Ask Joe."

Our conception of the parental response and the relinquishment of the executive role was that it pushed the child to look to his siblings in search of guidance, control, and direction as to how to cope with the familial and outside world. The *"parental children"* to whom authority was allocated by the parents and/or the siblings became the source of reference for executive guidance and control. If this sibling subgroup was oriented to a gang value system, these values were assimilated by the growing child.

With a sibling subgroup attempting independently and autonomously to compensate for an absence of parental guidance and executive control, special attention had to be paid to the importance of the developmental influence of the sibling subgroup upon the personality and adaptive patterns of the child. If the antecedents of acting-out and antisocial behavior rested in the relinquishment of the executive function by the parents and the formation of a sibling subsystem autonomous of parental guidance and control, certain therapeutic goals seemed indicated. These were seen as :(1) restoration or institution of executive functioning in the head of the family; (2) increase of areas of effective communication between parents and children; and (3) modification of the sibling subsystem's dynamic function and value system. These general goals helped us to develop our over-all therapeutic strategy as well as our specific interventive techniques.

The scoring variables we employed in our assessment techniques included not only the major variables described above, such as guidance, nurturance, and control, but also a number of other dimensions in the light of our early observations. It seemed to us, for example, that parental *attempts to control* the children should be of some significance, particularly in the context of assessing whether *effective control* would increase and *ineffective control* diminish as therapy progressed. *Aggression* was also seen as a variable of some importance, as was its converse, *harmonious* or *cooperative response.*

We also utilized additional variables because of their presumed importance to the therapeutic process or family dynamics, for example: *expression of positive and negative feelings, request for or giving information about feelings, acceptance of responsibility, disruptive behavior, affection, disagreement, competition,* and *leadership.*

On a gross level, we suspected that these variables, as well as a number of others not specifically mentioned here, played some part in the pathological structure and dynamics of our delinquent-producing families.[3] We expected, therefore—with more confidence in the case of some variables than others—that the families with delinquent children would: (1) differ from similar families without delinquents, and (2) show some desirable changes as therapy progressed.

Family Treatment in the Research

During our research, we evolved an over-all strategy of approach to therapy with our families which, though somewhat structured in the light of our early beliefs, allowed considerable room for expansion and modification. Our therapy sessions and the experiences of the therapist were constantly scrutinized and subjected to discussion, argument, and counter-argument. The fruits of such disputatious evaluation are now being tasted for the first time; our current therapeutic approach to such families is spelled out in some detail in Chapter 6, though it is still undergoing continuous scrutiny and modification. Our early experiences with therapy in the research phase were of extreme significance, however, for our early therapeutic methods allowed us to move in the direction of the more complex maneuvers we are using today.

We will describe the "structure" of our treatment approach in the research phase briefly below, primarily to provide a background for reading the illustrations from actual sessions in the chapters which follow and to orient the reader toward an understanding of our current procedures.

After an intake interview with a social worker, designed to secure

---

[3] Detailed description of the scoring variables employed in our instruments will be found in Chapter 7 and Appendixes B, C, and D. This section does not contain a complete list of the variables with which we worked.

background data and knowledge of the dynamics of the family, and a family interview with the therapists to structure some of the goals and procedures of therapy, the experimental families began a series of thirty weekly sessions with the understanding that these would continue for about eight months. The sessions, each of which was approximately one and one-half hours long, were designed to include all family members except children under six years of age.[4] Special arrangements were made to include the Wiltwyck child or children as well as children at various other institutions. (The index child was bussed in from upstate the night before the sessions, which he spent with his family. After the session was over he was bussed back.) Two therapists, the same two for any given family, and generally the Wiltwyck child's caseworker at the institution were involved in each family session.[5]

There were seven members on our team of therapists: three psychiatrists, two psychiatric social workers, and two clinical psychologists. The Preface to our book describes the backgrounds of the therapists in some detail. We might briefly note here that although all of them had had ample experience with our population and with group and individual therapy, they were "trained" and supervised with respect to our special techniques. Despite their heterogeneous backgrounds, all therapists performed the same functions in terms of our project. Their backgrounds were excellent; many had had specific experience with delinquent children, ethnic minorities, and the disadvantaged. Two of the therapists speak Spanish fluently (one is Argentinian and the other Puerto Rican); one is a Negro; and two had had substantial experience at the Wiltwyck School itself.

Each session was divided into three stages: Stage 1—the entire family

---

[4] Various assessment procedures (see pages 16–18) were introduced after the interviews but prior to the initiation of treatment.

[5] Sessions were conducted at the Wiltwyck School's New York City offices, in which special equipment such as one-way screens and various recording devices was available. In general, attendance of the family members was remarkably good, far exceeding our expectations in the light of their pathology and generally disorganized lives. Except for the children residing in institutions, family members came for the sessions "under their own steam." Although one of the families missed twelve of their thirty sessions, the rest canceled only infrequently and had their full quota of thirty sessions as dictated by the project plan and in accord with the original understanding. There were a number of practical difficulties in managing transportation, baby sitting, and so forth, which the therapists helped to overcome by financial aid and by their general willingness to be flexible. The Wiltwyck child's caseworker's role in the sessions was generally that of an observer and/or resource person rather than active participant. Because of her relationship to the index child, she was able to provide information concerning the child's immediate status at the residential center if necessary.

met as a group for about 30 to 40 minutes; Stage 2—two subgroups were formed, one of parents and one of children, each subgroup meeting separately with one therapist for about 30 to 40 minutes; Stage 3—the family met as a whole once again with both therapists for about 20 minutes. In addition, the index child's caseworker, when possible, was present in Stages 1 and 3 and in the sibling subgroup of Stage 2. It should also be mentioned that a post-therapy diagnostic and planning discussion by the therapists, referred to as "Stage 4" for convenience, followed each family session and usually lasted a minimum of 30 minutes. In practice, the timing of the various phases and even in some instances the procedure of breaking the sessions into stages were deliberately kept flexible and open to the clinical judgment of the therapists. All sessions were tape recorded.

Stage 1. Whole family, two therapists, and index child's caseworker. The purpose of this stage was to get the entire family to focus on a particular problem or area, and insofar as possible to assess the perceptions, attitudes, and feelings of the parental and sibling subsystems (as well as each individual's) concerning this problem. This, then, was intended to be the stage for problem-stating and initial exploration.

Stage 2. Two simultaneous, separated sessions of parents and children; one therapist (always the same one) in each session; and a caseworker in the sibling session. The intent of this stage was to explore the attitudes, perceptions, and feelings of the parents or children as individuals and in terms of subsystem cohesion in greater depth—particularly those aspects which might be inhibited in the presence of the other group. This stage also served the purpose of exploring problems which were important within one of the subsystems, but which involved the other only in a secondary way.

It was felt that when the parents were separated from the children, the children's specific value systems, perceptions, and ways of coping with the adult world would be more freely verbalized; similarly, parents removed from the intense impingement of the children on their sensibilities could begin to be helped to focus on *themselves* and their problems apart from their roles as parents.

Stage 3. Whole family, two therapists, and index child's caseworker. In this stage the therapists selectively reviewed the events which had transpired in the separate sessions for the group and the family again was encouraged to work jointly on various problems. Stage 3 was designed to enhance meaningful communication between parents and children through exploitation of the material that had emerged in the previous stages and to allow opportunity for resolving family problems important to both subsystems and particularly with respect to the interaction between subsystems. Discussion here often included suggestions as to how the family might approach certain problems at home or in future sessions.

"*Stage 4.*" Two therapists and the index child's caseworker. This "stage" followed the family sessions immediately. From the heat and light generated here—the post-session clinical discussions—we expected the emergence of an understanding of the families themselves, the effects of family therapy on them, and the modifications in certain procedures of family therapy that might be required. Whatever their deficiencies, clinical observation and judgment were regarded as the strongest weapons in our armamentarium. It was here that the specific dynamics of individuals and families on the one hand, and theory on the other, could come together to mesh or clash, thereby either providing confidence in our habitual ways of thinking or spurring new emphases and hypotheses.

Stages 1 and 3 and the children's Stage 2 sessions were conducted in a room which made it possible for these sessions to be monitored by one of the professional staff through the use of a one-way screen and a sound system. The observer recorded significant nonverbal behavior as well as who was speaking at a given moment on one track of the tape while that person was being recorded on the other track. Thus, when a session was being transcribed, the typist was not in doubt in attributing remarks to particular members of the family. The parents' Stage 2 and "Stage 4" sessions were conducted in another room and a tape recorder within the room was employed. Monitoring was not necessary in these stages, since there was no difficulty in distinguishing the remarks of the various participants from one another.

As already noted, Chapter 6 describes in considerable detail our therapeutic interventions as they emerged in the later phases of our work with families similar to those in our research population. There, primarily, we will be describing our current strategies and therapeutic procedures. These have necessarily developed out of our earlier experiences, but have departed considerably from the less sophisticated methods of our tentative beginnings in this area. Throughout, however, during our research as well as in our more complex therapeutic endeavors today, as therapists we are active, directive, and often essentially concerned with communicational patterns and processes of the family system as well as the ability of the members to perceive the issues and problems which underlie the ineffectiveness of their problem-solving attempts.

Measurement Procedures

The foregoing section on working hypotheses and relevant variables disclosed that our early thinking was based, essentially, on an inter-personal and intrafamilial framework. Since most standard psychological measuring instruments are intrapsychically and individually oriented, our task in selecting assessment procedures was not to be an easy one. The level at which to seek measurement—conscious report, "projective" report, or direct observation of interpersonal behavior—also involved much consideration. The subjects' low level of literacy, or in the case of some of the adults and many of the children, their very poor under-standing of English and inability to read created further problems. As a result, rather than attempting to stretch the interpretations of existing techniques to fit this population, and in order to tap the variables in which we were interested, we decided to devise measurement procedures of our own. We felt, too, that one should not (particularly when travel-ing unknown terrain) "put all one's eggs in one basket." And, again because we were on new terrain, we wanted our range of information to be as broad as we could reasonably make it. Thus we decided to seek measurements of these variables on more than one of the aforementioned levels. The resulting instruments and data on their reliability are described in detail in Chapter 7 and Appendixes B, C, and D. We shall describe them only briefly below.[6]

The Wiltwyck Family Interaction Apperception Technique (FIAT)

This instrument was designed to assess our major variables at a level deeper, and presumably less defensively distorted than that of conscious report. Moreover, the task required by the FIAT, although verbal, is game-like, informal, and only moderately structured and conceptual, re-quiring little or no skills in introspection.

---

[6] We also employed the Interpersonal Rating Form (IRF), which tapped the level of conscious report; that is, it was intended to provide a picture of how the various members of the family consciously perceived one another. The material which the IRF yielded was less useful for our purposes than that elicited by the other instru-ments which are mentioned in this section because the IRF taps a conscious, verbal level and requires at least some skills in introspection—areas of considerable defi-ciency in our population. We will not allude further to this instrument or results pertaining to it in this book.

The FIAT is a pictorial, apperceptive projective technique that was especially developed for use with our population in accordance with principles based on findings reported by workers using TAT-type material. Chapter 7 and Appendix D describe in detail the development of the instrument, rationale for certain methodological considerations such as the choice of the stimulus pictures, general administration and scoring procedures, results of reliability explorations, and quantitative findings.

The FIAT was individually administered to all available control and experimental family members over seven years of age and then again, in the post-treatment phase, to all available members of the experimental sample.

Analysis of Verbal Behavior in the Family Therapy Sessions

This procedure was intended to assess the nature of the family interaction and the interaction between family and therapists on the level of their overt verbal behavior. Our intent was to measure the variables of major interest as they displayed themselves in this context. Preselected sessions for all the experimental families were chosen for our analysis; neither the first nor last session was chosen because we did not want "hello" or "good-by" effects to be reflected in our data.

Our system for coding the verbal transactions of therapy sessions, although drawing on the earlier work of such men as Leary (1957) and Bales (1950), was specifically developed in terms of the particular needs of our research. A coding system was developed, pretested with transcripts of family therapy sessions with similar families, revised, and retested in attempts to make it true to clinical usage yet reliable enough to be used by nonprofessional technicians. Appendix B describes the coding system, its reliability, and the quantitative findings.

The Family Task

This assessment technique was designed to assess our major variables as shown at the level of overt behavior in an interactional context among family members but with no other participants. Our premise was that this procedure could be expected to reflect processes and changes independent of therapists' activities and of a more generalized character than those that could be observed in the therapy situation. Our method, in general, consisted of presenting to the family members as a group six "assignments" (tasks, questions) which were carried out under observation. Chapter 7 and Appendix C describe in detail the administration procedures of the Family Task, general scoring methods, reliability considerations, and qualitative as well as quantitative finding.

The Family Task was employed with all families, experimental and control, in the initial phase of our project, and again with experimental families in the post-treatment phase. All available family members over six years of age were asked to participate in the Family Task procedure.

Sample

As already indicated, we worked with two groups of disadvantaged families which we have called, for convenience, the experimental and control families. The former group was comprised of twelve families, each of which had more than one delinquent child; the control group contained ten "equivalent" families which, by the criteria noted below, had *no* delinquent children. Tables A and B (see Appendix A) summarize data on both types of families. Although detailed background data for the control families were not completely available to us, there was sufficient information about them to give us some confidence that the two groups were roughly equivalent across a number of variables except the crucial one—presence of more than one delinquent child vs. absence of any delinquent child within any family.

The experimental families were selected from a list compiled by a social worker, which contained background information on families with children at the Wiltwyck School. The criteria used for *excluding* Wiltwyck families from the project were: (1) there was only *one* delinquent child in the family; (2) the family lived outside of a reasonable commuting distance to Wiltwyck's office in New York City; (3) the mother was ill or pregnant; and (4) there were many children under five years of age. A delinquent child was defined as one who was judged so by the court, had been institutionalized or was on probation, was promiscuous or had had an out-of-wedlock child, or had been acting out in school to such a degree that he came to the attention of the Bureau of Child Guidance of the New York City Board of Education. Since Wiltwyck children are between eight and twelve years old, they were usually among the youngest of the delinquent children in the experimental families. Many of their siblings, in addition to those meeting the criteria for delinquency just designated, were troublesome in their schools and neighborhoods and could be classified as pre-delinquent.

Sixteen families were thus selected, but in the intake interview four declined to participate. A capsule description of each of the twelve experimental families and a bit of their background and circumstances at the time of first testing for the research are presented in Appendix A.

In obtaining the control group, cooperation was requested from twenty-five community centers and settlement houses, two public schools, two hospitals, a family agency, and the New York City Department of Welfare. Leads were actually secured, however, from only one of the centers and from the Department of Welfare, which was the main source. There were leads to 113 families.

Likely prospects were contacted by mail, advised of the project's needs and the fact that the family would be given twenty-five dollars in return for their cooperation, and asked to reply via an enclosed, self-addressed card. Since only about 20 per cent of the families responded in this fashion, each family was then personally visited by a social worker in an attempt to solicit participation. When a family expressed interest, they were given a screening interview and were required to give consent that the project workers could obtain confirming collateral data from schools and social agencies.

The main criterion for screening these families was that they not have any children who met the aforementioned criteria for delinquency. Severe pathology among the children in the age group desired also served as an excluding factor, for example, active psychosis, epilepsy, or mental retardation. Also, a distribution of ethnic factors, occupational level, family size, education, income, and family composition as similar as possible to that in the experimental group was sought.

Of the control family leads, the majority had to be eliminated for various reasons.[7] The remaining ten families comprise our control group.

As can be seen from Tables A and B, the two groups are roughly similar in source of support and income, ethnic composition, education of mothers, and total number of children in the family. They differ somewhat in that there is a higher proportion of absent father figures in the control families. Also, the children in the control group tend to be older than those in the experimental group. It might also be noted here (see footnote, Table B, page 389) that in the experimental group the younger

---

[7] Of these "leads," nine families were eliminated because they lived in middle-income housing projects; ten families were not reached because of having moved, or they were not at home in several attempts to contact them; forty-nine families were excluded because of: family size (10); family composition (12); delinquency (12); epilepsy (2); mental retardation (2); psychoses (3); and miscellaneous (8); thirty-five families were not interested.

category consists largely of boys, but this is not so true in the younger control group. These differences should be kept in mind when interpreting differences that are found between the two groups, as described later.

As for both groups of families, then, they are characterized by a striking absence of fathers or father-figures living at home, a plethora of children, ethnic minority status, low educational achievement of mothers, and dependence on public financial assistance (more than half of the families in each group). Apart from the absence of children designated as delinquents, the control group, in living styles and home arrangements, was generally similar to the experimental group. The control families definitely should not be regarded as "stable" or well-functioning low-income families.

Results

Our book is essentially a description of the results of our exploratory research—and more. We feel that our knowledge of the structure and dynamics of disorganized, impoverished families has been considerably expanded (see Chapter 5); we have developed appropriate new interventive techniques on the basis of our experiences with therapy in the research phase and in the light of our perspective and knowledge about these families as our research progressed (see Chapter 6). We have also developed some interesting and fruitful assessment procedures which have further expanded our knowledge (see Chapter 7 and Appendixes B, C, and D). And above all, we feel that our therapeutic attempts have been somewhat successfully applied to our research families. The chapters noted above and the final chapter of the book pull together some of the significant aspects of what we have learned.

REFERENCES

Bales, R. F., *Interaction process analysis: a method for the study of small groups*. Cambridge, Mass.: Addison-Wesley Press, Inc., 1950.
Leary, T. *Interpersonal diagnosis of personality*. New York: The Ronald Press Co., 1957.

*T*he plight of millions of impoverished Americans has captured the attention of the press, welfare agencies, local, state, and federal bureaus and the general public more than any other domestic aspect of our contemporary society, with the possible exception of civil rights. There is also a rapidly growing body of professional literature on poverty, coming from workers in many disciplines. Many of the researches on which these reports are based are relevant not only to applied, practical problems such as allocation of funds or administration of educational programs, but also to more theoretical considerations concerning human development, learning, and the relationship between culture and personality.

We are making no attempt to summarize in any way this already vast literature;[1] instead, we will raise some general considerations concerning certain characteristics of the disadvantaged.[2]

---

[1] We would like to mention, in addition to the authors discussed in these pages, Ferman, Kornbluh, and Haber (1965), and Brown (1965). The latter author has provided a personal account of his experiences growing up in Harlem, as well as of his life at the Wiltwyck School for Boys.

[2] Certain sociological features of poverty, such as geographical distribution, ethnic breakdown, or minimum baseline of income which can be used to define poverty,

Although the impoverished share many psychological characteristics with one another, groups such as the mountain people, migrant workers (e.g., Anglos and Mexicans), Southern Negroes, and Northern urban Negroes can be characterized by many cultural differences with respect to religion, dress, food habits, discrimination experienced, living conditions, and the like. We are especially interested in the ghetto-living, urban, minority group member who is experiencing poverty, discrimination, fear, crowdedness, and street-living in slums which are indescribably run down. And of this population we have concerned ourselves especially with the disorganized, pathological families that seem to possess certain characteristics which can be singled out in contrast to those of their equally impoverished but more stable neighbors. Other urban impoverished groups display special types of subcultures—the skid-row alcoholics; the rural poor living in big cities; the intellectual "beats" who are essentially aliens living in slums; the "junkies," etc. (see Harrington, 1962)—but these groups are not our immediate concern. It is the urban, disorganized family living in the midst of poverty which has drawn our interest.

The "Culture of Poverty"

One of the first writers to draw public attention to what has been called the "culture of poverty" was Harrington, who wrote: "Poverty in the United States is a culture, an institution, a way of life" (Harrington, 1962, p. 16). We are now familiar with certain characteristics of the disadvantaged such as their despair, apathy, hopelessness, and nonidentification with middle-class values. But we are also rapidly learning that the direct distribution of money or jobs and the availability of community facilities cannot make immediate inroads into the life of the poor (see Gordon, 1965).

For the psychological attributes of poverty are, to use Harrington's

---

can be found in the Appendix in Harrington (1962). Specialists differ somewhat with respect to baseline. Are there 20 million, 30 million, or 50 million Americans who can be subsumed under the designation, "the disadvantaged"? One such baseline of poverty, for example, includes families with an annual income of $3,000 or less and individuals with an income of $2,000 or less. There are a number of problems (and by no means agreement) in connection with defining the baseline of poverty. Some authors note that *inequality*, that is, the *relative* deprivation concerning the distribution of wealth and power (and in our society this is great) rather than the *absolute* deprivation is the significant variable in defining poverty and its effects.

phrase, "inherited"; that is, transmitted through the usual cultural means from generation to generation. The family is a key mechanism for transmitting these attributes. Some of the failures of public housing, for example ("old slums" vs. "new slums"), can in part be accounted for by the fact that the "personality of poverty" accompanies an impoverished family in its move from a rat-infested tenement into a shiny new housing project (Harrington, 1962).

What comprises this "inherited" "personality" of poverty? In writing about various general sociological and psychological attributes of the Negro American, Pettigrew (1964) contributed to our understanding of some of the consequences of poverty when it strikes at an ethnic minority family. Interacting variables such as economic discrimination, the ghetto subculture, a pattern of migration, and family disorganization (mother-centered families, divorce, desertion, separation, illegitimacy) result in confused masculine identity and a subsequent drive toward exaggerated masculinity. These are the concomitants of oppression and poverty, as are the self-hatred and lowering of self-esteem which have been shown to be in evidence in Negro children early in life. The world is viewed as hostile, and aspirations for achievement in this world are sharply lowered. The father has no job, or the job he does get is servile and menial; he deserts. The children grow up in a world in which success and money are associated with pimps, prostitutes, and sports celebrities, not with "middle-class respectability."[3] Pettigrew believes that certain types of stable family backgrounds can compensate for the inferior role into which the Negro is cast and which he must play at all costs.

The plight of the family is presented indirectly in Clark's documentation (1965) of the facts of life in the Harlem ghetto—the facts and figures of the crime, drug addiction, overcrowdedness, danger, disease, and joblessness. His vivid and impassioned descriptions of the despair, defeat, escapism, and agony of the slum dwellers go beyond the tables and convey the chronic and persistent pathology which neither exorcism nor excision can remove. And Sexton's description (1965) of Spanish Harlem, which is east of and borders on Harlem, further supplements this picture of poverty and despair. (Both Clark and Sexton, incidentally,

---

[3] Pettigrew is fully aware of the large numbers of middle- and upper-status Negroes for whom the above is not relevant. Actually, his set of three basic reactions to oppression—moving away from, moving toward, and moving against—further differentiates various patterns of behavior and subcultures among Negroes.

went beyond description, stressing the manner and means of organizing and utilizing the power of action and self-determination within these ghetto communities.)

We have some evidence that many of the same problems characterize different impoverished groups living in urban areas everywhere; that is, it seems that a number of variables cut across *all* cultures of poverty. For example, impoverished Arabic and Yemenite Jews in Israel are displaying familiar social and psychological problems such as dropping out of school, difficulties in deferring gratification, and difficulties in conceptualizing (Cohen, 1964). As a matter of fact, several reports coming out of urban centers in the Near and Far East confirm this general picture.

Oscar Lewis' touching portrayal of life and people in the slums of Mexico City (1959, 1961) reveals a striking familiarily and repetitiveness with respect to the overcrowded living arrangements, the plethora of children and their special sibling subsystems, the fluidity and transiency of marital bonds, and the precocity of sexual interest and activity among the children. And Gans's report of his study of a Boston slum (1962), in which he vividly described the life styles and patterns of the people (mostly of Italian extraction) who dwelled there, also contains familiar elements. For example, the "separate" lives that husbands and wives lead in their daily existence, the entrance of the children into peer group relationships almost exclusively, the action-seeking of the adolescents outside of their homes—these are familiar patterns which seem to cut across disadvantaged groups no matter what their ethnic and family composition may be.

As a matter of fact, an action-excitement orientation, special styles of communication, limited number of usable roles, etc. seem to characterize low-income groups in a wide variety of social settings; and there is every reason to believe that ethnic and racial factors do not account for these characteristics but that social class variables do (Gans, 1962).

Differences among "The Poor"

Having indicated that a number of general features characterize low-income groups, we hasten to add that failure to consider sampling and population problems when the disadvantaged are described may lead to invalid generalizations. Certain subsamples within the low-income group can be characterized by qualities of behavior, family organization, and communicational styles which set them apart from other equally impoverished samples.

Although various indices (such as employment status or education or income of household head) have been employed to differentiate certain low-income samples, it is quite common to find only global references to "the poor," "the disadvantaged," "the culturally deprived," etc. Such designations subsume what we now recognize to be a number of subgroupings and subcultures. We need to have much more information about differences along a number of dimensions among subgroups within the disadvantaged population itself.[4] Research along these lines is still in preliminary stages.

One differentiation which appears to be especially meaningful in the light of our own experiences with the poor is to separate the stable from the unstable and disorganized elements within a lower-class subculture. The latter group, although sharing certain characteristics with others in the low-income population, also shows social pathology: alcoholism, disease, mental illness, addiction, crime and delinquency, etc. (see, for example, Hylan Lewis, 1967). Pavenstedt, Malone and others have begun to make significant inroads into this area. Our book is similarly concerned with conceptualizations concerning disorganized, unstable, lower-class families rather than those coming from the working class or more stable elements of the lower class. As a matter of fact, as will be seen in the last

---

[4] One method of describing working-class and lower-class samples as well as differentiating them was proposed by Miller (1964), who used criteria based on both class (income) and status (style of life; lower class subculture; multiproblems; trouble children get into, etc.). Using a fourfold table (familial stability vs. instability; economic security vs. insecurity), Miller described four categories of low-income people; he suggested that since the strategies which could help each of these typologies vary, the correct identification of the "target" population is of utmost significance—a suggestion with which we are in agreement, since we feel, too, that the sample with which we are concerned differs considerably from many other segments of the disadvantaged population. Miller suggested that the designation "lower-class" be restricted to the fourth category in his fourfold typology, this category subsuming both economic insecurity and family instability, and the latter criterion involving a judgment which cuts across a number of variables. Riessman, Cohen, and Pearl (1964) differentiated working-class and lower-class subcultures with respect to such variables as amount of deprivation; access to middle-class goals and goods as well as groups such as unions; and degree of stability in connection with jobs, dwellings, and family composition. Both groups are similar, however, in the type of employment in which the males are involved (unskilled, manual), lack of concern with middle-class prestige, and life styles. Some authors (e.g. Cohen, 1964) differentiated lower-class from working-class cultures on the basis of a simpler criterion—degree of stability of employment patterns.

chapter, we have attempted to make differentiations *within* the disorganized group itself.

Pavenstedt (1965), on the basis of a comparative, longitudinal study of the child-rearing environments of pre-school to first-year grammar school children of upper-lower and very low lower-class families, reported a "vast difference" between them. She referred to the two types of families she studied as the stable group and the disorganized group and described the homes, attitudes, social activities, and child-rearing patterns of these two groups quite fully. Some of her vivid descriptive material does etch a striking contrast between these two types of impoverished families. Her details with respect to the disorganized families are especially relevant to our sample:

> The outstanding characteristic in these homes was that activities were impulse-determined; consistency was totally absent. The mother might stay in bed until noon while the children also were kept in bed or ran around unsupervised. Although families sometimes ate breakfast or dinner together, there was no pattern for anything. The parents often failed to discriminate between the children. A parent, incensed by the behavior of one child, was seen dealing a blow to another child who was closer. Communication by means of words hardly existed. Directions were indefinite or hung unfinished in mid-air. Reprimands were often high-pitched and angry. . . . As the children outgrew babyhood, the parents differentiated very little between the parent and child role. The parents' needs were as pressing and as often indulged as were those of the children. There was strong competition for the attention of helpful adults (pp. 94–95).

Malone (1963), in his detailed description of the behavior of preschool children from disorganized, skid-row, slum families, indicated that many aspects of their behavior predispose them to later chronic acting out and impulse disorders. They show low frustration tolerance, impulsivity and unreliable controls; dominant use of motor action for discharge; language retardation; tendency to concrete thinking; need-satisfying object relations; little evidence of constructive play or use of fantasy in play; poor sense of identity; and marked use of imitation.[5]

---

[5] Their behavior resembles that found in children with severe impulsive character disorders. Malone, however, was quick to indicate that the "developmental delay" found in such children and their general pattern of behavior are unique to disadvan-

Malone was describing a kind of pathology—a subculture of the culture of poverty—which we might bear in mind as we continue our discussion.

Gans (1962) also made a distinction between the stable and the disorganized poor. In his detailed presentation of findings based on an extensive study of native-born Americans of Italian parentage living in a Boston slum, he differentiated working-class and lower-class subcultures, stressing family structure. In the former families, the work-situation is important in maintaining the family as an intact unit despite the poverty surrounding it, although work for its own sake or work-success is of secondary importance. In the lower-class subculture, however, there is frequently only a female-based family and a marginal male, a lover or a husband, who is not a stable or important figure in the family unit. The man is generally "action-seeking," and floats from job to job and from action to action in episodic fashion.[6]

The evidence, then, in general suggests that the stable and unstable families differ considerably in patterns of family organization, child-rearing practices, and ability to withstand the demoralizing and shattering effects of poverty. Although both types of families possess a number of similar characteristics, the pathology of the unstable families is so severe as to require special inroads with respect to treatment, rehabilitation, and care.

"Strengths of the Poor" and "Cultural Deprivation"

In searching for inroads into unstable families, it is important to avoid the trap frequently encountered in early studies of a population of either overestimating or underestimating the qualities of this population and of drawing generalizations derived from observations of one segment for the total group. For instance, Gans (1962) described strengths and ad-

---

taged children, who can be differentiated from other children with severe ego problems in that the former ". . . are not withdrawn and do not attempt to become independent of people and directly gratify component instincts. . . . Rather they are hypersensitive to and almost constantly oriented to people in their efforts to obtain attention and interest and avoid pain" (p. 24). He also noted other factors such as their poor concept of time, magical thinking, the lack of "object constancy" in the home environment ("average expectable environment"), and the restriction of motor activity in their crowded homes.

[6] Gans's differentiation of "action-seekers" and "routine-seekers" was not intended to be a criterion distinguishing working-class and lower-class groups (his sample, he claimed, was composed essentially of working-class members). However, he did state that "If a class is defined by life-style . . . action-seekers can be described as lower class; routine-seekers, as working class. But not all action-seekers are lower class" (p. 31).

vantages of working-class life ("working-class culture is a positive response to the opportunities and deprivations which it encounters" [p.
267]) which, as he himself pointed out, do not fully apply to the lower-
class segments of his own sample.

Gans's description of certain aspects of the "community-life" of the
slum-dwellers with whom he worked suggests a sharing of problems, a
regularity of routine, and a leaning on one another which is in sharp
contrast to the lack of "community-life" of the disorganized families
with whom we are working.

Statements about the ingeniousness and resourcefulness of the poor in
facing their difficult life conditions imply a kind of survival-of-the-
fittest perspective—and this perspective may well be justifiable. We must
note again, however, that the strengths and assets[7] described by a number
of writers on poverty are simply not found in many individuals from
unstable, disorganized families (as in our sample), but characterize instead
(and apparently not consistently) those from the more stable families in
the low-income population. For example, Kohn (1963), in an outline of
working-class values, lists order and obedience, values which simply do
not correspond to those we found in *our* families. In fact, our material
shows a striking *absence* of some of the qualities described as "strengths
of the poor."

It could very well be that generalizations based on observations of one
segment of this large and complex population have created contradictory
trends, one slanted toward romanticizing the assets and strengths of poverty and another toward underestimating the strengths which are there.
The concept of "cultural deprivation" is an example of the latter.

---

[7] These "virtues" include variables such as: in-group spoken language and behavior
which exclude the outsider; narrowness of motivation, creativity, skills, aspirations,
and interests with the result that "job satisfaction" can be obtained from many
tedious, repetitive, rote activities; facility in a number of areas such as arithmetic
and in various manipulative, visual-motor, and mechanical activities; "creative potential" in language usage; a lack of conformity to middle-class values which might be
desirable; capacity for affectionate, loyal, intimate relationships with others; a good
sense of humor, playfulness, and gregariousness; lack of self-consciousness; informality
in peer relationships; a stress on endurance and physical prowess; ability to handle
aggressions directly, as opposed to repressing hostility or experiencing guilt; and a
basic reality-orientation. Among the children, in particular, the following qualities
have been noted: they are not overprotected, but show independence and confidence
in city traffic, self-care, care of siblings, etc. at an early age; they learn to cooperate
with siblings, and sibling rivalry is at a minimum; middle-class Oedipal conflicts are
rarely evidenced, and the child seems confident that he is loved despite frequent
physical punishment, which is not associated with loss of love; there is a lack of
intensity of parent-child relationships—as a matter of fact, Riessman (1962) suggested
that broken homes are not necessarily as "traumatic" as in the middle classes (p. 37).

We think it of some significance to indicate that the poor *do* have a culture of their own; consequently, any attempt to understand the cultural and familial patterns found in certain segments of our society necessitates a different set of research and professional tools than would be the case when we speak of deprivation. The latter concept denotes that by simply "enriching," teaching middle-class values, and building on a *tabula rasa*, we can modify the patterns of behavior found among the poor.

For example, some of the work of Deutsch and his colleagues (e.g., Deutsch, 1963) suggests that disadvantaged children grow up in an atmosphere of "stimulus deprivation" in the home and that this deprivation is in part responsible for difficulties as the children enter school. Deutsch speaks of the restricted range of experience in the home environment of the disadvantaged child. This includes, according to this author, a "minimal range" of visual stimuli, a "sparsity of objects," and a "lack of diversity of home artifacts." This creates for the child

> few opportunities to manipulate and organize the visual properties of his environment and thus perceptually to organize and discriminate the nuances of that environment. These would include figure-ground relationships and the spatial organization of the visual field. The sparsity of manipulable objects probably also hampers the development of these functions in the tactile area. For example, while these children have broomsticks and usually a ball, possibly a doll or a discarded kitchen pot to play with, they don't have the different shapes and colors and sizes to manipulate which the middle-class child has in the form of blocks which are bought just for him, or even in the variety of sizes and shapes of cooking utensils which might be available to him as playthings (p. 170).

We might note that there is by no means general agreement with Deutsch's reasoning, exemplified in the above quotation, from a strictly perceptual point of view. The visual stimulation in some sectors of such children's environments may well be richer, *more* varied, and *more* saturated with objects, especially in the world of the street and the city, than it is for their more protected middle-class peers.[8] These chil-

---

[8] The challenging issue here is the fact that these children are overdeveloped in some areas of ego functioning and underdeveloped in others. The nature of this unevenness remains to be studied.

dren have amazing ability to get around in the world with speed, facility, and agility. Figure-ground visual perception is not faulty when they roam the streets. Perhaps, on the other hand, they do poorly on a *test* of figure-ground spatial relations in a formal test situation.

We would suggest that the communicational, affective, and cognitive styles of the family members, as well as their aspirations, goals, and values are of significance, not merely the quantity or quality of playthings or the variety of pots in the home. The habitual modes of child care, parental handling, and the structure of the family system seem to be the crux of the issue because these modes create a distinctive set of behavioral, communicational, and cognitive styles in our population (described in Chapter 5) which actually *interfere* with the "enriching" and "building-block" approach. As we shall see in subsequent chapters, a treatment approach to our families involves, first, an offsetting of—an attempt to modify—their communicational, behavioral, and cognitive styles; this must take place so that other changes can occur.[9]

Poverty, Performance, and Psychological Attributes

Cognitive, Language, and Behavioral Styles

Familial patterns of interaction, on which styles of language and communication, the heightened noise levels in the crowded homes, and a number of other interpersonal variables hinge, contribute to a marked developmental delay in certain areas and serious difficulties in others. Disadvantaged children are particularly handicapped in school performance because of their atypical development of language, verbal, and conceptual skills (Bernstein, 1960, 1961, 1962, 1964; Deutsch, 1963, 1965, 1966; and John, 1963, 1965). Other stylistic features which may clash with the culture of the school are their action and excitement orientation and motoric pattern; aggression and physicalness in relating to others; reliance on paraverbal rather than verbal channels of communication; deficiencies in introspective as well as empathic skills; inattention and memory difficulties; poor time orientation; and lack of expectation of reward for successful performance. The accumulated literature even

---

[9] Riessman, in his book on the culturally deprived child (1962), despite his use of the term "deprivation," makes essentially the same point when he pleads for more effective methods of teaching the poor (see, for example, Chapter 1). His critique of the Higher Horizons program is in part based on the general orientation that it is not possible to "enrich" or "raise" the cultural level of a population without paying attention to other variables first.

suggests that marked differences in auditory discrimination exist among the different social classes, especially in the early grades, with lower-class children showing significantly poorer skills than middle-class children. Such differences decrease with age. Empirical findings have led to the conclusion, however, that although differences in perceptual skills diminish with age, language differences tend to increase (Deutsch, 1963; John, 1965).

Thus it is not surprising that disadvantaged children experience enormous difficulties in the formal school process. Poorly developed skills in a variety of areas (language, cognitive, attentive), lowered performance on timed tests and in other situations in which speed is required, as well as those special behavioral styles which characterize these children and their families create a composite picture of extremely inadequate resources for educational development in the formal school setting; "trauma" at the first school contact is to be expected for many of these children. There is evidence for believing, however, that many of these under-developed skills are subject to training and that striking increases in performance can be obtained.

In sum, there is growing agreement that interpersonal and familial relationships in severely deprived homes directly or indirectly contribute to a marked lack of the skills which are essential in the early school setting as well as in life in general—not only reading and writing, but also conceptualizing, paying attention, being task-oriented, and looking to adults for information, clarification, and reality-testing.

Psychological Testing

No wonder, then, that there is striking evidence as to the inappropriateness for this population of traditional measurement techniques and instruments of both the objective and projective variety in the school as well as the clinic.

It goes without saying that "objective" tests of personality, achievement, or intelligence (especially those which depend on reading and language skills and/or speed factors) are inadequate instruments with which to measure the performance or capacity of the disadvantaged.

Group-administered instruments are especially ineffective, and individually administered instruments do not fare much better, for motivation to do well, succeed on a test, or "impress" the examiner, and ability to sit still with sustained attention span are among a number of crucial variables which have been shown to differentiate lower-class from middle-class children. The inadequacy of the traditional intelligence tests to provide a reliable and valid measure of performance when Negroes are contrasted to whites and lower-class to middle-class children is too well known to warrant detailed specification here (for example, Semler and Iscoe [1963] have shown that WISC IQ's inadequately predict learning rates in an experimental situation for Negroes, as compared to whites; see also Deutsch and Brown [1964]). John (1965) briefly summarized some relevant material about the differential performance of white vs. non-white and lower-class vs. middle-class children on intelligence tests. She indicated some of the antecedent conditions as well as factors within the test situation itself which could account for these discrepancies (such as cultural bias within the test, extent of its verbal loading, test-taking skills of the subjects, etc.—the sort of factors noted below with respect to projective testing). For further discussion of the striking limitations of "standardized" tests when used with disadvantaged children, see Riessman (1962).

Projective techniques are also characterized by a number of serious problems when used indiscriminately with certain populations. Zubin, Eron, and Schumer (1965) have summarized many of these difficulties with respect to the use of these techniques in cross-cultural research. They have also noted, especially with regard to the Rorschach and the Thematic Apperception Test, an array of sociocultural variables which must be taken into consideration when evaluating a subject's performance. Riessman and Miller (1958) similarly discussed many of these factors, especially with regard to working- and lower-class subjects. These variables include language and verbal skills; motivational factors; cross-class rapport; hostility, or suspiciousness; educational factors; test-taking experience; response to timed situations as well as to authority figures (the examiner) and to the formal test situation itself; and the context of the testing situation (school? psychologist's office? etc.). The entire cognitive style of the subject, as a matter of fact, influences his performance to a remarkable degree, above and beyond the variable or variables presumably being tested. Moreover, norms, standardization, procedures for administration and scoring, etc. are generally not derived from lower socioeconomic populations.

Interpreter problems exist, too. Some suggestion of examiner bias in judging Rorschach protocols, for example, was reported by Haase (1964), who found that examiners consistently judged protocols which had been labeled as coming from middle-class subjects as showing greater adjustment than almost identical protocols labeled as having been produced by lower-class subjects.

Pictorial instruments involving familiar scenes, medium rather than extreme or too little ambiguity, and concrete situations are probably more appropriate than completely ambiguous instruments as far as projective techniques are concerned. Research with specially developed pictorial instruments (the Thompson TAT, for example) has indicated that a pictorial instrument which depicts Negro figures is not productive with Negroes—probably because the Negro is not familiar with taking a "Negro test" (Riessman and Miller, 1958). The development of the Wiltwyck Family Interaction Apperception Technique (FIAT) (see Chapter 7) took into account a number of these considerations.

Most of the accumulated evidence indicates in general that projective techniques, various "objective" instruments, and especially tests which have a high verbal loading or involve speed are biased against the lower-class child. Tests in which sheer productivity is related to a number of other scoring variables (such as the Rorschach and the TAT) are especially inappropriate, for there is ample evidence that productivity is related to class, educational, and cultural factors (as is, of course, verbal fluency—Zubin, Eron, and Schumer, 1965).

There is, thus, an increasing awareness that new instruments of assessment with this sample based on relevant normative data as well as more appropriate tasks are needed. The use of role-playing and various situational and behavioral situations is being explored. Beker *et al.* (1964), for example, have described a situational test which involves role-playing in standardized situations and ratings of behavior in these situations. The Family Task, a behavioral assessment technique described in Chapter 7, was developed in connection with our research. Suffice it to say that there is currently some agreement that most objective and projective techniques extant are inadequate and inappropriate for a large number of individuals in our society—ironically, precisely the segment of our population for whom various assessment techniques are becoming increasingly needed.

Psychopathology

In the last several years, a number of authors have become interested in the relationship between social status and the incidence of mental illness or degree of mental health and/or the nature of diagnosis, type of treatment utilized, duration of hospitalization, etc. (Hollingshead and Redlich, 1958; Hunt, 1960; Kornhauser, 1962; Langner, 1963; Pasamanick, *et al.*, 1959; Siegel *et al.*, 1962; and Srole *et al.*, 1962).[10]

Hollingshead and Redlich (1958), for example, reported the results of an extensive research which has often been quoted and sometimes criticized. They sought to discover whether a relationship existed between class status and the presence of mental illness in the population and whether or not the treatment received by a mentally ill person was affected by his class position. Their findings did, indeed, point to a significant relationship between class and (1) prevalence of psychiatric illness; (2) types of disorders; and (3) kind of treatment psychiatrists administered to their patients. One major criticism of this as well as similar studies, however, is that the unconscious middle-class bias of the diagnostician and/or psychiatrist may account for some of the findings in connection with variations in diagnostic entities and treatment procedures (Miller and Mishler, 1959).

Additional problems in interpreting some of the correlational findings in this area are discussed in some detail by Pasamanick *et al.* (1959) in connection with a mental disease survey of a large random sample from the city of Baltimore. For example:

> . . . it appears that on the whole lowered economic status is associated with more psychoses. How much of this is cause and how much effect we cannot state from our data. It is quite likely that both mechanisms are operative here. A certain number have probably been forced into the lower economic status because of psychosis, and it is also probable that because of a number of factors associated with low income a sizable group of elderly individuals have been forced into this psychotic group (pp. 194–195).

Despite theoretical and methodological problems, however, the empirical facts of the matter suggest that poverty and pathology are decidedly associated with each other. Of significance, then, is the fact that efforts to counsel or treat this population have been rather unsuccessful.

---

[10] Physical health variables such as prevalance of disease, type of medical service offered, frequency of medical service, incidence of specific disease entities, etc. are also related to social class.

Psychotherapy

The development of special psychotherapeutic techniques for this segment of the population was delayed because conceptualizations about treatment are dependent on the social and scientific setting of the theoretician and the population he studies.

It is a truism by now that the great psychoanalytic insights of Freud and his followers were largely derived from studies of a middle-class population. It is also well known that the theoretical richness of dynamic psychiatry was not accompanied by similar developments in the *techniques* of psychotherapy, so that until very recently we had to "make do" with a very limited armamentarium of psychotherapeutic tools. The low socioeconomic population became known as an "unreachable" group because individual psychotherapy traditionally stressed a permissive environment, a nondirective approach, and a free-associative atmosphere and relied on the patient's remembering past events and exploring affect—skills which are underdeveloped in this population.

The mental health movement, oriented toward the exploration of the field of intervention without concern for the "intervener," developed theories explaining why the low socioeconomic population was unreachable without an accompanying exploration of how therapeutic techniques could be adapted to the needs of this particular population. As a consequence, therefore, the stubborn demand of the mental health movement that the low socioeconomic population adapt their styles of pathology to available therapeutic techniques ended in a stalemate.

But now there is little doubt that traditional approaches and techniques of psychotherapy, treatment, counseling, and casework are not appropriate for most segments of the disadvantaged population (see Bernstein, 1964; Bredemeier, 1964; Gans, 1963; Gordon, 1965; Hunter, 1964; McMahon, 1964; and Visotsky, 1963, among others). Even when individual treatment programs are available to the lower classes, there is increasing evidence which suggests that they are neither efficient nor helpful. We do not know whether this is because individual therapy is not appropriate for this population or whether its failure is ascribable to the therapists' refusal to adapt their "one-to-one" techniques to the special needs of the low socioeconomic group. We do know that the goals of therapy differ between the therapist and patient. It is not surprising, therefore, that intensive individual therapy seems to be offered more frequently to the middle than to the lower classes.

Because of these problems, it has been suggested that the upper-working and middle classes have been profiting from the expanded social service and clinical facilities across the nation, but the members of disorganized, truly disadvantaged families, who need the most help in the light of their high incidence of pathology, poor school adjustment eventually leading to dropout, and marginal relationship to the main stream of society, have not been reached.

The general picture becomes more complicated when we consider the heterogeneous nature of the poor. There are, apparently, no rules-of-thumb. What might work with one subgroup might not fill the mental health needs of another. We might note, once again, the enormous need to specify the characteristics—the styles and cognitive approaches—of the subpopulations of the poor, in order to construct a frame of reference for various treatment approaches.

What are some of the specific attributes of the lower-class population as seen in the literature that serve to reduce the efficiency and success of traditional psychotherapeutic approaches? The range and content of their life experiences and value systems are in sharp contrast to those of the middle-class professional. Their lack of verbal and conceptual skills, special linguistic code, motoric "acting-out" orientation, nonintrospective approach, and the communicational difficulties between therapist and patient contribute to the serious limitations of the "talking therapies" in general. The "here-and-now" orientation of low-income patients prevents them from accepting long waiting lists, and they cannot endure a lengthy therapeutic relationship. And the one-to-one transference relationship of traditional therapies is regarded by many workers as inappropriate (Gordon, 1965; Spiegel, 1959; Visotsky, 1963).

It has been shown that the expectations of the poor when they seek help for personal problems are different from those of middle-class patients or clients. For example, the low-income patient expects and seeks suggestion, direct advice, attention to physical problems (medicine and physical treatment), warmth and support yet "authority" and structure, etc. Not finding his expectations met, he tends to drop out of therapy, often in bewilderment. (See Overall and Aronson [1963] and Hollingshead and Redlich [1958] for material concerning the expectations of the lower socioeconomic classes with respect to therapy. The former authors were concerned primarily with the reasons for the premature termination of therapy by lower-class patients.)

Although some of the suggestions for treating low-income patients are not "new" or startling in concept,[11] some attempt is being made to incorporate a number of these interventions into broader therapeutic frameworks which do represent a departure from the more conventional approaches. For example, Ruhig (1964) described a program aimed at reducing the hiatus between the physical-medical and psychiatric therapies (low-income people are suspicious of psychiatry) which consists of training and utilizing physicians in *medical* settings for psychiatric diagnosis and short-term treatment. Levine (1964) described a family treatment program (which was judged to be successful) which takes place in the *home*, and which involves the use of many auxiliary materials such as games, arts and crafts, and various other play materials as well as concrete services. And Scheidlinger (1960) reported success in the group treatment of severely deprived latency-age children utilizing a number of modifications of traditional procedures—actions instead of words were employed, for example.

The use of role-playing techniques has been strongly recommended by many workers. Riessman and Goldfarb (1964) noted the advantages of such techniques for low-income people, stressing the fact that role-playing is appropriate to the *style* of this population (motoric, action-oriented, concrete style with interest in informal, game-like situations, etc.); moreover, role-playing can reduce the distance and alienation between the middle-class professional and the lower-class patient.

While some workers speak of a need to modify and adapt the traditional techniques, and others of the need to integrate traditional, in-

---

[11] The following suggestions and techniques are among a large group culled from a sizable number of reports concerned with effective treatment of low-income groups: elimination of waiting lists, "red tape," and complicated initial interviews—that is, help should be made available immediately; short-range, practical, concrete goals; direct services, information, and advice, with a minimum stress on "talk"; direct interventions in crisis situations; elimination of psychological insight approach; involvement of more of the patient's family; financial aid for transportation, baby-sitters, etc.; coordinated, multiple interventions on any relevant level (medication, social services, financial aid, physical and medical treatment, etc.); adherence to the "presenting" problem with *specific* help around specific problems; aggressive "reaching out" to the patient; placebic and palliative approaches; short-term therapy which stresses the immediate, early stages of treatment; group methods; brief contacts only (a "20-minute hour" has been suggested; home visits (e.g., unannounced first visits to the home); the use of authority, yet warmth and support; encouraging *action* and *doing* on the part of the patient, etc.

dividual approaches with *community* facilities—church, job, school, recreation center, employment training program, etc. (e.g., Cottrell, 1964), still others are attempting to develop newer approaches which represent a departure from the traditional for use with the special subsample of the poor with which they are professionally concerned.

A number of workers concerned with the urban poor have been casting about for new ways to reach the multi-problem, "hard-core" family and to conceptualize its dynamics and structure (Geismar and La Sorte, 1964; Henry, 1958; Overton, 1953; Reiff and Scribner, 1963; Riessman, 1964a, 1964b; Tinker, 1959). Some of these workers are turning to a consideration of an approach which involves family diagnosis and family treatment.

Most of our book will be devoted to a presentation of what *we* have learned about the structure, dynamics, and family treatment of extremely disorganized families, based on, but going considerably beyond, our exploratory research.

The next two chapters illustrate parts of that exploratory research, giving transcripts of some of the interviews with the families we will call the Garcias, the Montgomerys, and the La Salles.

REFERENCES

Beker, J., Eliasoph, E., and Resnick, D. Situational testing of social psychological variables in personality. In F. Riessman, J. Cohen, and A. Pearl (Eds.), *Mental health of the poor.* New York: The Free Press of Glencoe, 1964. Pp. 259–266.

Bernstein, B. Language and social class. *Brit. J. Sociol.*, 1960, 11, 271–276.

Bernstein, B. Social class and linguistic development: a theory of social learning. In A. H. Halsey, Jean Floud, and C. A. Anderson (Eds.), *Education, economy, and society.* New York: The Free Press of Glencoe, 1961. Pp. 288–314.

Bernstein, B. Social class, linguistic codes and grammatical elements. *Lang. speech*, 1962, 5, 221–240.

Bernstein, B. Social class, speech systems, and psycho-therapy. *Brit. J. Sociol.*, 1964, 15, 54–64.

Bredemeier, H. C. The socially handicapped and the agencies: a market analysis. In F. Riessman, J. Cohen, and A. Pearl (Eds.), *Mental health of the poor.* New York: The Free Press of Glencoe, 1964. Pp. 88–109.

Brown, C. *Manchild in the promised land.* New York: The Macmillan Co., 1965.

Clark, K. *Dark ghetto: dilemmas of social power.* New York: Harper & Row, 1965.

Cohen, J. Social work and the culture of poverty. *Soc. Wk.*, 1964, **9**, 3–11.

Cottrell, L. S., Jr. Social planning, the competent community, and mental health. In *Urban America and the planning of mental health services.* Symposium No. 10. New York: Group for the Advancement of Psychiatry, 1964. Pp. 391–402.

Deutsch, M. The disadvantaged child and the learning process. In A. H. Passow (Ed.), *Education in depressed areas.* New York: Bureau of Publications, Teachers College, Columbia University, 1963. Pp. 163–179.

Deutsch, M. The role of social class in language development and cognition. *Amer. J. Orthopsychiat.*, 1965, **35**, 78–88.

Deutsch, M. Some psychosocial aspects of learning in the disadvantaged. *Teachers Coll. Rec.*, 1966, **67**, 260–275.

Deutsch, M., and Brown, B. Social influences in Negro-white intelligence differences. *J. soc. issues*, 1964, **20**, 24–35.

Ferman, L. A., Kornbluh, Joyce L., and Haber, A. (Eds.), *Poverty in America: a book of readings.* Ann Arbor: The University of Michigan Press, 1965.

Gans, H. J. *The urban villagers.* New York: The Free Press of Glencoe, 1962.

Gans, H. J. Social and physical planning for the elimination of urban poverty. *Washington Univ. law Quart.*, 1963, 2–18.

Geismar, L. L., and La Sorte, M. A. *Understanding the multi-problem family: a conceptual analysis and exploration in early identification.* New York: Association Press, 1964.

Gordon, J. E. Project CAUSE, the federal anti-poverty program, and some implications of subprofessional training. *Amer. Psychologist*, 1965, **20**, 334–343.

Haase, W. The role of socioeconomic class in examiner bias. In F. Riessman, J. Cohen, and A. Pearl (Eds.), *Mental health of the poor.* New York: The Free Press of Glencoe, 1964. Pp. 241–247.

Harrington, M. *The other America: poverty in the United States.* New York: The Macmillan Co., 1962.

Henry, Charlotte S. Motivation in non-voluntary clients. *Soc. Casewk.*, 1958, **39**, 130–138.

Hollingshead, A. B., and Redlich, F. C. *Social class and mental illness.* New York: John Wiley and Sons, 1958.

Hunt, R. G. Social class and mental illness: some implications for clinical theory and practice. *Amer. J. Psychiat.*, 1960, **116**, 1065–1069.

Hunter, D. R. Slums and social work or wishes and the double negative. In B. Rosenberg, I. Gerver, and F. W. Howton (Eds.), *Mass society in crisis: social problems and social pathology.* New York: The Macmillan Co., 1964. Pp. 594–603.

John, Vera P. The intellectual development of slum children: some preliminary findings. *Amer. J. Orthopsychiat.*, 1963, **33**, 813–822.

John, Vera P. A brief survey of research on the characteristics of children from low-income backgrounds. *Urban Educ.*, 1965, **1**, 215–222.

Kohn, M. L. Social class and parent-child relationships: an interpretation. *Amer. J. Sociol.*, 1963, **68**, 471–480.

Kornhauser, A. Toward an assessment of the mental health of factory workers: a Detroit study. *Hum. Org.*, 1962, **21**, 43–46.

Langner, T. S., *Life stress and mental health*. New York: The Free Press of Glencoe, 1963.

Levine, Rachel A. Treatment in the home. *Soc. Wk.*, 1964, **9**, 19–28.

Lewis, H. *Culture, class, and poverty*. Washington, D.C.: CROSS-TELL, 1967.

Lewis, O. *Five families*. New York: Basic Books, Inc., 1959.

Lewis, O. *The children of Sanchez*. New York: Random House, 1961.

McMahon, J. T. The working class psychiatric patient: a clinical view. In F. Riessman, J. Cohen, and A. Pearl (Eds.), *Mental health of the poor*. New York: The Free Press of Glencoe, 1964. Pp. 283–302.

Malone, C. A. Some observations on children of disorganized families and problems of acting out. *J. child Psychiat.*, 1963, **2**, 22–49.

Miller, S. M. The American lower class: a typological approach. *Soc. Res.*, 1964, **31**, 1–22.

Miller, S. M., and Mishler, E. G. Social class, mental illness, and American psychiatry: an expository review. *Milbank Memorial Fund Quart.*, 1959, **37**, 174–199.

Overall, Betty, and Aronson, H. Expectations of psychotherapy in patients of lower socioeconomic class. *Amer. J. Orthopsychiat.*, 1963, **33**, 421–430.

Overton, Alice. Serving families who "don't want help." *Soc. Casewk.*, 1953, **34**, 304–309.

Pasamanick, B., Roberts, D. W., Lemkau, P. W., and Krueger, D. B. A survey of mental disease in an urban population: prevalence by race and income. In B. Pasamanick (Ed.), *Epidemiology of mental disorder*. Washington, D.C.: The American Association for the Advancement of Science, 1959. Pp. 183–196.

Pavenstedt, Eleanor. A comparison of the child-rearing environment of upper-lower and very low-lower class families. *Amer. J. Orthopsychiat.*, 1965, **35**, 89–98. Quotation used by permission; © 1965 by the American Ortho-psychiatric Association, Inc.

Pettigrew, T. F. *A profile of the Negro American*. Princeton, N.J.: D. Van Nostrand Co., Inc., 1964.

Reiff, R., and Scribner, Sylvia. *Issues in the new national mental health program relating to labor and low-income groups*. New York: National Institute for Labor Education, June, 1963.

Riessman, F., *The culturally deprived child*. New York: Harper & Row, 1962.

Riessman, F. *New approaches to mental health treatment of labor and low income groups*. New York: National Institute for Labor Education. February, 1964. (a)

Riessman, F. New models for treatment of low income groups. *Trans-action*, 1964, **1**, 8–11 (b)

Riessman, F., Cohen, J., and Pearl, A. (Eds.), *Mental health of the poor*. New York: The Free Press of Glencoe, 1964.

Riessman, F., and Goldfarb, Jean. Role playing and the poor. *Group Psychother.*, 1964, **17**, 36–48.

Riessman, F., and Miller, S. M. Social class and projective tests. *J. proj. Tech.*, 1958, **22**, 432–439.

Ruhig, T. The Chicago Area Plan for workers' mental health. In F. Riessman, J. Cohen, and A. Pearl (Eds.), *Mental health of the poor*. New York: The Free Press of Glencoe, 1964. Pp. 422–426.

Scheidlinger, S. Experiential group treatment of severely deprived latency-age children. *Amer. J. Orthopsychiat.*, 1960, **30**, 356–368.

Semler, I. J., and Iscoe, I. Comparative and developmental study of the learning abilities of Negro and white children under four conditions. *J. educ. Psychol.*, 1963, **54**, 38–44.

Sexton, Patricia C. *Spanish Harlem: anatomy of poverty*. New York: Harper & Row, 1965.

Siegel, N. H., Kahn, R. L., Pollack, M., and Fink, M. Social class, diagnosis, and treatment in three psychiatric hospitals. *Soc. Prob.*, 1962, **10**, 191–196.

Spiegel, J. P. Some cultural aspects of transference and countertransference. In J. H. Masserman (Ed.), *Individual and familial dynamics*. New York: Grune & Stratton, Inc., 1959. Pp. 160–182.

Srole, L., Langner, T. S., Michael, S. T., Opler, M. K., and Rennie, T. A. C. *Mental health in the metropolis. Vol. I: the Midtown Manhattan study.* New York: McGraw-Hill Book Co., Inc., 1962.

Tinker, Katherine H. Casework with hard-to-reach families. *Amer. J. Orthopsychiat.*, 1959, **29**, 165–171.

Visotsky, H. M. Approaches to the treatment of the socially deprived and culturally different. In *Social work practice, 1963: selected papers, 90th annual forum, national conference on social welfare*. New York: Columbia University Press, 1963. Pp. 235–249.

Zubin, J., Eron, L., and Schumer, Florence. *An experimental approach to projective techniques*. New York: John Wiley and Sons, 1965.

CHAPTER *The Garcias and the Montgomerys: Excerpts from Transcripts of Family Treatment Sessions*[1]

*I*n the last analysis, the descriptive, clinical, and theoretical discussions which form the core of this book rest on what actually took place within the family sessions—on the behavior, verbal and nonverbal, of the family members toward each other and toward the therapists, and in addition on how the therapists responded to, initiated, reinforced, or helped in some way to modify this behavior. These transactions, interactions, or units of behavior form the raw data of our study; and the methods used to observe, record, and/or quantify these units constitute the methodology of our research.

Observations of specific task-oriented situations, projective testing, and the content analysis of verbal, interactional behavior have all yielded reportable data. Subsequent chapters will present some of this material. But we are now faced with an additional, perhaps central, task: how to communicate the "flavor" of our treatment sessions as they took place

---

[1] The reader is reminded once again that this chapter and the next present material from family therapy sessions at the time of our research. Chapter 6 discusses our *current* therapeutic strategies as they have evolved since then.

from the vantage point of the "here-and-now" of the actual interactions. The transitory shifts of mood, the fleeting, subtle exchanges and interchanges, the dramatic confrontations and insights, and the humdrum, prosaic, apathetic interactions in which nothing, it would seem, is happening—these are the warp and the woof, the very fabric of our raw material. And, further, there is a rich embroidery of other behaviors which provide a distinct, if not directly communicable, uniqueness to our sessions: the restlessness of the children, their constant distraction and seemingly senseless pattern of detachment from and involvement in what is going on, and their motor activities; the posture and stances of the family members—the facial expressions, the hopeless shrug, the direct actions, the desperate slap, the falling asleep, the walking out of the room; the sense of "things getting out of hand" on the part of the therapist or the parent; and the generally heightened noise level of our sessions.

If we can describe this framework, this brocade, as it were, we will have succeeded in providing the background for our primary objective —communication of what we have learned. We hope, in the light of this background, to present some generalizations concerning the dynamics and structures of our families, a description of the therapeutic techniques we have found to be effective with them, and a general evaluation of the expectations with which we initiated our explorations in this area.

Descriptions of case material alone will not suffice to accomplish our purpose. But excerpts from taped sessions, hopefully, will communicate more effectively and directly the transactions within the actual sessions. Although "noise," viewed as interference with the exchange of signals, was not always recorded (and "noise" often dominated the scene), our excerpts nevertheless convey some of the content (or lack of content) of what is going on, the problems with which the therapist and family members are trying to cope, and the "style" in which they talk about them. Moreover, these recorded segments convey the particular, *idiosyncratic* aspects of a specific family vividly and directly. And, indeed, it is precisely on the basis of careful listening to the taped sessions, again and again, that we have been able to isolate and scrutinize not only the more generic variables which cut across all of the families in our population, but also the more specific variables that characterize and are idiosyncratic to individual families and which assume great significance in the therapeutic goals for any particular family.

This chapter and the next, then, will present excerpts from taped sessions with three families. Two of these families were judged at the termination of our research to have developed more favorable patterns of coping with the world around them and with their own problems; one family was judged to be unchanged. Thus, in effect, we are presenting two successfully treated families and one unsuccessfully treated one. These particular families were selected for illustrative purposes not only because they are culturally and ethnically different from one another, but also because they provide us with an opportunity to present a rather broad range of comments in a number of areas.

The current chapter presents, first, excerpts from the family sessions with the Garcias—a changed family—in which the therapeutic focus was on the spouse subsystem. The second part of this chapter is devoted to a presentation of selected portions from the treatment transcripts of the Montgomerys, a more "primitive" family unit, unable to move in the direction of more adaptive patterns of behavior during treatment. The next chapter presents the La Salles, another family judged to be changed, especially with respect to the sibling subsystem.

The over-all clinical judgments of "change" or "nonchange" were based not only on our expectations and preconceptions of how these families function and what their internal structure is (see Chapter 5), but also on what we have learned during the course of our research and the resulting modifications of our original thinking. The question of why some families seemed to change and others (such as the Montgomerys) did not is a thorny one indeed. The answer is probably manifold: the depth and quality of the disorganization in a particular family system; the pathology of the individual members; the types of intrafamilial transactions that take place; the degree to which the therapist gets "trapped" by the meretricious operations of the members, and frankly, our limited knowledge not only of *how* these families function, but also of therapeutic techniques designed to treat, quite specifically, the families of our special population. But, after all, the very nature and aim of our research was to shed light on some of these issues. If we can but point the way, even tentatively, for future research in the shadowy corners of this general area, we will have fulfilled some of our goals. Some of the chapters ahead are devoted to these considerations.

It should be noted that excerpts from the transcripts are not placed in a sequential framework; we are not presenting a chronological summary of therapeutic events as they transpired. Nor is it our desire to utilize a narrative approach with despairing beginnings and happy or unhappy endings. Rather, we have isolated segments which illustrate and display some of the generic and stable variables which seem to cut across all of our disadvantaged families as well as the more specific, idiosyncratic, core problems which seem to bind the transactions of a given family into a consistent, albeit maladaptive, pattern. The very insistence of the latter type of family process created special therapeutic goals and interventions unique to some of our families, and these, too, will be highlighted when possible. Some of our interpretive comments may seem out of context or may yield the impression that we are stretching the facts to fit our preconceived notions. But we hasten to add that we have the advantage of really having known these families and their transactions over a long period of time. Chapters 5 and 6 will clarify and specify our conceptualizations with respect to all of our families (research as well as nonresearch), and give the details of our therapeutic techniques.

Since each family, despite certain generic aspects which inhere in our special population, presents a unique pattern of intrafamilial behavior, the taped sequences seem to differ for each family in terms of idiosyncratic, structural elements. As it turns out, the Garcia family, although we did not plan to use this format, does seem to communicate a sequential unfolding of familial interactions during the course of treatment. The structure and interactional processes of the Montgomery family, however, definitely prevented this unfolding in our illustrative sequences.

The segments chosen for presentation were pulled from any one of the three stages of the treatment process,[2] and from early or later sessions. The stage and session number will be indicated for each excerpt. Deletions due to poor transcription because of mechanical reasons are indicated by a series of dots. Sometimes, especially with the La Salle family transcripts presented in the next chapter, we have purposely deleted segments from the transcripts for clarity of exposition and in order to highlight certain aspects of the sequences. Deletions will always be indicated by dots. During the sessions monitors were designating the speakers on the tapes as well as indicating gross aspects of communication and

---

[2] As noted in Chapter 1, each family treatment session (two therapists, the Wiltwyck child's caseworker, and the whole family) was comprised of three stages:

Stage 1. The entire family met as a group for about 30–40 minutes.

Stage 2. Two subgroups were formed—parents and children—each subgroup meeting separately with a therapist for about 30–40 minutes. The Wiltwyck caseworker was generally present in the sibling subgroup of this phase.

Stage 3. The family members were reassembled for the final stage of the treatment session for about 20 minutes.

behavior such as nodding, leaving the room, falling asleep, etc. These will be indicated in our illustrations.

It is hoped, then, that our taped illustrations will create a background for the reader to understand the flavor of our families, the style of the individual family members, the nature of our therapeutic interventions, and some of the problems in connection with therapist-operations. Perhaps even more important, our illustrations can serve as a framework in which we can place a discussion of the significant dimensions which have emerged as a result of our explorations.

PART 1   The Garcia Family: A Profile of Change

There are four nuclear members of this family: Mrs. Garcia (Maria), who is 35 years old; Mr. Garcia (Pepe), who is 42 years old; and two sons, Juan and Felipe, who are 10 and 14 years old respectively.[3]

Mrs. Garcia is the youngest of six siblings. She grew up with a foster mother to whom she was sent with another sister at the age of one for reasons she cannot establish. She was raised in a small town in Puerto Rico. At 13 she married Mr. Garcia, whom she described during intake as "very much like my father." She portrayed her father as a promiscuous, abusive man who was also an alcoholic.

Mr. Garcia is also the youngest of six siblings. There were four sisters and an older brother. He grew up in the same town that Mrs. Garcia did. Shortly after his marriage, he entered the army for seven years of service.

According to case records, Mrs. Garcia left her husband because of a "beating" she received. She came to New York City with her infant son in 1947. A month after she arrived, Mr. Garcia followed her to New York for a reconciliation, but deserted the family when Felipe was only six months old. Mrs. Garcia then went to Family Court for nonsupport proceedings. Mr. Garcia came back to his wife in 1950 and left again in 1951. During this period Mr. Garcia lived with another woman for approximately five years.

Mr. Garcia attended school up to the eighth grade. His first job, at the age of 18, was in a grocery store owned by his sister and brother-in-law. He was later a truck driver, then a packer in a pickle factory. He

---

[3] This description of the family members is derived from a summary of their status at the time of the Wiltwyck intake. When treatment was initiated, these family members were older than indicated.

was described in a case record in a vaguely positive way: "In view of his lack of skills and poor English, Mr. Garcia seems to stay relatively long on one job."

The Garcia family first came to our attention through Juan, the younger son, who was a court referral to the Wiltwyck School. He was described by school authorities as an extremely provocative, hyperaggressive youngster who was a chronic truant, in need of residential treatment service. Juan had been examined by a school psychologist, who reported that he had obtained an IQ of 91 (WISC). A diagnostic appraisal by a Bureau of Child Guidance (Board of Education) psychiatrist suggested that Juan was a "schizoid personality with enormous hostility toward both parents." The report continued, however, that, "as he feels understood, he can respond to the benign, with his defenses against fear of isolation becoming less rigid."

At the time of our study the older son, Felipe, was institutionalized at one of the New York State training schools for behavior similar to Juan's. Arrangements were made for Felipe to be present at our family sessions, however. Felipe was described as an "enuretic, childish youngster who follows the crowd, but who makes a good, docile institutional adjustment." He was reported to have attained an IQ of 89 (WISC), and a reading grade level of 1.8. He was said to be making a "fair" school adjustment.

The material from the Garcia transcripts was taken from the first, sixth, nineteenth, and twenty-eighth sessions.[4] These segments seemed to fall into several areas: (1) husband-wife vs. mother-father; (2) father's attitude toward son's delinquency; (3) mistrust—husband and wife around money; (4) dissatisfaction—husband and wife around sexuality; (5) isolation—husband and wife; (6) mistrust to trust—father and son; (7) mistrust (revisited)—husband and wife around money; and (8) satisfaction—husband and wife around sexuality. Other aspects of the material will also be discussed from time to time. For example, attention will be drawn to certain therapeutic operations. It should be noted that the sequences in this chapter and the next are introduced primarily for illus-

---

[4] These excerpts, as noted, stress the spouse subsystem primarily. Even when first- or third-stage material is used, the parental, rather than the sibling, system is highlighted. We have deliberately not included very interesting transactions between the children, since our other case illustration families, the Montgomerys and the La Salles, do explore and illustrate such transactions at some length.

trative purposes; our brief remarks do not exhaust the multiplicity of interpretations or comments which might be made, nor are they designed to.

The Excerpts

Husband-Wife vs. Mother-Father

Sequences 1 to 5 are taken from the first session, Stage 2.

With this couple, at the outset, the therapist is trying to: (1) ascertain the degree to which family problems are seen only as reflections of "parenting" activities and roles; (2) explore their perceptions of each other as well as the history of the development of these perceptions; (3) delineate obstacles and problems in sharing; and (4) derive impressions of the over-all patterns of dominance and submission in their relationship. As will be seen, the therapist is clearly leading and orienting the direction and sequence of verbalizations. His rather directive approach is based not only on the fact that this is a first session, but also on the nature of the intellectual-cultural-conceptual-educational equipment and resources of most of the individuals in our population.

SEQUENCE 1

The sequence below demonstrates how the therapist attempts to establish a setting in which the couple is induced to do some differential, selective reporting about themselves. As can be seen, he orients his diagnostic inquiry to a particular framework: he wants the couple's attention focused on themselves as "husband and wife," rather than as "father and mother." The therapist has already formed a diagnostic impression of this family which causes him to choose husband-wife role conflicts as a focus of exploration, rather than parent-children conflicts.

Therapist: . . . So now, one of the things I feel—why I want to see husband and wife separately, is that I always think there are things that parents do not want to talk about when the children are there. And I think that that is right. There are some things that do not belong to children but belong to parents. And I think, also, that children talk—I am sure Felipe talks much more now that you aren't there than when you are, you know. It's just like that with all the children. So, I guess maybe we can talk a little bit about what's happening between you two. How are things? The things that are smooth in the family, the things that maybe could be changed a little bit. What are the areas in which you would like your wife to be a little bit different? What are the ways in which you would like your husband to be a little bit different, you know? In any marriage, there are things like that. So, you start to talk, whoever wants to talk.

Mrs. G.: You, uh, I will—you know—what I tried to say is that I would like my husband to understand more better the family, because he has been seven years out of the house. Maybe he don't have the experience of family. I didn't—I didn't have it before, you see, but now I understand that a family should be together, you see, and understand each other and . . .

SEQUENCE 2

After several minutes, dominated mostly by Mrs. Garcia's complaints about her husband's roughness to and lack of understanding of Felipe, the session continues:

Mr. G.: . . . I like to explain you something. You see, when Felipe was small kid, I loved very, very much everything he did. But when I returned back to home, I don't know, my son was different. Something different in Felipe that I don't like. In other words, I don't like the way he don't respect his mother . . . because he say—excuse me —he say "shit." . . .

Therapist: Uh-huh.

Mr. G.: He says "go to hell" to his mother. I don't like to see that, because I don't do that to my wife. You see, sometimes I feel mad about that.

Therapist: Uh-huh.

Mr. G.: When I tell something to him, I tell him "Felipe, don't do that." So he do it. He do it and he do it in bad way, sort of like, uh, to be in . . .

Therapist: Uh-huh, he's like a matador.

Mr. G.: Something like that. Like, somebody that's different, like an animal trainer. That's what he does. And I don't like to see that. When you tell "Felipe don't do this," he'll do it. He'll do it the bad way.

Therapist: Uh-huh. On purpose.

Mr. G.: And sometimes I don't just like to be in my house. Sometimes— and—I going to get a walk.

Therapist: You know, let me point out something here. I asked Maria, I said, what do you think are the difficulties, how would you like your husband to change. And I asked you how would you like your wife to change. And you know something? I am surprised. I'll tell you, Mrs. Garcia, why I am surprised. Because you told me that you would like him to change in terms of Felipe and you are telling me something about Felipe. But the life of people, it's more than being papa and mama. I wanted to know how you want him to change so that you will be satisfied. Not Felipe. I am not interested in that now. Here, I don't talk about the children. Here I talk about you as a wife and about you as a husband, not about you as a mother, and about you as a father. Here I want to talk about you as two people that are married to each other. I know you are also parents of the children . . .

Mrs. G.: Yes.

Therapist: You as *people*. You know what I mean?

Mrs. G.: I know.

Therapist: I get the feeling that you feel that it's more important to be parents than to be husband and wife. And I don't think that that's true. You know, you must have satisfactions besides being a mother. You must have satisfactions besides being a father.

Mrs. G.: I, I, I'm not—I'm not too happy.

Therapist: Okay, then talk.

Mrs. G.: No, I am not too happy, because first place, I feel he, he don't . . . he don't love me.

SEQUENCE 3

The following sequence discloses, in addition to interesting content, how quickly the basic structure of the relationship between Mr. and Mrs. Garcia is revealed. The articulateness of Mrs. Garcia and the dominance of her role in the husband-wife relationship become clear; and there are some indications that the therapist himself is responding to Mrs. Garcia's prominence in the web of interaction among them. The scanning of problem areas and the gathering of data as to their history are also clearly illustrated in this excerpt, which occurs a few minutes after the above sequence. Note that the structure which the therapist has tried to provide is already beginning to "pay off" in terms of the content which is emerging.

Mrs. G.: When, when we got married, you see, when we got married, the the first thing—uh—he—we got a lot of destructions. A lot of destructions. Maybe, maybe it was because he don't love me. When he—when he married me before, when he—when—how you say that? Can I speak in Spanish a little bit?

Therapist: Uh-huh.

Mrs. G.: (*Speaks in Spanish.*)

Therapist: Okay. Yes. You said . . .

Mrs. G.: Uh-huh. Oh, I think that when they do something like that they don't love the girl, because I was only thirteen years old.

Therapist: You were what?

Mrs. G.: Thirteen years old.

Therapist: Thirteen years old? You feel that—that—that he married you only because you had sexual relationship before?

Mrs. G.: Uh-huh.

Therapist: And if not, he wouldn't have married you?

Mrs. G.: No. And they, they force him to marry me, you see. They force him to marry.

Therapist: Who forced him?

Mrs. G.: Ah. My father. Because—uh—you know in Puerto Rico it's not the same as here.

Therapist: I know.

Mrs. G.: And when the—they take the honor of the girl, you know, how you say it, I don't know.

Therapist: Yeah . . .

Mrs. G.: Uh-huh. And they take the honor of the girl, so the father even if . . . they try to cover that with the marriage, you see?

Therapist: Uh-huh. So this is how your marriage started . . .

Mrs. G.: I—I loved him.

Therapist: You did—but he just . . .

Mrs. G.: But I thought—you—know—I—I think that he didn't, because if he do that to a girl thirteen years old, that means that he don't want me to be . . . a bride.

Therapist: Well, I do not know. . . . This happened . . . ?

Mrs. G.: . . . I don't know, but . . . about eighteen years ago . . .

Therapist: . . . and you always felt like that? . . . and—uh—

Mrs. G.: —and I feel these things—going the same . . .

Therapist: Uh-huh. Okay, then let's try to understand. You see, what happened eighteen years ago is something—what happened now— is . . .

Mrs. G.: . . . from there—from there . . . begins the problem.

Therapist: You feel, you feel that he never loved you? Really?

Mrs. G.: No. What I mean is, if he loved me first, he marry me. He don't—he don't make nobody force him to marry me.

Therapist: I do not know that, you know. You were youngsters. You were very young people, both of you.

Mrs. G.: But in that town you—you know—you don't act like kids.

Therapist: Well, thirteen years old, I don't know. Let's—let's talk a bit about that. You know—because I—I—I'm not, I do not feel so strong like Maria feels—uh—and I know that sometimes youngsters do have sexual relations without thinking of marrying. Uh—how did you feel when—when you were forced to marry her? Probably you were not prepared to marry her at all. Were you prepared to marry?

Mr. G.: Yeah, sure.

Therapist: Did you want to marry her? . . .

Mr. G.: . . . she think—she thought that I done wrong . . .

Therapist: Yes, she said that.

Mr. G.: Suppose I don't love her. She don't see me with another woman, right?

Mrs. G.: It was a woman in his life . . .

Therapist: Yeah. Okay. It was a woman in your life. If he was seven years away, I am sure that he must have had—during the seven years —some other woman—I am sure of that.

Mr. G.: . . .

Mrs. G.: And I didn't have nobody, you see?

Mrs. G.: . . .

Therapist: Huh? Okay, so because you are different. (*Mr. G. laughs.*) Because you are different, you didn't have anybody. But he lived a different life. So you had another woman, then?

Mr. G.: Yeah . . .

Mrs. G.: Yeah, but he got her before he left, he left home.

Therapist: Okay, so . . .

Mrs. G.: Before he left home.

The above excerpt, in addition to illustrating how two partners of a marriage—perhaps for the first time—are helped to verbalize deep attitudes toward each other, also discloses the importance of culturally determined values and beliefs in shaping the nature of these attitudes. This sociocultural orientation is familiar to those who work with a Puerto Rican population. Mrs. Garcia is convinced that her husband could never have loved her, since he had sexual relations with her before they were married. The husband, reciprocally, experiences considerable pressure because he feels he must display extraordinarily clear evidence of affection in order to prove that he *does* have tender and responsible feelings despite his premarital sexual experiences with his wife. Further, even if the husband had wanted an enduring marital commitment, he does not allow the awareness of this desire to alter his role perceptions: the culture has presumably "forced" him into an alliance. Bitterness and suspicion prevail, even at the beginning of a marriage. These crucial and significant attitudes toward one another, it should be noted, were brought to light when the *beginnings* of the marriage were reviewed, a diagnostic aid which is frequently highly revealing.[5]

SEQUENCE 4

After a brief interchange between the therapist and Mrs. Garcia, the session continues along lines already established; that is, further exploration of how each partner perceives the other.

Mrs. G.: I say that . . . a secret man.

Mr. G.: No, that's what she says.

Therapist: That he is a secret man?

Mrs. G.: Yeah, that he, uh, I don't know that he, I don't understand, but—every time I talk to him, I try to get him out of him. But he don't talk. He just make me laugh and—he—uh—make me tickles and everything. And and he don't tell me what I really want him to tell me.

Therapist: Like what?

Mrs. G.: Well, when I say something to him, you see, I tell him, "Pepe, you have to change and, if we want to, to be a very good wife, and, and husband and wife and raise children . . . and everything, we first, we have to, to love each other and, and we have to—ah—understand each other and everything." And I tell him, and you know, taking family out, and, uh, you know, I try, I try to . . .

Therapist: Now, let's talk with him a moment. Because you talk almost all the time, and let's give Pepe a chance to talk. Okay?

Mrs. G.: Okay.

Therapist: Now, Pepe, you come out now and you tell us. What do you think about—uh . . .

Mrs. G.: . . .

Mr. G.: . . .

Therapist: Your wife is complaining that you don't love her. She also is saying that, uh, it was because you didn't love her in the beginning.

---

[5] See Virginia Satir, *Conjoint family therapy*, Science and Behavior Books, Inc., 1964, Palo Alto, California, especially pp. 6–19, for further discussion of this point.

And she is saying that in some ways, you do not, uh, she would like you to be more . . . more—spend more time with the family and take them out and so on. Now, this is what she said. She also said that you probably don't love her, because when you were away seven years, you had another woman. Okay. Now instead of answering to all those things, I would like you to tell me in what ways your wife is not satisfying you, in the same way which she talked about in what way you don't satisfy her.

Mr. G.: . . .

Therapist: What are the things about your wife that you think should be different?

Mr. G.: Well, she says that I don't love her, but I—I don't think that is true, because—all the time . . . I got something in mind. I explain to her.

Therapist: Uh-huh.

Mr. G.: When I going to do something, I telling to her. When I go outside, I telling to her . . . You know, because I . . . (*Speaks in Spanish.*)

Therapist: Yeah.

Mr. G.: I have to say . . . (*Speaks in Spanish.*) So I take one day off, maybe Saturday or Sunday, but then it will be late, you see, because I don't want to miss on something like that. When I read too much, she don't like that.

Mrs. G.: Oh.

Mr. G.: And if she thinks I have thing with another woman, you want to know something?

Mrs. G.: It is a great difference . . .

Mr. G.: (*Speaks in Spanish.*) . . . because some people think that—uh—because they don't appreciate her. I appreciate my wife because I love my wife . . .

Mrs. G.: Appreciate and love is not the same. (*To the therapist:*) What do you think about it?

Therapist: Well, I still don't think anything. I am still listening.

Mrs. G.: Yes, you do.

Therapist: What?

Mr. G.: She said that I don't love her . . . I, when I don't love somebody, I telling to her. When I . . . telling to somebody, I don't love you—I don't love you.

Therapist: Uh-huh.

Mr. G.: . . . I telling to her.

Therapist: Uh-huh.

Mr. G.: But, she don't think it that way. She think . . . she think I got all my feelings on a secret. I don't got any secrets from nobody, because I am not a rich man. I am a working man, that's all. When I go outside I go, you know, different places. Sometimes I go to the movies . . .

Therapist: Do you go with her to the movies?

Mr. G.: No, because she don't go to the movies. She . . .

Therapist: Why doesn't she go to the movies?

Mr. G.: Because the religion don't permit her.

Therapist: This—the religion—does it . . .

Mr. G.: Religion, not for me.

Therapist: Does she go out to parties?

Mr. G.: No. Sometimes (*Spanish.*) . . . other things . . .

Mrs. G.: Yeah, I go to parties . . .

Therapist: Huh?

Mrs. G.: I—I'm going to parties, but that depends on what kind of party, you see. We don't drink. And in almost all the parties that—uh—

Therapist: Yeah, but you don't need to drink. He can drink, and you don't need to.

Mr. G.: . . .

Mrs. G.: Yeah, but—uh—you know, he don't go to parties. He just go to bar, and I don't use to go to bar . . .

After a brief interchange between the therapist and Mr. Garcia, primarily about whether or not Mr. Garcia dances, the sequence continues:

Therapist: So, tell me something. Is it that you are telling me that one of the ways in which you would like your wife to change is that she should love more fun? That she—that you like still a life in which you have more satisfactions, that you feel that she's—uh—in English you call it "a wet towel"? You know what a wet towel is?

Mr. G.: . . .

Therapist: Uh—they call that someone that—that doesn't like to enjoy life.

The therapist, in the above sequences, is helping Mr. Garcia to articulate his feelings about his wife, and similarly, is encouraging Mrs. Garcia to be specific in her verbalizations of feelings about her husband. Mrs. Garcia talks about her husband's remoteness and uncommunicativeness; and he, in turn, talks about her Puritanism, and her suspiciousness of his reserved style. Problems in sharing and in feeling alienated from one another are beginning to emerge, and these are expressed in terms of concrete activities such as going together to the movies, a bar, parties, etc. The therapist is also making some attempt to help the couple perceive an important aspect of their relationship—the wife's needs to dominate and to monopolize; she even tries to force the therapist to take sides. He defines his role: "Well, I still don't think anything. I am still listening." And he prevents the wife (and at the same time makes her aware of her behavior) from excluding her husband: "Now, let's talk with him a moment. Because you talk almost all the time, and let's give Pepe a chance to talk. Okay?"

SEQUENCE 5

The session continues with the following segment. The therapist is beginning to identify, label, and characterize the problems between Mr. and Mrs. Garcia. Problems are rephrased and restated to obtain a focus on target areas which will reappear in coming sessions. The emphasis is on "What you are saying about each other."

Mrs. G.: But I used to like it . . . and—and—and I used to go with him dancing and the bar, and—uh—movies and everything before.

Therapist: Uh-huh.

Mrs. G.: I used to go every place for him—oh, I used to go—we—we dance in the—you know—in dancings and . . . and everything.

Therapist: Uh-huh.

Mrs. G.: And—uh—things was worse.

Therapist: No, but you see, I am wondering. Because you said first that you would like him to go out more with the family, with the kids.

Mrs. G.: Oh, but what I mean . . .

Therapist: . . . But let's say that you said that you would like him to take *you*. You are a very important part of the family. You see, here in this meeting I have with both of you, I want to forget that you have children. I want to remember you, at this moment, only as husband and wife. Now, it, correct me if I am wrong, it seemed to me that you are saying, seemed to me that you are saying "He doesn't love me because he doesn't spend enough time really with—with me," and—uh—I think that he is saying, "Well, I would like to spend time with you if you would like to do the kind of things that I would like to do." Does he say that or not? Are you saying that?

Mrs. G.: ...

Mr. G.: No, I wouldn't say that.

Therapist: Well, then I am wrong.

Mr. G.: In one way, sometimes she invite me to go to a party ... a wedding or something like that—but ... (*in Spanish.*)

Therapist: ...?

Mr. G.: ... wedding ...

Mrs. G.: Party or wedding that they make in church, and sisters—

Therapist: Uh-huh.

Mr. G.: ... the religion. But, what I going to do about it? Because I don't ... Sometimes they eat a piece of cake. What you gonna do with ... her to realize that?

Therapist: Uh-huh. You don't think that's fun?

Mr. G.: I don't think that it's fair to me, because the only thing they have. They married in the—they married in the same house—and, you see—

Therapist: Uh-huh.

Mr. G.: I don't want to go ... over there, looking like that, because I ...

Therapist: He feels—he feels out of place.

Mrs. G.: And I feel out of place to be in the bar.

Therapist: Uh-huh.

Mrs. G.: —and to be in a place that I never use to go—I just don't like it.

Therapist: Uh-huh. So we are trying to understand what are the kinds of things that do not work. I feel that you are saying that—uh—you —that you have different ways of life. And that the things that would satisfy him do not satisfy you. And the things that satisfy you do not satisfy him. Are you saying something like that? ...

Father's Attitude toward Son's Delinquency

The sequences below convey some of the parent-operations evident in many of our families. Value is placed mainly on the whereabouts, the physical presence, of the stolen object; that is, the tangible, concrete evidence resulting *from* the child's behavior. The child, or the behavior itself, and the complex of motivations involved are seemingly ignored, as are opportunities for the child to appreciate the rightness or wrongness of his acts and the self-detrimental nature of his behavior. For Mr. Garcia is primarily concerned with the child's actions as a poor reflection on himself.

SEQUENCE 6 SIXTH SESSION, STAGE 2

There had been some interchange, just before the following sequence, about the presence of an electric saw (stolen object) inside the home, which dissipated into a desultory reporting of incidental, not entirely relevant events.

Therapist: So, what happened then?

Mrs. G.: And he still have one pigeon at home.

Therapist: Ah, but let's not run away from the electric saw. So, what did he do with the electric saw?

Mrs. G.: He took it out. I think that my husband told him. I was not there.

Mr. G.: Yes.

Mrs. G.: My husband told me to take it out from the house.

Mr. G.: Yeah, because I don't want things like that—I don't want in my home. Somebody come around, and he maybe think that I was asking my son to steal.

Mrs. G.: You know something, Pepe? You don't suppose to tell him to take it out. You take it out. Maybe you put it in the garbage can or something. You know what he did? When you tell him to take it out, he sell it, and he buy a knife. This knife like that, you know, like a Jim Bowie knife.

Therapist: Yes.

Mrs. G.: . . . That's what he did. The other time he told me to take the box—uh—the bicycle out of our house. He did, you know? He took it out, but he sell it and buy this BB gun, right? Now, he told him to take that thing out, so he sell it—and—and—he buy a knife.

Mr. G.: He told me—he told me—not now—because that belongs to a friend of his. Because—I don't want to see that thing over here.

Therapist: Tell me something, Pepe. Why didn't you give it back to the police?

Mr. G.: I tried to do my best, you know.

Therapist: No, no. Why didn't you take Felipe with this thing, and take both to the police and say . . .

Mrs. G.: I used to do that—but—uh—you know . . .

Mr. G.: . . . do that before.

Therapist: . . . but, I think that this is necessary, because, if not, what Felipe feels is you are concerned only with safety. But then, he will go steal and put that and—and hide it some place. It seems to me that—are you concerned only with your safety, or are you concerned only with what he does?

Mr. G.: Thinking to take him over there, but every time, the next day, when I wake up, you know, he's woke up and run away. He come late, you know.

The therapist, in the above segment, refocuses the attention of the family on the matter at hand. If this is not done, the interchanges in our sessions often become disjointed monologues in which problems are not articulated or verbalized—or even experienced, perhaps, as problems. Mr. Garcia has been verbalizing attitudes about the stolen object and its removal, and, as noted, not about the child himself or the act of stealing. The therapist not only informs Mr. Garcia that there are alternative patterns of behavior, but does so rather insistently. He poses a conflict between Mr. Garcia's emphasis on his own safety and the behavior of the child. The problem and its inherent conflict are thus directly articulated by the therapist. Mrs. Garcia apparently delegates to Mr. Garcia the responsibility for handling the family members' antisocial acts. She questions, and obviously attempts to guide him. She has salience in the family structure. But the therapist is not, at this time, responding correctively to the implied power distribution in the family or to its particular structural characteristics, for Mrs. Garcia has expressed a positive, helpful approach with which the therapist is in agreement. He is thus, in a sense, allying himself with her and reinforcing her dominant position in relation to Mr. Garcia.

Sequences 7 and 8 are from the sixth session, Stage 3.

SEQUENCE 7

The overemphasis on the external rather than the internal consequences of the child's behavior presents Mr. Garcia with a boomerang when he attempts to clarify the issues pertaining to his son's delinquent act.

Therapist: But then, how is it you are saying you didn't do anything? Where did the saw come from?

Felipe: The saw? My friend.

Mr. G.: He all the time—every time—he say his friend. Uh—when he—he stole a bicycle over there, he say, "That belong to a friend."

Felipe: (*To Mr. G.*) It do!

Mr. G.: I don't—I don't say that you stole it.

Therapist: Felipe . . .

Mr. G.: Every time anything happen, you never stole. You never do something. You never do nothing. I don't know . . . (*Spanish.*) . . .

But—uh—you don't always tell me if you got something in my house. I—I telling you, "I don't want that in the house!"
Felipe: I took it out, right?

"I don't say that you stole it," says Mr. Garcia hesitantly after his son has been denying what he did; but he also seems to be saying, "I suspect that you are doing something more than what you say." Felipe rebels against this interpretation, and Mr. Garcia retreats. This is a frequently observed "father-son" interaction, which gives the son a feeling of power over a weak authority-figure.

Mr. Garcia's comeback, "Every time anything happens you never stole. You never do something. You never do nothing. I don't know . . ." shows the kind of bitter helplessness and doubt that he is experiencing. He never fully explores the situation of the stolen bike. He is in an "I-don't-know" situation. This simple but significant plight is a chronic one of the parents in many of our families. Having insufficient information to make a meaningful confrontation, they must retreat: "I don't say that you stole it." The absence of responsible, intermediate steps of "finding out" robs them of conviction in their accusatory statements. They are left with little but suspicion and a vague sense of guilt about mistrusting or suspecting the child without really "knowing."

SEQUENCE 8

As suggested earlier, the stress by the parents on the *object*, rather than on the *act* of stealing, must eventually dull the child's awareness of and responsibility for his own behavior. Perhaps the "delinquent attitude" of the child is developed and nurtured by the parental attitude: "It's the object that counts." This cognitive attitude allows the child to defy or comply with a rather simple parental demand ("I took it out, right?") and still be free to engage in further delinquent acts. In short, if the significant issue is the stolen object, the child can relate exclusively to that issue. Below is a brief interchange, occurring a few minutes after the above sequence, which illustrates the stress on "what they are looking for," so typical of our delinquent children:

Therapist: For five dollars. To whom did you sell it?
Felipe: To a man.
Therapist: To a man? Do you know him? Because the police . . . [?]
Felipe: For what?
Therapist: Because—because it's stolen. Stolen goods that you had in your house.
Felipe: What's the police looking for? Nothing . . .

Therapist: How do you think—your father just said they were in the house.

Felipe: They wasn't looking for the saw!

Therapist: How do you know?

Felipe: Because, that saw, I had for a long time in my house. I had to hide it.

Mistrust—Husband and Wife around Money

Sequences 9 to 11 are from the sixth session, Stage 2.

In some of our families, mistrust prevails; in such families, mistrust stems from a generalized pattern of attitude among and between individual members rather than, say, from a particular relationship between one parent and one child. Mistrust in the Garcia family appears consistently, and on all levels of relationship. In particular, we find a stabilized pattern between husband and wife through frequent "delinquent" interchanges. Interpersonal skirmishes, on the adult level, characterized by lack of openness in communication, suspicion, and deception help, in this family, to establish mistrust as a central family affect; as a result, the climate in which the children are socialized is drenched with open and accepted suspiciousness, accusation and counteraccusation, mistrust, and dishonesty.

SEQUENCE 9

A sample of the covert delinquency operations on the parental level which parallels the overt delinquency operations on the children's level is disclosed in the following monologue by Mrs. Garcia. The handling of money is under scrutiny as an important area which reflects the difficulties in the development of mutuality between Mr. and Mrs. Garcia.

Therapist: You got a what?

Mrs. G.: I got a lot—uh—

Therapist: Bills?

Mrs. G.: Bills to cover. And I don't have enough money. So I went to the bank to get—I got fifty dollars in the bank. So I get to—to go over there and get twenty-five to cover my—you know—my bills and the—and the grocery store and everything. So, when I went there, the man told me—uh—"Aren't you glad that you received the check the end of the week?" I said, "What check?" He said, "The amount," uh—"the loan you took. The three hundred dollars. You already have the check, don't you?" I told him, I don't want to tell him what—what—what he told me, you know, but I said, "Well, maybe—maybe my husband got it and I don't know. Maybe it was in the mailbox and I don't have no key. But thank you anyway. I'm so glad about it," I told him. And—uh—I keep quiet because that was in my heart that I have to take a little amount of my money to pay—to pay all the bills . . . so today, I was so upset that if I—I start telling him—yesterday—I might cry or I might scream or something like that. I don't know. So I—I decide to—qu—be quiet, you know, to—so to mor—this morning he told me, he—again he told me, "Gee—uh—you know—I went to the bank yesterday and—uh—they still saying that they don't give me the money because I uh—I owe some money in the corporation." And I say, "What—you—you have the nerve to tell me that when the man told me that you already got the check and it's already changed? You know. And that upset me—and—and—he's upset me, 'cause he think that I'm trying to find out about himself. But it's not that. If I give him the signature, he don't have to hide things from me. I know that it's—uh—for the car, or to send it to Puerto Rico to—you know—to put it in an account for a house.[6] I know, but, if he is trying to hide something, maybe another thing, that it's not for those two things. So maybe, maybe, I think that it's for something else.

Therapist: Something else, like what?

Some of the intrapersonal obstacles which emerge when a marital partner attempts to assert or defend his or her rights within the marriage are evident in the above sequence. Problem-solving is delayed; there is a decision to "be quiet" under the fearful expectation of losing behavioral control or meeting a paranoid-like counterattack from her husband ("'cause he think that I'm trying to find out about himself"). To assert one's rights often means to be intrusive, to violate the unstated but essential rules of interpersonal behavior which have evolved and have become stabilized into a kind of implicit contract between the partners. To change the terms of this contract implies a revision of a long-standing policy of nonintrusion which, in the guise of respect for each partner's privacy and self-sufficiency, supports and sanctions the lack of shared responsibility and the denial of delinquency between them.

---

[6] Note that in this family there is a capacity for long-range planning and a striving for social mobility. The talk about a house, car, savings, etc., reflects aspirations and dreams which we do not find in many of our disadvantaged families. These motivational elements have facilitated therapy with this family. It might also be noted, as an aside, that installment buying characterizes many of the purchases of our Puerto Rican families. (A piano that the Garcia family had bought was repossessed after they had paid more than half its value.)

SEQUENCE 10

In this sequence, which almost immediately followed sequence 9, the therapist begins to link the delinquency on the parental level to the delinquency on the children's level. Mr. Garcia looks for avenues to escape or rationalize responsibility. He appeals to the terms of the "contract": "I never ask what you gonna do with *your* money." In effect, he seems to be saying, "It's not that I'm delinquent in hiding money from you; we agreed not to meddle into each other's business."

Therapist: Pepe, you see, that means there are just, just two things that are happening. One is delinquent behavior on the part of Felipe. And the other thing is in some way delinquent behavior with your wife on your part. So just—you were—hiding from her something. Why did you hide it from her—that?

Mr. G.: I don't hide anything.

Therapist: But you did.

Mr. G.: You know. I telling you. Sometimes when I got a hundred dollars, and—uh—or less than that—all the time when she got money, I never ask, "What you gonna do with *your* money?" You see, I said I need you to sign because I need three hundred dollars. I have to go, so maybe I send to Puerto Rico because I am interested in a house.

Mrs. G.: That's what you sent?

Mr. G.: That's right. Sometimes I got money, so I have to pay. I have to pay that—you know—so on—so on—so, I, I do my best. I help her sometimes. I have to pay some others. I have to pay another bill in finance in August, and other things. I got a hundred dollar bill. All the time she is telling me, "Ah, the first thing you going to do, to go to—to the bar." And I don't like that thing. Because she knows that.

Therapist: I think that you are attacking because you are defending yourself, you know?

SEQUENCE 11

The therapist, in the above sequence, has already begun to focus attention on certain characteristics of Mr. Garcia. He continues, in the following sequence, which flows directly from sequence 10, to articulate certain aspects of Mr. Garcia's behavior: elusiveness, and mislabeling his own delinquent behavior; delinquent behavior toward his wife as a substitute for appropriate alternatives in problem-solving; unawakened experiential resources for empathy with, or understanding of, his wife's feelings, and no understanding that mutuality is essential to the framework of marriage and family life. These are all tackled here in quick succession, without immediately evident success.

Mr. G.: Well, I—I—I don't . . .

Therapist: Pepe, why—why—why did you—why couldn't you tell her? You are deliberately lying to her. Because—because you could have said, "Look, I need the three hundred dollars and I got the three hundred dollars." Why did you need to say, "No, I didn't get it"?

Mr. G.: Well, I tell you. Sometimes you have to—to—to—

Therapist: Okay, you got some—some reason why you need this money. Okay? But . . . This reason can be all right . . . maybe—uh—you have a special debt, or maybe you need to do something.

After some brief interchanges, the therapist continues:

Therapist: Pepe, tell me something. If she would hide something from you, how would you feel? You remember how you used to feel when you were in the army? It was the same thing. You thought she was doing what you are doing now.[7]

Mr. G.: I never ask what you do with the money.

Mrs. G.: You don't have to ask me. I tell you. I—I tell you. No—nobody have to ask. How can I ask you? You are my husband.

Therapist: Pepe . . .

Mrs. G.: I—I tell you. They give me a raise. I took thirty-five dollars from the bank.

Mr. G.: That ain't my business if they give you a raise.

Mrs. G.: Well, it's your business.

Therapist: Pepe, Pepe . . . I think you are wrong. All the money that she makes is your business, because you are married. You are married and you have two children. The same way, you are sharing all the troubles with Felipe. Aren't you sharing the same troubles?

Mr. G.: Yeah.

Therapist: Well, why, then? You say that it's not your business what she makes. It *is*, because you are a family. You remember what I tell you last session? I talk about how you are not in marriage yet, you remember?

Mr. G.: Yeah, I remember.

Therapist: Well, this is one instance that shows how though you are

---

[7] When Mr. Garcia was in the army, away from home, he was plagued by suspiciousness and anger.

married, you are not in marriage. Yet, because you are, you are so separated in some ways. You see, if you would be in marriage, you know what would happen? You could have said to your wife, "Listen, there is something—that—for which I need three hundred dollars. And I cannot tell you now. And I need your help, I need your sympathy." And she would certainly, she would feel very bad and very curious and so on, but she wouldn't ask it. But she would feel bad. She has the right to feel bad. Because you would also feel bad in a situation like that. Wouldn't you feel bad?

Therapeutic neutrality toward this couple, in the above sequence, is superseded by immediate considerations of clinical appropriateness. In work with these families, it is often necessary for the therapist to take sides, and sometimes even to "sermonize" as well as to teach. Here, the therapist deliberately adopts an intimate attitude that has the components of "frankness" and "sincerity" that are so valued by segments of the Puerto Rican population.

The therapist stresses the desirability of honest and open communication and "pins down" the elusive partner, Mr. Garcia. His evasive behavior is handled by a confronting attitude and by clearly labeling the behavior in question: "deliberate lying." Alternatives to lying and being secretive are presented. Training in making empathic responses is attempted to help Mr. Garcia understand the reasonableness of his wife's feelings, such as suspicion and anger. And redefinition of the terms of the marriage contract—the rights and duties within a marriage—is openly introduced.

Dissatisfaction—Husband and Wife around Sexuality

Sequences 12 and 13 are from the nineteenth session, Stage 2.

The coming to terms with basic arrangements of mutual sexual satisfaction is an inevitable process of interpersonal problem-solving on the husband-wife level. The possibility that disturbances in this area, because of affectional deficits on the husband-wife level, may create disturbances in the entire family makes the pattern of sexual adjustment an important aspect of family study. The area is crucial to any understanding of the family's affective equilibrium.

SEQUENCE 12

Some of the patterns in which mutuality problems find expression in the sexual area begin to be seen in the following sequence:

Therapist: You see, I—I really—she said that you don't have loving words for her. Well, I would wonder very much if Pepe could have loving words for you. You know why? Because I think that Pepe is very angry at you.

Mrs. G.: I don't know why.

Therapist: I think that you are very angry at Pepe, also.

Mrs. G.: No, no. I try him—you know—I try him—I'm—I—uh . . . (*Spanish.*) . . .

Therapist: Pepe, is that true what she said?

Mr. G.: Well—sometimes . . . (*Spanish.*)

Therapist: Please, answer her. She's talking to you. I don't want you to talk, both of you, to *me*. I want you to talk to each other.

From the emergence of Mrs. Garcia's simple complaint that her husband has no loving words for her begins the unraveling of information as to the partners' perception of each other. There is an attempt to induce them into the rudimentaries of mutuality in the here-and-now interaction. Simple interventions of this sort, which attempt to guide and promote a new form of interaction ("I want you to talk to each other"), are, of course, as essential to diagnostic information-gathering as to therapeutic goals. After a few minutes of interchange, the sequence continues:

SEQUENCE 13

Therapist: She's challenging you, Pepe. Is that true, that you never have any loving words for her?

Mrs. G.: That's true.

Mr. G.: No, I don't think it's true. (*Small laugh from Mrs. G.*) . . . (*Mrs. G. speaks in Spanish. Therapist asks her to talk in English.*)

Mrs. G.: He stay the whole week, working, the whole week. Then we got two days only. And—uh—and I—and I don't even hear from him a word of love. Never. So, you know how I feel? Sometimes I feel mad, you know? And then when we—uh—like we talk over there in the other room, when—when we gonna have—uh—a little enjoyment, and then he—he's li—rough—like—uh—li—like in the—after life—no? (*Spanish.*) . . . (*Pause.*)

Therapist: Pepe, you are there in the corner and I don't know what you are thinking. She's saying something. What do you think about what she's saying?

Mr. G.: Well, I am saying that—that—she talk about herself. But—uh—she got this opinion about me.

Therapist: Yes, and what's her opinion about you?

Mr. G.: Well—uh—you know. She said it.

Therapist: Huh? What did she say? That's not love?

Mr. G.: That's not true.

Therapist: But this is what she's feeling. Isn't that so?

Mr. G.: That's so.

Therapist: And why does she feel that you are not loving her, Pepe?

Mr. G.: I don't know.

Therapist: No? On what does she base—that you don't love her?

Mr. G.: Well, I don't know.

Therapist: Mm. Is it true what she said?

Mr. G.: Certainly (?) true.

Mrs. G.: Sometimes I go through the day—and—

Therapist: Don't tell (me). Here is your husband.

Mrs. G.: Well, sometimes I go through the day. And he's—you are sleeping. But I go and I—how you say—tickle? And I tickle him. Or I—
uh—uh—and he say, "Get outta here, the bed is getting down." . . .
(*Spanish.*) "And you don't let me sleep. Go away from here. What's
the matter with you? Just let me sleep." He know that—uh— (*Mrs.
G. speaks Spanish at length.*) . . .

Therapist: That you did not enjoy sex?

Mrs. G.: Uh-huh. Right.

Mr. G.: That's right. Why you didn't talk about this first, huh? (*They
speak Spanish for a while.*)

Therapist: It means, you told the doctor that you are not enjoying sexual
relations?

Mrs. G.: Yes. And he says, "Oh, don't worry. That's only in your head."

Therapist: This is all in your mind?

Mrs. G.: Right. And I say, "Well—uh—well you can help me." He
didn't say nothing. And always I try to help myself. You see, I—uh
—read—uh—sexology and everything, to find out—uh—what can it
help me.

(*The session continues in Spanish.*)

The wife's sense of rejection and deprivation as well as her frigidity
symptoms are now open to exploration. The husband's, "That's right.
Why didn't you talk about this first, huh?" is especially noteworthy in
that up to now his lack of initiative and his typically "one-down" position
had left *his* side, the extent of his dissatisfactions in the relationship, un-
expressed. We can reconstruct some of their problems through a state-

ment by one of the therapists in the postsession ("Stage 4") discussion after the nineteenth session:

> I feel that the second stage had to be all in Spanish. They just could not, at all, express themselves in English with a problem that was so intimate. But I think that something is coming out. . . . She is stating that he masturbates himself in order to have an arousal and when he is excited, then he calls her and he is demanding from her sex at this moment, because he is stimulated. She gets very angry and then she would respond to him: "OK. If that's what you want, have sex," and she just lies down completely numb. And she does not act at all. He gets angry because he says, "You are not participating at all." Besides, she expressed that she reads a lot of books about sex. She reads sexology and she found out that her . . . [another therapist completes the thought] life can be different.

Isolation—Husband and Wife

Sequences 14 and 15 are from the nineteenth session, Stage 1.

Religion is a convenient arena in which to express problems in lack of mutuality. Here Mr. Garcia discloses his wife's demands in this area.

SEQUENCE 14

Therapist B.: What makes you angry?

Mr. G.: Yeah because when I come, when we start living again, the first day she told me she know I—I don't belong to this religion—I am a Catholic. Sometimes we used to get a—a picture of a saint or something like that or a rosary or something like that. The first thing she said, "I don't want that thing ever here in the house."

Mrs. G.: (*Spanish.*) . . . they won't let me talk.

Therapist B.: Well, Mama was saying before you came back there was a discussion. Well, what was the discussion with Mr. G.?

Mrs. G.: When he came home, oh, I invite him to live with me. No, but I want to tell you. He knows I—uh—when—when I make him come to my house, I told my husband I got a lot of problem with the children. And I decide him to come to my house again and live with me and take care of the children with me, you know? And I told him, "But one thing I'm gonna tell you. And it's that—because I am a Christian—and I don't like things . . . (*Spanish.*) and I don't like that."

Therapist A.: Rosaries, papers, or . . . ? [Holy pictures?]

Therapist B.: Yes.

Mrs. G.: Right. Uh—because I don't like that. And I have my house clean of that stuff. I wish that you will do the same thing to me. Not to bring those things over here. And we will be happy. And he do it. He did it for—for about three years he did it.

Therapist A.: And?

Mrs. G.: And now he wants to bring it to my house. And now—because —I got a right to tell him because I told him before he came home. I got a right when he gonna bring something like that to tell him, "Pepe, don't I tell you when you came here not to bring those things to my house?" And now he's angry because I told him. First he accept it, now he reject it.

SEQUENCE 15

This arena can itself be used, by any member, as an obstacle to open communication and problem-solving. Mrs. Garcia's defensive use of religious ideas is tackled directly, a few minutes after the above sequence, in which the therapist shifted his alliance toward Mr. Garcia.

Therapist A.: You—you know—no, no. Wait a moment. Don't agree so fast with me because maybe you will not agree when I finish. (*Slight laugh from Mrs. G.*) I think that many, many things that happen in the family are put as if they are in this religion. And they don't have anything to do with the religion. But it's impossible to discuss it because in the moment in which we begin to discuss it, you said, "Well we cannot. God is holy." In that nobody's disagreeing with you—or that we can. You see, I think that sometimes Pepe, your husband, is talking about his feeling that you don't like him. This is all that he's saying.

SEQUENCE 16   NINETEENTH SESSION, STAGE 2

The mutuality issue must be constantly stressed as central to family problems by seizing upon any of its manifestations:

Therapist: Well, you know, one of the things, for instance, that I noticed is that—what's your first name?

Mrs. G.: Uh, Maria.

Therapist: That Maria said "my house" and that you, Pepe, say "my house."

Mrs. G.: And we never say "our."

Therapist: Never. You never say "our house." Maria said that, "My husband will not bring saints to my house." . . . I actually think that you, Pepe, also think that the house is your wife's house and not your house.

Mrs. G.: You'll never explain [anything to] me. (*Statement directed to Mr. G.*)

Therapist: Why—why is that? Because you never say "our house." Do you notice that, Pepe?

Mr. G.: (*Spanish.*) . . .

Mrs. G.: Uh—you know what happened? When I say "my house" and, and it's because of that—uh—when—uh—he left me—the—I was living in a furnished room, and the housing project later gave me an apartment. I—uh—I found the apartment by myself. And I say "my house" always . . .

SEQUENCE 17 NINETEENTH SESSION, STAGE 1

Clarification as to why each partner lacks satisfaction in family life is made explicit. Some of Mrs. Garcia's dissatisfactions have already been brought to light through explorations around money (in which, it was seen, she met delinquent behavior from her husband), sex, and family activity. Here are some of Mr. Garcia's dissatisfactions. Notice that his description is rather bland, centering on external behavior. Only with interpretive help is the full depth of his loneliness brought to the surface. (Many of the fathers in our families have come to accept isolation from family life and have difficulty in expressing and experiencing feelings. They act as if they have no right to receive consideration or tenderness.) In this sequence, the therapist is transforming Mr. Garcia's description of what to him is an external set of events and reactions into a broader meaning. The therapist is guiding this couple into an awareness of the internal events which are paralleling the circumstances that Mr. Garcia is describing. Notice how Mr. Garcia's rather incidental use of the word "alone" is employed to disclose his role in the family structure.

Mr. G.: What I mean to say, if I'm alone, you know, all the day or something, so I take a bath, change my clothes and take a walk.

After a few interchanges, the sequence continues:

Therapist A.: May I ask you—did you feel alone?

Mr. G.: Yeah, that's right.

Therapist A.: Huh?

Mr. G.: That's right.

Therapist A.: You—that means, you see, that it seemed to me that Pepe

is not talking now of religion. He is talking about a feeling that he
had on Sunday.

Therapist B.: Separated from the family.

Therapist A.: . . . that he was separated from the family. That Felipe
was, let's see first if this is what Pepe feels, that Felipe went to the
movie by himself, wife went to the church by herself, and then you
remained alone. Is that—is that it?

Mr. G.: Yeah, I stay at home alone.

Therapist A.: Huh?

Mr. G.: I stay, I stay home. So I change my mind. So I take a bath,
change my clothes, I go to the movies . . .

Therapist A.: Were you annoyed at your wife because she was not with
you?

Mr. G.: . . . That's right.

SEQUENCE 18   NINETEENTH SESSION, STAGE 2

Lack of acceptance or even awareness of the feeling that one has rights
leads directly to an inability to defend them or to explore the reasons
why satisfaction is not forthcoming. Therapeutic technique, therefore,
frequently centers on mobilizing not only the spouse's sense of responsibility and obligation to the partner, as was evident in the interchanges
between the therapist and Mr. Garcia revolving around his delinquency
to his wife, but also in giving him an awareness that he can make certain
demands from her:

Therapist A.: I really think that, you know, what she's—what Ther. B.
is bringing, Pepe, is that you are not—uh—fighting—fighting enough
to be a member of the family; that you are not working strong
enough in telling your wife, "Look, Maria, today is Sunday. I would
like to enjoy this Sunday with you in some way or another. And I
know that you have the church at two o'clock, but maybe you can
skip the church today, because I would like to spend the day with
you."

SEQUENCE 19

Sequences 19, 20, and 21 are from the nineteenth session, Stage 1.

The beginnings of change at the parental level often are accompanied
by or follow an increased ability of one partner to display his feelings
more openly. The following sequence shows Mrs. Garcia's increased
attentiveness to Mr. Garcia's feelings while the therapists are, at the same
time, attempting to help the children perceive the issue under scrutiny
as a family problem.

Therapist A.: Now, let's—maybe we can ask Felipe. Do you know what they are talking, Felipe, what Papa and Mama are talking? (*Felipe nods yes.*) What do you think is the problem that we are discussing here?

Felipe: About their church.

Therapist B.: Yeah.

Therapist A.: No, I don't think it is about the church. I think that it is . . .

Therapist B.: Well, let's see. What about the church?

Felipe: So she says, go down to the church . . .

Therapist B.: Yes? Well, why do you think we are talking about it?

Therapist A.: How is Papa feeling? (*Juan is tapping the therapist's chair.*)

Felipe: He don't like that. You know, he don't feel good.

Therapist B.: He doesn't feel good. He told you about it?

Felipe: No, I just heard him say it.

Therapist B.: Uh-huh. But Papa, do you know why he didn't feel good? (*Felipe shakes head no.*) Well, he said it.

Therapist A.: Juan, why do you think Papa doesn't feel good? (*Juan shrugs.*) You can guess.

Juan: He may be sick.

Therapist A.: May be sick? What other—didn't you hear him when—say—why . . . doesn't feel good?

Juan: He don't like to be the monkey.

Therapist B.: Uh-huh.

Therapist A.: Yeah. That means Papa feels that he doesn't have a family. You are away. Felipe is away. And he feels alone. You know, we have talked about that. It's really a big family problem.

Therapist B.: Uh-huh.

Mrs. G.: . . . (*Spanish.*)

Therapist A.: Because—because Pepe goes to work and you go to work, so the only time that you have together . . .

Therapist B.: —is the weekend.

Therapist A.: —is the weekend—this—during the day you don't see each other.

Mrs. G.: Right.

Therapist A.: So—uh—I don't think that here we are really talking about church, Felipe. We are talking about this feeling that Papa and Mama have about being able to be together and to be able to enjoy themselves when they are together.

SEQUENCE 20

The long-standing pattern of isolation between Mr. and Mrs. Garcia is complemented by their respective anchorage in mutually inaccessible social groups. Their extrafamilial frameworks needed to be explored, since they widened and crystallized their alienated positions. For Mrs. Garcia, this might be stated as: "I want you to participate with me in church life, but also I wish you wouldn't, since this gives me a measure of independence which I find rather convenient." And for Mr. Garcia: "I wish you would give me as much of your companionship as you give the church brethren, but I also wish you wouldn't, since your business with church gives me much freedom." A sample of these contradictory messages which strengthen the family's resistance to change is revealed in the following sequence:

Mrs. G.: . . . then he goes . . . yeah—yeah—and he's complaining a lot. But before, he was the one—even when—even when I have to stay with him on Saturday, he say, "Hey. You don't go to church to-night?" You see?

Therapist B.: Yeah?

Mrs. G.: And—uh—sometimes on Sunday at one o'clock, "Listen, it's late, very late for you to go to church."

Mr. G.: I didn't say that.

Mrs. G.: Oh, yes.

Mr. G.: Ah.

Mrs. G.: Oh, yes. That's right.

Therapist B.: What do you mean by that? You mean—sometimes—

Mrs. G.: He's reminding—reminding me—

Therapist B.: So what does that mean? He reminds you that he doesn't want you home—that he—

Mrs. G.: I—I don't know—I think that—

Therapist B.: —he respects your religion? What does it mean?

Mrs. G.: I think that, in that time, I saying to me, "Well, my husband wants me to go."

Therapist B.: To church?

Mrs. G.: To church.

Therapist B.: Well, let's see.

SEQUENCE 21

Confusing communications are sometimes clarified by full exploration and elaboration of the two contradictory messages, but therapeutic considerations often require the dismissal of one aspect of the communication and the focusing on just one of the messages—the one which family dynamics tend to obfuscate. A minute or so after the above interchange, the therapist says:

Therapist A.: You know, I hear both of you and I am trying to make sense. If there is some kind of communication that makes sense. And I can't because you say one thing and you say another thing. To me, Pepe, you are saying that the amount of time that your wife spends in church in some way hurts you, because it takes her away from your companionship—and that in some way you resent that. You told that many, many times . . . that your feeling is that you are in competition with the church, that she loves more other people in the church than she loves you.

SEQUENCE 22   NINETEENTH SESSION, STAGE 2

Many of the therapist's statements concentrate, of necessity, on tackling the behavioral manifestations of lack of mutuality in the sessions.

Therapist: Please, answer to *her*. She's talking to you. I don't want you to talk—both of you—to me. I want you to talk to each other.

Mr. G.: (*Spanish.*) . . . sometimes.

Therapist: What "sometimes"? She's saying—

Mrs. G.: . . . (*Spanish.*)

Therapist: You don't talk with me. You talk with *him*.

Mrs. G.: (*Spanish.*) . . .

Therapist: No, no, tell *him*. Tell him, whatever you want to say. Tell him now.

Mrs. G.: He knows already.

Therapist: No—uh—is that true, Pepe?

We see in the above sequence that although the therapist has made a number of attempts to establish direct communications between the Garcias, he nevertheless becomes part of the system he is trying to break up by finally using himself as the contact-point between husband and wife.

SEQUENCE 23   NINETEENTH SESSION, STAGE 1

Some of the child's wish for maintaining strict generational lines—for the parents to display aggression between themselves only—is disclosed in the continuation of the above sequence. Here, the child "wants no part" of the intense, emotional battle between his mother and father, and he repeats, "That's their business." But there is no consistency in his desire to uphold generational lines, for he also feels free, probably because he feels threatened and frightened, to cross these lines and to ridicule his mother out of her executive or adult position in the family.

There is an implicit power-struggle with the father, it would seem, as well as an almost furtive alliance of mother and son against the father, but this coalition boomerangs, apparently, to Mrs. Garcia's disadvantage. (Although this process is not strikingly illustrated in the segment below, the therapists state that it is a central operation in the Garcia family.)

This brief sequence also suggests the style in which the child handles strong feelings in connection with parental strife. He retreats, or tries to detach himself, talks behind his father's back and allies himself with his mother, and then derogates her.

Therapist B.: What does that mean, Felipe, when Mama and Papa fight? How do you feel?

Felipe: Nothing. That's their business.

Therapist B.: You feel what?

Felipe: That's their business. That ain't my business.

Therapist B.: It ain't your business? Well, are you sorry? Are you happy? Are you mad? Are you depressed? Sad?

Felipe: I don't know.

Mrs. G.: He's happy.

Therapist A.: He's happy?

Therapist B.: Why? Why do you say that?

Mrs. G.: Because—uh—when—when Pepe, my husband, is saying something to me he (Felipe) wait for me in the kitchen and he laugh. And he say a lot of things to me.

Therapist B.: What does he say?

Mrs. G.: He laugh at me and he and he say, "You see? You see? Now you got it." You see—and—and—

SEQUENCE 24   NINETEENTH SESSION, STAGE 3

The preceding fragments, it is hoped, communicate the flavor of our work with some of these families and some of the problems which beset them. The following sequence, in which the therapist begins to summarize, discloses echoes of confirmation, first from Mr. Garcia, and soon after that from both Mr. and Mrs. Garcia in quick succession:

Therapist A.: Okay. I will try to summarize something that what I think is that one of the things that we talked is that Papa, for instance, says "my" house, and Mama says "my" house. And in the twenty or nineteen sessions that we have here not once they say "our" house.

Therapist B.: That's right. That's right.

Mr. G.: I never say that.

Therapist A.: Not once they say "our" house. And this is something that they need to work together. Because up to now, though they are married many, many years, still they operate as if they are two separate people. And this is one of the things that we talked. The other thing that we talked, and I think that this can be said here, is that I think that Papa and Mama are more interested sometimes in blaming each other than in finding a solution. Is that correct?

Therapist B.: Than finding ways, than finding ways.

Mr. G.: That's right. That's right.

Therapist A.: . . . is that what we talked? That there is a lot of blame and—and Felipe, for instance, I want to bring you into that. There was in the beginning, you remember, everything for the first five, six sessions—everything that happened in the home was Felipe's fault. You remember that? Huh?

Therapist B.: . . .

Therapist A.: Papa's anger was Felipe's fault. Mama's anxiety was Felipe's fault. Everything was Felipe's fault, for at least six, seven, eight—you remember this, the beginning?

Mrs. G.: Right.

Mr. G.: Yes, I remember.

Therapist A.: Everything was put on Felipe's shoulders. It is a very heavy burden to wear on his shoulders, you know? Now things are changing and we know that not everything that happened at home is Felipe's fault. We are putting the problem where it belongs. The problem belongs—a lot of the problem belongs—between Papa and Mama. And when Papa and Mama solve many of the problems (*Mrs. G. nods yes.*) then many things will become better. But still there is a lot of work for Juan and there is a lot of work for Felipe.

From Mistrust to Trust—Father and Son

Sequences 25 to 35 are from the twenty-eighth session, Stage 1.

The fragments to be presented are from a family session quite late in the series. They disclose the beginnings of mutuality between Mr. and Mrs. Garcia in terms of cooperative problem-solving in relation to the children's behavior; they also disclose an incident between father and son that contrasts markedly with the one concerned with stealing which was discussed in the sixth session (see sequences 6 to 8). Mrs. Garcia's relationship to her husband no longer emerges as detached "advisor and critic," as seemed to be the case during the sixth session. She seems to be a more active participant in Mr. Garcia's handling of the child, and more capable of allowing her husband some initiative.

SEQUENCE 25

The following sequence leads into the family's perception of change—of increased ability to do problem-solving on their own. Ability for conflict-resolution on the interspouse level results, it is hoped, in better understanding and care of the children.

Mr. G.: Everything is all right for us this week, you know. It goes all right.

Therapist A.: Pepe, you always start that way, but then slowly you come out with more. (*Mr. G. laughs.*) The first thing that you said is that everything is okay, and then other things come out. Okay, then, you remember that you were going to discuss certain things? So, well, what did happen?

Mr. G.: Well, we—I talked with my wife about the plan that we had last week, but I don't think that it work out.

Therapist B.: What plans do you mean, Mr. G.?

Mr. G.: . . . and we can try and find something in him, see? Something to help him. But I don't think this plan work because at the time I have to go to work, he come from school, you see? Saturday morning, we—we try to do our best, you know? Because he was home, but he going away and he return back about seven o'clock in the afternoon. I was at home, but I don't think this plan work this way.

Therapist A.: What?

Mr. G.: We just only try to find another way to, you know, to catch him in the same position, so we can talk and—

Therapist B.: What happened Saturday, though? What time did he get up? When did you get up—and—

Mr. G.: Well, about nine or ten, something like that.

Therapist A.: And?

Mr. G.: . . . he was in the living room, talking with Juan.

Therapist B.: Juan was home this weekend?

Mr. G.: Yeah.

Therapist B.: This was your visiting weekend, Juan?

Juan: Yeah.

Mr. G.: So he said, "I have to go downstairs." I think that he was playing downstairs but as soon as I woke up—he was not downstairs . . .

Therapist A.: Did you discuss the problem with you, Maria?

Mr. G.: Yeah. We, I discussed to her what—what . . .

Therapist A.: Did you discuss it?

Therapist B.: When you say it didn't work out, what do you mean? What didn't?

Mr. G.: . . . It can work out. What I mean, if we can catch him in time, because I have to go at four o'clock, you see?

Therapist B.: Uh-huh.

Mr. G.: And this time, he don't come here from school.

Therapist B.: Yeah.

Mr. G.: That's every day. Yeah.

Therapist A.: He comes from school at three o'clock?—Three-thirty?

Mr. G.: And that, that's the thing I tell you, in this way it don't work.

(*Therapist A. suggests that Mrs. G. said that it did or could work.*)

Therapist B.: Did you say that it did work?

Mrs. G.: It did work.

Therapist B.: Uh-huh.

Therapist A.: Okay, let's try to see here—there is some—

Mrs. G.: Yeah . . . because he talked to him—and I saw him talk.

In the above sequence, one can notice the therapists' efforts to help the family to perceive change, any change, no matter how dimly it is perceived by any member of the parental team. Changes highlighted by one member are used in guiding the perception of the other family members. "Did you say that it did work?" says the therapist to Mrs. Garcia immediately after Mr. Garcia's ". . . it don't work."

SEQUENCE 26 (CONTINUATION OF SEQUENCE 25)

Therapist A.: You mean to Felipe?

Mrs. G.: Yeah, I saw my husband talking to him, and you know what? He was so quiet. Felipe was so nice. Even that I asked him to do favors, and he did it, and he was in his room and everything. I can see that little change.

Therapist A.: May I ask you first, you could see a little change, but may I ask you, what did you discuss together first?

Mr. G.: Well, I talk with my wife and I told her the same thing we discussed here, last week over here.

Therapist A.: . . .

Mr. G.: —and I talked to my wife that in case we meet together . . . we can do the best—to talk with Felipe together, and to find out, you see, something in him. Something like—to see if he feel very good, in the family. But . . . the only way I catch him was on Saturday afternoon. I was home. And he was maybe with a friend.

A new problem-solving role is being tested. Here Mr. Garcia is attempting to reach his wife to discuss ways of approaching the children. It is interesting to notice Mr. Garcia's leadership in the situation and the carry-over of problem-solving approaches suggested and developed for use *within* the sessions. These are now employed in the natural living situation; they are generalized to the "outside" to tackle the tangible problems the family meets in everyday reality.

SEQUENCE 27

Therapist B.: What time did he come back?

Mr. G.: He was over there about seven o'clock, something like that.

Therapist B.: And then what happened?

Mr. G.: But he was home and—and we talked . . . and we pass a good time.

Therapist B.: Oh, you did have a nice evening?

Mr. G.: Yeah—with him and Juan.

Therapist B.: Uh-huh.

The above sequence, occurring a few seconds after sequence 26, is a reference to a positive experience, a scarce event in our families.

SEQUENCE 28 (CONTINUATION OF SEQUENCE 27)

Mr. G.: And we just—I got my brother at home, you see, he come and visit me . . . and we talk—and . . .

Therapist B.: Well, why did you say it didn't work out?

Mr. G.: Well. You know why. Because I can't see him in the day, you see, that's (*Spanish.*) . . .

Mrs. G.: What he means is—what he means is—that he wants to see him every day, you know, to get more and more . . .

In this sequence, Mr. Garcia communicates his need for a more involved and intense relationship to his son. He sees as a problem the fact that he is unable to meet with his son very often. Their schedules do not overlap because of work and school obligations that they have to meet.

SEQUENCE 29

The Garcia family structure has not changed in that Mrs. Garcia still has considerable salience within the family. She continues to mediate communications, to "help" her husband and to serve as his interpreter. But now Mrs. Garcia's salience is oriented toward the family's welfare. She is helping her husband, rather than obstructing him. Her interference with a constructive father-son relationship has been strikingly reduced. Let us follow this development further:

Mr. G.: Well, I told my wife that—that we get a plan to help Felipe. Just, not too much, just a little bit—in case—we decide to—in case . . . you know, we meet all together, and to find out what's going on from him, and sometimes . . . to work in the family.

Therapist A.: So, this is what you told her?

Mr. G.: Yeah, that's right. That's what I told her.

Therapist B.: What did you hear, Maria? I mean, this is what Pepe . . . You hear that?

Mrs. G.: I hear the same thing.

Mr. G.: Yeah.

Therapist B.: What do you think of that plan? Pepe thought it would, it might—he wanted to try it. What do you think?

Mrs. G.: I was, you know, surprised, because on that day Felipe was mad, and . . . he find a paper at home and my husband was so nice to him in the paper, and he read it.

Therapist A.: The paper? Paper where?

Therapist B.: What kind of paper? (*Mrs. G looks at Mr. G.*)

Mr. G.: Yeah, about last week. Because he feel mad about me, because I take him, you know, he got a knife—

Therapist B.: Oh!

Mr. G.: —in his room.

Therapist A.: Yes?

Mr. G.: So I bring him away. He feel mad because he think that I take the knife.

Mrs. G.: And he feel very mad.

Mr. G.: You see?

Mrs. G.: So my husband, he have to go to work, so he left a paper to Felipe.

Therapist A.: You mean a letter?

Despite the language difficulties, the content of the material comes across. Mr. Garcia is trying very, very hard to find a way to contact his son. This is particularly important in the context of the former constant interactions of mistrust between father and son, in which Mr. Garcia was constantly afraid of being attacked by Felipe, and in which he would never even try to reach his son directly about these issues. The sequence continues:

Therapist B.: A note?

Mrs. G.: A note. Felipe read it, and he say with the head—he don't say
it's so good, but he say, "Ain't bad."
Therapist B.: Yeah? What was in the note?
Therapist A.: What did you write?
Mr. G.: Well, I wrote to him, because—I say, "Dear son. I think that
you get mad because you think that I take the knife. And I didn't
take it. I found the knife after you went to school. I find the knife
in another place, in the place you say, in the place you put the knife.
I don't take it. I find in another place. I am very sorry about what
happen this morning. . . . (*Apparently in the morning he had spoken
strongly to the boy when discovering the knife in the house.*) I was
sorry what happen this morning, but that's not the way you said
that I take the knife. I didn't take the knife."
Therapist A.: That's very nice.
Therapist B.: That's wonderful.
Mrs. G.: So even Felipe, when he leave, he was sorry too.
Therapist B.: How wonderful!

There is general rejoicing, and the therapists share in the Garcias'
feelings of excitement and joy at the tenderness shown by the father in
trying to reach his son in order to repair what he had done during the
morning. Perhaps a significant aspect of the following continuation of
sequence 29 is Mrs. Garcia's expressions of confirmation. She is perceiving a different interaction between father and son. The sequence continues:

Therapist A.: This was a very nice thing that you did, Pepe, you know?
(*Mrs. G. nods yes.*)
Therapist B.: Wonderful.
Mrs. G.: . . . I saw that . . .
Therapist B.: And Pepe received it well, you say, Mrs. G.?
Mrs. G.: Right.
Therapist B.: How wonderful.
Mrs. G.: And the other day, you know, I thought that the knife would
come back again, you know, the discussion. My husband called him,
so nice and kind, and they was talking in the kitchen there, you
know, like friendship . . .
Therapist A.: Yes.
Mrs. G.: In between them, I was so happy. I didn't know it. Later, Pepe
told me.

The above sequence is particularly illustrative of the family's perception of some change and of Mrs. Garcia's reactions to the change—Mr. Garcia's efforts to reach the child. There is open happiness at seeing the conflict-resolution attempts between father and son. Mr. Garcia seems to share in this new perception, for Mrs. Garcia says, "Later, Pepe told me." Her description of the dialogue between father and son is particularly poignant: "My husband . . . so nice and kind, and they was talking in the kitchen there, you know, like friendship." Her experience of seeing her husband able to be a different type of father is of vital significance in terms of further changes which may occur between husband and wife. When she sees that as "father" her husband is quite a person, he quite possibly grows as "husband."

SEQUENCE 30

The sequence below discloses, quite directly, a growing, shared tenderness in the family, especially between husband and wife. Note the contrast to the excerpts from the sixth session (Sequences 9 to 11), in which mistrust and lack of mutuality characterized their relationship. Here we see affectionate, positive themes in the relationship between husband and wife. The nonverbal atmosphere of this session reflects a shy embarrassment over the fact that there is love and tenderness. There is a tone and mood in this sequence that prevails when one discusses intimate things.

Mr. G.: Yeah, you see, I have to be friends with my wife . . . (*Mrs. G. nods yes.*)

Therapist A.: Why, may I ask you, why do you call it "my wife"? At home you call . . . Maria.

Mr. G.: Oh yeah, my wife.

Therapist A.: You don't call it "my wife"?

Mr. G.: Yeah, uh, no, sometimes Maria. I call her everything. (*He laughs.*)

Mrs. G.: He calls me Pepita.

Therapist A.: Pepita. Okay.

Therapist B.: Pepita meaning what?

Therapist A.: Pepita—it's—uh—

Therapist B.: Is it a diminutive, an affectionate name?

Mr. G.: Yeah, the same thing.

Therapist A.: It's a nickname.

Mr. G.: Yeah.

Therapist B.: It's a nickname, Pepita?

Mrs. G.: Yeah, only that's a little affectionate, so he don't want to call me Pepita, so he says "my wife."

Therapist A.: Oh, well, because . . .

Therapist B.: Uh-hum.

Therapist A.: Let's call her Pepita if that's the name that you call her. (*Mr. G. laughs.*) You know, there is a big change. I think that the big change . . . I see is in Pepe's attitude, you know?

Therapist B.: Uh-huh. And mother's also—I think.

Therapist A.: Yes.

Therapist B.: To father.

Therapist A.: Yes.

Therapist B.: And father to Felipe, and to mother.

Therapist A.: What do you think, Maria, is the way in which Pepe wrote this letter to Felipe—what do you think is the change? I mean, what do you see that is different than before?

Mrs. G.: Well, I feel that he want to try—to try Felipe to understand him. To be friends, you know? That's what I think. I saw that . . .

Mr. G.: Sure, because I didn't tell [him] . . . in other ways before. But— he don't want that.

SEQUENCE 31

Mrs. Garcia again acknowledges the efforts of Mr. Garcia—his attempts to reach Felipe in a positive way. Mr. Garcia realizes, makes the differentiation, that his "other ways" of problem-solving were not effective.

Therapist B.: . . . Tell me, what happened about the knife, actually?

Mrs. G.: He still got it.

Therapist B.: Who?

Mrs. G.: Felipe.

Therapist B.: You gave it back to him?

Mr. G.: Yeah, because I decided to give it to him. I saw it in the closet the other day. He don't use it.

Therapist B.: He doesn't? This is different too.

Mr. G.: No, he don't use it. You see? That's why, I just think, I just looking in the closet and I found it over there. You see? He don't use it.

Therapist B.: But, why did you give it to him? Let's see.

Mr. G.: Well, because, you know, in that way—I just only thinkin'. I just only thinking in my way that if I give it to him, the boy, he don't feel mad at me.

Therapist B.: Uh-hum.

Mr. G.: See? So I decide to give it to him in another way. So I left the knife there—I left the paper. I put the knife on the top of the table. When he return back, maybe he read the paper.

Therapist B.: Yes, yes.

Mr. G.: So he keep the knife in some place. And I saw this morning over there in the closet.

Therapist A.: You see, Pepe, I remember the first time, when Felipe, what was—he had? Also some . . .

Therapist B.: A big dagger—a knife.

Therapist A.: Yes, a knife. And I remember at this time, the first time that we discussed that, you were in some way afraid that Felipe was going to do something, like attack you, or something like that. Wasn't that what?

Mr. G.: Yeah.

Therapist B.: Yes.

Therapist A.: What it seems, then, is that your feelings have changed in the sense that you—in the way in which you think now of Felipe— is that he will not attack you. (*Mr. G. nods yes.*)

Therapist B.: That you can trust him.

Therapist A.: That you can trust him. This is the big difference that I see. Instead, before you were saying, "Well, I need to give it to him, because he will do something bad," and now you are saying, "I can give it to him, and he will not use it for any bad thing." This is the change in your—in the way that you are thinking.

Mr. G.: In the way he act, you see. I don't think he's a bad boy. In his feeling, I don't think he's a bad boy.

Therapist B.: Uh-hum.

Mr. G.: Because he got good points, friends, I know. And, you know, when he's not home, I used to talk with his friends, and everybody's looking for him. Somebody knock on the door, "Is Felipe . . ."

Therapist B.: Yes.

The above sequence is particularly significant in that Mr. Garcia is not only trusting his son, but trying to look for positives in him. The rediscovery of the son and of his different facets and roles is of particular significance. The strategy in the therapist-operations is also important to note. Mr. Garcia's verbalization, "I just only thinking in my way that if I give it to him, the boy, he don't feel mad at me," could easily have been misinterpreted to be a repetition of his "giving in" in order not to be confronted with an angry, rebellious son. The therapist, however, responds to the nonverbal subtleties of change: ". . . now you are saying, I can give it to him and he will not use it for any bad thing." This recognition that Mr. Garcia's motivation is now different contains a "releasing" power, for it is exactly after this that Mr. Garcia states, ". . . I don't think he's a bad boy . . . he got good points . . ." Mr. Garcia further verbalizes his discovery that the child is liked by others, by his peers.

SEQUENCE 32

The changed perspective toward the child—the ushering of trust into the relationship between father and son—permits the son's actions to be seen in a completely different context:

Therapist A.: But, what do you think about Felipe having a knife now? You think that he should have it anyway, you think that's—that's what you're feeling now?

Mr. G.: You see, I in my own way, I think when a boy is interested in something, maybe a knife for one day, day and a half, later he forget . . . So that's why he try to make some distrust. So I lookin' this morning, no yesterday, and he got the knife in the closet. And he don't use it. I know that.

Mrs. G.: Now that you are in the—in a better—you know—how you say it? Friendly—

Therapist B.: Relations.

Mrs. G.: Friendly relations? It is friendly, that's right. Now you can tell him that's no good 'cause he can throw it away.

Mr. G.: Yeah, yeah. I telling to him. It's no good. I explain in the letter too . . . you know, that sooner or later, maybe something happen to him . . . maybe the boy understand better—you see?

Mrs. Garcia's statement in the context of the friendly relations between father and son, "Now you can tell him that's no good 'cause he can throw it away," is also interesting to note. The type of problem-solving she suggests could not have emerged if the basic problem-solving obstacle, the fundamental mistrust, had not been somewhat dissipated. Mrs. Garcia assumes that the fundamental attitude problem between father and son is diminishing and that Mr. Garcia has more freedom and alternatives in solving the problem of the child's having a knife.

SEQUENCE 33

This sequence, which is a continuation of sequence 32, highlights the therapists' efforts to verbalize any evidence of change in the family.

Change in the interactional here-and-now is immediately relayed to the family, emphasizing how and where they are moving:

Therapist A.: You know something that happened just now? Usually Pepe talks to me or to Therapist B., and you talk to me or to Therapist B. And I saw just now that you talked to Pepe directly. And this is something that very rarely happens, here, that you begin to talk more with each other. (*Turns to Juan.*) That is, I think, one of the bases of making a family, Juan, that has a motor. You remember about your car with the difficult motor, the motor that doesn't work? I think that something has happened . . .

The therapist is not only reflecting a sense of change for the benefit of Mr. and Mrs. Garcia, but he is including other family members by expressing the change in the fantasy language of the Wiltwyck child. The child had seen his family, symbolically, as a car without a motor.

Mistrust Revisited—Husband and Wife around Money

Sequences 34 to 36 are from the twenty-eighth session, Stage 2.

Some features of family interaction change quickly; others are more resistant to change.

SEQUENCE 34

Mr. and Mrs. Garcia relate an incident which shows continued difficulties with respect to sharing financial responsibilities:

Mrs. G.: I told him I was mad. I'm telling you. I told, "Well, Pepe, I'm sorry, but next time you go with me. I don't go alone anymore to the store. You have to go with me and you have to find out the prices."

Therapist A.: Were you ashamed when you were taking . . .

Mrs. G.: Well I was ashamed. And I was so—spendin' the money he gave me for the furniture, because I just want him to take from $22, $15, you know? So I decide to take $2 out and I give him $20.

Therapist A.: Uh-hum.

Mrs. G.: And I don't leave no money for the furniture.

Therapist A.: And then?

Mrs. G.: And I told him even $20 was not enough.

Therapist A.: Well, did you . . .

Mrs. G.: And you gave me only $15, and I want you to go with me. (*Mr. G. . . . Spanish.*)

Therapist A.: Pepe, what did you feel when she—

Mr. G.: I telling her . . . I do my best.

Mrs. G.: Tell him what you told me.

Mr. G.: I don't remember what I told you.

Mrs. G.: Well, he says, "You, what did you want, $50?"

Mr. G.: If I don't get money . . . I do my best . . . with that money do your best until I find [about?] some more money.

Therapist A.: What did you say to her?

Mr. G.: "What you needing about $50 to . . ." (*Laughing.*)

Therapist B.: Well, how much does Maria need to manage?

Mrs. G.: He don't even know. If I go—

Therapist B.: Well, let's see, do you know?

Mrs. G.: (*Spanish.*) . . .

Therapist B.: Pepe?

Mrs. G.: I tell him, when I was taking care of the food, I used to spend $22 and $25 every week in food and milk and everything.

Therapist B.: $22 to $25?

Mrs. G.: . . . Right. But I know he can't afford it because it's hard for him. But he can give me $20 or $22.

Mr. G.: Because sometimes I have to pay the rent. I have to pay some bills . . .

Therapist A.: You know, may I say something? This is a problem, you know, it is a problem.

Mrs. G.: It's not so big, but it's a problem.

Although problems in connection with the use and sharing of money still indicate considerable conflict between Mr. and Mrs. Garcia with little evidence of change (see sixth session, sequences 9 to 11), there seems to be some indication of a change in perspective. Problems in this area dominated many of the interactions between husband and wife, yielding only mistrust and conflict, with no solutions in sight. Now these same problems are seen as much more manageable. Therapist A. immediately follows with:

SEQUENCE 35

Therapist A.: It is a problem. First, of trying between both of you, of talking and coming to some arrangement.

Mrs. G.: Right.

Mr. G.: . . .

Therapist A.: You see, the feeling, Maria, that you had when you went to Pepe, you were annoyed and you responded to him with annoyance, with anger. And Pepe answered you with the feeling: "What do you want from me, my flesh, my blood? You want $50?" And it seemed to me that this—

Mrs. G.: And I told him no. I say, "No, I don't want no $50, I just want for you to go and see the prices with me, so you . . ."

Therapist B.: Yeah, but I think that Therapist A. is trying to say that even though you were getting along, and you are not mad at each other, that you treated this important problem with a little bit of anger, and Therapist A. is saying that even in this problem you can have family cooperation. You said, "I want him to go with me to see the prices." You were right, but maybe you could say, "Pepe, you know, I need your help to go shopping, because the prices . . ."

Mrs. Garcia is trying to get Mr. Garcia to join her in appraising and confronting their financial problems with respect to marketing. There is a pull toward "come with me and share my troubles in this area."

SEQUENCE 36

The following is a continuation of sequence 35.

Mrs. Garcia has achieved some success in her efforts to get her husband to share her problems in this area, and both therapists respond to this success, indicating the conditions under which this success can occur.

Mrs. G.: I used to say to him, tell him every time, but he don't feel like it—

Therapist B.: But he went Thanksgiving to shop with you. And we were very pleased to hear it. (*Mr. G. laughs.*) I hear you had a beautiful dinner.

Mrs. G.: That's right.

Therapist B.: Felipe, he said it was excellent, and a big family, you had guests, and he was very proud that he went to shop with your husband. But Therapist A. is saying now that maybe, on every problem, you will find a way if you are not too mad, but if you are so mad—

Therapist A.: If you talk to each other, you see?

We have already seen that covert delinquency was the rule in the handling of money between husband and wife. This was deeply affecting their parenting roles, for conflicts around money-sharing were contaminating all family relationships with mistrust. Now Mr. and Mrs. Garcia seem able to enter more directly, less covertly, into dealing with their problems in sharing money.

Satisfaction—Husband and Wife around Sexuality

Sequences 37 to 39 are from the twenty-eighth session, Stage 2.

SEQUENCE 37

The following sequence is fairly explicit. Mr. Garcia gets his message across clearly. There is increased mutuality between husband and wife, and Mr. Garcia clearly perceives his wife as more responsive to him.

Therapist B.: . . . How is it, as man and wife, how is it getting on?

Mrs. G.: Fine.

Therapist B.: I'm speaking about sex, how is it?

Mrs. G.: Fine, fine.

Therapist B.: It's better?

Mrs. G.: It's better.

Therapist B.: Well, if she says it's better, she was always complaining. How is it for you, Pepe?

Mr. G.: Oh, it feels all right. In other words, I feel, you know, so different. Like before, you see, in other words, in appreciation or something like that. She's much better.

Therapist B.: How do you explain this? What do you think happened?

Mr. G.: Well—

Therapist A.: What is the difference?

Mr. G.: Well, it's different. Before it was different in . . . because sometimes she don't get feelings, you know. Now I notice, now—maybe —because she went to the hospital—maybe they got something over there—I think—

Mrs. G.: *He's* changed.

Therapist B.: Uh-hum. He says that you have the feeling now.

This is obviously in reference to Mrs. Garcia's previous frigidity symptoms, which had made the husband feel that he was not being sexually reciprocated. The sequence continues:

Mrs. G.: No. Doctor do nothing. It feels unchanged.

Therapist A.: In what way is Pepe changed?

Mr. G.: Well, that's what I feel. But she never told me what happen. The only thing is I notice a difference, you see?

Mrs. G.: You know what happened?

Therapist A.: You noticed a difference?

There is again an interchange in which Mr. Garcia expresses his feelings that Mrs. Garcia was told what to do by the doctor, which she denies. The sequence continues:

Therapist B.: Listen to her. She says it's not true.

Mrs. G.: No, it wasn't.

Therapist A.: Well, tell him what is the difference. Tell him, Maria. What's the difference?

SEQUENCE 38

After a few minutes, the above sequence continues. Both husband and wife are able to verbalize the changes they see in each other.

Therapist B.: But this is not every time?

Mr. G.: No.

Mrs. G.: Oh, no, no!

Therapist A.: What is, in what way, Maria, is Pepe, why do you say that things are better in sex? Why, Pepe says that you show feelings toward him. Is that Pepe—

Mrs. G.: That's right.

Mr. G.: She show to me some feeling when it was sometimes, when some person . . . like it's another thing . . . now she do it with feelings. Right, but she—before—she don't do it that way. Something, like, it was not interesting before. Something like that. I notice a little difference in her.

Therapist A.: In what way? How do you notice now?

Mr. G.: Well, she try to love, love me more, you see, something like that—uh—in other words, she is close to me.

Therapist A.: How does she show it? Physically? She comes to you?

Mr. G.: That's right. I know the difference.

Therapist A.: What do you think, Maria, what's the difference in your opinion?

Mrs. G.: That he understands more—you know—he understands me more.

Therapist A.: How?

Mrs. G.: Uh—my feelings.

Therapist A.: How does he? Explain better. How? Can you give me an example of how?

Mrs. G.: Uh—no—I don't know how.

Therapist B.: Well, I think you used to tell me, Maria, exactly what he says now about you. You used to say, "He has no feelings. He's just mechanical, and he does not respond to me with feelings, and he only does it because the therapists want him to," you remember?

Mrs. G.: Right.

Therapist B.: So, what is it, how is it now?

Mrs. G.: One of the things I don't know—but—uh—we were both trying.
Therapist B.: Uh-hum.
Mrs. G.: Now, it's not only me or him, alone, but we both trying. But what I think is very good understanding in each other.
Therapist B.: Well, this sounds very good . . .

The sense of reciprocity, of giving while receiving contrasts sharply with what we learned of this problem in the sixth session (see sequences 12 and 13.)

SEQUENCE 39

A few minutes after the above sequence, the therapist verbalizes and differentiates for the Garcias some important changes within the nonverbal interaction of the here-and-now:

Therapist A.: May I interrupt just a moment here? I want to say something that has just happened now. Maria made a gesture that Pepe should—
Therapist B.: Take over?
Therapist A.: Yes, take over and express. And this is, in itself, a big change, you know, that you let him express himself first.
Therapist B.: Good. Well, what were you going to say?
Mr. G.: Well, the only thing I feel from the beginning, we come over here and we don't understand that we live in different worlds, you see? Living like—persons try to fight, or something like that—uh— we live in this world. Now, as soon as the session, we come over here every Monday, we discuss about problems. I just understand that everything is coming all right, anyway for me. I know about the rest, but I think in the family—everything comes all right.

The reference to "different worlds" is explanatory enough. The alienation that characterized the relationship between Mr. and Mrs. Garcia has been somewhat reduced, and there is, furthermore, awareness and reflectiveness concerning their relationship.

Summary

The Garcia family system had certain outstanding, intertwined characteristics: (1) Mrs. Garcia was used as a central pathway, a relay station of communications between her sons and her husband; and (2) the "husband" and "wife" roles were submerged or absorbed by the "parent" roles.

In their day-to-day living Mr. Garcia was peripheral, and inaccessible to his children. Contact between the older son and the father (when the mother was circumvented) was confined to antagonistic and rebellious interactions. These interactional characteristics were requirements of the system, and compelled the younger son to rely almost exclusively on Mrs. Garcia or on the older son for guidance.

The therapist adopted a particular approach toward the Garcia family configuration. His over-all focus was to define and enrich the spouse subsystem. The general orientation guiding the therapist was that if changes could be produced in the *spouse* subsystem, the *parent* subsystem would show concomitant changes benefiting the web of interaction in the family as a whole.

This approach involved helping Mr. and Mrs. Garcia to: (1) broaden the areas of contact and experience in their roles as husband and wife per se; (2) gradually curtail Mrs. Garcia's power as a central and "over-available" figure; and (3) expand the areas for Mr. Garcia's participation and sense of interpersonal competence in the family. The general goal was to encourage the containment of adult problems within the spouse subsystem, for these problems were contaminating the parent roles and the socialization of the children. At the termination of treatment, the clinical team felt that the Garcia family had made some progress in the direction of these over-all therapeutic goals.

PART 2   The Montgomery Family: A Profile of Unchanged Disorganization

Several years ago, the vast records of the Children's Court were expanded by the addition of the following terse but dramatic statement:

> The M. children were under such improper guardianship and control by the mother and Mr. M., with whom the mother has been living for the past 10 years without benefit of marriage, as to injure and endanger their health, morals and general welfare in that Mr. M., on or about . . . 1956, attempted to have an act of sexual intercourse with Marguerite, the older girl, and on other occasions has asked the child to come to bed with him, (and) that this paramour drinks alcoholic beverages to excess and fights and abuses the mother physically in the presence of the children. Further, the mother was aware of the advances which Mr. M. made to the child, Marguerite, but took no action whatsoever.

The Montgomerys, a Negro family, were subsequently to become members of our research population. The rest of this chapter attempts to communicate the quality of the interpersonal transactions of the members of this family as it was disclosed during treatment.

The clinical staff of our research team judged the Montgomery family to be "nonchanged" when the family pattern of interaction at the beginning, during, and at the termination of therapy was reviewed. Whether or not "nonchange," as viewed therapeutically, is a prognostication for the future actions of the Montgomery family members raises other considerations. Only long-range follow-up research can provide the answers. Our guess would be that certain members of this family will continue to behave in such a way as to come to the serious attention of the police, the courts, and various other institutions—that is, unless there is some powerful, preventive intervention. What such intervention could be, or might be, is not within the scope of either our research or our discussion. The label "nonchanged," then, viewed in the more limited sense of our continuous observation of this family during the treatment process, is based not on the behavior of this family in the community, but on the nature of their interpersonal transactions (with each other and with the therapists) during the course of therapy.

Without (except indirectly) focusing our attention on *why* this family did not seem to change during the course of treatment, we will attempt to illustrate the *ways* in which it did not change. The segments from the tape-recorded transcripts of treatment sessions with this family were taken from the sixth, thirteenth, twentieth, and twenty-eighth sessions. It will be noted that the quality of the interactions seems to be the same throughout. Indeed, sequences from the later sessions could easily have been transposed directly into earlier sessions without a break or shift in continuity, quality, or narrative sequence. As contrasted with the Garcia family (see earlier), there is no unfolding of a story, no discernible learning process, and, in a sense, no beginning and no ending. The same material, and more important, the same operations, are manifested throughout the sessions.

The material seemed to fall into four general areas: (1) communication processes; (2) mother-child interactions; (3) delinquent and aggressive operations; and (4) the world in which the Montgomerys—especially the children—live. As contrasted to the sequences pertaining to the Garcias, stress will be placed on certain aspects of the sibling subsystem in this family. Although these areas serve as the framework for our illustrations, we will also indicate, from time to time, additional aspects of the sequences which might be of interest. As with the Garcias, attention will also be drawn to some of the therapists' operations.

At the time of intake of one of the children (Richard) at the Wiltwyck School, the members of the Montgomery family were described as follows (see footnote 3, page 46):

Mrs. Montgomery, 38 years old, was born in North Carolina, the second of seven children. Her mother died when she was 10 years old, and she was raised by a grandmother. After she finished high school, she entered college, only to leave because of her first out-of-wedlock pregnancy. At the age of 17, she bore her first son, whom she left with her sister in North Carolina.

She came to New York City in 1940 when she was 18 years old, but returned to North Carolina after a few months. She had a relationship there with a Mr. H. who is the father of Marguerite (17 years old) and Phyllis (16 years old). She never lived with Mr. H., but "for some reason, couldn't avoid intimacies with him." At the age of 23, Mrs. Montgomery came once again to New York City, bringing her two daughters with her. Shortly afterward, she met Mr. Montgomery and lived with him for the next thirteen years. The sons, Clark, 14, Henry or "Laddy," 13, Michael, 11, Richard, 10, and Thomas, 9, were born of this relationship.

Mr. Montgomery, 45 years old, whereabouts unknown, was ordered out of the household by the court in 1957, three years prior to Richard's intake at the Wiltwyck School. He had been a patient at the neurological clinic in a city hospital in Harlem, with several physical complaints and frequent headaches which had made him unable to work since 1951. Since then, the family has been on public assistance.

Marguerite, who was 17 years old when Richard entered the Wiltwyck School, was the target of the family members' anger at that time. They had accused her of having "kicked" her stepfather out of the home, for when she was sexually attacked by three boys and taken to court, she told the court about her previous sexual experience with Mr. M., who was then ordered by the court to leave the home. (Mrs. M. had asked Marguerite not to tell anybody about her sexual contacts with him.) In 1962, when the family began therapy, Marguerite was the mother of an out-of-wedlock baby who was then a few months old. At this time, she was regarded as "the good daughter," and was considering the possibility of marrying the father of her baby.

Phyllis, at the age of 16, had a 2½-year-old out-of-wedlock child, and had been involved in several stealing episodes. She was caught up in intense power transactions with her mother, these struggles being acted out in almost every interaction between them but centering mostly around issues concerning her truancy, staying out late, and not taking care of her baby.

Clark, 14, had had meningitis when he was younger, was mentally retarded, and living in a New York State institution for retarded children.

Henry ("Laddy"), 13 years old, had been involved in a stealing incident and had a court record as a juvenile delinquent. He had spent one year in one of the New York State training schools. Though he had had difficulties with his mother prior to his going to "the school," he was considered, at this time, a "good child" by Mrs. Montgomery. He was attending a New York City "600" school.[8] He was acting quite autonomously in some areas, and Mrs. Montgomery gave him the "right" to come home late (sometimes as late as 1 or 2 A.M.) because of his status as the older boy.

Michael, 11 years old, was the scapegoat of the family. Whenever there was some stealing within the family, suspicion was immediately directed toward him. Michael was labeled by the family members as "dope," "stupid," "brainless," as well as "the robber." He had had difficulties in school and had been transferred to a "600" school. He also had a juvenile delinquency record with the courts.

Richard, at intake, was 10 years old (he had been at the Wiltwyck School for two years when our research was initiated). He had been referred by the court with a delinquency petition because of multiple acting-out in school. In the last incident he had manhandled a classmate in front of a teacher, flung a rock at another teacher, and seemed "impossible to contain." At Wiltwyck, he was described as a bully, and as

---

[8] New York City's "600" schools (labeled as such because the Board of Education designated them by numbers in the six hundreds, e.g., P.S. 637) were public elementary schools to which children considered to be "difficult" in ordinary school settings were assigned. These schools were populated by disturbed, rebellious children to an unusually high degree, and had a disproportionately large number of Puerto Rican and Negro youngsters. They were often "problem" schools in a number of respects: their physical location (in overcrowded, poorly housed areas—often "ghettos"); run-down physical plant; and considerable staff turnover.

having a number of "slaves" whom he exploited for food and sex.[9] With adults, he was clinging and submissive, yet extremely suspicious.

Thomas, 9 years old, was the "baby." He was considered by Mrs. Montgomery to be the only one who "can do no wrong." He was very attached to his mother, as she was to him. He was doing reasonably well in school, according to the records at the time of Wiltwyck intake.

Our clinical team was impressed with the fact that there was not one "well" child in the family despite the foregoing statements about Thomas. Each child was or had been involved in antisocial activities, and/or displayed behavior which was not age-appropriate.

The Excerpts

Communication Processes

As will be seen in the following pages, the pattern and flow of communication in the Montgomery family has a distinctive flavor. There is a chaotic, disorganized quality in the content that emerges; indeed, the explicit content itself seems to be sacrificed for other types of messages. Logical inconsistencies, the shifting of content, contradictory statements, confusions about time, place, and specifics of an event being discussed, and constant and frequent interruptions characterize the spoken messages. Seemingly *implicit* in these chaotic overt communications is another type of content: the Montgomery family members are constantly involved in competitive aggression with each other and in the need to rank one another in some hierarchical fashion. The theme constantly being transacted is some variation of, "I am more powerful than you," or "You are worse than me." In these interactions, in which such global, interpersonal struggles are at stake, formal rules of logic do not apply.

Overt, explicit content of the Montgomerys' communications seems to revolve, repetitively and endlessly, around aggression and stealing. As already noted, these themes are disclosed in almost all phases of the

---

[9] In such residential centers (see H. W. Polsky, *Cottage six*, New York: Russell Sage Foundation, 1962), a subculture—a peer culture, so to speak—thrives and regulates the members therein, often without control, supervision, or impact from the staff, professional and otherwise. Rules, mores, and codes emerge, with a language and structure which frequently defy or mystify the authorities. "Pecking orders" develop, and those higher up in the hierarchy literally extract "favors" from those who are lower. Among these are homosexual "servicing," stealing of food, etc. The peer culture cannot even be termed *sub rosa* because many of the children talk freely about their roles within this subculture, and use the relevant slang and jargon quite openly when queried.

therapy, early and late, with little variation, not only in the issues bandied about, but also in the *manner* and *style* of the interactions. Themes contain subthemes, and the conflicts, arguments, accusations, and counter-accusations flow from one area to another with unusual fluidity; there is no attempt to resolve or to conclude a phase, and even more important, there is a striking lack of awareness or concern on the part of family members that issues are not resolved and that there are no beginnings or endings.

An integral aspect of the mood, quality, and distinctiveness of the sessions with the Montgomery family relates not only to the type of communications noted above, but also to the level of disengagement that the children displayed when they were not directly involved in verbal interaction with the therapist or other family members. The children brought comic books to the sessions and would frequently read them, even when content directly concerning them was being verbalized. Sometimes one, two, or even three of them would fall asleep or would engage in some kind of autistic playing with one object or another. Occasionally, one of the children would put his coat over his head, creating an impression of total isolation from his environment. Such behavior is, of course, not directly disclosed by the sequences which follow. But the impact of this disengagement on the quality of the sessions is striking.

The therapists, of course, must handle in some way such extreme detachment and disengagement. Because our excerpts do not directly convey all therapist activities with respect to the disengagement process, we feel we should indicate some of these. The therapist would activate the children by taking away their comics, by prodding them into interaction, by asking their mother to wake them up, or in some way interacting with them. The need of the therapist to "activate" these children sometimes produced a rather strange type of dialogue. A significant theme might at times be interrupted by an intervention of one of the disengaged children; the therapist would then "detour" to follow the meanderings of the newly engaged child. The essential purpose of this detour was to make the child experience some contact with the therapist.

After such attempts to establish some contact with the child, the therapist would often return to the main theme and go along with it for a while until the need to engage *another* child would produce still another meandering away from the main theme or themes. And so on. This gave the sessions a characteristic chaotic jumping from theme to theme. It should be noted that the family members as well as the therapist contributed to this quality. The therapist's participation in the disorganized patterns of the Montgomerys' communication processes may have contributed to some of the difficulties in working with this family. But we might suggest that the situational factors ("mood" of the session, as it were) which motivated the therapist to contact the child regardless of the expense are certainly not captured by the sequences which follow or even by the reading of entire transcripts.[10]

SEQUENCE 1   THIRTEENTH SESSION, STAGE 1

The dialogue between Mrs. Montgomery and Phyllis, below, illustrates the family members' use of and response to language. For them it is a vehicle to communicate affect. For language generally is not used functionally by the Montgomerys to solve problems or mutually explore issues.

Phyllis: Maybe somebody'll be in the house fighting. She don't even wait to see what it is. She just comes in there hollering at me. Now say you don't do that.

Mrs. M.: Yeah, because I know how . . .

Phyllis: I don't start arguing.

Mrs. M.: . . . I know how you . . .

Phyllis: So, you should find out what happened first. Not just come in there and argue . . . so, it's no way to say it, the way you been telling me something.

Therapist: Is there a way to say it, Phyllis?

Phyllis: Sure, there's a way to say it.

Mrs. M.: Why don't you learn it then? How to talk to people.

Phyllis: I know that way. I've been learning it *your* way. I'm learning it *your* way.

Note above that at the point when the therapist is trying to explore and to neutralize affect, Mrs. Montgomery interrupts with an attack. His question is designed to introduce some appropriate "distance" that could allow exploration, but Mrs. Montgomery's interruption, which engages

---

[10] This disengagement process and the consequent therapist activities to disrupt and break through it characterized most of our treatment sessions. The directive quality of many of the therapist statements, the queries, the information-seeking, and the concrete explorations of seemingly neutral areas were necessarily part of this therapist activity, yielding verbal material on the part of the family members which to some extent was shaped by these therapeutic procedures. Appendix B, which describes in some detail the results of an analysis of the verbal interactions that took place, highlights this point.

Phyllis in a power struggle with her, precludes the kind of exploration toward which the therapist is trying to orient the discussion. The sequence continues:

Therapist: Well, what way?

Phyllis: If I wasn't . . . Laddy asked me if I was coming downtown. I'm supposed to say no or yes. So I don't feel like being bothered.

Therapist: I didn't really understand you. You said no or yes?

Phyllis: If I was coming I'm supposed to say yes. If I'm not coming, I'm supposed to say no. But I just don't feel like being bothered.

Therapist: In other words, the way to say it is the direct way?

Phyllis: Yes.

Therapist: You mean, when your mother says something to you, it's not direct?

Phyllis: No, she just hollers. What's all that hollering for? I'm not deaf.

Mrs. M.: Phyllis, when I try to get you to get out of bed and go dry the baby, I do holler then? What do I say? I come in there . . .

Phyllis: "Get out of this bed!"

In the above segment, Phyllis is bitterly complaining that her mother "hollers" at her continually. In their dyadic interactions, in which negative affect is kept invariant, the meaning of verbal content is subordinated to the sign of the affect. Words lose, or never acquire, the freedom necessary for their use as instruments for exchange of neutral information. Phyllis learns that in her interactions with her mother words are used primarily for the delineation of power. Thus, although she is presumably agreeing with the therapist that "the way to say it is the direct way," she amply demonstrates that the "direct way" elicits no response from her. "If I was coming I'm supposed to say yes. If I'm not coming I'm supposed to say no. But I just don't feel like being bothered." For Phyllis, her mother's "hollering" and Laddy's direct question seem to be emotionally equivalent.

SEQUENCE 2 SIXTH SESSION, STAGE 1

The segment below illustrates the difficulties the therapist faces when he attempts to establish a meaningful dialogue in a significant area with one of the children. His goal, seemingly, is to *involve* Tommy, but he fails repeatedly. The incident under discussion concerns Tommy's attempts to escape from home through the window.

Therapist: Tommy, do you go out of the window because Mike does?

Tommy: No.

Therapist: What do you think about going out of the window, your escape?

Tommy: Uh? Nothing.

Therapist: Do you think all this stuff we are talking about concerns you in any way? Hmmm?

Tommy: I don't know.

Therapist: Hmmm? Well let's think about this for a moment. Do you see yourself as heading for trouble? (*Tommy shrugs his shoulders.*)

Therapist: Do you understand the question, Tommy? Do you see yourself heading for trouble?

Tommy: I don't know.

Therapist: I think this is something he should know. Don't you, Laddy? Is he doing anything that's sending him to trouble right now? Do you think so?

Henry (Laddy): No.

The therapist is greeted with noncommittal replies at every turn; he tries different inroads, but unsuccessfully. Does Tommy feel that he is personally involved in the discussion? Does Tommy anticipate some of the consequences of his act? The child's inability to relate to these issues is extreme. The therapist appeals to a sibling for support—perhaps also to involve the *new* child in some of the discussion—to no avail.

SEQUENCE 3   THIRTEENTH SESSION, STAGE 1

Several minutes after sequence 1, the interchange between Phyllis and her mother continues:

Mrs. M.: . . . You don't listen to me.

Phyllis: So you don't say nothing. Somebody . . . you are always hollering.

Therapist: Phyllis, you don't hear your mother very well when she does say things to you, do you? You don't listen to her.

Phyllis: No.

Therapist: That doesn't make it very easy for her to . . .

Phyllis: So I listen to what I want to hear, and something the way she says it don't even make no sense.

Therapist: You mean, the other side of that is you don't listen to things you don't want to hear.

Phyllis: That's right.

Therapist: So that some of the things you tell *her* and *she* doesn't want to hear and she refuses to listen, is what you're saying. What happens to your mother, does she listen to you?

Phyllis: I don't never say nothing to her. I don't ask her nothing about nothing. I'll go ask somebody else before I ask her. I ask my god-mother.[11]

Therapist: Well, do you see what message that sends your mother?

Phyllis: No, why should I? I ain't never been talked to . . . She ain't never talked to me about nothing.

In the above segment, Phyllis' bitterness continues. There is little ex-pectation that language between herself and her mother can be used for the exchange of information ("I don't never say nothing to her." "I ain't never been talked to. She ain't never talked to me about nothing.") The pattern of "hollering" and "nonlistening" goes something like this: "If I know what you will say to me, and if that is something derogatory to me, I will not listen." "If you don't listen to me, I need to increase the volume of my voice so you will listen." "If you yell at me as a way of com-municating your dislike of me, I will cut you off by closing my ears or by never talking to you." Obviously, this type of operation results in considerable static and interference in the communication among the family members.

SEQUENCE 4   THIRTEENTH SESSION, STAGE 1

Later on, in the same session, Phyllis and Mrs. Montgomery continue their exchange, illustrating once more the "nonlistening" and "nonhear-ing" so characteristic of their dialogue.

Mrs. M.: Yes, I take your clothes out because you refuse to do anything in the house. I asked you one day to take the baby's clothes. You wouldn't even do that.

Phyllis: When was this?

Mrs. M.: I asked you one day last week.

Phyllis: You didn't ask me. Don't say that. That wasn't last week.

Mrs. M.: And those clothes stayed in that bag until I got through that night and took them to the Bendix.

Phyllis: Well, I don't remember that. I don't remember that. I sure didn't hear you.

Mrs. M.: I guess not, because you went right on upstairs to Louise's house and went to bed.

---

[11] Significant people on the periphery of the family can support or disrupt family members' efforts toward resolving their role conflicts. In our current work (see Chapter 6, pages 272–274) the relationship of Mrs. M. Phyllis, and her godmother would be explored as a unit for therapeutic intervention.

Phyllis: I don't know nothing about it. You didn't say it to me or I didn't hear you.

Phyllis refuses to discuss the issue of responsibility for the care of her baby's clothes. Her line of defense, even in the above brief interchange, is a constantly shifting one, indeed: (1) when was this; (2) you didn't ask me; (3) that wasn't last week; (4) I don't remember that; (5) I sure didn't hear you; (6) I don't know nothing about it; (7) (again) you didn't say it to me; and (8) (again) I didn't hear you. This shifting of the content of verbal defenses characterizes a communication that deals essentially with relationship messages. If one pays attention to the interpersonal transactions involved here, one can see that Phyllis is consistently stating that her mother's accusations, regardless of content, are unfair.

SEQUENCE 5   TWENTIETH SESSION, STAGE 1

The sudden interjection of a new theme (and the therapist's "going along" with the shift) is illustrated below. Mrs. Montgomery had been talking about her stealing money from her husband and how the children were witnessing the operation.

Mrs. M.: Yeah, I—uh—usually, I took it when I be by myself, but everyone seem to be peeking. They all seemed to be peeking.

Therapist A.: Tommy was the one most likely to be peeking and watching what you were doing, huh?

Henry: (*Showing a picture.*) This is a sister that won the beauty contest in October.

Therapist A.: Oh, really? That's wonderful.

Therapist B.: Yeah, she is pretty.

Therapist A.: Beautiful. Do you all know about that picture? Do you feel the same way about it as he does?

Richard: I knew about it before he did!

Therapist A.: You did? Who told you?

Richard: I was down there. And our cousin won second. She come in second place, right?

We see here that Henry is interrupting a significant issue that was being explored by introducing a seemingly unrelated theme. He shows a picture of his half-sister to the therapist and the therapist follows him by exploring this new theme for some minutes. But later on, the therapist attempts to return to the main issue:

Therapist A.: Well, they are shifting us pretty fast away from this money bit everyone is . . . concerned about.

Here, then, after permitting and encouraging an irrelevant shift, presumably in order to contact the children (see earlier discussion in this chapter), the therapist comes back to the main theme: Mrs. Montgomery's delinquency under the observation of her children. But the therapist fails to reflect this shift *when it happens* or the possible reasons underlying Henry's decided interruption (embarrassment? protectiveness toward his mother or his siblings?); further, the therapist's comment, "they are shifting us pretty fast away from this money bit . . ." fails to recognize his *own* participation in the shift.

The above sequence also illustrates a characteristic competitiveness between the siblings ("I knew about it before he did!") transforming the communication from one in which one child is sharing an event with the therapist to one in which both siblings are involved in the competitive interaction of who is more powerful.

SEQUENCE 6   TWENTIETH SESSION, STAGE 1

Communication with the outside world has the same lack of effectiveness and the same level of confusion that exist among the family members. For example, below there is an exchange between Mrs. Montgomery and Tommy about an injection that he received in school.

Tommy: (The doctor asked me) "Do you still have headaches?" I said, "For what?" He looked at me and said, "When you got hit in the head." And I said, "Oh, no."

Therapist: What man asked you this, Tommy?

Tommy: The doctor. And so . . . he got out this thing and I said, "I don't want no needle," and he said, "It's just an injection."

Therapist: Maybe Tommy didn't understand it before, because I don't understand it. Do you know what the injection was for?

Mrs. M.: I don't know, I don't know what it was for.

Tommy: Remember that day I brought you a paper?

Mrs. M.: I didn't sign. I didn't sign anything for you to get an injection.

Tommy: You did, you know. Remember that day I came home and that day when I got put back and they wrote down . . . ?

Mrs. M.: Yeah, that day I sent just a message and signed it . . .

Again, in this world of confusing messages, Mrs. Montgomery received a communication from the school without receiving it; she apparently signed a paper but states that she did not sign anything. She knows nothing about the injection of which Tommy claims she *had* been informed.

SEQUENCE 7   TWENTY-EIGHTH SESSION, STAGE 1

Another instance of confused communication between Mrs. Montgomery and one of her children is illustrated in the following sequence:

Therapist A.: Did you two guys hear about the birthday party we had that you missed? (*In the previous session, the therapist had brought a birthday cake for one of the siblings.*)

Michael: She told me not to come (*indicating mother*).

Therapist A.: Who told you not to come? (*At this point, Mrs. M. is reading a newspaper, and Tommy a comic book.*) Told you not to come to the party?

Mrs. M.: I didn't tell him not to come. I told him that he had to go to school. And the way he was looking, I told him he'd better not come down here looking the way he was looking, that's what I told him. He didn't want to wear what I wanted him to wear.

Therapist A.: And that meant your not coming to the party, Michael?

Michael: I went to school and just signed up and came home.

Mrs. M.: . . .

Therapist A.: You mean he signed up to come down here and instead he went home?

Therapist B.: . . .

Michael: Because she told me not to come.

Therapist A.: Why didn't you stay in school, then?

Michael: . . .

Therapist: Henry, did you hear about the party?

Henry: Yeah.

Therapist: Now, let's get the whole thing straight. You told him that . . .

Mrs. M.: Yeah, I told him to go to school and check out. He didn't want to wear what I wanted him to. (*Continues looking at newspaper.*)

Therapist A.: I see.

Mrs. M.: So, he didn't wear it. Didn't want to wear it.

Therapist A.: What did you want him to wear?

Mrs. M.: Wanted him to change his pants, I think, and his shirt. He had on a sports shirt, you know.

Therapist A.: Michael got the message then that he couldn't come here unless he was dressed.

In the above excerpt, Mrs. Montgomery sends the message, "I want you to change your clothing," but the child receives it as, "I cannot make you obey me, therefore, I punish you by not letting you come to the party dressed like that." Although there is an implicit alternative in the message that she sends, "You could come if you would change," the child has become engaged in a power struggle, hearing only, "Do not come to the party." He, in turn, punishes his mother by not staying in school. Note, too, Mrs. Montgomery's disengagement from the proceedings, indicated by her reading a newspaper. The therapist seems to accept this. He seems, at least in this session, to have been inducted into the family system.

Mother-Child Interaction: Helplessness and Defeat

Mrs. Montgomery is a big woman, bright and verbal. She impressed those in direct interaction with her as being insightful, and well able to differentiate her children by pointing to their individual characteristics. In view of this, her inability to manage her children and her "giving up" (by abandoning the parental field) were regarded by the clinician who worked with this family as "relinquishment of executive functions." It should be noted, in this connection, that this view was consistent with our early formulations (see Chapter 1) concerning the parental roles in our families. This interpretation of Mrs. Montgomery's behavior motivated the therapist to continue to "prod" her to look at her own behavior as a disorganizing influence in the family field. The therapist focused on her "not doing" and on the children's "not accepting" whenever she "did." These therapeutic biases prevented an important observation: that Mrs. Montgomery was enmeshed in her children's lives and that she felt a constant need to "take over" when they failed to do things. She was a continuation of her children, replacing them and taking over their responsibilities, not as a matter of choice, but as part of her concept of motherhood.

Her chronic feelings of depression and of being overburdened and trapped by her children were not dealt with, and the therapeutic demands for her to "assume executive functions" increased her derogatory self-image, her guilt, and her resistance to change. Moreover, the complementarity of the children's role and their constant and insistent demands on her were also not adequately handled by therapeutic strategies.

The lack of focus on certain significant aspects of the Montgomery family system is in part a reflection of initial expectations concerning these families which have been modified in the light of our subsequent experiences (see Chapter 6). The hypothesis concerning the "relinquishment of executive functions" is an overly simple formulation which did not seem to tie in with our findings. Note, for example, the Garcia family, described earlier in this chapter. With Mr. and Mrs. Garcia, the therapist focused, with some degree of success, on issues concerning their perceptions of themselves as people, husband and wife, or man and woman, rather than on their "assuming executive functions."

SEQUENCE 8 SIXTH SESSION, STAGE 1

Most of the excerpts of the mother-child interaction deal with Mrs. Montgomery's expressed helplessness in controlling her children. An instance of this is in the sixth session.

Mrs. M.: (*In relation to Phyllis*.) We got into a fuss about me taking care of the baby and she going free, you know. So I don't really think I have to take care of her, but I only do what she won't, but the baby has to be bathed, and has to be clean, and has to have clean clothes. So I just go on and do it, and I'm sorry. And I made her get up out of bed. She stayed up for the Late Late Show and she wants to sleep all day. I resent that, being that I am doing for the baby . . . I take over all the responsibility. . . . She didn't do the dishes, and she wasn't doing anything, and everybody has something to do, and she didn't do them. She just sits down and refuses.

Mrs. Montgomery, in the above statements, expresses her resentment of caring for Phyllis' baby while "she [is] going free." That the situation remained unchanged several weeks later is seen in the sequence below.

SEQUENCE 9 THIRTEENTH SESSION, STAGE 1

Mrs. M.: . . . Because you don't even be in the house to help me take care of the baby, and I get tired all day long taking care of that baby. I have things to do that I have to go out.

Phyllis: When I get ready to do something for her, you always holler, "I am taking care of this baby. Don't holler at her. Don't do this. Don't do that." So I don't say nothing to her. You are taking care of her. Everything! . . . Bathe her, put her to bed, too. That's the way I feel about you since you are taking care of her.

Earlier in the same session, the following interchange took place:

Therapist: Phyllis, what are you saying? That you have given up doing things for the baby since your mother is doing it?

Phyllis: That's right. Why should I do it when she does it?

Mrs. M.: Because you will not do it.

Phyllis: I will do it. I know what I do.

Mrs. M.: You do not. I ask you to get up and dry the baby. You lay up there on the bed until 12 or 1 o'clock and refuse to get up and dry the baby. Well, I can't see the baby neglected so I go on and do it, that's why. 'Cause if you mean right, you'd go and do it without me asking you and I get tired of asking you . . . So, to keep from my asking, I go and do it. The baby don't eat breakfast. I have to go out and fix breakfast. You won't even get up to fix the baby's breakfast. The baby goes to sleep starved, and it's wrong to let the baby be neglected like that, so I just go and do it . . . and you don't do these things that I ask you to do. I ask you to come in the house and do something in the house, or help me do something in the house . . .

Phyllis: (*Interrupting.*) You don't ask me nothing. You don't ask me nothing.

Mrs. M.: I ask you.

Phyllis: I clean up that room like I'm supposed to and leave.

Mrs. M.: Then you leave the baby there on me.

Therapist: Phyllis, why do you leave?

Phyllis: So I won't be arguing.

Mrs. M.: I do not. I don't have anything to say to you, Phyllis.

Phyllis: You do. You be around there saying things.

Mrs. M.: I do not tell you anything to do.

Phyllis: (*With tears in her eyes.*) You do so. You be around there telling me, "Get you a man, and this and that."

Mrs. M.: Well, you can stay with your baby. That's not my baby. She comes in the morning at 5:30.

Phyllis: So how was I going to sleep in that room?

Mrs. M.: You have slept in there. You have slept in there in that bed . . .

Phyllis: Henry had thrown up so nobody could sleep in there. So I wasn't going to sleep in there. (*Phyllis is very upset.*)

Mrs. M.: (*Speaks while Phyllis is speaking.*)

Phyllis: So what time did Henry come in?

Mrs. M.: Henry . . .

Phyllis: (*Interrupting.*) He came in there five minutes before.

Mrs. M.: He did not . . .

Phyllis: He did so, because he left Frances' house five minutes before.

Mrs. M.: It doesn't make sense, you coming in there.

Phyllis: So why should I . . . be telling a story?

Mrs. M.: I am not telling a story.

Phyllis: You are so. (*Her voice gets louder.*)

Mrs. M.: I do not . . . and I have other people I need to worry about . . . The same statement I made . . . that this child come in . . .

Phyllis: What time does Henry come in?

The bickering continues about whether Phyllis had come in before or after Henry, and after an attempt by the therapist to find a solution to this conflict, they shift to another area of disagreement (Phyllis is the aggressive one, at this point) around the fact that Mrs. Montgomery doesn't buy her clothing. And before this discussion is resolved, they enter another conflict, this time about Phyllis' sleeping in the house of a neighbor. This is followed by still another power operation, the content "always and never" changing.

Mrs. Montgomery discloses that she feels a sense of responsibility for her daughter's behavior, and because she is unable to make her responsible for her own activities, she automatically steps in herself—repairing, fulfilling obligations, and acting, in a sense, in her daughter's behalf. She enters this role, but feels overburdened and resentful, nevertheless. Phyllis responds to all of this by feeling that her mother is taking away her own responsibility as a mother. She acts resentful, relinquishing *all* the responsibilities that are being met by her mother. The therapist, in these interactions, seemingly accuses Mrs. Montgomery of being unable to make her daughter assume responsibility.

In these power struggles between mother and daughter, it should be noted, the strong affect displayed permeates all areas. There is, it would seem, no differentiation, no hierarchical structuring of values as to what is important and what is less important. In the above sequence, for example, the conflict is allowed to run rampant even in a primary life-area of the baby. The baby might well go without breakfast, be wet, go to sleep starved. This issue is dropped with the same complete nonresolution as transactions and interchanges with respect to whether Phyllis or Henry came home later.

SEQUENCE 10 SIXTH SESSION, STAGE 1

Mrs. Montgomery experiences the same helplessness with her other children:

Mrs. M.: . . . I had a time getting them out, I had a terrible time. And I was . . . to come on all by myself, or [even] not to come myself, because Laddy and Mike, both of them, both of them didn't want to come. And Richard said, "As long as they won't come, I can't come home no more." So then he say, "Well, I guess they don't want me home," and he . . . went to the door . . .

Later in this session, also in relation to bringing the children to the sessions, Mrs. Montgomery says:

Mrs. M.: Well, in general, I—uh—it's all right with me, but it makes . . .
I fight with the kids back there all the time.

Therapist: You have to fight with the kids all the time?

Mrs. M.: Yeah. And then too, some will cooperate and some won't and
I—uh—can't make them. Michael is the only one that I count on, and
that makes me a little bit disagreeable, and fighting with them . . .

Therapist: . . . What I mean is that you were at the point of giving up?

Mrs. M.: Uh-huh.

Therapist: You had said that sometimes they had fought with you and
you had fought as much as you could and then they said, "No."
What Laddy and Mike are saying is that they wouldn't have come
if it hadn't been for Richard. They are not coming for you, they are
coming because of him. You said the same thing about Phyllis and
the baby. You said, "It's your baby and take care of it" and Phyllis
said, "No." You give up and you take care of the baby. What do
you think about that? How does it strike you? Do you understand
what I am saying?

Mrs. M.: I—ah—I—ah—I think I do.

Mrs. Montgomery has been verbalizing her profound feelings of helplessness with respect to getting the children to obey her. The therapist
restates her feelings and attempts also to indicate how her "taking over"
and her being "at the point of giving up" both reflect her despair. Again
there is a message to the mother that *she* is the only one responsible and
that she is the only one who can change that system in the family. (Mrs.
Montgomery's weak "I think I do" is a tentative "agreeing" response,
probably not reflecting true understanding, but rather compliance.) He
continues along these lines a little later, in the same session.

SEQUENCE 11   SIXTH SESSION, STAGE 1

Tommy: I came [to the session] because of Richard.

Mrs. M.: You only came because of that? So you didn't come because
I said so. . . .

      . . . .

Tommy: I was going to get up early in the morning to get my bird.

Therapist: . . .

Mrs. M.: You only got up to get your bird?

Richard: When Mama came back she would have caught you.

Tommy: Then, I would have come down here.

Mrs. M.: Don't you think I would have whipped you when I did catch
you? You'd have to come home, wouldn't you?

Tommy: Yes.

Mrs. M.: Would you rather take the whipping than come home?

. . .

Therapist: It's very important in terms of why the kids get in trouble.

Mrs. M.: That's the first time I ever heard him say anything.

Therapist: I know. I know what a shock it is to you. I know, because
what you are really saying is that he'll defy you and he'll get away
with it. This is what gets him in trouble out there because the school
and the community won't take that from your kids. They won't take
what you have taken. They won't give up. They'll send them away
some place. The truant officer will pick them up, like Laddy, and
he'll go away soon afterward. You see, you have to take it in a sense.
And we are questioning really whether you have to take it.

In the above sequence, it is clear that the therapist is trying to show
Mrs. Montgomery that what she "takes" from her children is just the
kind of behavior that will get them into trouble with the authorities. He
is "throwing the book" at her and is invoking a number of frightening
images at the same time ("They'll send them away some place"). He is
attacking her helplessness by contrasting it to the nonhelplessness of society ("They won't take what you have taken. They won't give up").
The "attack" may well serve to enhance Mrs. Montgomery's negative
self-image and feelings of complete incapacity to cope with her problems.[12]

SEQUENCE 12   TWENTIETH SESSION, STAGE 1

The segment below, taken from a session rather late in the series,
discloses the same helplessness and defeat that Mrs. Montgomery had
expressed earlier with respect to the children. The incident under discussion occurred a few days before the session, on a bus.

Mrs. M.: . . . He just had to be doing something. The other day he gets
on Henry's and their nerves, jumping up and down in the bus. He is
back there in the back of the bus, beating on the bus.

Tommy: Yeah, but I stopped when you said.

Mrs. M.: Yeah? You didn't stop when I said stop, did you?

Tommy: You didn't tell me to sit down.

---

[12] It should be noted, despite the ineffectiveness of this therapeutic operation with
Mrs. Montgomery, that many therapists treating delinquent children and their families
generally tend to confront them with societal values, for example, pointing out the
consequences of antisocial acts, or their "wrongness," etc.

Mrs. M.: No, I didn't tell you to sit down, I told you to stop.

Therapist: They [siblings] told you to sit down?

Tommy: Yeah.

Therapist: Did you?

Tommy: Nope.

Henry: No.

Therapist: No? Why not?

Tommy: 'Cause.

Therapist: Why?

Tommy: I ask them. I told them to go and ask Mommy, and . . . when they came back and said, Mom said to sit down, and I asked her and she ain't telling me nothing.

Therapist: Well, Tommy, why do you think they were telling you to sit down? You don't think about it that way, huh?

Tommy: I don't know why they told me to sit down.

Therapist: You have no idea?

Tommy: And then when Richard started, and I got tired of standing up, and I sat down, Richard started acting up just as bad as I. He was putting on a strange act.

The above sequence illustrates the lack of communication of clearly stated rules in this family. Tommy did not stop what he was doing because his mother did not specifically tell him to sit down. (The child uses concreteness as a defense.) When the other siblings told him to sit down, he continued to disobey, but requested a formal command from his mother. They solicited and communicated this command to him, but this, apparently, was not sufficient for Tommy. He asked her himself, "and she ain't telling me nothing." Tommy was then free to persist in his "bad" behavior, stopping only because of fatigue, and when another sibling took over his role.

From this interchange, it becomes clear that the children look to their mother for control. Delegated authority is not accepted. But when she is directly asked for a clearcut statement, she no longer specifically states what she wants. Tommy in no way sees within himself any resources for controlling his own behavior. Apparently, however, he perceives his behavior as "bad," and he can even make an objective statement about it as well as the behavior of a sibling: ". . . Richard started acting up just as bad as I. He was putting on a strange act." The bickering about "who has the authority" may well be a reflection of "I want to stop my bad behavior, but I can't unless someone in complete authority makes me."

SEQUENCE 13   TWENTIETH SESSION, STAGE 1

Another incident portraying Mrs. Montgomery's feelings of confusion and helplessness as well as the aura of adventure, confusion, and helplessness in which the children are caught (and generate) is disclosed in the following sequence (Richard had apparently given a burning object [paper] to Bambi, Phyllis' 2½-year-old daughter):

Richard: Well, the thing I gave Bambi—when I took it from her I blew it out and she had it.

. . .

Tommy: You should have blew it out in the kitchen and . . . thrown it away anyway.

Richard: That's what I did, Tommy.

Tommy: She had it, 'cause you know it was burned down. Soon as I see it's burned down, and then like you blow it out and then you see this is fire . . .

. . .

Mrs. M.: Why didn't you all tell me this morning when I, when you were at home?

Michael: I told you Bambi had some fire.

Tommy: That's right.

Mrs. M.: You told me?

Tommy: Yeah.

Michael: I did.

Mrs. M.: About Bambi?

Tommy: Yup. Yup.

Therapist: And what did your mother . . . ?

Tommy: And then you went to . . . and I went to lay down and you said, "Tommy, don't go to sleep again." Yeah, you did and then you woke me up.

. . .

Mrs. M.: Honestly?

Richard: Do you think I am trying to set your house on fire?

Therapist: Yeah, sure, your house and their house. Exactly.

Richard: You think I tried to do it, right?

. . .

Therapist: I think that they do think that. The thing that amazes me about it is that nobody took it from Bambi.

Tommy: I did.

Therapist: You did? Fine, that's good.

Tommy: That's why she was crying.

Therapist: Well, Richard, how else would you understand what you did, I'd like to know. Why would you do it?

Richard: I blew the thing out and put it on the floor.

Therapist: It wasn't out, it was still burning. Now what else am I to think? Maybe he thinks I'm stupid.

Richard: It must have had some sparks on it.

. . .

Mrs. M.: Did you give it to her?

Richard: No.

Therapist: How did she get it?

Richard: I put it on the floor, and Jo [a neighbor?] was in there with her.

Tommy: So you shouldn't have left her in there anyway.

Richard: And the stove was lit anyway.

Richard's narration shifts continuously: First, he gave the "fire" to Bambi, but blew it out. Later he states that he put it on the floor, implying that Jo either gave it to her or should have prevented her from taking it. (Mrs. Montgomery, it should be noted, helps Richard to withdraw his earlier "confession," reinforcing his pattern of talking himself out of a negative situation without directly assuming responsibility for his own role in it.)

The therapist has difficulty, as does the family, in pinning Richard down. He seems to be constantly justifying his behavior by maintaining a continuously shifting line of defense. His elusiveness works, for it seems to be accepted by the family members along with other confused communications and illogical explanations.

The above sequence highlights an additional aspect of cognitive behavior—this time with respect to Mrs. Montgomery. Michael had apparently told his mother that Bambi had "fire," but she had dismissed this communication and attended to something which was even more "immediate": Tommy had gone to sleep again and needed to be reawakened. Apparently, in this situation of confused and multiple demands, Mrs. Montgomery attended to the one which was *immediately* within her cognitive field, even though a dangerous emergency had been brought to her attention. Communication of an event that was not as directly tangible as the one which was occupying her made no impact on Mrs. Montgomery, who was concentrating only on the here-and-now. Once again, as in other episodes we have illustrated (on the bus, for example), her attempts to be effective, to control, to assert herself, and to maintain for herself some order in a chaotic, threatening, and confusing atmosphere fail dramatically. She is being drowned in a sea of impinging demands.

Delinquent and Aggressive Operations

The themes of delinquency and aggression permeate many of the interchanges in the Montgomery family, and there is little change in this respect when early and late sessions are compared. As a matter of fact, an analysis of the transcripts would disclose that more than half of the time the family members are involved in verbal transactions concerning some conflict with respect to a delinquent or aggressive act.

The starting point can be a stolen coin, or somebody's taking the records belonging to a brother, or one of the children's stealing the mother's jewelry, or the children and the mother stealing from the father. No matter what the initial stimulus is, however, the interaction among the Montgomerys follows a predictable pattern. After global accusatory statements that take the form of "who stole *x*," some of the siblings specifically accuse Michael, who defends himself by a counteraccusation. This is followed by interactions in which successively one or the other of the children is perceived as a potential "criminal" until the presentation of some alibi or a disruption by another member "closes" the situation without any resolution. Or the accusations jump from one to another of the children *without* a "closing." In either case, the situation ends as it started, with general accusations afloat that say, in effect, "some one of you is the guilty one." At times, when one of the children seems to be confronted directly—that is, the delinquency can be definitely "pinned" on him—Mrs. Montgomery or one of the children will come to his defense, so that once more the anticipated and familiar nonsolution prevails. There is a general suspiciousness that is directed to each one of the family members, but there is rarely a specific, individualized, and logical confrontation or resolution.

It should be noted, too, that in this as well as many of our other families, the delinquent and aggressive act is not simply an outer-directed hostility to authority, the community, or society. The latter may well be present, but hostility, suspicion, aggression, and "delinquent" activities are directed to members of the family unit with even more frequency than to outside authority figures; moreover, these behavioral "styles" spill over to peers, neighbors, friends, etc.

In sequence 5 there is a dialogue between Mrs. Montgomery and the therapist pertaining to the fact that she took money from under the rug, where Mr. Montgomery had hidden it, with all of the children "peeking." Sequence 2 discloses Tommy's attempted "escapes" from his home through the window. In sequence 7 there is a description of an event in which Michael is truant from school to "punish" his mother. In sequence 13 the baby is involved in a dangerous incident with fire. These sequences were discussed in other contexts, but now we specifically turn to segments from the transcripts which illustrate the delinquent and aggressive atmosphere and climate in which the Montgomerys breathe, talk, and conduct their lives.

SEQUENCE 14   TWENTIETH SESSION, STAGE 1

In the following sequence the children are discussing a quarter stolen from Mrs. Montgomery.

Therapist: You ever find out who took it?

Richard: I know who took it.

Therapist: Who?

Richard: He told me.

Therapist: Who told you?

Richard: He told me, but he didn't want to take it.

Therapist: Who was it, huh, Richard? Who?

Mrs. M.: Tell him. Wish you could tell me who took the $20 later on.

Therapist: I think it would be very important for us to know.

Richard: It wasn't Michael.

Therapist: It was not Michael, then who was it?

Henry: It was Tommy.

Therapist: Tommy, did you take that quarter? Are you positive?

Mrs. M.: Tommy, did you take that quarter?

Tommy: No, I didn't take it.

Therapist: Well, did you tell Richard you took it, Tommy?

Tommy: I didn't tell . . .

Richard: Was it on the radio?

Mrs. M.: No, it was on the top of my wallet.

Richard: See, Tommy told me that he didn't mean to take it, but he thought it was part of his . . . fare.

Tommy: Well, somebody else probably told him that.

Therapist: Somebody else?

Tommy: Because I had a dollar and some change.

Henry: What about that money in your wallet?

Michael: Yeah, and I had no money on me. I had not one red cent, until Tommy came and gave me a dime.

Mrs. M.: When? That same thing?

Michael: What?

Mrs. M.: What are you talking about, the same . . . ?

Michael: When you said I took the quarter. Tommy came and gave me a dime, and then Laddy came and gave me . . .

Therapist: You know, one of the main things might be, Mrs. M. and fellows, uh, Laddy, why do you feel you have to take from your mother? Everybody at one time has taken something.

Tommy: Not me.

Therapist: You never have? And you never have? That's not what you just said.

Therapist B.: Did Tommy say he never did?

Therapist: Yeah, he just said he never had.

In the above exchange, just when the accusatory sallies are beginning to bear fruit, the therapist suddenly intervenes by introducing the general question (addressed to *all*), ". . . why do you feel you have to take from your mother?" He is aiding the family in acting-out their usual pattern: failure to resolve the *specific* conflict facing them. This type of therapeutic intervention was described earlier, and is an illustration of how, in some instances, the therapist may be unwittingly "trapped" into using the same type of communication patterns that the family uses. In the following sequence, a continuation of the above exchange, the family moves away from the pseudo-resolution of the particular theft under discussion and considers another (acknowledged) "delinquency": the participation of all members of the family in stealing from the father.

SEQUENCE 15   TWENTIETH SESSION, STAGE 1

This is a continuation of sequence 14.

Michael: Tommy did because my mother used to let him take, uh, Daddy used to put pennies under the rug and every time my brother Tommy wanted money he used to go and get it and Dad don't do nothing. But when we'd do it, he'd get after us.

Therapist: You mean Tommy was Daddy's favorite?

Richard: Yup, him, Laddy, and Phyllis.

Therapist: Him, Laddy, and Phyllis were Daddy's favorites. Why did he put the money under the rug?

Michael: I don't know. Good luck.

Therapist: Good luck?

Richard: He put dollars, a lot of dollars, under the rug.

Therapist: Is that true, Mrs. M.? What they are saying, is it true?

Mrs. M.: Sometimes he hid it, big money, you know, he used to hide it under the rug.

Therapist: Big money, he used to hide under the rug? Well, that sounds to me that it might be kind of tempting.

Mrs. M.: . . .

Therapist: Yeah, you too. I would think so. Would he get angry when it was taken?

Mrs. M.: Yes.

Richard: Not at Tommy.

Therapist: I see, but he would never get angry at Tommy.

Mrs. M.: He didn't think that Tommy would have taken it.

Richard: He used to take a little stick and say . . .

. . .

Therapist: You mean, you don't think Tommy would take your money?

Mrs. M.: Well, I'll tell you. I—I—to me—I don't think he's even taken anything from me and I don't think he would. You know—I mean— he could.

Therapist: Oh, but you see you got the same story with Tommy. He's able to take the money because nobody believes that he will, except his brothers. . . . But he has been able to, you know. Tommy, did you used to take the pennies when your daddy hid them under the rug?

Tommy: Yup.

The above interaction clearly illustrates a training-process in delinquency. Mr. Montgomery's method of giving money to the children was via a stealing process. We do not know why he would not *directly* give money to the children; but in any case this shows us an operation in which each one of the Montgomery children was involved in stealing from Mr. and Mrs. Montgomery, and Mr. Montgomery was involved in providing the provocation for this stealing. We have also seen how the children were aware of Mrs. Montgomery's stealing from Mr. Montgomery (see sequence 5).

The implicit parental sanction as well as participation in these delinquent operations is accompanied by a denial process on the part of Mrs. Montgomery. For example, Tommy says that he had taken money from his father; Mrs. Montgomery nevertheless insists that he could not have done it. For Mrs. Montgomery, awareness of her own participation and her children's in certain operations does not become a sufficient building-block for the next step: a consideration of the consequences of these acts in the delinquent socialization of her children.

SEQUENCE 16   SIXTH SESSION, STAGE 1

In the following segment, Henry describes some of his feelings and activities with respect to stealing. He had said, just a little earlier, in relation to Tommy, "He is always playing and that will help to keep him out of trouble." He is acknowledging, at the beginning of this sequence, that other activities became more "exciting" to him than football.

Henry: I used to play football. On a Saturday they played, but they didn't make out so good.

Therapist A.: You mean other things became more important to you or more exciting?

Henry: More exciting.

Therapist A.: Like what? What were some of the things?

Henry: Well, robbing.

Therapist A.: Robbing?

Therapist B.: Did your brothers know you were doing that at that time?

Therapist A.: Did your brothers know you were out robbing at this point? Did you try to keep them from knowing?

Henry: Yeah.

Therapist A.: You did? Richard, did Laddy ever turn up with anything? You know. What did you steal, Laddy? Some of the things? You shook down the other kids?

Henry: No, not all the time. I didn't shake down nobody.

Therapist A.: Well, what did you do?

Henry: I asked someone to give me a nickel.

Therapist A.: You asked them to give you a nickel? They give it to you because you think they love you or something?

Henry: No.

Therapist A.: No, well?

Henry: They lend me.

Therapist A.: You name it.

Henry: Yeah, I . . .

Therapist A.: Umhmm. What about the robbing part?

Henry: Like, if I see somebody with some money and I don't have none, I try to get it.

Therapist A.: Did you know any of this was even in his mind, Mrs. M.?

Mrs. M.: No, I know in school he used to bully children and take their money. Then in court once his brother . . . some little boy said he beat him up and . . .

Henry: Oh, that was Mike by himself alone. I didn't know anything about that.

. . .

Therapist A.: Is that the time you took the rap for Mike?

Henry: . . .

Therapist A.: I see. You know what I mean about taking the rap, don't you, Mrs. M.?

Mrs. M.: Yeah.

Therapist A.: Yeah. So, he still has this good feeling, this good closeness in the family, but it doesn't work so good. What did Mike say after you took that rap for him? Did he say thank you at least?

Henry: No.

Therapist A.: Did you feel you wasted your time doing that?

Henry: Oh, he was going to . . .

Therapist A.: Uh.

Henry: But I ain't nothing to do with it.

Therapist: That was the time down in the subway?

Mrs. M.: No, not that time.

Henry: This was a little boy and it happened while I was in Youth House the first time.

Therapist A.: You mean the actual thing happened when you weren't even around?

Henry: Yeah, I was in Youth House. All the other boys they were in on it and they only took Mike, and the boy said it was me.

Therapist A.: Did this boy know you?

Henry: I never saw him before and he said he knew me.

Therapist A.: Oh, I was wondering if he had some beef against you. Why did he pick you?

Henry: I don't know.

In this interaction we see once again some of the operations described above. Mrs. Montgomery's implicit sanction of the delinquencies of her children while she is denying them is dramatically illustrated. Henry has stated quite directly: "Like, if I see somebody with some money and I don't have none, I try to get it." When the therapist inquires of Mrs.

Montgomery whether or not she knew ". . . any of this was even in his mind," she responds flatly with a "No," followed immediately by an explicit and open statement of her awareness of this activity, which she had just denied ("I know in school he used to bully children and take their money"). Then she closes the direct confrontation with a shift of the entire exchange to an episode in which Henry was not only *not guilty*, but was actually the "good" brother who was sacrificed because of family loyalty. And once more the therapist aids and abets the shift and the nonresolution by falling in step with the new tune. The change in content because of this process is illustrated by the sequence below, which follows the above exchange by a minute or two.

SEQUENCE 17 SIXTH SESSION, STAGE 1

Henry: . . . and anyway, if I had done it, they should have took the boys that were with me, right?

Therapist: The whole crew?

Henry: Yeah.

Therapist: That's the usual procedure. And what happened, they didn't take the other guy?

Henry: They only took Mike out of the crowd. And me.

Therapist: Well, could it be that whoever it was that was accusing, only picked you two out and said the other guys had nothing to do with it. . . . Could that be what happened?

Henry: Michael was there and he told them and everyone else told them he didn't.

Therapist: So you think they, the whole thing was wrong and that they only took you?

Henry: Yeah.

Therapist: I see. Could be it happened that way.

As already noted, Mrs. Montgomery has helped Henry to "escape" from a direct confrontation with his delinquencies by providing an instance in which he was clearly wrongly accused by society. By this procedure she is providing her son with a projective mechanism which allows him to avoid awareness of his own responsibility for his acts. The child is now free to engage the therapist in an exploration of this new, "safe" situation, which seems, essentially, an operation directed toward blaming society.

In sequence 16, the therapist had made explicit a family feeling concerning Henry's "taking the rap" for Michael as a "good feeling, this good closeness in the family . . ."[13] In this situation, cooperation and affection between the siblings are expressed around the delinquent act, and the family members (and to some extent, the therapist) then join in accusing society.

The therapist, in the end, finds himself needing to defend society on the grounds that it could have been just a mistake and not an act aimed at hurting the particular members of the family. But, interestingly, an interaction that started with the exploration of the delinquent activities of one of the children finishes up with an accusation of the family as a group against society as a whole.

SEQUENCE 18 TWENTIETH SESSION, STAGE 1

The encouragement by Mrs. Montgomery of her children's delinquency is illustrated in the following transaction concerning one of the children.

Therapist: Is he generous though? Will he offer to buy you things?

Mrs. M.: Yes, he will.

Therapist: Where does he get money though? Do you ask him where he gets it?

Mrs. M.: Well, I do sometimes, yeah, I ask him all the time if I find him with money. He—uh—

Therapist: What's his story?

Mrs. M.: He—uh—says that he used to have his papers, you know . . . and Safeway.[14]

Therapist: I see.

Mrs. M.: And one time he did say that he found a man drunk and then the boys had taken his money from him. Later on, I did find out that that was true because a lady came and told me.

Therapist: I see. What did you do about that?

Mrs. M.: Well, that was, uh, was too far afterwards to find out but he told me that and there was nothing for me to do. I told him it wasn't nice and to leave people alone when they was drunk.

Therapist: That you shouldn't roll drunks?

Mrs. M.: That's right.

Therapist: But he did tell you, so . . .

Mrs. M.: But he could get in trouble, you know. Even though the man

---

[13] It should be noted that one of the approaches in the therapist's orientation to this family involved looking for, and then making articulate, any positive, "good" element that could be found in its generally disorganized structure. In this instance, the feeling of family ties and loyalty was thought to be a "positive" and was stressed as such.

[14] A metropolitan supermarket chainstore.

is drunk. And, someone might see him and call a cop and the cop would take him, and you know, he would get in trouble even though the man is drunk and don't know what he's doing. And—uh—so—

Therapist: Did you tell him that maybe it would be a very tough thing for the man to lose his money?

Mrs. M.: Uh?

Therapist: Did you tell him that it might be a very tough thing for that man to lose his money?

Mrs. M.: Yeah, well I did, so he told me that if I didn't get it somebody else would so he wouldn't have it anyway. That's what he tells me.

Therapist: Boy, he was really having the reasons going for that one, wasn't he? Mrs. M., what do you think he expected you to do when he told you about it? It's good he told you, but I . . .

Mrs. M.: Well, I guess he knew he did it. He let me know, just go and steal from somebody and take something, that I wouldn't, uh, you know, wouldn't fuss at him as much as I would have.

Therapist: In other words, he expected you to feel the same way about it as he did?

Mrs. M.: As he did, yeah. Yeah, that's why he said he—if he didn't get it somebody else would. Which the other boys did, you know.

In the above interaction, we see that Mrs. Montgomery makes use of the money that the children give to her and that she encourages them to lie or to be vague about the source of their money. In addition, she and her children apparently agree in their perception of the world around them as "dog eat dog"; this becomes a justification for stealing from a drunk—if they do not reap the benefit, someone else will. When the child tells his mother about what he has done, he knows that she will condone his act because she feels the same way he does. Further, there seems to be no concern with the rightness or wrongness of the act of stealing—only with the danger or trouble involved. Mrs. Montgomery had stated to her son that ". . . it wasn't nice and to leave people alone when they was drunk." But she admits, a few seconds later, that her real concern is that "he could get in trouble."

SEQUENCE 19   TWENTY-EIGHTH SESSION, STAGE 1

In the light of the "encouragement" the children receive, it is not surprising to find repeated situations in which the children steal from their mother, outsiders, and each other. Let us follow an exchange concerning an object stolen from Mrs. Montgomery. She is directly confronting the children.

Mrs. M.: I am going to ask you something right in front of the therapist and them. One of them—I don't know which—stole a locket out of my drawer, out of my dresser.

Later on, in the same session, Mrs. Montgomery continues:

Mrs. M.: It was [a Christmas present] for one of the children at the church. I had bought two . . . and they had taken one and left the other one there. Now I can't find the other one. . . . And I don't allow anybody in there.

Richard: Michael . . .

Mrs. M.: No, he didn't. Michael said he bought . . .

(*Richard and Michael speak together as if to drown each other out.*)

Richard: Well, where did Michael get money from?

Therapist: . . .

Mrs. M.: I don't say it is the boys. I say it is between the boys and Phyllis.

Henry: I don't think Phyllis has it.

(*The boys are carrying on with each other over the dialogue.*)

Therapist: Why would they take your locket?

Mrs. M.: I don't know why they would.

In the above sequence, immediately after Mrs. Montgomery presents a general accusation to the children, one of the siblings accuses another. Mrs. Montgomery then says the accused sibling did *not* do it, but the accusing sibling insists on an exploration of the accused's actions. But Mrs. Montgomery sees to it that no one is "pinned down": "I don't say it is the boys. I say it is between the boys and Phyllis."

SEQUENCE 20   TWENTY-EIGHTH SESSION, STAGE 1

The stage is now set for a "free-for-all" in which there is no attempt to resolve the conflict of who stole the locket. Michael says with respect to Tommy:

Michael: Everything that is stolen he blames it on me.

Tommy: . . . stealing in the house and you don't say nothing, do you?

Mrs. M.: I don't blame it on nobody. I said between you all. Somebody.

Tommy: You said I stole your quarter and I didn't.

Michael: You said *I* stole your quarter, and I didn't.

Tommy: You and Phyllis were the only ones in the house . . . I said she wouldn't steal it.

Michael: You didn't have no money either. I wonder how you got all that money so quick.

Tommy: Ah-ha—ha. It was given to me.

    . . .

Tommy: I believe Michael did steal it. Where did you get that quarter from?

Michael: What quarter? I didn't have no quarter, ha—ha. I had a dime.

Tommy: How did you buy a cake and a 15-cent soda and then bought another? . . .

Michael: I had 35 cents and a dime.

So in the end, the transaction about the stolen locket remains vague and amorphous; and a general suspicion of *all* members of the family prevails. Even when one of the members can almost be pinpointed in his guilt, the mother or some other sibling defends the person who is specifically accused. As a result, the accusation remains general (*somebody* took it), *all* the children are categorized as a group, and nobody is really guilty. The issue is dropped because the family finds itself in another delinquent conflict in which Tommy and Michael accuse each other of having stolen a quarter. The family evades one accusation about a stealing episode by verbalizing other accusations over a new stealing episode.

Caught in a lie ("I didn't have no quarter . . . I had a dime"), Michael changes his previous statement and stands pat on his new statement, "I had 35 cents and a dime." In effect, reality can be continuously shifted because the problems are not related to the objective situation but to the atmosphere of delinquency: accusation, counteraccusation, and a need to escape from accusation.

SEQUENCE 21   TWENTY-EIGHTH SESSION, STAGE 1

Finally, Mrs. Montgomery finds a delinquent solution to the issue of the stolen locket. The therapist inquires:

Therapist: Let me ask you, do you think you have any chance of getting the locket back?

Mrs. M.: No.

Therapist: Why not?

(*The children and the two therapists start to talk, all at once.*)

Mrs. M.: Put it back in the drawer, back in the drawer, and lay it there. . . . And I'm telling you, good, that's all right . . . And I won't ask them . . .

In effect, Mrs. Montgomery is allowing the children to solve the problem by suggesting that they put the stolen object back where it came from so that nobody will know who stole it. This, of course, does not really resolve the issue, but Mrs. Montgomery is apparently not at all concerned with the act of stealing—only with the return of the stolen object. It might be noted that the therapist helps to orient her in the direction of this pseudo-solution: when, after many family shifts and pulls away from the issue, he brings the interchanges back to the chief issue at hand (who stole the locket), he does so with an unfortunate query, ". . . do you think you have any chance of getting the locket back?" The issue is immediately perceived as one which involves the *object* and its whereabouts, rather than as one which is concerned with interpersonal transactions and with personal responsibility for the act itself. The Montgomerys, it goes without saying, thus receive reinforcement for cognitive attitudes that are overlearned to begin with.

SEQUENCE 22   TWENTY-EIGHTH SESSION, STAGE 1

The following is still another sequence illustrating the chaotic atmosphere of accusation and counteraccusation between and among the siblings with respect to stealing from one another.

Therapist: Well, what are you saying, Mike . . . he stole a record, somebody else's record, you found?

Michael: Uhhm . . . because he stole my glasses.

Therapist: Who?

Michael: Him.

Therapist: Tommy?

Michael: No.

Therapist: Who? Laddy?

Michael: Yeah . . . I'm gonna sell his record.

. . .

Therapist: You are stealing again, Laddy?

Henry: (*Laddy*) No . . .

Michael: Up in the roof . . . it's still there.

Therapist: You mean the record is still up on the roof?

Michael: Umhm.

Mrs. M.: (*To Michael*) You don't have any business taking other people's records.

Therapist: In other words, Henry took your glasses and sold them to Tommy?

Michael: No.

Mrs. M.: (*To Michael*) Who did he sell them to?

Michael: He said he was going to get me another pair, then he didn't. I was going to take the things that he had . . .

Therapist: It sounds as though they are back to stealing again, Mrs. M.

Mrs. M.: I don't think . . . pick up something.

Henry: Then he just wanted his jaw cracked.

Therapist: Who is going to crack it for him, Laddy?

Henry: If he takes anything of mine, I will!

Michael: If you take anything of mine, I'll crack yours.

Mrs. M.: (*To Michael*) You're not supposed to take things that don't belong to you. You're not supposed to take it.

Michael: Well, he took my glasses, you didn't say anything.

> (*Richard and Tommy are reading comic books during the above sequence. A minute later:*)

Mrs. M.: Those glasses of Michael were taken over since before the . . . summer. I mean . . . sunglasses.

Michael: And they cost a dollar.

. . .

Therapist: I would suggest that Tommy put the funnies away. Richard.

Mrs. M.: Richard, Tommy.

> (*They continue to read.*)

Therapist: She just said something about putting the funnybook away, Richard.

> (*Richard puts the comic book down.*)

Mrs. M.: Put it on the table, Richard. Put it on the table.

> (*The children play with other objects. Meanwhile Richard tries to get something out of his satchel. Tommy and Michael talk. Richard takes a record from the satchel, and Michael makes faces at the hole in the record. Richard teases Henry with it. Henry asks Richard for the record. Michael tries to get it, Henry gets it, but Michael gives it back to Richard. A few minutes later:*)

Therapist: Is this the record, Laddy?

Henry: Yeah.

Therapist: Everything is all right now?

Henry: Yeah.

Therapist: Good.

We see from the above that the code of behavior among the siblings is, "If he takes, I take." In the absence of other "rules" to guide behavior and the lack of communication skills in conflict-resolution, there is no other way to negotiate. A child can *take* or *steal;* this is the only "resolution" he is familiar with.

Further, the generally disruptive atmosphere subsides somewhat when the record (a stolen óbject to begin with) is returned to the "rightful" owner. Once again, the "Everything is all right now?" becomes a terminal point at which the "resolution" is vague, confused, and reinforcing to ineffective and maladaptive attitudes and behavior. There is no concern with the *why* of stealing or with an evaluation of the siblings' behavior toward each other. There is no real repair, either—just a concrete exchange of temporary ownership of the object (the record). Attitudinal, verbal, and behavioral patterns have not changed, for two minutes later, in the same session, we have a reappearance of the same type of exchange between siblings (two different ones) over a coveted object (this time, a wristband):

Tommy: Laddy, give me my wristband.

Richard: Let him have it!

Tommy: Next time, I'll leave it there.

And so on.

The Surrounding World: Money, Action, the Victims, and the Victimized

The following pages attempt to communicate the Montgomerys' perceptions (the children's, in particular) of the world around them and their descriptions of how they move around, attempt to manipulate, cope with, and derive excitement and stimulation from this world. Strangers, neighbors, "cops," schoolmates, friends, and relatives move through this world, and so do the shadowy, transient lovers of some of these people. There are money and adventures to be taken, and victims to be "took." There is action: the excitement of the chase or the being chased. There are risks. The world is peopled by adults who can be counted on and adults whom you cannot trust. Sometimes, like the shifting accusations and counter-accusations around a stolen article, an adult can be giving, kind, generous, and a "pal" at one time, and mean, cruel, and sadistic at another time. And there is the stubborn, insistent reality of the slum, the welfare check, the drunkard, and the addict.

SEQUENCE 23   TWENTIETH SESSION, STAGE 1

The therapist prompts Michael to tell his mother of an incident about which he has already told the therapist:

Michael: Remember that Saturday night, that man, that drunk, downstairs . . . and said he'd slap my face and cut my . . . of the . . . ?

Henry: Yeah.

Therapist: You remember that, Laddy, huh?

Mrs. M.: Oh, when? That night when you had . . .

Henry: No, in the daytime, on Saturday.

Mrs. M.: Recently?

Henry: Hmm?

Mrs. M.: Recently?

Therapist: . . .

Henry:About two months ago, Mike went in the house and got two knives. I followed behind him, he was getting ready to . . . He didn't want to cut him because he was a dope addict and everybody . . . and so we went back.

Therapist: He has a hard time controlling himself when he gets angry.

Mrs. M.: What were you going to do with two knives? Come on, son.

Michael: Cut him on the face so he would remember he saw me.

Therapist: Mike says he really has to hit back and mark him and everything. What do you mean, why should you want him to remember you, Mike?

Michael: 'Cause he won't mess with me no more.

This is the world in which these children live. Drug addicts and drunkards loiter or sprawl on the sidewalks. The children learn to live in a world that is threatening and aggressive. Michael went for knives to cut the man who wanted to slap and cut *him* ("So he won't mess with me no more"), and Henry came after him, indicating that in some way he accepts this philosophy. Probably some fortunate event intervened, so that Michael did not go through with his plan. The next time, in similar circumstances, the hitting back and the "marking" ritual might indeed occur.[15] As a matter of fact, there is an implicit acceptance by Mrs. Montgomery and Henry that this is how life is. Michael defends himself by direct attack, it might be noted. (On another occasion, he attacked his older brother with a knife because he had accused him of stealing something from him.)

SEQUENCE 24   SIXTH SESSION, STAGE 2

The surrounding world of the Montgomery family includes neighbors who give them money and feed them. The sequence below is about one of these people who in some way are part of the extended family. Some of these individuals enter into the family life only at certain times, others during the entire span of the family life. The relationship with the family can be peripheral or a more intense relationship can exist. These relation-

---

[15] There is a prototype for "marking him so that he would remember me" in many subcultures in our own as well as other societies. For Michael, the "marking" is a concrete, dramatic way of making an impact on the other person and of guaranteeing that he, as an individual, is acknowledged. Michael's need to leave an imprint on the other is expressed literally. He lacks more subtle skills for defending his ego against attack.

ships are sometimes extremely difficult to assess. Here the children are talking about a man, Frank Smith:

Richard: He always takes them to the show. He takes them to . . .

Therapist: You said takes them. Doesn't he take you too?

Richard: No. He takes Tommy the most.

Therapist: He takes him the most? Did he ever take you, Henry?

Henry: No, uh yeah, to the movies.

Therapist: The movies. Does he pay your way?

Richard: Yup.

Therapist: Why is he so nice to everybody?

Henry: He likes my aunt.

Therapist: Oh, he likes your aunt. I see. Is he nice to the girls, too?

Henry: Yeah, he took Phyllis and Marguerite to the . . . but everytime he takes Marguerite, he argues with her.

(*A few minutes later, Michael says:*)

Michael: When he comes around he gives the boys a lot of money.

Tommy: Boy, he took Mike, he took Martha and Elizabeth to his house and so he told us to give him our money, and I gave him a dollar, and Richard gave him a dollar, and my friend, you know. And all of us were giving him our money and then we said . . . "Let's get a cab." He told the man to follow the cab in front of him so he followed the cab around and they say, "Oh, yeah." . . . He was gonna take us home and you know he said, "You all wait here," and he told me and my friend to wait at the . . . and he would be back with his car and he don't have a car. We waited and waited.

Therapist: You mean you're still waiting?

Tommy: Yeah. We just kept waiting and he never came back. He gave me my dollar back, but my friend didn't get his back.

Therapist: Well, why does he play tricks like that on everybody?

Henry: He's a sneak.

Therapist: He's a sneak?

Henry: Yeah. And then he'd give money, he'd give money to all of us.

The same man whom they describe as extremely generous, and who takes the children to the movies, gives them money, etc., now is described as leaving them stranded. He has played a mean trick on the boys. Apparently, he is generous or sneaky by turns, depending only on his own whims and impulses. Here is a model for adult identification who responds to the children by giving and taking away only as part of his own need without taking into consideration the children's needs.

SEQUENCE 25   SIXTH SESSION, STAGE 2

The children are continuing to talk about Mr. Smith's interaction with them, and it is clear that he is identified in their minds with unsolicited, generous gifts of money, the source of which is not at all clear to them (or to the therapist).

Henry: He always, you know, he always [gives money].

Tommy: He gave me a hundred dollars.

Therapist: A hundred dollars!

Tommy: A whole hundred dollars. He took it back.

Therapist: Did you know about him giving Tommy a hundred dollars?

Henry: Yeah.

Therapist: What kind of bills was it in, Tommy?

Tommy: Ones.

Therapist: Ones, in a hundred dollars?

Tommy: And he took it back the same day.

Henry: He gave Mary forty dollars. He gave her twenty, but there was another twenty with it, you know, like a buck here and now for cabfare.

Therapist: She kept the other twenty?

Henry: Yeah.

Therapist: What does he do that he gives you that money . . . ?

Henry: He told her . . . Mary, and giving her the extra twenty and I don't remember getting it back and then he say to keep the whole thing.

Therapist: Oh, he did. Where does Frank get all this money?

Henry: He—uh—a painter. He used to be an electrician.

Therapist: Well, does he work most of the time?

Henry: Umhmm. Hard.

These children live with inconsistencies. At times, the welfare check is not enough for the mere elements of survival, and there is no food in the house. And yet, there is a considerable amount of easy money floating around (or *talk* about easy money).

Later on:

Tommy: And the man, uh, he gave us a lot of money in the cab and we ran out of money because we didn't count on the show and we saw Frank Smith and he told us, uh, he gave us money for the cab and me and my friend and my cousin. He gave me the money to give the cab and so he gave them a quarter and so it cost us sixty— sixty-five cents, 'cause I tipped, and then I kept the rest of it.

I didn't want to, but I didn't have much choice.

These children go to shows, take cabs to get around, and somehow manage the financing of these excursions with considerable resourcefulness. As can be seen in the following sequence, they learn to get or to take whatever they can and to resolve their problems in the best way that they can.

SEQUENCE 26 SIXTH SESSION, STAGE 2

Michael: One time we did that over in the park. We got a cab ride hitch for free. We were, you know, we were way up on the hill, me, Jimmy, and Billy, and a guy named Rusty, and Benny, and we were way up on a hill, you know. And we couldn't find our way so, and the cabdriver he knew his way so all we had to do was find a taxicab driver and say, "West 138th Street." And we couldn't find our way so he took us all the way down street and we said, "Right here." We stopped off by the pool on Bradley. We stopped right there with him. "Wait a minute," he said. "Wait a minute." . . . And didn't you know, okay, and then he holds Billy's hand and then he holds my hand. Bam! Billy says, "I got loose from him." Then I got loose from him and bam! And we all jumped out of the car . . . We only had a dollar, you know . . . We showed him a five, we made it like it was five and we said, "We've got five." When we jumped out, we said, "Here," but then he held our hand, so we went, bam!

(*After a few minutes, the sequence continues:*)

Therapist: You didn't give him the dollar? You said you had that much. You didn't give him the dollar?

Michael: Nope. It wasn't my money. So we picked it up out of the cab and started running. And he was driving by in the street and he say, "Come on back, come on back." He was driving down the street and we started running. And Billy, and the cab was moving a little, and Billy was in there and the cab was moving. Billy just jumped out and kept running.

Therapist: You mean one guy he still kept in there?

Michael: Yup. He just jumped out the door, you know, as it was moving he jumped out the door and slammed the door. Everyone said, "Hey, hey you, come back here." Then he started running down—

Tommy: He should have started running down a one-way street.

Therapist: Oh, I see, Tommy, you said they should have gotten away. You feel that they should have gotten away with this, huh?

Tommy: Just like that man was mean.

. . .

Richard: We was going to pay him. We were going to pay him, but he said, "Give me your hand," and he held Billy's hand, and then I asked him, "What'd you say?" and then Michael said, "Jump out." . . .

We see, from the above, the way in which the children shift grounds in terms of the description of the situation. First they had a dollar, then the money was not theirs, then they *were* going to pay the driver but they jumped away from the car because the man was "mean." It is at the moment when they can confirm their expectations that "the world around us is against us" that all acts become justified. There is no guilt then, for they are reacting to the action of the cabdriver who seemingly did not trust them. Note, too, Tommy's suggestion for outwitting the driver: "running down a one-way street" (so that the driver could not follow). Even the youngest of the Montgomery children employ tactics and stratagems for outmaneuvering the authority figure.

SEQUENCE 27   SIXTH SESSION, STAGE 2

The children live in a world in which no one can be trusted, even friends, who are capable of playing cruel tricks on them. Below, we have a description of an incident that involved Tommy and some of his friends.

Tommy: My friends . . . all of them. They was on a ship . . . they don't belong on it. . . . So they got off of the ship and him and his—my three—there were three of them—friends I know. And so they stayed on and the other boys cut the rope. Johnny got off and then there was two on it. And my friend says, "Come on, Marty," because then Marty and Bobby were on deck. Marty stayed and Bobby jumped off on the shore and then he sailed all the way out there. They called the police boat and they had a search warrant.

Therapist: A search warrant?

Tommy: Yeah. They was looking for him.

. . .

Tommy: And he was scared and his friends jumped. His best friend jumped off and he stayed on and he sailed out there.

Therapist: You saw all this happen?

Tommy: Yeah. First we were on it and we have rocks . . . and we . . . cross the bridge to get there and Fred said, "Let's go over there," and I said, "No." So they said I'm going to have to go, and I said, "I am going to stay over here." So they all went and stayed over there. I went home and when they came back they told me that the policeman brought him home. He got a whipping.

The incident Tommy describes above appeared in the New York City newspapers. Tommy's account is somewhat garbled. What actually happened was this: Several of the children had gained access to a houseboat tied up in one of the rivers surrounding the city, and as a "prank," cut the mooring. All but one of the children were able to get ashore. The stranded child was afloat alone for several hours until he was rescued by a police boat.

Note the accessibility of ships, docks, etc., in the lives of these children and their constant need to experience danger, excitement, and adventure. Action, motion, and excitement, even when there are no immediate gains, help to define and identify them as individuals and give them a sense, it would seem, of knowing who they are.

SEQUENCE 28   TWENTIETH SESSION, STAGE 1

It is already apparent that the children stress money in their interactions and that a great deal of their activities and their give-and-take with each other are in the context of the ownership, possession, transfer, stealing, finding, or being given money. Not only is there free-floating talk about money, but also, apparently, a free-floating exchange of money. This household receives welfare assistance. Where does the money the children have in their possession come from? Tommy said (see earlier sequence) that Mr. Smith had given him one hundred dollars! It is not always possible to separate fact from fantasy, especially in the area of "money-boasting," but we know that the children are constantly stealing money from each other, talking about money, and that there is money in fluid circulation among them. For example, Henry had been saying that Michael had stolen money from him:

Henry: What about my dollar?

Tommy: I don't know anything about your dollar . . .

Therapist: . . .

Tommy: I didn't take the quarter. She gave me fifty cents, and the boys gave me fifty cents.

Richard: I thought you had a dollar and a quarter.

Tommy: That's right. That's right. Anita . . . gave me a quarter.

Again we see the ease with which the children shift grounds. First Tommy says, "I don't know nothing about your dollar." Then he says he had a dollar which was given to him, but Richard says, "I thought you had a dollar and a quarter." Tommy then says, "Anita gave me a quarter." Who is Anita? Why did she give him a quarter? Why does Tommy, who is eleven years old, have so much money? All of this is pretty difficult to assess.

Sizable amounts of money are discussed, and their sources never disclosed. For example, a few minutes later:

Tommy: One time my mother gave a party and there was ten dollars on the floor, and I looked down there and then I took it and the next day in class Jimmy had lost it because he said so. Some cheap son-of-a-gun is going to keep it . . .

And a minute after the above:

Richard: Hey Mike, remember that ten dollars you had when we were going out to the movie? That was it? On Sunday?

SEQUENCE 29   TWENTIETH SESSION, STAGE 1

The shifting story-line and the vagueness of detail concerning the source of money are again illustrated below:

Mrs. M.: . . . Richard—one day he was reminding me of the five dollars he had one day. And I asked him where he got it from and he told me he found it. He found it in a trash can, you know.

Therapist: Yeah.

Richard: Oh, yeah. I thought it was a piece of a dollar. It was a five-dollar bill . . . Everybody thought it was a piece of a dollar, so they left me. Then when I went outside, I opened it and it was a real dollar.

Therapist: . . .

Richard: They claim we took it.

Therapist: . . . There is another part to this story, hmm? You don't believe he found it, huh, Tommy?

Tommy: No. Somebody told me it was in his clothes.

Therapist: That he had stolen it?

Tommy: Yes.

Richard: And I bought a gun with it.

Therapist: Umhm.

Richard, above, is relating an unlikely incident. He found five dollars (or one dollar?). One of his siblings challenges him, suggesting that he knows it was stolen, but Richard continues his story as if the question as to whether he had stolen or found it was really of no importance. His story ends with a statement about his purchase—a gun. There is no concern about handling the confrontation as to *where* the money came from.

SEQUENCE 30   TWENTIETH SESSION, STAGE 1

And finally, below, we see Tommy's need to spend his money immediately, in order to prevent his siblings from stealing it:

Tommy: I made seventy-five cents off of bottles.

Therapist A.: . . .

Therapist B.: What do you have to do with that seventy-five cents, Tommy? Are you going to hide it so that some other kid doesn't get it?

Tommy: Nope. I spent it before they came home.

It appears, then, from an examination of the Montgomery family's attitudes toward money that these reflect an experience with money that is not related in any way to a plan of organizing efforts in order to gain a reward that is appropriate to the effort spent. Broken down, these attitudes seem to be: money is something you just get, or you get it from the confused, surrounding world by stealing it from a drunk, getting it from a member of the extended family (like a neighbor or somebody who is interested in your aunt), or it comes as a check from a reluctant, anonymous giver—welfare; it serves only to satisfy immediate needs; you cannot get more by working more; you do not accumulate it to serve distant goals; and if you want something, you get it now.

Summary

Initially, Mrs. Montgomery was described as an ineffective controller who functioned at her best when she was in a nurturant role. In addition, she was thought to be dependent on her children for protection, nurturance, and guidance. She relied on her oldest daughter, Marguerite, for the management of household duties and on Henry for control of the other children. The Montgomery family was felt to be organized around the myth that the father's return would solve all problems, for then in a magical way he would become the organizing, focal force which they lacked. The children functioned fairly autonomously, with little or no reliance on their mother for guidance. Sibling interaction, either competitive or cooperative, occurred almost exclusively in delinquent and/or aggressive activities. They looked to one another for guidance, but often resisted it when it was offered.

In general, Phyllis and Michael were allied as the isolates, scapegoats, and underdogs in the family system; the other family members were constantly derogating them. Marguerite and Henry were functioning at the top of the power-hierarchy in the sibling subsystem, participating, as it were, in an alliance of power-holders. Mrs. Montgomery and Tommy, the "baby," were engaged in a strictly nurturant alliance, and she was in a continuous power-conflict with Phyllis.

Family transactions centered around the allocation of power that remained unstable. These transactions—continuous and never-ending negotiations—were acted-out in a field of confused communications in which "noise" and disruption dominated; the content of these transactions dealt primarily with delinquent or aggressive operations or the distribution and availability of love, nurturance, or ownership. Implicit as well as explicit training and socialization in delinquency were proffered by all members of the system. Guilt was never pinned down, and conflicts never resolved in the generally chaotic atmosphere of accusation and counteraccusation.

Therapeutic goals were: (1) to help Mrs. Montgomery organize herself into a leadership and controlling position; (2) to buttress the siblings' executive functioning by helping them to implement Mrs. Montgomery's efforts, which were acknowledged as insufficient; and (3) to encourage the family members to accept one of the therapists as a temporary replacement for the father who was perceived by the family as a "miracleworker," even in his absence.

Although the foregoing goals were aimed at introducing basic changes in the Montgomery family structure by using the third as an intermediate step to the first, they resulted only in temporary and fleeting changes which were dependent on the presence of the therapist within the system. The family members continued to rely on one of the therapists as the only problem-solver within the system as well as a parental substitute. Moreover, therapist-operations, contrary to explicit aims and expectations, kept Mrs. Montgomery in a dependent and helpless position by reinforcing the children's perception of her as well as her own self-perception as incompetent. In general, little change in the family system was found when the sessions at the beginning of the treatment series were compared with those at the end.

The La Salles: Excerpts from Transcripts of Family Treatment Sessions

*W*hen Tim La Salle was admitted to the Wiltwyck School, the La Salle family consisted of Mrs. La Salle, age 40, her father, age 75, and three children, Meredith, Tim, and George, ages 12, 10, and 8, respectively. (See footnote 3, page 46.) The La Salles are a West Indian Negro family. They had been receiving public assistance for a number of years prior to Tim's admission. Mr. La Salle, the father of the three boys, had deserted his wife and children before Tim was one year old but returned occasionally to visit them. During one of these visits, he fathered George.

Mr. La Salle's first contact with the courts was in 1944 for carrying firearms; he was deported to Nassau, but illegally returned to the States shortly afterwards. After being deported once more, he re-entered the States again, and was rearrested in 1946 for assault and vagrancy. He was deported for a third time. But Mr. La Salle found his way into the country again! In 1952, he was arrested for disorderly conduct; in 1955, he was sentenced for third-degree robbery; in 1958, he was released under parole and deported again; and in 1961, he returned illegally (violation of parole) once again. He is now an inmate in one of the federal prisons.

Although Mrs. La Salle forbids the children to talk about their father, they describe how he taught them to make zip guns, and they display the bullet hole in the wall which was made when Mr. La Salle shot at his father-in-law and missed. Mr. La Salle is described as a high-strung person who shouted a great deal and struck his children on little provocation. He was a heavy drinker who had always been an inadequate provider for his family.

When Tim was admitted to the Wiltwyck School, the family was described as follows:

Mrs. La Salle is a shabbily dressed, obese woman who seems to be unconcerned with her physical appearance. She is rather bright and articulate, a high school graduate, and she makes a point of displaying "good" books (Kipling, Maugham, etc.) on the shelves of her bedroom. She lived with her parents until her marriage, returning intermittently during her marriage to live with them. In 1954, Mrs. La Salle moved permanently into her parents' home, and has been living there since that time. Mrs. La Salle's mother, who was a diabetic and had congestive heart failure, has recently died. Despite severe physical incapacitation until her death, her mother had exercised considerable control over the household: "Whatever mother said was law." Mrs. La Salle describes her enormous respect for her mother, but points out at the same time how she "spoiled" the children. For example, the grandmother would not allow her daughter to "touch or reprimand" Tim. In addition, she would send the children after Mrs. La Salle whenever she went out, and if it were after 5 P.M., she would threaten to call the police to report that the children were left alone.

Mrs. La Salle's father had a stroke six years ago, and since then, he "wanders through the house, his mind wanders, and then comes back." He might say that someone is knocking at the door, or that the police came while everybody was out. He smokes, and once burned the furniture with a cigarette. Mrs. La Salle describes her fear that he might burn himself alive if she leaves him alone in the house.

For the last few years, Mrs. La Salle has had a paramour who frequently stays in her home, but who has his own room in the neighborhood. His relationship with the family is tangential. Mrs. La Salle makes it clear that he should not "mix in my business." Her sense of being overwhelmed is best reflected in a statement that she made about her mother's illness and death, her father's stroke, and Meredith's leaving for training school: "At least one has been eliminated!"

Meredith, the oldest boy, is the grandfather's favorite child. Six months prior to Tim's admission to Wiltwyck, Meredith was sent to a New York State training school. He is a hyperactive, enuretic youngster of average intelligence who has been truant continuously from school. He is immature and reacts to stress with depressive withdrawals. Meredith was a leader among his siblings in various antisocial activities such as stealing and starting a fire in a synagogue. Mrs. La Salle describes him as "a convincing thief and liar."

Tim was characterized as "hyperactive, disorganized, and unable to settle down and focus on anything." Mrs. La Salle identifies him with Mr. La Salle, who would fight at the drop of a hat. She calls him "The Great I Am." He is an obese boy who looks like his mother. Tim's behavior in school is described as follows: "He cannot get along with other children; he is insolent, has too much money to waste, endangers the safety of other children, fights, kicks, spits, steals, and at times tries to choke children. He feels that the 'teachers are wrong and pick on me.'" Mrs. La Salle states that he is influenced by the other neighborhood boys; she has difficulty in keeping him away from the street gangs. He comes home as late as 10 P.M. at night, and runs away when he anticipates a beating. When he does come home, Mrs. La Salle says, "I can't punish him. He's already been out. What can I do, beat him again?" Yet he is very clinging to his mother. When she goes to the store he looks for her from store to store. He wants her around physically, but he "won't be petted."

George is the baby of the family, and physically rather underdeveloped for his age. His language skills are immature, and he disrupts conversations by making inappropriate statements which he repeats in stereotyped fashion until his mother asserts control. He is a hyperactive youngster who is very attached to both of his siblings. He is having difficulties at school, where his behavior is similar to Tim's.

The La Salles live in the Bronx in a neighborhood that was once mostly Negro but now has a large Puerto Rican population. The area is notorious for ethnic fights between gangs of Negro and Puerto Rican adolescents, as well as for pockets of drug addiction and alcoholism. The family occupies a four-room, fourth-floor apartment in a run-down tenement building.[1] Mrs. La Salle has her own bedroom (with a double bed) that opens into the next bedroom. There is no door between the rooms. In this room Tim and Meredith had always shared the same bed, while George slept in his own bed. The grandfather has his own bed in the same room, too. When Meredith left for training school, George moved into the bed with Tim, and his own bed remains empty. Mrs. La Salle explains that both George and Tim refuse to sleep alone.

The material from the transcripts was taken from the third, eighth, twentieth, and twenty-sixth sessions. As noted earlier, deletions (for mechanical or other reasons) will always be indicated by a series of dots. The La Salle material was organized under the following headings: (1) communication patterns; (2) the family world—perception of and behavior toward one another; (3) attitudes toward the surrounding world —suspicion, mistrust, and misinformation; (4) therapist-operations; and (5) change. The stress in the last section—change—is on the evidence of modification of the style of communication in this family. Certain aspects of the sibling subsystem in this family will be especially stressed.

As was indicated with respect to the material in Chapter 3, the sequences from the transcripts are presented for illustrative purposes, and although they lend themselves to certain interpretive remarks, these comments do not exhaust the multiplicity of interpretations which might be made.

The Excerpts

Communication Patterns

Neither a written exposition nor the transcripts themselves can convey the paraverbal quality of the sessions as they transpired: the noise-level, the inflections of the voice, the frequency and intensity of the shouting and yelling, the grimaces, grunts, and groans, the actions of the children when they fight over objects and chairs, the gross and chaotic motor activity—the pushing, pulling, shoving, standing up, sitting down, etc.[2]

---

[1] The La Salles were not eligible for public housing because Mr. La Salle was a felon. In this connection, it might be noted that eligibility for public housing is frequently determined by various "unwritten," subjective criteria applied by an investigator in an effort to establish a family's ability to manage a budget, maintain an apartment, and the like. Couples in common-law marriages, families with illegitimate children, etc., are usually ineligible, according to this unwritten code.

[2] This family, as do the majority of our families, loads the field with numerous paraverbal transactions which complicate the task of deriving meaning from the verbal transcripts of their interactions. At the worst moments, paraverbal transactions

In addition, there is disruptive and disjointed *verbal* communication. Communication difficulties in the transactions of the La Salle family dominate the sessions. The extent to which disruptive communications interfere with the development of meaningful dialogue between the therapist and the family members can best be demonstrated by comparing sequences 1 and 2. In the first sequence, we have deleted all the interferences and disruptive content in a dialogue between the therapists and Meredith, who has been complaining that his mother always calls on him to help her with chores when he is engaged in a pleasurable activity.

SEQUENCE 1   TWENTIETH SESSION, STAGE 2

Meredith: I don't like nobody bothering me when I'm doing something.

Therapist B.: You don't like to be bothered when you're doing something?

Meredith: Uh-uh.

Therapist A.: Is there no way you can let your mother know that you're doing something that you don't want her to interfere with? Why not? What have you tried? How have you tried to tell her that?

Therapist A.: Well, tell me some of the things you do that she interferes with. Maybe I could help. What are you pulling that she gets in your way, huh?

Meredith: She'll see I be doing something.

Therapist A.: Like what? Just give me an example.

Therapist A.: . . . Meredith, well, give me an idea of what you're doing that Mommy bothers you about, 'cause . . .

Therapist A.: . . . Maybe we can make her understand.

Meredith. I'll be watching TV.

Therapist A.: Go ahead, Meredith.

Meredith: I'll be doing something and she'll come and bother me.

Therapist A.: What does she do while you're watching TV? What does she do?

Meredith: I got to go to the store or something.

Therapist A.: You think she picks that time to ask you to go to the store?

Meredith: Yeah.

Therapist B.: Does she ask you to go to the store at other times?

---

obscure every other level of communication. Research data based on an analysis of strictly *verbal* material must be interpreted with considerable caution in the light of this methodological difficulty. Appendix B, which presents data based on an analysis of verbal behavior, will raise these as well as other considerations again.

Meredith: Yeah.

Therapist B.: But mostly when you're watching TV?

Meredith: But mostly good pictures get on and I get 'em . . . I got to go to the store.

Therapist B.: Oh. Can you think of any way that you can work that out? Because I'm thinking of something.

Therapist B.: Did you ever try asking your mother before you went to watch the picture if there's anything she wanted?

Meredith: (*To Therapist B.*) She say, "No," but then after she says, "Yes."

SEQUENCE 2

Below is the same sequence as it actually transpired in the session. It is hoped that the quality of the disjointed communications among the siblings can be conveyed by the following segment. Note, too, the difficulties that the therapists encounter when they attempt to carry the thread of a particular theme through the static of the disruptive comments, as well as the need to control the behavior of the children.

George: (*Makes squealing noises in rear.*)

Meredith: I don't like nobody bothering me when I'm doing something.

George: Tim, take me to the bathroom.

Therapist B.: You don't like to be bothered when you're doing something?

Meredith: Uh-uh.

George: Tim, I got to go to the bathroom.

Therapist A.: You've got to go to the bathroom, Tim? Hurry back. (*Tim leaves the room.*)

Tim: See you all. (*Several voices mumble here.*)

Therapist A.: Is there no way you can let your mother know that you're doing something that you don't want her to interfere with? Why not? What have you tried? How have you tried to tell her that?

Meredith: . . .

Therapist A.: Well, tell me some of things you do that she interferes with. Maybe I could help. What are you pulling that she gets in your way, huh?

Meredith: She'll see I be doing something.

Therapist A.: Like what? Just give me an example.

George: I got to go to the bathroom.

Therapist A.: You're not going to the bathroom. Miss —— [Case aide] will bring you back in here.

George: Yes, I am! I am!

Therapist A.: Now you better sit down there.

Meredith: Aw, sit down and shut up.

George: I got to go to the bathroom.

Therapist A.: Sit down.

Tim: You had your chance. Now it's my chance to go.

George: I did not.

Therapist A.: You went, Tim.

Meredith: You went already.

Tim: I know, but I got to go again.

Therapist A.: Sit down, George.

George: I got to go to the bathroom.

   . . .

George: I didn't go to the bathroom.

Meredith: You try it.

Tim: I won't try it.

Therapist B.: Which way were you, this way or that way?

Therapist A.: Meredith? Well, Miss —— [Case aide] will bring him back
    in here if he goes to the bathroom. Meredith, well, give me an idea
    of what you're doing that Mommy bothers you about, 'cause . . .

George: Let me go to the bathroom.

Therapist A.: Maybe we can make her understand.

Meredith: I'll be watching TV.

George: I ain't watching no—I want to go to the bathroom.

Therapist A.: George, you have to keep quiet for the moment.

George: But I want to go to the bathroom.

Therapist A.: . . .

Tim: Hey, can I take him, to make sure he goes to the bathroom?

George: No, let me go.

Tim: I got to go, too.

Therapist A.: Go ahead, Meredith.

Meredith: I'll be doing something and she'll come and bother me.

George: Please, please can I go to the bathroom?

Tim: Be quiet, George.

George: (*Mumbles in background.*)

Therapist A.: What does she do while you're watching TV? What does
    she do?

Meredith: I got to go to the store or something.

Therapist A.: You think she picks that time to ask you to go to the store?

Meredith: Yeah.

Therapist B.: Does she ask you to go to the store at other times?

Meredith: Yeah.

Therapist B.: But mostly when you're watching TV?

Meredith: But mostly good pictures get on and I get 'em . . . I got to go to the store.

Therapist B.: Oh. Can you think of any way that you can work that out? Because I'm thinking of something.

Therapist A.: Put the chair down, George, and sit in it.

Therapist B.: Did you ever try asking your mother before you went to watch the picture if there's anything she wanted?

Tim: (*To George*) Put the chair down.

George: I want to go to the bathroom, Tim.

Tim: Therapist A., I'll take him.

Therapist A.: He can go by himself when it's time to go, but not now.

Meredith: (*To Therapist B.*) She say, "No," but then after she says, "Yes."

Tim: Can I go then?

Therapist A.: George, we want to pay attention and hear what you have to say too, but you have to wait 'cause Meredith is talking right now. Okay?

Tim: Can I go then?

Therapist A.: You, too, Tim, hear what Meredith has to say. Go ahead, Meredith.

The therapists, as can be seen from the above, are enmeshed in the communication patterns of the family. Although in earlier sessions they had required a reasonably quiet background, they appear now to be accepting noise in order to communicate meaningfully. They accept the "static" that two of the siblings are emitting, so to speak, in order to communicate with a third. The trip to the bathroom had become a frequent strategy in the sessions; as a matter of fact George repeatedly used this ploy to capture the therapists' attention whenever their attention was not directly focused on him. In any one session he might go to the bathroom, return, and soon after his return, request permission to leave again. We shall see later that George attempts to elicit external controls in order to achieve a sense of security (see sequence 17, for example).

We state that the therapists in the foregoing transactions are involved in an essentially uneconomical and noneffective method of establishing communication with the children. In effect, they are operating *within* the communication system that the family members use, rather than outside it, in an attempt to modify it. If this had been a "natural" transaction (siblings without therapists), the thread of communications would have undoubtedly shifted or waned without closure. But the therapist(s) is attempting to sustain attention through a storm of unruly communications. In this role, he forcefully contacts the family members, struggling to maintain a thread of meaningful continuity. The experience thus generated is undoubtedly a new one for the family members, for often this type of therapeutic intervention yields the first genuine exchange of information among them. However, this phase of therapeutic intervention —the overpowering of "noise" by the therapist—should yield "rules" for future sensible, orderly, and focused communications if the family is to learn a new system of sustaining exchanges around a particular topic. Judgments as to what extent the therapist should initially accommodate to the family's system of communication and to what extent he should reject it depend on the artistry of the therapist and the idiosyncratic characteristics of the system of communications of the family as they are disclosed in therapy.

One might wonder whether or not it is worthwhile to attempt *family* therapy (as opposed to *individual* therapy) under such difficult conditions. We therefore stress our belief that it is precisely under conditions of family therapy that poor communication systems can be observed and an attempt made to establish more effective communications. In other words, rather than being contraindicated, family therapy can be shown to be fundamental to the job that needs to be done. Chapter 6 returns to this issue and those raised in the above paragraphs.

SEQUENCE 3   TWENTIETH SESSION, STAGE 2

Communications in the La Salle family are often vague, the referents unclear, and the yield quite sparse when the level of exchange of information is considered. There seems to be little need felt by the family members to make explicit their communications and to expand their familial "boundaries," so to speak.[3] The sequence below illustrates this pattern of communications, which, it should be noted, is a central feature of this family's transactions.

Therapist: You got the same teacher?
Meredith: Yep.
Therapist: Yeah?

---

[3] See Chapter 5, which presents a full discussion of the communication patterns in our families.

George: There was a mean teacher in my class.
Therapist: It's the same one as before, right?
George: Huh?
Therapist: It's the same teacher you had before?
George: It ain't . . . but that one ain't mean.
Therapist: Huh?
George: The other is a lady that's mean.
Therapist: Oh, you have a man teacher, too?
George: Huh? That was a lady.
Therapist: Oh, there was a lady who was mean.

Notice the problem that the therapist has in defining the subject to which George is referring. "It's the same one as before, right?" "Huh?" "The other is a lady that's mean." "Oh, you have a man teacher, too?" This basic confusion in identifying whom the conversation is about is an aspect of disruptive communications. It takes many exchanges just to arrive at a consensus as to what the subject is. Defining the "referent" is a laborsome operation for the therapist as well as for the children. The La Salles tend to assume that the other person has an implicit understanding of what is being talked about; they feel no need to clarify or make their references explicit before proceeding to further exchanges.

SEQUENCE 4 EIGHTH SESSION, STAGE 2

The La Salles' inability to utilize an efficient framework of communications rules which could help them to sustain focus on the subject under discussion allows the individual members to disrupt, shift, or introduce a new referent into the conversation without a signal or cue that the new thought is unrelated to the shared (implicit or explicit) context. For example, in the sequence below, Tim changes the subjective referent under discussion to a new one, as if either referent would suffice equally well to create a semblance of conversational continuity.

George has been talking about his fears and the monsters he sees on TV, which assume for him concrete reality. The therapist tries to recruit Tim to help George.

Therapist A.: . . . Tim, did you ever tell George and Meredith that there really are no monsters?
Tim: He knows it, but George don't. The day that he dropped the garbage can off the back fire escape and had to go down and get it 'cause in the night time the janitor found out that he had dropped it down there. Then, when he went down there to get it, he took a stick with him.

Therapist A.: Who did? George did?

Therapist B.: He's talking about one of the boys at the school. Why do you think he took a stick?

We see in the above sequence that although the talk is about George, Tim subjectively associates to another boy in school; he talks about this boy and George interchangeably, probably because they had engaged in similar behavior (or had similar fears). Here, a similarity of content makes the individuals interchangeable. At other times, a similarity of individuals can make content interchangeable.

SEQUENCE 5   TWENTY-SIXTH SESSION, STAGE 1

The sequence below illustrates Mrs. La Salle's inability to make communicational impact on her children. Note that the impression one gets from reading the written transcript is that she is insistently unresponsive to Tim and is in no way acknowledging the fact that Tim *is*, seemingly, responding to her. The family members and the therapist are discussing Tim's impending discharge from the Wiltwyck School. Thus:

Therapist A.: Yeah, but is there any reason why you think you should come home now, you think?

Tim: Yeah.

Therapist A.: Why?

Tim: 'Cause I want to.

Therapist A.: Oh, that's all fine, but that's . . .

Mrs. L.: Are you ready?

Tim: Yeah, I am.

Mrs. L.: Are you actually ready for it?

Tim: Yeah, I am.

Mrs. L.: You're certain that you're ready?

Tim: Huh?

Mrs. L.: You are certain that you're ready?

Meredith: He won't listen to you.

Tim: What did you say?

Mrs. L.: I said, "Are you certain that you are ready?"

Tim: Yeah, I am.

The fact is that at the paraverbal level Tim is feeding cues to his mother which convey to her that he is not at all attending to what she is saying. When she asks, "Are you ready?" and he says, "Yeah, I am," we would like to stress that her repetition ("Are you actually ready for it?") is based on her experience that the children do not focus selectively on *most* communications. Mrs. La Salle constantly feels that she is never reaching or making contact with her children. Impotence in "making contact" is implicit in all of the La Salle transactions. The plight of Mrs. La Salle is obvious when Meredith says, "He won't listen to you." Meredith's correct diagnosis of the situation hits precisely at the core of the problem and underlies Mrs. La Salle's insistent repetition of some variation of, "Are you certain that you're ready?"

SEQUENCE 6 TWENTY-SIXTH SESSION, STAGE 7

A characteristic of the La Salles' disjointed communications is the easy spread of disruption, once it is initiated. For example:

(*Meredith gets up from his chair and gets his coat.*)

Mrs. L.: Who said we're going home?

Meredith: I'm getting tired.

Mrs. L.: Tired of doing what?

George: Mommy?

Mrs. L.: Yes, George?

George: Can I go to the bathroom?

Mrs. L.: Yes, George.

(*George and Tim speak at the same time.*)

Mrs. L.: (*To Tim*) You should be minding your own business.

(*To George*) And you don't come through that room.

(*George leaves the room.*)

Meredith attempts to leave, complaining of tiredness; George asks to go to the bathroom; then George and Tim speak at the same time. Disruptive activity has quickly spread. Note that Mrs. La Salle's response suddenly becomes punitive and restrictive in order to "contain" the demands the children are making. She has issued two controlling commands to two of the children. Mrs. La Salle's plight and her sense of being burdened by the multiple "pulls" from her children elicit frequent and intense (but ineffective) control responses from her. Some aspects of this interactional process—the overdemandingness of the children and Mrs. La Salle's resultant responses—will be illustrated in the next section along with other aspects of the family members' perception of and behavior toward one another.

The Family World: The La Salles' Perception of and Behavior toward One Another

This section, as noted, attempts to illustrate through recorded transcripts the views, attitudes, perceptions, and behavior that the La Salle family members display toward one another; in addition, some emergent self-perceptions and self-attitudes will be disclosed. The material to be covered includes Mrs. La Salle's views about her own upbringing as they relate to her children; mother-children interaction; and various aspects of sibling behavior and sibling interaction. We turn first to sequences relevant to Mrs. La Salle's description of her own upbringing.

SEQUENCE 7   THIRD SESSION, STAGES 1 AND 2

Below are excerpts from two stages of a single session. The sequence of this material has been altered in order to communicate a sense of the content. Mrs. La Salle, in these segments, is describing her own upbringing, her feelings about her mother's expectations of her as a child and of her children. She also verbalizes her feelings about how her own early development and upbringing affected her attitudes toward and interaction with her children.

Mrs. L.: You see, what I am trying to bring out? I myself, I have been brought up, what would you call it? Ah, what's the word?

Therapist A.: Say what you mean.

Mrs. L.: Well, I want the word, but maybe she can help me with the word.

Therapist A.: Well, just say what you feel.

Mrs. L.: I know, but I have spoken to you about it and I was hoping you could give me that one word, at least.

Therapist A.: Are your parents from Bermuda, the West Indies?

Mrs. L.: My parents are from the West Indies.

Therapist A.: All right, that tells me something. In other words, I think what you are—if I can help a bit—I can't think of the one word.

Mrs. L.: Yeah, but you are brought up . . .

Therapist A.: (*Finishes her sentence.*) . . . differently.

Mrs. L.: Straight on the line. I'll put it like that.

Therapist A.: Okay.

Therapist B.: Do you mean rigidly?

Mrs. L.: Rigid, rigid, rigid. Thank you. That's the word I really wanted. You're brought up rigidly.

Therapist A.: Yeah.

Mrs. L.: And then, on the other hand, I had no sisters, no brothers. I was brought up, you know, as you say, rigid.

. . .

Mrs. L.: And I will give her credit, she did the best she could with me. Naturally I turn around, I try to do the same thing . . . with my children as she did with me. There is only one difference though.

There is more than one difference. The thing of it is . . . she was so rigid with me, that I have tried to break it down. Maybe I broke it down too much.

Therapist A.: You mean you try to be less rigid and more understanding?

Mrs. L.: More, yes, more lenient.

. . .

Mrs. L.: Well, yet may I say this? I mean my parents were very rigid with me in bringing me up.

Therapist A.: Uhm, with your kids?

Mrs. L.: They were too lenient with the children.

. . .

Therapist A.: You were sort of caught in the middle, between not quite knowing what to do.

Mrs. L.: Well, yeah, yes. Because I didn't want to hurt one or the other [parents or children]. Remember, all this came up with the children, got themselves messed up as they did, just about three weeks to the day, practically, of my mother's death.

. . .

Mrs. L.: It all came on about three weeks to the day, and my mother has told the children, which made it very hard, where she has told them that when she was gone, they would suffer.

. . .

Mrs. L.: Well, what I thought, to my feeling of what I thought she meant, as long as she wasn't around they wouldn't have their way . . . Maybe now, to a certain extent, she really meant, too, what I knew she meant. I should say she figured that as long as I—that *she* wasn't around, they would not get the direct care that they should get. That is what she tried to put into their minds.

Therapist A.: In other words, she was saying that they had to depend on *her* for the mother, really.

Mrs. L.: Well, at one time, Therapist A., those children did not know that I was their mother . . . But with the children she was too lenient.

. . .

In a manner of speaking, I'll put it this way: As a child, like say, from George on until my oldest son, I didn't actually have what you call a childhood. She never took me around to any clubs or anything like that. There were always church people, very good friends, and things like that. But to say, actually to be among children of my own age group, I really . . . I didn't have any. Because whenever she went she took me. She never left me by myself . . . well, I guess any mother would do that with a younger child.

. . .

But . . . my children, I had all three of them, so you know it's not the matter that they were just infants . . . I never had a chance to go out . . . alone . . . I couldn't take in a movie. I couldn't go anywhere on my own. Everywhere I went, I had to take the children with me.

. . .

Up until [Meredith] he was, say 3½ years old, he and my mother and all of us were together . . . Then my husband and I were together to a separate place . . . I left my mother before I took Meredith, and after I made the home, I took Meredith with us.

. . .

Mrs. L.: Well there was a lot of contentions there, too, because she didn't want me to take the child. . . . And when she came to the house to see me, she would criticize.

. . .

And then if I spoke to Meredith, it was wrong. I couldn't spank him. "Don't do this to him." "Don't do the other to him." Anything I would say to him, it would be wrong.

We see from the above an explicit, repeated statement of Mrs. La Salle's feelings that her own upbringing was excessively rigid and cloistered. She is confused and inconsistent in her views, however. First she states that she is repeating the pattern, "Naturally I turn around, I try to do the same thing . . . with my children as she did with me." Then she modifies this somewhat by stating soon afterward, ". . . but I have tried to break it down. Maybe I broke it down too much." She suggests that she *is* overcontrolling, however, by describing her mother's intervention and leniency with respect to the children. Some superstitious elements in Mrs. La Salle's views are further disclosed when she describes her mother's ominous prediction to the children that when "she was gone, they would suffer." She points out that the children "got themselves messed up as they did, just about three weeks, to the day, practically, of my mother's death." Her feelings of awe, admiration, resentment, and fear of her mother are apparent in her verbalizations, as are feelings of confusion and insecurity about her fulfillment of her own role as a mother. For she indicates that she has attempted (unsuccessfully) to change the pattern of upbringing that *she* received when she relates to her own children.

SEQUENCE 8   EIGHTH SESSION, STAGE 3

We turn now to illustrating Mrs. La Salle's actual behavior toward her children and her implicit attitudes toward them, as they emerged in our sessions. In the sequence below, Mrs. La Salle is responding to the therapist's questions concerning her handling of George's imaginary fears:

Therapist: Do you say to him directly that there are no monsters?

Mrs. L.: Well, I won't tell him that there are such things . . . and he wants to know about the clouds, and about how rain comes, and all of that. "Are there monsters up in the clouds?" he might say. And you know yourself that there are times when the formation of the clouds makes things, and he'll look at it and decide what it is. And there are times when he decides what he sees up there is a monster.

Therapist: Uhmm.

Mrs. L.: But I have to try to explain to him, so that he'll understand that it's not actually monsters; it's just the formation of the clouds.

Therapist: Uhmm. I see.

Mrs. L.: But, ah, he will question me about things like that and I try to answer him. I try to give him a sensible answer, but in a way that he will understand.

The above suggests that Mrs. La Salle has a conscious picture of herself as a guiding, sensitive mother who is attuned to her child's fears and needs. She describes herself as always willing to provide him with sensible information, reassurance, and guidance.

SEQUENCE 9   THIRD SESSION, STAGE 1

The conscious, verbalized, positive image of herself that Mrs. La Salle discloses in her dialogue with the therapist is in sharp contrast to her actual transactions with the children in the sessions:

Mrs. L.: Is there any way that he can bring me some water?

Therapist A.: Oh, yeah, sure.

Mrs. L.: I'd appreciate it.

(*Meredith and therapist get Mrs. L. a cup of water.*)

George: Mommy, I want water.

(*All talk at once at this point.*)

George: Mommy, I want water.

Mrs. L.: I told you about acting up.

George: I'll shut my big mouth.

Therapist: What did you say about your big mouth?

George: I talk too much.

SEQUENCE 10 THIRD SESSION, STAGE 1

Another instance of contrast between Mrs. La Salle's projected self-attitudes and her actual behavior is found in the sequence below. Meredith is getting ready to leave the session to return to his institution. Preceding this segment, the therapist stated that there was a change in Meredith, who, in the previous two sessions, had been depressed and tearful just before leaving for the institution.

Meredith: The earlier we leave, the more fun we have.

Therapist: The more fun you have going back? Well, that's a change, Meredith.

Mrs. L.: Tell her why you like to get back on the bus, and why not.
. . .

Mrs. L.: Well, which getting back? Which way did you mean? Getting back to school or getting back home? Which?

Meredith: School.

Mrs. L.: Oh, it's fun on the way back.

Meredith: Uh-huh.

Mrs. L.: On the bus.

Meredith: Uh-huh.

Mrs. L.: But you don't have much fun coming home? Well in other words, what I think he is trying to say, he doesn't care much about coming home.

Therapist: Well, I don't know if he said that, Mrs. La Salle . . . and I think that it was quite different than saying, "I don't like to come home." Is that right, Meredith?

Meredith: I guess so.

Mrs. L.: Do you like to come home?

Meredith: Yeah.

Mrs. L.: Are you sure? (*Meredith nods yes.*) Don't look so pitiful.

Meredith: Yes, um.

The discrepancy between Mrs. La Salle's self-descriptions and what actually happens in the interactions between mother and child is of special interest because diagnostic and therapeutic data along this dimension are usually obtained in an *individual* interview. It seems quite likely that conceptualizations about mother-child interactions based on individual interview data may often be invalid; the actual facts of a dyadic system are more accessible when unfolded in a real interaction.

SEQUENCE 11   TWENTY-SIXTH SESSION, STAGE 1

The sequence below highlights Mrs. La Salle's manner of handling what she possibly interprets as the beginning of disruptive behavior. In response to George's, "Mommy, I got a sore on my finger," she verbalizes a threat which contains a global, nonspecific, punitive quality.

George: Mommy, I got a sore on my finger.

Mrs. L.: That's not the only place you're going to have one.

George: You mean, I'll have one on my head?

Mrs. L.: No.

George: My popo?

Mrs. L.: Uh-huh.

George: Why?

Mrs. L.: (*No response to George's question.*)

Therapist: He wants to know why.

We see from the above that George's request for nurturance elicits only, "That's not the only place you're going to have one." The response is sharp and threatening in tone ("I will hurt you even more"), and there is no hint to the child as to why he will be punished, or where, or in what way. To his mother's undefined and nonspecific threat, George responds with a series of exploratory questions oriented to clarify the issue and to put the global aggression into smaller units and more manageable form. He succeeds, partially, for his mother's global threat is pinpointed to a spanking on his behind. Now he asks, "Why?" but no response is forthcoming. It is interesting that in this session, late in the series, George is beginning to display some capacity for cognitive coping —for exploration, expressing curiosity, and confronting his mother. In prior sessions he would have chosen to go to the bathroom. And Mrs. La Salle is undergoing a complementary change, for she is allowing the confrontation to take place without curtailing George completely.

SEQUENCE 12   (CONTINUATION OF ABOVE)

A minute after Mrs. La Salle responded to George's demand for nurturance with undifferentiated aggression, she addressed herself to him with a nurturant response. His specific question about his sore finger remains unanswered.

Mrs. L.: (*To George*) Come on.

Tim: Yeah, bring him over there.

Mrs. L.: Have a seat. (*George sits next to mother.*)

Characteristic of the interaction between Mrs. La Salle and her children is the alternate presence of two different modalities of contact. She often squelches their freedom, curtails exploratory responses on their part, establishes rigid control over their behavior, and demands immediate and absolute obedience on her own terms. At other times, however, as in the above interaction, she encourages a closeness which is defined and acted out in terms of sheer physical proximity. Her emotional contact with the children generally has an either/or quality. On the one hand, there is the global aggression and the assertion of absolute rule; on the other hand, we find attempts to offer complete nurturance. But the latter, too, is expressed in global terms—physical proximity and concrete, tangible closeness—which keep George's specific concern (the sore on his finger) unfocused and unattended to.

SEQUENCE 13   EIGHTH SESSION, STAGE 3

That the children develop and are socialized in this climate of extremes and display an intense need for proximity is indicated not only by their demand for the mother's physical presence in a room, but by their involvement with her *bed*:

Therapist B.: The minute he came in the door, and you were gone, he wanted to get out.

Therapist A.: An immediate reaction: Where were you? He wanted to check on where you were, you know. And I think that's part of the same picture, but I don't know that for sure.

Mrs. L.: I understand.

Therapist A.: It's just a feeling.

Therapist C.: Does he hang on to you when you're at home, too?

Mrs. L.: Yes, ah, he's very . . . and, ah, he will get in my bed with me, if I let him.

Therapist C.: Do you let him, sometimes?

Mrs. L.: At times I do, and at times I don't, but ah . . .

Therapist A.: What does it depend on? I'm curious.

Mrs. L.: (*Inaudible.*)

Therapist A.: Oh, I see, now I know what that look means. Okay.

Mrs. L.: Sometimes I do and sometimes I don't.

Therapist A.: If you're free, you can let him.

Mrs. L.: That's right.

Therapist A.: I'm glad you told me that. I think it's very interesting. I think it has some bearing on . . .

Mrs. L.: Sometimes I let him in my bed, and sometimes I don't.

Therapist B.: Does Meredith try and get in your bed?

Mrs. L.: Well, Meredith's always in my bed. As soon as I'm not in it,

Meredith and all the kids want to be in my bed. I don't know why. And, at times, when they're all home, I let them sleep in it. They all get in the bed. They all want to sleep in my bed. Why I don't know.

Therapist C.: You mean, whether you're there or not, or with you?

Mrs. L.: Well, yes with me, if I'm in the bed, which is very seldom. But they say, "Mommy, can I sleep in your bed tonight?" "Go ahead, sleep in my bed if you want to." They all sleep in my bed. I don't know if it's just more comfortable, but they all like sleeping in my bed. So I let them sleep in it.

Therapist C.: Well, I think it shows that they are needing you and that they are wanting you.

Mrs. L.: Yeah, they're all like that.

SEQUENCE 14   EIGHTH SESSION, STAGE 3

A few minutes later, the therapist explores the sexual aspects of the La Salle family's intense need for physical proximity, which is being expressed in the rivalry for the mother's bed. He does not, however, explore, clarify, and really make explicit the role that Mrs. La Salle plays in encouraging and condoning this behavior, nor does he raise the question concerning her *own* needs in this particular family process.

Therapist A.: Talk about how they behave when they're in the bed. What they do, and all these things, which can be very important.

Mrs. L.: Uh huh.

Therapist A.: And it's quite different, as you know, between three two-year-olds getting in a bed and a boy of 13.

Mrs. L.: That's right.

Therapist A.: You know, there is a big, big difference. Right? When a boy of 13 wants to do that it means several things. When a boy of two wants to do that, it means only one.

Mrs. L.: It's a different thing altogether.

Therapist A.: That's right. Even at four, he begins to . . .

Mrs. L.: I know what you mean.

SEQUENCE 15   EIGHTH SESSION, STAGE 2

The foregoing sequences illustrate an aspect of the La Salle family's interactional pattern: the need for physical proximity to the mother and even to her things (bed). In the following sequences, we turn to a closer look at the sibling subsystem. We find that physical proximity is a requisite here, too, as a "unifying" and cohesive factor among them. In particular, aggression and aggressive contact, that is, physical proximity in its crudest form, seem to act as an organizing force among the siblings. Below, for example, is an excerpt illustrating an instance of cooperative sibling interaction through the use of aggression:

Tim: Why can't I go with him [Meredith]?

Therapist A.: You think he needs you?

Tim: Yeah.

Therapist A.: For what?

Tim: So I could do things, so I could help him.

Therapist A.: What would you help him do?

Tim: Stay out of trouble.

Therapist A.: You could? You think he needs help to stay out of trouble?

Tim: Yeah.

Therapist A.: Well, what would you do to help him?

Tim: Every time he'd go to get into trouble, I'd hit him, and keep on hitting him and then I'd run upstairs and then I'd get him upstairs that way.

Therapist A.: You hear that, Meredith?

Meredith: Yes, sir.

Therapist A.: What do you think of what he says? What does it mean to you? Hmm? What? Anything?

Meredith: That he would help me.

. . .

Therapist B.: Tim, do you remember when you were home and you followed Meredith everywhere he went?

Tim: Yeah.

Therapist B.: Well, why did you do that?

Tim: I wanted to keep him out of trouble, but he got me in trouble, too.

Aggression acts as an integrating and cohesive force in the La Salle family: Tim assumes a protective and aggressive role simultaneously and interchangeably. His aggression is aimed to keep Meredith out of trouble. Notice, also, that Tim follows Meredith, presumably to "keep him out of trouble." This kind of physical proximity, in the form of following each other or "watching over" each other, is frequently found at the sibling level in this family. Tim's statement, ". . . but he got me in trouble, too" shows the ineffectiveness of his attempts to guide and protect his brother.

SEQUENCE 16 EIGHTH SESSION, STAGE 2

Later on, in the same session, an anxious interaction among the siblings occurs after Mrs. La Salle leaves the room. The lack of an organizing agent is immediately felt. Her physical proximity had served to keep disruptive behavior somewhat under control.

George: I would tear everything up down there.

Tim: (*Noticing someone in the observation room.*) There's a lady in there.

Therapist A.: There is? Oh, that's all right.

George: Why is she in there?

Therapist A.: She's watching what's going on. We let them do that. (*The children all talk at once and play with the microphone.*)

Therapist A.: Well, nothing is going to happen to you . . .

George: I want my mother.

Therapist A.: Why?

George: I want to know where she's at. I know where she's at.

Tim: (*Gets up from his seat.*) I know where she's at, too.

George: I'm going to get her.

Therapist A.: No, you're not. Sit down, Tim.

George: Let me go get her.

Therapist A.: No, you're not going to get her.

George: Why?

Therapist A.: 'Cause you're not supposed to right now. Sit down, Tim.

George: Tim, that was my chair.

Therapist A.: . . .

Therapist B.: Tim, why all of a sudden do you want to know where your mother is, and see her?

Tim: I don't know.

Therapist A.: Miss her?

George: . . .

Therapist B.: Tim is pretty concerned about his mother.

Therapist A.: I was going to say he is. When she's not around he gets very scared. Thinks things are going to happen to him.

George: . . . Hey, Tim, why do you eat snakes for dinner?

Tim: You don't know what you're talking about.

Therapist B.: Tell me, Tim.

George: You do eat snakes for dinner.

Therapist B.: When George says things that don't make much sense, what do you do, just don't pay any attention to him?

Tim: I don't pay no attention to him.

Therapist B.: What do you do?

Tim: I don't pay no attention to him.

George: He knocks me out the window.
Therapist A.: Oh, we're on that again.

It can be seen from the above that when Mrs. La Salle leaves the room and can no longer help to establish and to delineate inner and outer reality for the children, Tim becomes overconcerned with and alert to danger from without, and George becomes concerned with diffuse and global attacks and aggression.[4] George says, "I would tear everything up down there." Tim suddenly becomes concerned with the observer behind the one-way screen; although the observer had previously been accepted, she is now a threat. The children's hyperactivity is based on fear. Both children want their mother to return. George baits Tim about eating snakes.

The process can be described as follows: (1) loss of the mother implies falling back on one's own resources; (2) fear and anxiety now predominate, essentially having to do with aggression either from within or without; (3) the children sense the inadequacy of their coping operations and attempt to decrease the uncertainty in the environment and their own feelings by bringing back the mother as an organizing and structuring agent; and (4) when these attempts fail, one of the siblings, George, introduces a provocation (". . . why do you eat snakes for dinner?"), for he needs to elicit an aggressive response from the outside as a security measure for himself. Further, George's "joke," although a barb, is his own bid for contact and for relationship with his sibling. (Humor, baiting, sometimes cruel "joking" are often employed in certain subcultures as organizing, reaching-out-to-the-other contact mechanisms.)

SEQUENCE 17   EIGHTH SESSION, STAGE 2

When the children cannot gain access to orientation cues (in this instance, from their mother), and when their coping mechanisms fail to work, the level of disorganization increases rapidly and with mounting intensity. Below, in a sequence which occurs a few minutes after the above, Tim wants to leave the field altogether, but George invokes a mechanism with which we are already familiar—he seeks physical controls from without:

Therapist A.: Sit down, George. Where are you going, Tim?
George: To look for his mother.

---

[4] The clinicians working with this family have noted that George's predominant fear is that of being overwhelmed from within because there is no external check upon his impulse repertoire. Tim's is that he will be overwhelmed from without, by a hostile, intrusive environment (see C. A. Malone, Safety first: comments on the influence of external danger in the lives of children of disorganized families, *Amer. J. Orthopsychiat.*, 1966, 36, 3-12).

Tim: To the bathroom.

Therapist A.: You've just been. You have to go again?

Tim: I know, but I'm thirsty.

Therapist A.: You really want water? Okay.

George: Oh, me too . . .

Therapist A.: Sit down, George. (*George slaps himself at this point.*)

Therapist B.: Why did you slap yourself, George, and so hard? Why?

George: Because I just wanted to slap myself so no one would think I'm a crybaby.

George artificially introduces physical controls by slapping himself. In a sense, he does to himself what his family (mother and siblings) usually do to him. He is creating the boundaries that he needs by supplementing or reinforcing the verbal command of the therapist with a self-imposed direct and aggressive act. He literally reconstructs a family pattern of interaction: aggression and punishment are vital for the handling of anxiety and for the sense of organization, control, and orientation of the individual children in the family.

SEQUENCE 18   EIGHTH SESSION, STAGE 2

But aggression does not always unify and organize the transactions among the siblings. In the following interaction between George and Tim, George verbalizes a fantasy about "Me and Tim going to be out playing in the snow." He is expressing a wish for a positive and enjoyable inter-action with his brother, but is immediately rebuffed: "You're gonna be out there by yourself. I'm not going to be out there freezing." George's behavior suddenly changes:

George: Me and Tim going to be out playing in the snow, come Christmas.

Tim: You're gonna be out there by yourself. I'm not going to be out there freezing.

George: . . .

Tim: You better get your . . .

George: No, I won't . . .

Tim: You better shut up about that.

George: (*Inaudible—something about the pipe in the ceiling.*)

Therapist B.: What pipe?

George: That pipe up there.

Therapist B.: That pipe isn't going to fall.

George: What kind of pipe?

Tim: It's a water pipe, or a heat pipe.

Therapist B.: They're not going to fall on you.

George: If a bomb come, this whole house will fall.

Therapist A.: Are you worried about there being a fire, with these two guys in it? Why should that concern . . .

George: No, I'm not worried about there being no fire.

Tim: He said, "If there is."

Therapist A.: Oh, if there is.

George: You know what? If there were a fire in here, I would try to bust through the glass.

Tim: Bust through the glass? What good is that going to do?

George: To help me get out. I know what I would do. I would go down the stairs and bring water over and put out the fire.

Therapist A.: Good. And that you could do.

The transaction continues around the issue of the threat of fire and the handling of it, for several minutes.

We see from the above sequence that George responds to Tim's rebuff and aggression by speaking of danger. Tim's aggressive responses, in this instance, acted as a powerful disorganizing force. Aggression this time did not function as an organizing force, but as a disruptive one; it is likely that the timing of aggression (the context, as it were) as well as the momentary balance of security resources within the family enter into the determination of the role such aggression plays in the La Salle family interactions, especially among the siblings.

The therapist attempts to support the child by channeling his amorphous, vague fears into the more familiar, concrete threat of fire, around which he explores coping behavior. Fire is a familiar context: fire was set in the house by the senile grandfather of this family, George and Meredith once set fire to a synagogue, and George himself set the house on fire when he was five years old. The therapist uses fire as a concrete focal point, representing the child's basic insecurity with respect to his immediate environment.

SEQUENCE 19   TWENTIETH SESSION, STAGE 2

George is in the second grade at school. The therapists, George, and Meredith have been talking about George's first day in school. Meredith had taken him to school that day. Sequence 3 (see earlier), which illustrates some of the difficulties in establishing communications in this family, immediately precedes the following sequence. We see here how Meredith

trains and socializes his younger brother to adopt certain views toward
the outside world,[5] in this instance, school and authority. Further, Meredith instructs George how to cope with this world, providing him with
an antisocial model.

George: But anyway, I don't even care if they do call the officer on me.

Therapist B.: You don't care what?

George: I don't care if they call the officer on me.

Therapist A.: Call the officer on you?

Therapist B.: . . .

George: I don't care if she calls the officer on me 'cause I could run.

Therapist B.: . . . Does she call the officer on you?

Therapist A.: Why do you smile, Meredith? Where is there for him to
run, uh?

George: I got word that she's gonna call the officer on me.

Therapist B.: Has she called the officer on you since she's been in school?

Meredith: Sometimes.

Therapist A.: What happens when he doesn't?

George: Anyway, I don't like that teacher.

Therapist A.: I mean what does he do when he doesn't do what you
say? . . .

Meredith: He can run up and down. I don't care what he does.

Therapist B.: You mean you get disgusted?

George: And yeah, you told me . . . you told me . . . you told me if
the teacher don't let me go to the bathroom, run and come home.

Meredith: That's right.

George: Yeah, I'll run out of the school and don't never come back.

Therapists A. and B.: You told him to do that, Meredith?

Therapist A.: Why did you say that?

Meredith: I didn't tell him to do that. I said—(*interrupted.*)

Therapist A.: You just told him now to do it. Why did you tell him?

George: Yeah, and I did it and I didn't come home.

Therapist A.: You be quiet, George. You know George will do it. Why
did you tell him to do a thing like that?

Meredith: I didn't . . . I was just playing with him. If he do it, he just
do it.

Therapist A.: Yeah, but don't you know you can't play with him that

---

[5] See Chapter 5 for a detailed discussion of the "parental child" as a socializer in these
families. Meredith seems to feel the need to take over much of the adult responsibility
for guiding and protecting his younger siblings.

way? Huh? Don't you? You know George will do what you tell him, mostly. Who'll get blamed for it?

George: (*Points to Meredith.*) You.

Therapist A.: Won't you? Won't you?

George: If he wouldn't let me.

Therapist B.: That's not one . . . that's not a way to help him, Meredith. Tell him to do what you think he should do.

George: I don't care if she calls the officer on me.

Therapist B.: 'Cause when you joke he doesn't always understand the difference, you know that?

George: I don't care.

Therapist A.: I think Meredith . . . why do you do that, Meredith? Let's understand that at least.

Meredith: I didn't do it.

George: If an officer catch you and the . . . (*interrupted.*)

Therapist A.: You don't want to be bothered with this guy, do you?

Meredith: No.

Therapist A.: That's it.

George: If an officer catch you that you don't . . . if an officer catches you that you don't go to school, what do they do to you?

Therapist A.: He wouldn't do anything to you.

George: Well, what . . . what, what?

Therapist A.: What do you think he would do to you, George?

George: I don't know.

Therapist A.: What are you afraid of?

George: What if he catch you doing something you don't have no . . . what if he catch you doing something you don't have no business doing, then what he do?

Therapist B.: . . .

George: He'll take you to the teacher.

Therapist A.: (*Nods yes.*)

George: And then what she would do?

Therapist A.: She might scold you . . . tell you not to do that again.

George: Well, I still would do it . . . no, I wouldn't do it, but I would run out of that class.

There is a "paranoid" flavor in the training to which Meredith is exposing George. It should be noted that the world is depicted as hostile and foreboding, but it is especially the school and the teacher that symbolize and represent this world. The irony, of course, is that it is precisely the world of the school and of education which is vital to the social mobility, hopefulness, job opportunities, and the development of skills which these children sorely lack. Meredith's bitter experiences and confusion in the school setting as well as his method of handling these feelings are transmitted directly to George; in a sense, George does not even have to *learn* his own ways of coping. He anticipates difficulties, and has already decided how to handle them.

The above sequence also discloses the constant, pervasive tricking and teasing that characterize the interactions of the siblings in the La Salle family. (Sequence 16 provides an example of how George maliciously teases Tim.) Meredith smiles, aware, perhaps, that he is tricking and deceiving his brother in regard to what to expect from the teacher.

SEQUENCE 20   TWENTIETH SESSION, STAGE 2

The sequence below illustrates how the La Salle children cope with mounting disruptive interactions. Notice their futile attempts to recover control, and how they all contribute to extremely disruptive activity in their attempts to establish control over each other.

George: Can't I go to the bathroom?

Tim: I said sit down.

Therapist: Sit down. You can go to the bathroom later, just sit down. You know why we're not letting you go to the bathroom?

Tim: It looks like I'm gonna have to put you down.

Therapist: Sit down, George.

Tim: Sit down.

Therapist: Sit down, break it up. Come on, sit down.

Tim: Come on, George, stop playing around. Sit down.

Therapist: Sit down, Tim. You sit down and George sit down.

Meredith: (*To Tim*) You sit down, too.

Therapist: Sit down, Tim.

Meredith: Sit down.

Tim: (*To George*) Sit down, and stay there.

Therapist: George, sit.

Meredith: Sit down, George.

George: No.

Therapist: Sit, George.

Meredith: (*Gets up and shoves George into chair.*)

Therapist: Okay, Meredith, that's it.

Meredith: Now sit down.

Therapist: (*To George*) Now stay that way. Come over here by me,

George. Bring your chair. Come over here. Bring your chair over. Now sit down.

The La Salle children become globally aggressive in their attempts to control each other. Each child, in turn, seems to assume his proper hierarchical rank in a kind of age-determined pecking order, but all the children (as well as the therapist) come to perceive George, the youngest, as the real trouble-maker and as an excess burden. As a matter of fact, the therapist, becoming increasingly enmeshed in the communication and control patterns of the La Salle family, regulates the situation by using a tactic that is decidedly characteristic of the family members. He employs the very primitive maneuver of using physical proximity as a means of control. He says to George, ". . . Come over here by me, George. Bring your chair. Come over here. Bring your chair over. Now sit down." (Note, Mrs. La Salle used this tactic after an aggressive interaction with George. See sequence 12.) His controlling the child's disruptive behavior in this manner is an illustration of how the therapist can become inducted into the family system. This issue will be raised again in greater detail in Chapter 6.

Both Mrs. La Salle and the therapist, perhaps, are also attempting to handle the aggression which has been displayed toward George by evincing a nurturance-by-proximity response to him—a response which he tends to elicit from others due to his infantile needs.

Attitudes toward the Surrounding World: Suspicion, Mistrust, and Misinformation

All sequences in this section are from the twenty-sixth session, Stage 3.

The La Salles live in a world that is heavily populated with aggressors. So when members of the family talk about an incident in the neighborhood, they will frequently fasten on an incident with aggressive connotations. Aggression forms a significant part of their daily encounters.

For this reason, it is no easy task for the clinician to differentiate the instances in which family members are being realistically descriptive from those in which they are imaginatively suspicious and mistrustful. Perhaps it is unnecessary to distinguish in order to understand, for in this family there is a merging of fears and anxieties whether or not the source is real: the true dangers of the external realities become confused with the overflow of inner insecurities and uncertainties.

If the inner organization of this family included trust and acceptance, one wonders what the effect of these continuously external threats would be. In what way would these realistic threats then impinge on family equilibrium? How is the emotional development of individuals who are forced to live in a world that requires continuous awareness of danger affected?

SEQUENCE 21 TWENTY-SIXTH SESSION, STAGE 3

Below, Mrs. La Salle is talking about what happens when she leaves her father alone at home:

Mrs. L.: . . . When I ask him if anyone came or anyone knocked at the door, "No," he tells me, "no one was there." But yet after a time . . .

Therapist: He may not remember it.

Mrs. L.: Yeah. But then after a time I'll meet someone or they'll come back and then they'll tell me, "I was here at such-and-such a time. Your father let me in and I waited." Maybe if I'm away too long then they'll go. I know one day he opened the door and let some man who called himself an inspector go all through the house. So that's why I don't take the chance on leaving him alone anymore. And he didn't necessarily have to be an inspector.

We share with Mrs. La Salle her feelings of uncertainty: was it an inspector that came into the house? Who was it?

SEQUENCE 22 TWENTY-SIXTH SESSION, STAGE 3

Despite the "fluidity" of the children in and out of the neighborhood and apartment, there is little participation or communication with others in the neighborhood and community on Mrs. La Salle's part. She is emotionally isolated, and seems to live alone in a strange world which she contacts only occasionally. In the sequence below, Mrs. La Salle is talking about the need for Tim to have a friend when he leaves the Wiltwyck School and returns home:

Mrs. L.: And it would be nice to have a companion for him around. It doesn't have to be his age. It could be 90 years old.

Therapist: Yeah, he could be older.

Mrs. L.: Someone that he could talk to a little bit, too.

Therapist: Yeah.

Mrs. L.: And still he wouldn't be getting into any trouble.

Therapist: No, that's right.

Mrs. L.: It would be good for him because what's out where we live?

Therapist: Not much, uh-uh, that's what I was thinking.

Mrs. L.: That's definitely out.

Therapist: Uhhmm.

Mrs. L.: And I'm not the only mother around there that thinks so. There is another young boy that comes up to the house to see him now and then. At least I let him in. Ah, he's younger than you, isn't he, by a year or so?

Meredith: Twelve.

Mrs. L.: Well, I know he's younger than you, and this boy, on the weekends, his mother sends him away because there are certain ones around there that she doesn't want him involved with.

Therapist: Uh-huh, she wants to keep him out of mischief.

Mrs. L.: And they are the same ones that I had told him to try to stay away from. And I was amazed when he told me about this other fellow's mother thought that way too.

Mrs. La Salle discloses her surprise at learning that there are other mothers who share her point of view. She has apparently never discussed these and related problems with her neighbors, nor does she particularly possess a sense of "community" or "neighborhood-consciousness." She feels no identification with a group or social organization, and she does not have ties within a larger context than her own immediate family. She senses the fluidity of many people in her neighborhood as well as of her own children, and would like to barricade herself against possible on-slaughts, psychological and tangible. But barricades shut out reality, too. Mrs. La Salle's world is a barren world in which people do not know each other, barricade themselves behind locked doors,[6] and always feel unsure and anxious about possible invaders.

Mrs. La Salle's cognitive attitudes toward her world, indeed, her behavior within her world, are in sharp contrast to those of low-income, disadvantaged, but stable families. Members of the latter families possess abilities to navigate through a known world. There are identifiable companions for the children and a local meeting place, perhaps at the bottom of the stairs or at a grocery store, where social activity goes on. Mothers meet and share news and gossip with each other, usually supporting one another with respect to problems. The significance of deprivation and isolation from these larger community props might well be explored in

---

[6] It might be noted that our clinicians often reported difficulty in gaining access to the homes of some of our families in connection with home visits. It took them several minutes, on the other side of a barricaded door, to properly identify themselves before they were admitted. For they were regarded as dangerous invaders from the outside, and had to disprove expectations of aggression. The reality aspects of such suspiciousness should not be ignored, of course.

differentiating the lower-class multi-problem family from the stable lower-class family.

SEQUENCE 23   TWENTY-SIXTH SESSION, STAGE 3

Mrs. La Salle's alienation from her community extends to her children's activities—especially the world of their school. In the sequence below, she discloses her surprise with respect to some new information she has learned as to what goes on at school. For Mrs. La Salle, this information confirms her suspicions and mistrust about the alien, uncertain world in which she and her children live, providing her with a negative image of school.

Meredith: The school yard.

Therapist: You mean the kids are good kids there? I mean the kids stay out of trouble, is all I mean by good, huh?

Meredith: (*Nods yes*.) Except for shooting crap.

Mrs. L.: They shoot crap . . . ?

Meredith: Yeah, they shoot crap.

Therapist: You don't have to get involved in that.

Mrs. L.: On the corner?

Meredith: Yeah.

Mrs. L.: Not in the school?

Tim: What's crap? Dice?

Therapist: Yeah.

Meredith: (*To mother*) Yes, they do.

Mrs. L.: The teacher doesn't see that?

Meredith: They be on the stoop shooting crap.

SEQUENCE 24   TWENTY-SIXTH SESSION, STAGE 3

Meredith's verbalizations about the "antisocial" activities in the school yard supplement an earlier description by George as to how he would run from school, the teacher, and the officer (see earlier—sequence 19). In that sequence George, trained by Meredith, reveals his expectations of a hostile teacher who will deprive him and who ". . . calls the officer on me."

We have seen (see sequence 19) that George, the "baby," is thoroughly trained to view the teacher as a restrictive authority who appeals to stronger forces to implement her controls. Moreover, teachers are not straightforward—they do not disclose their intentions directly ("I got word that she's gonna call the officer on me")—and must be "figured out" by relying on indirect sources of information. Teachers even interfere with basic and essential needs (going to the bathroom).[7] The child has no alternative but to rely on physical escape maneuvers ("I'll run out of the school and don't never come back").

The world of school authority is comprised of inscrutable adults whose intentions are never clear; there is vagueness and fear about how they will handle the child ("If an officer catches you that you don't go to school, what do they do to you?"). We might add that George is a child who does not know and cannot predict what his mother will do in certain situations; he has not developed a sense of the pattern of responses his behavior will elicit from her. He transfers his confused expectations of how his mother behaves toward him to *other* authority figures. The teacher also becomes a vague, globally restrictive adult who behaves in ways that defy prediction.

The sequence below illustrates Tim's perceptions and expectations of the teacher's functions and role. His verbalizations in this area are presented with the intervening dialogue deleted:

Tim: No, it's not that. It's that she don't give me no more arithmetic after I get through with that first assignment.

. . .

Yeah. I was the last one to start with my arithmetic book in my class.

. . .

Then when I start going fast to catch up, she slows me down.

. . .

She gives me something else to do instead of arithmetic.

. . .

Yeah, that's why she gives me something else, 'cause I'm going too fast. She must maybe don't want me to catch up.

From the above, we can see Tim's perception of the teacher as someone who is out of pace with his needs, who obstructs him, slows him down, and never acknowledges his productions. This might be interpreted as a reflection of an idiosyncratic perception because of Tim's particular personality dynamics. But in our population, Tim's views often represent

---

[7] Note that George is seemingly unaware of the fact that others attempt to "control" him in this way, too—the therapist, for example, as well as his siblings (see sequences 2, 17, and 20). These children, especially George, attempt to "solve" problems crudely and globally through physical action, motility, and leaving "the field" altogether. The teacher may well prevent him from constantly "going to the bathroom" (as does the therapist). George undoubtedly elicits this kind of restrictive, nonpermissive control from the adults in the world around him repeatedly.

a consensus—a shared configuration—as to what the functions and role of "teacher" are.[8] The teacher is a depriver who puts you in situations in which you are doomed to fail, to be slow, and never able to catch up or measure up to group expectations. "She gives me something else to do instead of arithmetic," says Tim, and then adds his opinion of her motive: "She must maybe don't want me to catch up."

Therapist Operations

One of the chief characteristics of this family's transactions is related to Mrs. La Salle's restrictive demands for immediate obedience and her parallel curtailment of cognitive exploration and autonomy in her children. That is, her lack of differentiated responses to the children reinforces and encourages styles of interaction and communication on their part which are characterized by disjointed, disruptive, and isolated content and by inability to focus on a specific issue with any degree of continuity. As a result, focused problem-solving behavior becomes almost impossible to elicit in the various interactions of the family members.

In the light of the above, the therapists' strategies were concerned with attempts to modify the style of the La Salles' communication processes and patterns in the direction of increasing development of skills in sustaining subject- and issue-centered dialogue and in learning how to respect and to help explore each other's productions. The therapists' view was that no change was feasible in a field of ineffective and indiscriminate communication. They spent a great deal of time trying to teach the La Salle family some of the rudiments of communication: when to talk; how to listen; when not to disrupt; and how to continue relating to the same theme. Further, they attempted to help the children focus their attention on temporal elements in their presentations so that they could begin to organize and conceptualize their thoughts sequentially in order to communicate and share *meaning*.

It was felt that any change in the machinery of communication in this family would be an essential precursor of other types of change: increasing the range and discrimination of their perception of the world around them; re-evaluating and understanding mislabeled feelings toward each other and toward adults around them; and developing skills in problem-

---

[8] Observation of teachers in slum schools seems to indicate that the children's perception of the teacher as globally restrictive, out of pace with their needs, etc., is often based on realistic assessment of the teachers' behavior and of the dynamics of the slum school as a social institution.

solving on a cognitive-affective level. The maneuvers in which the therapists were engaged were manifold. Some of them will be illustrated in the following excerpts.

SEQUENCE 25   EIGHTH SESSION, STAGE 2

The therapist places a great deal of stress upon the teaching of time limits, time organization, and, as illustrated below, on an understanding of the calendar.

Therapist: Hey, George, you want to talk with us about Meredith. He's coming home in June. You know when June is? It's not too long from now. What do you think it's going to be like for you when your brother . . . ?

George: June is a lot of Saturdays.

Therapist: No, it's a lot of days, but it's not . . .

George: It's one Saturday.

Therapist: Is it? Tell me how long June is, Meredith.

George: 145 days.

Therapist: George, you have to keep quiet when your brother's talking.

Meredith: Two weeks away.

Therapist: It's two weeks away. So you mean you're going to come home by June first.

Notice George's basic confusion with respect to his time-map and his primitive organization of the most essential and elementary aspects of the calendar. And notice, too, how the therapist encourages Meredith to convey corrective information to his brother. It is no accident that the therapist chooses an area in which Meredith is competent to teach his brother. The therapist encourages George to *listen*, to curtail his disruptive intervention (". . . you have to be quiet when your brother's talking").

SEQUENCE 26   EIGHTH SESSION, STAGE 2

The therapist also encourages the children to increase the range of their communications to each other not only in terms of objective content, but also in terms of relaying to one another their experiences in order to clarify, delineate, and structure the vague, global world outside. He wants to increase the communicational exchange between and among the children.

Therapist A.: . . . Do you guys ever talk about Wiltwyck and what it is like? What do you talk about?

Meredith: Nothing but TV.

Therapist A.: That's all you talk about?

Therapist B.: You don't tell about the boys at Wiltwyck, Tim?

SEQUENCE 27   EIGHTH SESSION, STAGE 2

The importance of the above operation can be seen in the light of the deep need these children have for information about the world. Notice below the need for corrective information and how it intertwines with the problems of deep insecurity in George. The therapist interacts with him around his informational hunger; George wants to know whether the environment is stable and reassuring, and how his siblings are placed in this environment. The transaction below concerns Tim's life at the Wiltwyck School:

George: Therapist A., does Therapist B. live with Tim up at the school?

Therapist A.: Oh, you mean up at the school? What made you think that?

George: I don't know.

Therapist A.: Why do you say Therapist B.?

George: I don't know. Does he stay here all night?

Therapist A.: No, this is not where Tim is. You know that. Tim goes upstate, on a bus. Didn't you know that? Hmm? Did you think he stayed here all the time?[9] Huh?

George: Then he couldn't get out.

Therapist A.: Oh, he could get out okay.

George: How could he?

Therapist A.: Well, you know, there are doors and elevators and all that. Can't you see . . .

George: Yeah, but after they lock the doors and all that, how is he going to get out?

Therapist A.: Did you ever ask Tim or Meredith this? Think the same thing about Meredith? Why don't you ask him now?

George: I want to ask you.

Therapist A.: You don't think . . .

George: Uh-uh.

Therapist A.: Ask him where he lives. Ask him what it's like upstate.

George: But I want to know how if they lock the doors, how do you get out?

Therapist A.: Well, they don't lock the doors.

Tim: They don't lock the doors at —— either?

---

[9] George is confusing the central offices where the therapy sessions take place (New York City) with the institution at which Tim actually lives (upstate, in Esopus, N.Y., at that time).

Therapist B.: No, they don't lock the doors. They don't lock the doors at Wiltwyck, either. Where Tim is, they don't lock the doors, either.

This is one of the paramount functions of the therapist, especially when working with the sibling subsystem in this family. He must become a source of corrective information, allowing himself to be employed in this way until the children are ready to feel that he is not only a safe "presence," but also a safe "knower." The therapist actively teaches the siblings to employ each other as resources. These children, though able to teach each other in many areas concerning aggression and the escape from implacable authority, seldom employ the same exploratory attitudes in checking and ascertaining basic information about their environment. George, for example, doesn't know where one of his siblings lives; the therapist actively teaches him an exploratory device with, "Did you ever ask Tim or Meredith this?"

SEQUENCE 28   EIGHTH SESSION, STAGE 2

The therapist is faced with the task of "forcing" the family members to look at themselves and to perceive the situation they are in and the events that surround them as personally meaningful and significant. Shortly before the following sequence Tim had stated, "I am ready to go home now." He is referring to leaving the Wiltwyck School, and is implying that there is "nothing wrong with me." His feelings of magical omnipotence and of unawareness of or unwillingness to recognize his troubles must be shaken and uprooted before he can change his behavior:

Therapist A.: . . . Well, you may not be ready to go home because some of the things that caused you to get into trouble may not be settled at that time.

Tim: (*Inaudible.*)

Therapist A.: That's your view. That's your opinion.

Therapist B.: But I tell you, there are a lot of things that you're not ready for. For example, being able to stay in school and sit down and think. You get tired. You can't do that yet. You can't think very long, you say. You have to have recesses. You have to ask to go to the bathroom, even though you don't need to go, just to get out of the classroom.

The sequence above illustrates how, on occasion, the therapist must "crack down" on the child in order to make impact on him. Tim cannot deal with these issues on a conceptual level. The therapist, perforce, must be specific and concrete, hoping, in effect, to involve the child emotionally by having him look at the realities of his life. A realization of his futility and some sense of discomfort about it may be his first steps on the path of involvement and engagement.

SEQUENCE 29   EIGHTH SESSION, STAGE 1

But at times the therapist must transcend the concrete and the specific so that a shared affect in the family system can be brought to light and handled. He helps the family members generalize from the concrete issue, however, with simple, manageable steps and direct questions. In the sequence below, the children are talking about George's fear of television monsters, which he perceives as almost real:

Therapist: Well, I was interested in knowing what you're so concerned with. George sounds awfully worried when someone is getting or going to get killed. You think that's so, Tim? (*Mother nods yes.*)

Tim: Nobody's really getting killed. He's talking about the person that's getting killed in the picture.

Therapist: Yeah, but he's always talking about killing so much. (*To Mother*) Does he do this to you, too?

Mrs. L.: Oh, every now and then he talks about things like that.

Therapist: I wonder if you boys have some of the same feelings. Huh? You know what I'm talking about, Meredith? (*Meredith shakes his head no.*)

Therapist: What? You tell me.

Meredith: About George.

Therapist: Well, I started about George, but—

Meredith: About people getting shot.

Therapist: Yes, you're absolutely right. Thank you.

The therapist is attempting to involve the children in a discussion of their overconcern and persistent involvement with killing, shooting, and fear of aggression and death in the family.[10] He uses George's fear of television monsters as the stepping-stone to a consideration of a broader issue concerning a central family affect. Note, for example, that as Meredith becomes less and less productive, he is brought back to the issue through a few simple, concrete questions which present manageable material for him to handle. Meredith has been helped to enter the communicational interactions revolving around this issue.

Without making any assumptions as to whether or not the children

---

[10] As already noted, the children witnessed their father's shooting at their grandfather. Mr. La Salle also taught the children how to make zip guns.

truly come to understand the full implication of what the fear of people getting killed on television is about, it should be noted that this kind of therapeutic operation is necessary in work with these families. The therapist must constantly segment the communicational sequence by concrete questions that review the area of focus in order to help the family members explore the meaning of what is being said.

SEQUENCE 30   TWENTIETH SESSION, STAGE 2

At times the therapist needs to provide the child with a label to frame new knowledge and to make this knowledge part of the child's repertoire. Meredith, below, is trying to describe his inner experiences in relation to his mother's demands that he do chores when he is engaged in a pleasurable activity. (See sequence 2, which precedes the following sequence by a minute or so.)

Meredith: She say, "No," and then later on it's, "Yes."

Therapist A.: She's always switching, you mean, huh? . . .

Meredith: Yeah.

Therapist A.: Back and forth?

Meredith: That's what she always calls it.

Therapist A.: Huh?

Meredith: That's what she always calls it.

Therapist A.: Well, what do you call it, I don't know.

Meredith: In fact . . .

Therapist A.: Go ahead, what do you want to call it? What? Like what, huh? Go ahead. What? You started to say "In fact . . ." something. In fact what, Meredith?

Meredith: I can't pronounce it.

Therapist A.: Well, let's try. I'll help you with it. Huh?

Meredith: I can't pronounce it. In fact . . . I can't pronounce it.

Therapist A.: Well, tell me what it means. Maybe I can find the word.

Meredith: Like bothering me.

Therapist B.: You mean aggravating?

Meredith: Yeah.

Although the supplying of labels to help a patient examine a particular affective content is an aspect of most therapies, such an operation is of particular importance in work with our families. For here the therapist is not only providing the child with a new word, "aggravating," but also he is providing him with an opportunity to organize his perceptions of his interactions with his mother along a new qualitative dimension. These children need specific training so they can learn how to conceptualize their experiences.

SEQUENCE 31   EIGHTH SESSION, STAGE 1

The clear labeling of reality in terms of structure as well as function (the cognitive map of the world) is insufficiently developed in the La Salle children. As a result, efficient coping behavior with the world around them is markedly handicapped. Mrs. La Salle often does not spontaneously correct the mislabeling that frequently occurs. During the following sequence, Meredith is crying because he must leave the session to return to his institution.[11] Mrs. La Salle and the therapist have just asked George why Meredith is crying.

George: Because he has to go home.

Therapist: George, you think that the school is home?

Mrs. L.: Yeah, he calls the school home. Quite often he wants to know if he can go home again.

The therapist, above, helps the family to apply correct labels to their surrounding world. In particular, he is attempting to help Mrs. La Salle to perceive the mislabeling. It is interesting that she does not interrupt George or correct him about the fact that the institution is not Meredith's home; she brings forth the explanation only after the therapist focuses on the issue.

SEQUENCE 32   EIGHTH SESSION, STAGE 1

Therapists with these families must develop skills with respect to actional information in order to move into intrapsychic and affective dimensions. Notice in the following sequence how the therapist employs Tim's need to go to the bathroom to explore Mrs. La Salle's feelings concerning his frequent trips. The therapist uses this exploration as a jumping-off point to offer the child information about how his behavior affects other people. He tries to explain the actions of the teacher, for example in terms of Tim's own behavior.

Therapist A.: Tim, you still have to go to the bathroom? (*Tim nods yes.*)

Therapist A.: Then why can't you convince your mother that you have to go? Think it might be because she didn't trust you?

Tim: I don't know.

Therapist A.: Maybe we could talk about that.

---

[11] Note, a few sessions prior to this (see sequence 10) Meredith was attacked by his mother because he saw his return to the institution as fun.

Mrs. L.: I trust him going to the bathroom, but the idea is that it isn't that he needs to go to the bathroom, he's trying to get away from us.

Therapist A.: You really don't think he needs to go?

Mrs. L.: No, he just came from there.

Therapist A.: He looks as though he's about to burst his bladder.

Mrs. L.: I don't know about that, but . . .

Therapist B.: This is something like what happens at school?

Mrs. L.: Yes.

Therapist B.: You ask to go to the bathroom and then you play around and the teacher thinks that you don't need to go, and she won't let you go.

Therapist A.: I think that's a very important point and I'll be ready to talk about it when he gets back.

Mrs. L.: Let's just see how long it takes you to get back.

It is interesting that Mrs. La Salle expects the worst from Tim. She is training him into delinquent expectations. But in effect, the child has already trained his mother (and the therapist and teacher, as well) to expect these minor delinquencies from him. The people in Tim's world encourage him to live up to a delinquent identity; they mistrust his actions (but they have good cause to do so). This circle of interaction in which Tim is revolving must receive some therapeutic attention before Tim can change his "image" as well as his behavior, and others can begin to trust him.

SEQUENCE 33   TWENTY-SIXTH SESSION, STAGE 3

Below, in a session quite late in the series, the therapist explores the bathroom issue with George:

(*George re-enters the room through the observation room.*)

Mrs. L.: (*To George*) What are you doing in there?

George: I drank some water.

Mrs. L.: And you have to be in there to drink water? Well, then sit down here and don't ask me to go out any more.

George: I had to go to the bathroom.

Therapist A.: George, do you know what happens the next time you really have to go to the bathroom now?

Meredith: He don't go.

Mrs. L.: He didn't ask you.

Therapist A.: Huh? You know what? Huh?

George: Huh?

Therapist A.: You know that the next time you're going to have a hard time convincing your mother, telling your mother you really have to go to the bathroom? Huh?

George: Huh?

Therapist A.: Do you know that?

George: Yeah.

Therapist C.: Do you know why, George? Tell Therapist A. why.

Tim: Huh, Mommy?

Mrs. L.: What?

Tim: Can I go to the bathroom now?

Mrs. L.: Yeah, go and come back, and sit down.

George: 'Cause I didn't do what I said I'll do.

Therapist A.: That's right. That's absolutely right, George. That's great thought. That's very good, George, for you to be able to understand that. Now you have to try to act it, you know. You have to try to do it. When she says to go the bathroom, okay? (*George nods yes.*)

Above, the therapist is not only upholding the parental role, but also is helping George to explore the possible consequences of his behavior and to anticipate the effect of his behavior on his mother. The concept of interpersonal causality, the issue that the therapist is helping George to understand, is one that is poorly understood in this family.

SEQUENCE 34   TWENTY-SIXTH SESSION, STAGE 3

Another operation that is rather commonly engaged in by the therapist may appear to be a set of instructions on manipulation. The therapist is teaching Meredith how to make the teacher recognize and differentiate him. He had asked the child to ask the teacher about some books that he needs.

Therapist: But I was thinking that the advantage is that if you ask your teacher . . . [he] should know better than anybody I know what kind of books are important. And the second thing, he ought to know you are interested. And then he picks you out of class . . . as an interested boy. And he won't pick you out as he picked you out before, somebody who is making trouble. Do you follow what I am saying? You understand what I am saying?

In therapy with more differentiated children, one would look askance at this type of operation which seems to be oriented toward manipulating the environment. But the therapist is concerned with helping Meredith to see the ways in which his behavior impinges on the other person's perception of him. The La Salle children need training, as already noted, in looking at the consequences of their own behavior in terms of the other person's attitudes and responses toward them.

Change

In the preceding pages some of the La Salle family transactions as they transpired in the treatment sessions were illustrated. These transactions seemed to fall into several areas. Although the designation of areas to present this material was somewhat arbitrary and was based on convenience and clarity for presentation purposes, there is one salient feature of this family's transactions which dominated all of the interchanges: the primitive, crude, and ineffective communication patterns which permeated any and all of the exchanges within the family. We have already noted that therapeutic strategy with the La Salles was directed toward raising the level of the communication between and among the family members —specifically, in encouraging exploratory operations and responses. It was hoped that this therapeutic orientation would result in increased discrimination of the family members in their perception of one another and in an increased differentiation of the surrounding world. Evidences of change in this family are based on (and will be chiefly illustrated by) changes relevant to these considerations.

The following pages present sequences from exchanges involving the children, primarily. Although the children displayed the greatest change, it should be noted that in subtle, perhaps not so dramatic ways, Mrs. La Salle was changing too, for she was complementing her children's changed behavior. In sequence 11, for example, a segment from the twenty-sixth session, George asks "Why?" when he is confronted with a global, illogical threat of aggression from his mother. He is exploring, confronting, and examining the situation he is in. He feels freer to assert his needs for clarification. We have seen innumerable instances in the earlier sessions of George's usual mode of handling threat: going to the bathroom, or seeking physical proximity. Now he is beginning to relinquish some of these usual behavioral patterns and substitute more adaptive ones. He must be feeling that his mother is allowing this newer behavior to emerge.

In general, the La Salles' behavior was changed in the following ways: Disruptive communications diminished considerably. George and Tim, who had made their presence felt essentially through noise-making, displayed a notable modification of this pattern. George, who had sought contact by extreme disruptiveness and with a total disregard of the content of a dialogue, was becoming more self-contained. He was beginning to express his needs to his mother and siblings through more appropriate verbalizations, while Tim was beginning to communicate through more elaborate verbal forms, showing less of an actional orientation.

Mrs. La Salle complemented these changes in the children by permitting and sustaining their more rationally expressed requests while displaying less of a need to control them. As a result of her change, there was increased expression of cooperation among the siblings in neutral areas. (The characteristic mode of "cooperation" between Tim and Meredith, for example, had been based on a pattern of substituting for a felt lack of parental protection—(see footnote 5, page 162). This characteristic pattern was giving way to more appropriate, peerlike, cooperative interaction.) Tim and Meredith were tending to "scapegoat" and tease George less frequently and were showing an increase of frankly "nurturing" and guiding responses toward him.

All three children were beginning to display an increase in autonomous behavior. Meredith became less depressed and began to assume leadership among his siblings while demonstrating some ability to withstand his mother's pressures. In general, he was showing some capacity to cope more effectively with situations outside the family, too. In Tim, we see the appearance of more age-appropriate behavior in his relinquishment of infantile methods of contacting his mother, increased self-awareness, decreased anxiety about growing up, and increased skills in exploring unknown areas. George's "psychotic-like" productions became conspicuous by their absence, reflecting a fundamental change in the rest of the family, who were showing increased capacity to acknowledge him as a separate and coherent individual.

Mrs. La Salle's changes, as noted, were more subtly expressed and were evidenced more by her accommodation to the children's change than by autonomous changes. Her controlling responses were becoming less devious and less overwhelming in nature. Though still unable to display a frank change toward a more nurturing orientation, she became, by the end of treatment, more direct in her guiding and controlling remarks and more attuned to positives in her children.

Attitudes of the children toward school and the teacher were changing, too. Sometimes, however, change represents only a first step; the modification of attitude continues to reflect distortion and ineffective coping. For example, in sequence 19, we have seen George's global fear of the teacher and of physical aggression on the part of school authorities. Later on, George obtained some insight with respect to the fact that teachers are generally limited in their physical aggression and in what "they can do to you." But George continued to regard physical aggression as vital for control and for containing behavior. The teacher is now seen as completely impotent; he (the teacher) has shifted from being a totally frightening and omnipotent power to a completely helpless and manageable entity. (If the teacher cannot hit you, there is very little he can do to you.) For George, the shift in attitude toward the teacher represented a shift to the other extreme, and indicates a need for further exploration of this area.

Finally, before turning to the sequences, a word about the nature of change within the La Salle family system. Change did not occur simultaneously in all of the members. Rather, change was a reflection of a process of accommodation between the changed and unchanged members. As a result, a healthy strain was brought to bear on family equilibrium. Furthermore, a particular family member may have adopted new communicational and attitudinal patterns without yet manifesting change in other ways and without modifying old and characteristic ways of behaving. "Old ways" in the family and among individual members were retained while new and subtle changes were taking place. As a result, signs of incipient change frequently eluded the clinician who was involved in the family transactions.

SEQUENCE 35   TWENTY-SIXTH SESSION, STAGE 3

Below is an illustration of cooperative exploration among the La Salles of changes in Tim's behavior. Notice that there is sustained ability to focus at some length on a specific issue.

Therapist A.: Yeah. You think anything has changed, Tim, since you been coming to sit in on these family sessions?

Tim: Uh-hmm.

Therapist A.: What's different for you?

Mrs. L.: You think something has changed, but you don't know?

George: . . .

Tim: Yeah, I don't get in trouble as much.

. . .

Therapist A.: And you mean you think your coming here has something to do with that?

Tim: Huh?

Therapist A.: You think coming down here keeps you out of trouble?

Tim: No.

Mrs. L.: So what keeps you out of trouble?

Tim: Talking.

Therapist A.: Huh?

Tim: Talking.

Therapist A.: Talking keeps you out of trouble?

Tim: Talking stops me from messing up.

Mrs. L.: Talking where and to whom and about what?

Tim: Talking in the meeting, that's where.

Mrs. L.: Oh, talking here.

Tim: Um-hmm.

. . .

Mrs. L.: That's all right. He doesn't have that aggressive attitude he used to have, and he's not as stubborn.

Therapist A.: Has he had a temper tantrum in the last . . .

Mrs. L.: Yes, he used to have them.

Therapist A: Does he now? Has he had one?

Mrs. L.: No.

Therapist A.: When has he had the last one home, do you know?

Mrs. L.: Oh, it's been a long time ago.

Therapist A.: Uh-huh.

Meredith: When school started back.

Mrs. L.: It must have been . . . he hasn't started that about since after the third or fourth meeting.

Therapist A.: He hasn't had one since then?

Mrs. L.: (*Nods no.*) He's learned how to cope with things more.

. . .

Therapist C.: And he doesn't run out of the room the way he used to.

Mrs. L.: Uh-hmm.

Meredith: Or lock himself in the bathroom anymore.

. . .

Mrs. L.: In a way of speaking, he's getting more grown up like.

Mrs. La Salle's participation in the above interchange can be seen from several viewpoints. First, she encourages Tim's exploration of his own behavior; by being specific in her questions as well as in her evaluation of her child, she encourages and elicits his self-evaluation. Second, supported by the therapist, she labels Tim in positive terms, and, by doing so, helps another sibling to perceive Tim differently, too. Third, by sustaining focused interest and attention on the issue being discussed, she helps to create an atmosphere in which other family members can be directly and specifically involved in the communication process.[12] Meredith, for example, participates in a focused manner by providing information, introducing an independent observation about Tim's behavior, and contributing a time-oriented comment. It is interesting to note that Tim links the change in his behavior to opportunities to participate in verbal explorations.

SEQUENCE 36   TWENTY-SIXTH SESSION, STAGE 3

In this family, George is consistently victimized. He is a scapegoat for the family's hostilities and aggression. This attitude toward him continues even in the later sessions. For example:

George: I want to be a policeman.

Meredith: A carpenter or an electrician, they're both good jobs.

Tim: (*To George*) You? You couldn't beat a fly.

Therapist A.: Tim, he said he wanted to *be* a policeman.

Mrs. L.: You don't have to beat people 'cause you're a policeman.

Tim: So, he couldn't beat a fly for looking at him.

George: So, a policeman is a policeman.

Meredith: So you couldn't fight your way out of a paper bag.

Therapist C.: But he didn't say he's going to be one now, Tim.

Tim: Huh?

Mrs. L.: If he acts like a lot of policemen act today, he could be one.

It is interesting that Mrs. La Salle supports George, and repeatedly attempts to modify and correct the other children's focus on aggression as the chief function of a policeman. (Both therapists, in attempting to inject a time perspective into the evaluation of George's explorations of identification, seem to be unwittingly reinforcing the siblings' attitude toward George as a weakling. By stressing the fact that he does not want to be a policeman *now*, they fail to stress that aspect of the issue to which Mrs. La Salle is responding, that is, that a policeman and aggressive force are not synonymous.)

---

[12] Mrs. La Salle's changed attitudes toward the children, as noted, are subtly expressed. She has become in many ways, however, more consistently positive and reinforcing with respect to them. For example, later on in the same session, Tim became rather discouraged when he was confronted with his inability to do an arithmetic problem. Mrs. La Salle said to him, "Now listen, Tim, you musn't get disgusted with yourself so quickly because you don't do things correctly. You have to continue at it until you actually get it."

SEQUENCE 37   TWENTIETH SESSION, STAGE 2

But a few sessions earlier, we see evidence that the consistency of hostile attitudes toward George is beginning to give way. George, at times, *can* be seen in a positive light.

Therapist: Who's left [at home]?

Tim: What?

Therapist: Who's left?

Tim: Me and George.

Therapist: George can't go to the store.

Meredith: Yes, he can.

George: Yes, I can.

Therapist: He can?

Tim: He can buy cigarettes and everything else.

The above interchange discloses the beginnings of ability on the part of the siblings to perceive George more positively: Meredith and Tim, although still labeling George essentially with negatives, are showing evidences of increased flexibility in their cognitive approach to him. The rigid focus on negatives and on the "disapproved self" in the sibling subsystem is beginning to lose some of its underpinnings.

SEQUENCE 38   TWENTIETH SESSION, STAGE 2

Several minutes after the interchange presented in sequence 2 (the extremely disjointed and chaotic exchange between Meredith and the therapist around the child's displeasure at constantly being interrupted by his mother to do chores when he is enjoying himself), the following interchange took place:

Therapist B.: He doesn't ask?

Tim: See, he don't ask my mother "if she wants me to go to the store." That's how come he's always getting interrupted when the good programs come on.

Therapist B.: So you're suggesting that's one way. Can you think of anything else he could do?

Tim: Yeah, maybe he could stay out of the house a little more often.

Therapist A.: You mean stay away from her?

Tim: No, like go downstairs.

Therapist A.: So he wouldn't be around . . . so he wouldn't be around to be bothered.

Tim is offering or attempting to offer a helpful suggestion to Meredith concerning his coping with problems he has verbalized. Helpfulness and support with respect to nonaggressive areas have not been frequently manifested in the exchanges among the siblings in this family. It is interesting to note, too, the endurance, persistence, and patience of the therapists in sustaining the main theme (see sequences 1 and 2) despite the continuous disruptive maneuvers of Tim and George finally permit the emergence of a focused, mildly positive, helpful interaction at the sibling level.

SEQUENCE 39   TWENTY-SIXTH SESSION, STAGE 3

Changes in the style of communication in the La Salle family were frequently subtle and often embedded in the context of "old" patterns. Consider, for example, the following interchange:

Therapist A.: Now we just asked if you think Tim is going to mess up when he comes home.

Meredith: No.

Tim: Hey, Meredith, how old you got to be to go to PAL?

Meredith: Ten.

Tim: Ten?

Therapist C.: When are you going to be . . .

Mrs. L.: That's not the idea right now, Tim. It's not the idea of the PAL. The idea is, are you ready to come home?

Tim: Yeah.

Mrs. L.: Ah, in what way do you consider yourself ready?

Tim: Every way.

Although Tim's interjection about PAL might be regarded as a reflection of his thoughts about coming home and activities at home and in the community, it does disrupt the continuity and flow of discussion around the issue of his "messing up" when he comes home. (Note: Therapist C. seems to be "going along" with Tim's shift.) The significant aspect of the above interchange is Mrs. La Salle's "That's not the idea right now, Tim. It's not the idea of the PAL . . ." She is beginning to respond to shifts and disruptions with an attempt to redirect and refocus the subject matter back to the chief issue. She is providing an opportunity for the children to perceive the disruption as such and is helping them to relate and respond to a direct confrontation about their behavior. Such attempts are indeed rare in the communicational exchanges in this family.

SEQUENCE 40   TWENTY-SIXTH SESSION, STAGE 3

Again, subtle but significant changes in communicational patterns are seen in attempts to signal a disruptive communication. The use of such cues or signals denotes that the speaker is aware that the communication *is* disruptive and does not follow the content of the interchange, so it can be regarded as a reflection of considerable development along lines of more effective communication in this family.

Therapist A.: Miss ——? Oh, I know her. She's been there a long time.

Therapist C.: Tim, how are you learning? What does she think about it?

Meredith: Excuse me! Did you find out that man's name yet?

Therapist A.: Which one?

Meredith: That you said don't forget last week.

George: Mr. ——

Mrs. L.: No.

Therapist A.: You don't mean the probation officer? Which man?

Meredith: That man that you said was up there . . .

Therapist A.: Oh, no, no. I may have a hard time finding out now . . .

Note Meredith's "Excuse me!" Although he continues to introduce material more related to his inner stress and ruminations than to the dialogue in process, this time his disruption is clearly signaled, allowing the family members to shift their attention. The awareness of a disruption and the signaling of it are of vital significance in the development of new communication patterns. We feel that to the extent that such operations emerge, higher-level processes can emerge—for example, introspection and sustained attempts at symbolic problem-solving.

SEQUENCE 41   TWENTY-SIXTH SESSION, STAGE 3

Changes in the interactional processes in this family are reflected on the sibling level by evidences of the children's increased ability in autonomous exploration of various neutral areas and by the focused communication of this exploration.

Therapist A.: Have you moved, Mrs. L.? The reason I ask you is that we sent a letter out and—(*Interrupted.*)

Mrs. L.: And I didn't get it.

Therapist A.: No, that's right. It came back unclaimed from your old address.

Mrs. L.: No, no. I'm still in the same place. And I thought about it. Remember I told you I wanted to move?

Meredith: The mailbox is jammed up.

Mrs. L.: What do you mean the mailbox is jammed up?

Meredith: You can't get in the top of it, to put the mail in. You know the part where you put the mail in at? It's jammed up and you can't get any mail. If you want any mail you got to go down while the mailman is there.

Mrs. L.: Well, then he should call you.

Tim: That's right.

Therapist C.: What is it jammed up with, Meredith?

Meredith: I don't know.

Therapist C.: Other mail or letters? I mean—(*Interrupted.*)

Mrs. L.: There's no other mail in there.

Meredith: There's nothing in there. If there was something in there the person who has the box underneath the key, the key lock would get it.

Therapist A.: Gee, how did you discover that in itself?

Meredith: Last Wednesday I was, when I left and came back home, the mailman had just come out so I went down and got the mail and he said that I couldn't get it out. So I had to wait until I took it from him. I asked him if he could give it to me so I got it from him. He said the mailbox was jammed up.

Meredith's statements have direction and meaningfulness. His observations are organized around a clearly defined problem: how to open the mailbox. He reveals himself, in general, to be capable of exploration and of arriving at inference and synthesis in a problem-centered way. He is in the role of "able knower." The therapist, toward the end of this sequence, reinforces him, "Gee, how did you discover that in itself?" We consider the operations underlying Meredith's cognitive exploration to be essential in helping the family patterns of communication to change, especially when these are brought to light in a shared context of conversation.

SEQUENCE 42 TWENTY-SIXTH SESSION, STAGE 3

The children are beginning to show signs of increased ability to withstand their mother's demands for complete and absolute obedience. These changes are reflections not only of emotional development in the children, but also, as the following sequence illustrates, are an indication of a growing concern with the defense of one's assessment and coding of reality. Such operations must emerge if there is to be a more adaptive and effective relationship to the world of reality. Note Meredith's behavior toward his mother in the following sequence, which occurs a minute or so after sequence 41. The conversation is about the jammed mailbox.

Therapist: I'm curious about one thing, Meredith. Why didn't you tell your mother this, you know?

Meredith: I did.

Therapist: Oh, you did tell your mother.

Mrs. L.: What did you tell me?

Meredith: I told you the other day, when we came in.

Mrs. L.: I don't recall your telling me that.

Meredith: You forgot.

Mrs. L.: I don't even remember it and that's strange that I'd forget something like that. Or, you thought you told me?

Meredith: I told you.

Mrs. L.: I don't recall it.

In this instance, Meredith feels that he can adequately account for his "knowing"; he adheres to his observation of reality. He eludes his mother's trap, in which she seems to be presenting herself as omniscient and implying, at the same time, that he is "cognitively unable." He repeats, "I told you." His resistance to her attempts to influence his autonomous coding of reality reflects improvement in the La Salle family's communication pattern. Meredith's cognitive "challenging," his pitting of his evaluation of reality against his mother's can now emerge without his feeling totally alienated from the family system. He can be capable of cognitive independence; he can be a "knower" without endangering his sense of linkage with his mother.

SEQUENCE 43   TWENTY-SIXTH SESSION, STAGE 3

And finally, an instance of a focused, reality-oriented exchange between Meredith and Tim (they are talking about the letter carrier):

Mrs. L.: Oh. Yeah, he talks to everybody. He knows everybody. But he still makes time.

Meredith: If you put him out the last one in the morning and I'll bet he'll be finished before all them other men and he'll talk too.

Mrs. L.: He talks while he goes back and forth.

Meredith: See, he don't carry no push cart. He carries it on his shoulder.

Mrs. L.: Yeah, that's amazing.

Tim: Yeah, you go faster.

Meredith: No, you don't either. Not with that push cart.

Tim: I said you go faster with the one on your shoulder.

Meredith: Oh. 'Cause with that push cart you got to push it. You got to push it and stop it so it don't move. I'd rather put it on my back.

Therapist: You mean if you were a mailman.

Meredith: Yeah.

Meredith and Tim, in the above sequence, are really communicating with each other and are in contact with the material being discussed: they remain sufficiently focused on the subject matter as well as responsive to the content of each other's responses to produce a brief sequence of coherent communication. There is exploration as well as a true exchange of information—elements of communicational interaction which were felt to be absent to a striking degree in the earlier transactions of the La Salle family.

Summary

This family was characterized by an absent father who had left his impact on the children by previously training and socializing them into aggressive activity. When the research was initiated, Mrs. La Salle had a paramour who occupied a fleeting, tangential relationship to the family and did not participate in the guidance or control of the children. Mrs. La Salle, who had come from a strict, rigid West Indian background, was unable to fill the executive role in the family because of her own mother's presence—her mother consistently undermined her in her parental efforts and prevented her from feeling secure and competent in handling the demands made upon her by the children. To these constant, persistent, overwhelming demands from the children, Mrs. La Salle responded in a crude, global fashion, striking out in an undifferentiated manner against them. Her verbalized self-image as a guiding, sensitive mother was in marked contrast to her actual behavior. Because of her rigid, punitive, and extremely ineffective control attempts, the children's ability for autonomous exploring responses never became sufficiently developed.

Certain salient characteristics of the La Salles' transactions came to the attention of the therapists when they worked with the family members. One of these was related to the special features of the communication processes in this family system: the tremendous stress on paraverbal exchanges; constant disruption and easy spread of disruption among the children and their actional as opposed to verbal orientation; their extreme inattention and inability to focus on an issue, etc. These aspects of the members' behavior often trapped the therapists into the role of controlling, regulating, and directing the flow of transactions at the expense of conflict-resolution and other content considerations.

Another outstanding characteristic of the transactions of the La Salles concerned the expression and experience of affect: the children and Mrs. La Salle displayed a need either for direct, crude, global aggression or for complete nurturance. In either case, physical contact and crude proximity served as organizing and integrating forces. The children needed to elicit external controls, often in the form of aggression from the outside, for their own security. With respect to this family dimension, too, the therapists at times were inducted into the family system, for they frequently attempted to control and organize some of the family members through using physical proximity as a maneuver.

The sibling subsystem was an extremely active force in the socialization of the children. One of the children, Meredith, performed in the role of "parental child," training his siblings into delinquent activities and expectations, negative attitudes toward school and various authority figures, and mistrust and suspicion of the outside world.

Therapeutic goals with this family were concerned chiefly with helping the members in the area of communicational skills to sustain issue-centered dialogue; to learn skills of cognitive exploration and how to use language as a tool in this connection; to know when and how to listen and attend to others' dialogue; to learn to look at one's own behavior as it affects the outside world; to develop skills in sharing meaning, etc. This therapeutic framework was based on a conviction that successful intervention along the foregoing lines was an essential precursor of other types of change in the family members. Actual therapeutic strategies were manifold, for the therapists seized upon any opportunity that presented itself to train the family members.

Although changes as a result of these therapeutic maneuvers were not dramatic, the clinical team felt that over-all therapeutic goals were realized, for attempts to raise the general level of the communicational style of the La Salles were somewhat successful, primarily among the children. It was also thought that Mrs. La Salle's behavioral changes were complementing the children's growth and that she was becoming more consistently positive and reinforcing with regard to her children.

As a whole, toward the end of treatment, the family system was characterized by a drop in disruptive communications and by generally more self-contained, age-commensurate behavior among the children. They became less action-oriented, and more cooperative in neutral, rather than antisocial areas. More autonomous, exploratory behavior also began to appear.

The next two chapters present a discussion of the structure and dynamics of the family systems of our special group of disadvantaged families (Chapter 5) and our interventive techniques with respect to these systems (Chapter 6).

We note again that these chapters are based on intensive clinical experience *subsequent* to our research. The transcripts we have just presented show our thinking in the early phases of our investigation. We presented them to provide an understanding of the kinds of people and families we worked with. We now turn to our conceptualizations and techniques as we are employing them today.

CHAPTER *The Disorganized and Disadvantaged Family: Structure and Process*[1]

*I*n the first few pages of this book we presented an episode involving two children, Peter and Jimmy. In Chapters 3 and 4 we introduced other children and their families—the Garcias, the La Salles, and the Montgomerys. These children and these families, as different from one another as they may appear to be, view their worlds from a common vantage point. For the very differences through which they approach their life environments highlight how "everyone and anyone is much more simply human than otherwise, more like everyone else than different," as Harry Stack Sullivan (1962, frontispiece) once said. These families share the culture of the slum but also transcend it; they share with all of us the generic characteristics of being human.

When families are viewed as members of a sociocultural group, though their idiosyncratic features are clearly discernible, even more striking is the observation that many of their so-called "unique" characteristics

[1] Some sections of this and the next chapter appeared in slightly different form in Minuchin (1965, 1968), Minuchin, Auerswald, King, and Rabinowitz (1964), and Minuchin and Montalvo (1966).

are, in actuality, shared features of the sociocultural group to which they belong. Thus, these three families as well as the families of Peter and Jimmy present shared difficulties in helping their children learn how to cope with the world around them, how to communicate, and how to experience nuances in their own affective lives. And Peter, Jimmy, George La Salle, Felipe Garcia, Richard Montgomery, their brothers and sisters, and a multitude of children in the institutions and slums of our big cities share with each other a style of thinking, coping, communicating, and behaving, aspects of which can be directly traced to the structure and processes of the family systems of which they are, or were, a part.

The stereotyped way in which our children relate to the surrounding world reflects a quality of experience that seems to be comprised of several factors: a sense that "the world stimulates me and I am only a passive recipient of stimuli"; an either/or experience of aggression without the ability to tune in nuances of affective experience; an accompanying lack of flexibility within an extremely narrow range of verbal response; and a concomitant inability to focus on an event in such a way as to be able to store, or, later on, recover the experience.[2] This cluster of features reflects a style of experiencing life in the midst of the family and the home, for it is here that much basic learning takes place. We have been impressed by certain qualities of the physical and social environment of our children and by the reaction patterns which they seem to foster.

One essential feature of the family and home environment is its impermanence and unpredictability. These characteristics make it difficult for the growing child to define himself in relation to his world. In home visits we encountered a world in which objects and events have a transient quality. For example, a bed shared by two or more children can be turned over to a different child or to a semi-permanent visitor while its original occupants are crowded into a section of another bed. The geography of the home and its arrangements impede the development of a sense that "I have my place in the world." Meals have no set time, order, or place. A mother who prepares four individual and different dinners one day, according to the wishes of the children, will prepare

---

[2] On the basis of our intensive clinical contacts we have concluded that the children's inability to recover their affective experiences is not simply a reflection of being reluctant to do so because an authority figure has made the request, nor simply a question of limited verbal skills. We are positing actual limitations and distinctive qualities in the way affect is *experienced*.

nothing another day, so that the children have to look in closets for available food, making their meals out of potato chips and soda.

Interpersonal contacts have these same erratic and impermanent qualities. In these large families, care of the young children is divided among many figures. Mother, aunts, grandmother, as well as older siblings, care for the young child. Sometimes they shower him with stimulation, and at other times he is left alone for long periods while he wanders through the house unattended. There can be elements of security in this multiple care, but danger lurks in those periods when the child is lost between the interstices of responsibility. Multiple, erratic nurturing figures can increase the child's sense of an unstable world and hinder his movement from a diffuse to a more focused sense of self.

In the socialization of the child, these families seem to be characterized by two major features: parents' responses to children's behavior are relatively random and therefore deficient in the qualities that convey rules which can be internalized; and the parental emphasis is on the control and inhibition of behavior rather than on guidance.

One sees in these families patterns of parental reaction that operate like traffic signals: they carry the instructions of "don't" at the moment, but they do not carry instructions for behavior in the future (Hess and Shipman, 1965). The unpredictability of parental controlling signals handicaps the development and internalization of rules, for the child cannot determine what part of his behavior is inappropriate. As a result, he learns to define the limits of permissible behavior by reacting mostly to his parents' *mood* responses. He learns that the "don'ts" of behavior are related to the pain or power of the mother or other powerful figures. "Don't do this because I say so," or, "Don't do this because you make me nervous," or "Don't do this or I'll beat you." Lacking norms to regulate behavior, and caught in experiences that hinge on immediate interpersonal control, the children need continuous parental participation to organize their interpersonal transactions. The transactions are inevitably ineffective; they perpetuate a situation in which an overtaxed mother responds erratically to a confused child who behaves in ways that will assure him of continuous contact with an outside controlling figure.

In these families, as noted, life experiences are characterized by impermanence, randomness, fast changes in mood, either accelerated tempo in interpersonal transactions or lack of contact, control boundaries that shift with the parents' mood, and lack of guidance and orientation to norms. This kaleidoscope of moving and shifting stimuli hinders the ability of the child to develop the object constancy essential for keeping hold of an object in thought, and it hinders the development of control over impulsivity. Action-oriented, impulsive reactions characterize the child who grows up in this environment, even at ages when more complex and reflective controls are possible. The kind of reactivity perpetuated in the child represents both an emotional organization and a cognitive style. The child is impulsive and global in his responses, tends to search the immediate reactions of others for clues to the solution of conflict situations, and remains relatively unexercised in the use of focal attention for observing himself or the specific characteristics of a situation.

That these qualities form a coherent syndrome has been suggested by the reports of several investigators working with other populations. Wolff, for example, working with infants, reported a positive correlation between attention and inhibition of motor discharge (Wolff, 1965; Wolff and White, 1965). Kagan, Moss, and Sigel (1963), who studied middle-class children of various ages, noted a relationship among response time, focal attention, and cognitive style. The ability to inhibit motor discharge and modulate behavior in the face of irrelevant stimulation is correlated in his studies with an analytic, differentiating, cognitive style. The tendency toward motoric impulse discharge is associated with poor focal attention and a conceptual style that is global and nonanalytic. It is this latter syndrome that seems characteristic of the children we have seen. This is an observation corroborated by Bernstein (1962), whose study of time reactivity in speech related the fast tempo and "lack of hesitation" of the deprived working-class child to a restricted type of language that encourages unfocused, nonanalytic behavior.

We are now ready to examine the family system in greater detail. In order to do so, we have organized our material into three major sections for ease of presentation. We hasten to note that *all* of the material is derived from an over-all consideration of the family transactions as they were unfolded to us as we worked with our families. There is some unavoidable overlap among the sections, and the division of our chapter is both arbitrary and artificial. Yet only in this way are we able to focus on and highlight certain salient features of our families that deserve close attention.

The major sections of our chapter are: (1) self-observation and communication; (2) socialization of affect; and (3) family structure. The first section considers the capacity our children have for self-observation as well as their ability to communicate the observed. The second section presents material relating to anger and nurturance as interchangeable forms of contact and to the modalities of contact within the family system. There is some stress on the *children* in these first two sections, it should be noted. The remaining pages of this chapter are devoted to a consideration of the family in terms of its structure. Specifically, the husband-wife and sibling subsystems are examined as well as certain features of our families: the "peripheral" and "transient" males in our Negro families; various characteristics of our Puerto Rican families; and the failure of the grandmother to assume her role-functions in many of our families.

Self-Observation and Communication

Self-Observation

We posit that the epigenetic development of self-observation in a normal child requires: (1) a grasp of reality as organized along a certain order; and (2) the experience that "I am affecting my environment."

The development in the normal child of object constancy (see foregoing discussion), which is essential for a grasp of reality, requires the experience of repetitive encounter with things and people in similar situations. A child needs to develop trust that the significant objects in his environment continue to exist and retain their basic characteristics even when they cannot be seen or touched. Schachtel (1959) focused on the progressive interrelation among the following factors:

> (a) the discovery of object constancy; (b) the power to make an object reappear—be it the mother by crying, or the spool, by pulling at a thread; (c) the capacity to recover an object by going after it and finding it in reality; (d) the confidence that an object will continue to exist and eventually will be available again even if, for the time being, one can neither make it reappear nor go and look for it; and (e) the capacity to keep hold of an object in *thought*—that is, to develop focal attention to the idea of an object even when the object is not available for present need satisfaction, manipulation, perception and exploration (p. 264).

The child's developing sense of reality and of himself in action in this reality, in other words, depends on the predictability of his environment.

The concept of the discovery of "myself" through "my effect on my environment," which has been explored by so many writers, is given a new perspective in White's concept of competence and the feeling of efficacy in the child (1963, 1965). White pointed out that the child's sense of self-esteem grows with his competence in mastering and affecting his world of things and people:

> Our knowledge consists of the several consequences of our several actions; it is a knowledge, in other words, of action possibilities. . . . Concepts consist of information that is coded for action. . . . Effects produced without focalized attention, intention, and directed effort . . . seem to have happened to us; they are not felt as products of ourselves as agents (1965, pp. 200, 201, 203).

It becomes important, therefore, in the development of the observing ego, that the child should have a focused experience of himself as an agent of change.

In what ways do these processes have a chance to develop in disadvantaged families? Various writers have described the immediate environment in which the lower-class child grows up, pointing out some of the factors that would tend, in our terms, to block the development of a strong sense of self and the capacity for self-observation. Deutsch (1963), for instance, observed that in the overcrowded living conditions of this population privacy is almost nonexistent; families are large with little opportunity for individualization. Further, he noted that:

> the child learns to be inattentive in the pre-school environment. . . . If this trained inattention comes about as a result of his being insufficiently called upon to respond to particular stimuli, then his general level of responsiveness will also be diminished. The nature of the total environment and the child-adult interaction is such that reinforcement is too infrequent, and, as a result, the quantity of response is diminished (p. 171).

Or:

> Another area in which the lower-class child lacks pre-school orientation is the well-inculcated expectation of reward for performance, especially for successful task completion. The lack of such expectation, of course, reduces motivation for beginning a task and, therefore, also makes less likely the self-reinforcement

of activity through the gaining of feelings of competence. In these impoverished, broken homes there is very little of the type of interaction seen so commonly in middle-class homes, in which the parent sets a task for the child, observes its performance, and in some way rewards its completion (p. 172).

When we consider the kind of growth experiences that normally fosters a capacity for self-observation, as described earlier, then it becomes clear that a sizable portion of the low socioeconomic population does not have these experiences and therefore cannot develop this capacity. Circumstances do not allow them to develop either an increasingly objective grasp of reality or a sense of efficacy in interaction with their environment. The inconstancy of the environment, the features that make it difficult to internalize a sense of power and identity, the fast and externally geared resolution of cognitive-affective stress that becomes the dominant coping style—these make for multiple difficulties, including a poor capacity to focus attention and to observe the self, with an attendant inability to make use of most therapeutic efforts.

Ability to Communicate the Observed

A child growing into an increasingly complex and confusing world needs for his development significant adults to process necessary information in ways that will help him in the ordering of his universe. Though for the young child learning of basic emotions and of simple realities can occur in nonverbal modalities, transmission of complex information to him requires the use of language and the development of dialogues. Parents, in communicating with the child, orient their attention toward certain prevalent segments of the surrounding world that therefore acquire a special affective tinge. The clarity, order, and degree of differentiation in parental communication will affect the child's ability to grasp the nuances of his inanimate and interpersonal surroundings. The model presented to the child will affect his evolving style of interpersonal communication and, more significantly, his inner dialogues and the quality of his self-observation.

When the child exchanges information with his parents, his concern for his relationship with them sometimes outweighs the informational content of his message. To communicate his observations, thoughts, and feelings, the child must learn to express himself in ways in which the relationship messages and the content messages do not obscure each other.

We will later contend that the child growing up in disorganized, disadvantaged families is frequently handicapped in the development of this communication skill.

In the process of communication between parents and children in which exchange of information and reciprocal learning occur, there is normally a development of a body of implicit, shared rules among them which regulates their communication. These rules deal with formal aspects of the "how" of communications. These formal processes eventually develop to the point at which they occur "on automatic pilot," allowing such economy of interaction that parents and children can take for granted the rules of communication and move their attention to content without having to negotiate each time *how* content is going to be transacted.

In general, the formal rules that participants in a dialogue share have to do with how to signal that one has heard, understood, agreed, or disagreed, etc. Then the possibility of carrying themes to conclusions is realizable. The signaling closure is shared by others. There are possibilities for reviewing and recovering information and for signaling shifts in content matter. Important in this process is the capacity to differentiate relevant information from accompanying static which may blur clarity of information. When these rules have been developed, communication and reception of content become autonomous and useful for problem-solving functions.

Most middle-class children develop a system of rules of communication which allows them to exchange information with minimal regard for the implicit, formal rules that regulate their communicational flow. The situation with the deprived child is quite different.

Bernstein (1961) noted that the restricted language code used by low socioeconomic English individuals is not appropriate for use in reciprocal learning relationships because it does not facilitate a verbal elaboration of meaning and does not permit verbalization of intent, belief, or motivation. The restricted code is used as a vehicle for expressing and receiving global descriptive relationship messages organized at a relatively low level of conceptualization. Deutsch (1963), with similar emphasis, pointed out that the disadvantaged child is restricted "to a segment of the spectrum of stimulation potentially available" (p. 168) and that he is handicapped by training that discourages the development of a differentiated language. Both authors were concerned with deficits in the structural organization of language and its influence on cognitive organization and learning.

Our work with multi-problem low socioeconomic families, however, has given us a somewhat broader perspective. We have become increasingly aware that the entire process by which our family members relate to each other is affected by the characteristics and quality of their communicational system.

The low socioeconomic disorganized family shows deficits in the knowledge of the implicit rules that regulate the communicational flow. In the overcrowded conditions of these large families, parents pay little attention to the requests of the individual children, and the children in turn accept the fact that they will not be heard. In the development of necessary techniques for attracting attention to themselves, the children find that intensity of sound is more effective than the power of the themes; assertion by power is more important than knowledge.

Ways of transacting power operations occupy a large part of the siblings' interaction, and "ranking"[3] of each other can occur around an almost infinite variety of subjects. They attempt to resolve conflict by a series of escalated threats and counterthreats. This process frequently maintains the conflict, unresolved, as an issue that will reappear in another context. Diffuse affect is communicated through kinetic modifiers, through the pitch and intensity of the tone of voice, etc. Sometimes it seems that in the resolution of conflict it is unnecessary to hear the content of what is being transacted; one can almost predict the "winner" by noncontent clues. And sometimes there is no "winner."

The total amount of words—the vocabulary available in the family— is usually scarce. Not only are the parents limited in their verbal education, but they also tend to employ the best of their verbal equipment in situations outside the family. In the one-parent family, this trend has even more deprivational significance. The model of adults communicating among themselves is unavailable to the child. The role of verbal negotiation in solving interpersonal situations remains undeveloped, and the opportunity to sharpen capacities for abstract, relational thinking is largely unexercised.[4] The parent's attention is absorbed in issues of inter-

---

[3] Ranking: a process by which the children assign to one another positions in the hierarchical order according to various criteria of power.

[4] Smilansky's work (1965) is pertinent to our observations. She noted that in "primitive" Israeli children what seemed significantly lacking was not the *quantity* of labels but rather the ability to establish relationships between labels. She implied that any teaching with regard to increasing the *number* of labels introduced added confusion in a warehouse already full of single, unrelated numbers of objects. She recommended training in the fundamental ways in which objects are related.

personal regulation, and he thus fails to focus attention on the continuity and development of themes. Specific subject matter in his family will rarely be carried to any conclusion. A small number of interactions around a topic is usually interrupted by a disconnected intervention of another family member. It is rare for more than two family members to participate in an interaction around a specific point. When another member intervenes, the subject usually changes. The family threshold for accepting abrupt shifts in content matter is much higher than that of most middle-class therapists.

The result is a style of communication wherein people do not expect to be heard and in which they assert themselves by yelling. Conflicts do not have closure; there is faulty development of themes, a restricted affective range, and lack of training in the elaboration of questions to gather information. This style is perhaps adequate for the transaction of gross nurturing and power relationships, but it is insufficient for dealing with chronic and more subtle conflicts, for this requires the search for, ordering of, and sharing of different or new information.

The child is trained to pay attention to the *person* with whom he is dealing rather than to the *content* of the message received. The focus on the hierarchical organization of social relationships in the family curtails the child's freedom to address himself to the more objective aspects of the transaction, to the *content* of what is being transacted at the moment. What seems characteristic of our families is that the constant defining of relationships between and among family members outweighs the meaning of the content of messages. This type of communicational exchange, which is developmentally correct in interactions between young children and parents, seems to be dominant in the low socioeconomic population at all age levels. It plays an important role in the communication process among adults. The object of communication is to provide a vehicle through which attempts to define the status relationship of "me" dealing with "you" in a specific role are acted out. People who are unclear about their effectiveness and their impingement on other people need continuous use of other people for definition of themselves and of their social situation.

Formal Characteristics of Communication in Our Families

The problems in defining "self" and "other"—that is, a sense of mutual impingement and an awareness of interpersonal causality—can be clarified by presenting some of the salient formal characteristics of communication within our families:

LISTENING

a. Subjects do not expect to be heard. For example, Phyllis Montgomery finished a "monologue" about a painful school experience, which was prompted by a specific question of the therapist. Immediately after finishing, she initiated another activity, as though once she had performed the requested act the interaction ended. She did not think her communicative behavior would have any effect on the rest of her family or that it could prompt a response. Her assumption was complemented by the behavior of the mother and siblings, who showed no signs of involvement in or response to her verbalization.

If family members are heard, they do not expect a response. When the therapist attempted to elicit specific feedbacks, checking with each family member, "Tell me, what did Phyllis say?" the following emerged: The two boys were completely disengaged and had "tuned her out," while the mother and the other daughter, although they had heard Phyllis' message, did not feel that their responses would be significant. Mother: "What am I supposed to say?" Older daughter: "So she said it, so . . . it's her business."

b. If someone responds, it is not necessarily along the lines of the preceding communication. Any irrelevant response can be forthcoming and accepted. These are generally responses regulating the hierarchical relation between the member who talked first and the second speaker, for example, "You are always talking." (Language, as already noted, is not generally used as a medium for the exchange of thematic information, but rather as a way of establishing and regulating contact.)

DEVELOPMENT OF THEMES

a. A subject will rarely be carried to any conclusion: a small number of interactions around one subject are usually discontinued by an unrelated intervention of another member, which initiates the emergence of a new subject. That is, it is rare for more than two family members to participate around a specific content; when the third person intervenes the subject is usually changed.

b. Members can endure a dislocated shift in content matter by using the following coping mechanisms: following the newly introduced subject matter; disengaging, while some other members continue; and letting the new theme die at the end of a monologue. Some families fluctuate between "noise" and "quiet," depending on the theme or composition of the group, while others remain predominantly at one or the other extreme of the continuum.

NOISE

a. Intensity of sound frequently displaces the theme content. Two or more family members can engage in parallel talk for some minutes, spiraling, increasing the intensity of sound, and trying to outtalk each other.[5]

Many different types of kinetic activities accompany such verbal communication—children standing, going to each other, trying to exchange chairs, taking each other's property, throwing things, etc. The net effect of such interactions is to multiply the "noise" of paraverbal transactions. Noise has a contagious quality, and disruptions by one member can be observed spreading immediately to others. Members do not wait until someone finishes talking; they interrupt according to their inner pressures, sometimes around the same topic, but most often with the introduction of new themes.

b. The opposite of this picture of multiple engagement is illustrated by the disengaged family member or members. Examples are a child's putting his hat over his eyes, or covering himself with his jacket in typical foetal position, answering questions monosyllabically, or with "I don't know." At times children fall asleep successively until they are activated again.

c. In all families the mother's role as "regulator" is of significance; the exclusion of the mother from the group (in the second stage) produces a large increase in the level of noise, as if the mother's mere presence controls and regulates the extent of noise.

PATHWAYS

a. The mother is a central pathway for most transactions among family members when they are together.[6] Sometimes children relate to her as the target of their anger; at other times they respond to questions only if a signal from her indicates that it is all right. At times the mother acts, prompting a child to respond, or she functions as a "traffic officer," regulating the flow and direction of transactions, "shushing" a child, putting her hand on another, yelling at the third that he should not rock in his chair, etc. Sometimes she withdraws in sudden anger or depression; even then, many of the children's activities continue to be oriented toward her.

---

[5] This operation has been described as "symmetric escalation" by workers such as Jackson and Haley at The Mental Research Institute, Palo Alto, California.
[6] This clinical observation was confirmed in the Family Task situation (see Chapter 7), where it was found that the children either talked through their mother exclusively, or not at all. Our verbal behavior analysis (see Appendix B) did not yield this finding, however.

The disruptive activities of the children seem focused on activating the mother's role as a controller. When she is behind the one-way mirror, the children press their faces against the mirror to see her and touch her.

b. The spouses very rarely talk to each other. They talk to the therapist or to the children, or about the children. In general, they are in a "parallel" and not "reciprocal" orientation toward each other as spouses.

c. The children's sustained talk is mostly to the mother. Sustained dialogues among the children are rare, although they constantly "bump" competitively against each other.

CONTENT

a. Variations on the theme of a "dangerous world" are central. Aggressive antisocial themes can be the expression of inner pressures, but also the description and handling of outer realities. Drug addiction, "rolling" drunkards, setting fire to synagogues, the unfairness of the police or the court, the details of the ways in which children extract money and sometimes sex from other children, the excitement of stealing a car, or perhaps just the mastery of driving a car that incidentally has been stolen, or the "conning" of cabdrivers are all examples of themes repeated with infinite variations.

b. Ways of transacting power operations occupy a large part of the siblings' interactions. This "ranking" of each other occurs around an endless variety of subjects: "I will not give you your record until you pay me back for my glasses"; "This chair is mine, you lost it when you got up"; "I play better baseball"; "You are stupid"; "I read better than you," etc. They attempt to resolve power conflicts by a series of escalated threats and counterthreats, underlined by motoric activity. The issues end without resolution, only to reappear within another context in another power struggle. Siblings almost never relate to or emphasize positives in other siblings.

c. (1) The mother's messages to the children are mostly framed in "don'ts." She restricts their behavior with the repeated phrase, "Don't do that," which is seldom accompanied by a "because" that would imply a system of ordering outside of herself. When the child misbehaves and the mother responds to his action, her response may be a form of control directed to "stop" rather than to explore behavior. Her response, moreover, is usually couched in terms of "what you are doing to me." This type of message emphasizes how difficult "they" make her life, how helpless she is to cope with "them," and how "they" make her "sick." She leaves the child's behavior vague and unexplored. A few mothers who are strongly religious respond to their children's actions with long sermons that are more related to "the good life under the Lord" than to the child's activity.

(2) The mother's responses to one child's disruptive behavior are often generalized to the whole group. For example, Mrs. Smith may sometimes respond to one child's stealing or playing hooky by stating that, "These are the ways of the Smiths." Or a mother may respond to stress induced by the behavior of a child out of her reach by overcontrolling the child who is near her. This type of response encourages an undifferentiated evaluation of behavior and a diffusion of responsibility for certain actions; it raises the threshold for experiencing guilt and imposes limits on the development of self-differentiation among the children.

(3) Rarely do the mothers' messages to the children emphasize positives. She neither acknowledges their attempts to change nor verbally rewards achievement, coping, or exploration.

FROM CONTENT MATTER TO INTERPERSONAL CONTACT

We have stressed that a central characteristic of communication among family members is the selective attention to relationship messages at the expense of content messages. We have often been impressed, while observing conversation between family members, with the ways in which reality grounds seem to shift. Only by focusing on the significance of the relationship messages can one clarify the meaning of the shifting content. For instance, in one family session, we observed an adolescent girl, eight months pregnant, shift three times from a statement of wanting to leave her baby in the hospital to one of wishing to give it to her own mother. From an intrapsychic focus one could emphasize the undeniable ambivalence of this girl toward her unborn baby. From an *interpersonal* viewpoint, however, a consistent message in her shifting content becomes obvious. She was stating to the mother, "I will do whatever will bring me your acceptance." The mother was sending alternating messages. One stated, "I want to have the baby with me," responded to by the daughter, "I will do it." The other was, "It will be very difficult to have the baby with us—I am very anxious and nervous and having the baby will remind me of your sins and of my own second child that I gave away to my sister." To this other message, the daughter would respond, "Then I will leave the baby in the hospital," which would prompt the reappearance of the first message from the mother.

The irrelevance of content in negotiating and clarifying interpersonal positions is of major significance in the freezing of roles in the family, yielding a nonmodifiable structure. Many verbal transactions among family members have this characteristic, and only by paying attention to the basic "me-you" messages exchanged can one make sense of the seemingly disjointed character of family communication. Only then does the continual shifting of themes without exploration or attempts to reach consensual validation of their meaning make sense. The attempts to define interpersonal positions are merely continued in the next theme, and the shift of content is more illusory than real.

We turn now to a consideration of the family system with respect to affective behavior.

Socialization of Affect

As previously stated, transactions among family members seem to have an all-or-nothing pattern. Members can be totally disengaged or they can relate with intense involvement. The shift from one modality of interaction to the other sometimes has the characteristic of swift mood changes without clearly observable transitions. Intense involvement of family members occurs mostly around two affective poles: aggressive and nurturant.

Affect is communicated mostly through paraverbal channels in the pitch, tempo, and intensity of the verbal messages and the accompanying kinesthetic modifiers. Rarely do members talk about their feelings or comment on the feelings of others. When the therapist requests verbal expression of feelings, the response is usually a global positive or negative stereotype: sad or happy, angry or well, and bad or okay are the major descriptions of feeling. Clinical examples serve to point out some of the ways in which children are socialized into this global pattern of experiencing affect.[7]

Jimmy, at four, learns about aggression. Jimmy is a member of the

---

[7] Although generalizing about the experiencing of affect on the basis of observable behavior involves a series of assumptions, we feel safe in making such assumptions because of consistency with our observations in other areas. Further, we believe that restricted language skills, distinctive cognitive style, paucity and lack of gradients in experienced or expressed affect, and the structural problems in the family are all differing aspects of an over-all family system which seeps into and controls all parts *within* it. In this sense, then, as already noted, our division of this chapter into sections concerned with communication, affect, and family structure is, perforce, arbitrary and artificial.

Martinez family, of Puerto Rican extraction.[8] The father is bright, verbal, alcoholic, phobic, and given to shifting from excessive love to excessive rage. The mother is slow and depressed, with psychosomatic symptoms, suicidal ideas, and chronic resentment. They have four children. The two oldest boys show acting-out behavior. The eleven-year-old girl shows psychosomatic symptoms and depression. Jimmy, the youngest, is a delightful, hyperactive youngster. He wanders about from one spot to another and from one activity to another. Seemingly, he does not expect any reaction from his parents. Every once in a while he seems to reach the limit of the permissible, at which time his mother or father yells at him or extends an inattentive hand to push him in another direction. The moment at which such parental response is elicited is unpredictable; one cannot see how the child's activity differs at this time, when a parental response is elicited, from the times when no such response is forthcoming. At times the parents seem to "correct" him when the interviewers show signs of annoyance.

This vignette, which is repeated in many forms, seems to indicate a lack of selective reactivity on the parents' part to the children's actions; it suggests that parental reactions are to their own internal stress rather than to the behavior of the child. It is as if the interpersonal framework within which the child grows were made of an elastic band. The child acts and gets no response. The child acts again and again; the band gives until it comes to the limits of its elasticity. The child is then hit by the forceful strength of the band returning to its natural form. The parental mode of response at this point is usually violence in some form.

This phenomenon is pervasive enough to merit status as an "integrative" force in the family. The violent reaction, if viewed over the long sweep of the child's development, is at least predictable in the sense that it will come and it has a somewhat reorganizing effect. For at certain points, Mr. and Mrs. Martinez responded with an attempt to create boundaries by a sudden and irrational interruption of Jimmy's activity. The child experienced a deficit of response at one extreme of the continuum and a violent response at the other, with nothing in between. This response of the parents is not clearly related to the nature of Jimmy's action. His encounter with the reaction of violence is frequent, capricious, and in-

---

[8] See Appendix A for a brief description of this family, as well as others which comprise our research population. Unless otherwise indicated, our illustrations are from our research sample. Ages of children are at time of treatment, rather than intake or initiation of research.

comprehensible. It creates in him the sense of being helpless. He experiences a violent world which cannot be modified by his own actions. The different intensities and gradients in the continuum of aggression are not perceived or experienced because they are not there.

Another example from the Martinez family highlights some of the operations in the socialization for aggression and nurturance. Rafael, 12, the oldest boy, has been at Wiltwyck for one year. His father bought him a phonograph because the boy was sad; he also bought him three records. Later that day, Rafael asked his mother to give him another dollar to buy records, which she did. Still later, Rafael accompanied his mother to the store, asked for and got 50 cents to buy a toy. Ten minutes later, while still in the store, he asked for another 50 cents. His mother said that she had no more money, at which point Rafael stormed out of the store, yelling at her. When the therapist asked Mrs. Martinez why she didn't give Rafael the money he requested, she answered that she had given him her last 50 cents. The discussion which followed between the therapist and the family members was as follows:

Therapist: Would you have given him more if you had the money?

Mrs. M.: Of course I would. If the child needs something and the parents have it, they should give it to him.

Therapist: What do you think, Mr. Martinez, do you agree with your wife?

Mr. M.: Yes, I know that when I want something I want to have it. If I want a drink I'll get it, so if Rafael wants a toy and I have the money I'll give it to him.

Therapist: What do you think of that, Arturo? [*Arturo is the ten-year-old.*]

Arturo: Well, if he loves him, he will give him the money.

We wish to point out the equation of love and giving, the concrete nature of the giving, and the all-or-nothing quality of these transactions. As in the previous example, the lack of differentiation of nuances within an affective dimension is apparent here. The child is trained to respond at an extreme of the affective range. If money and giving are equated with nurturance and love, when these are held back, even for realistic reasons, the child's response is rage.

These parents are at the same time extremely depriving. Mrs. Martinez, for example, often leaves the children without food. (But she will at times prepare individualized lunches for each one of the children according to his wishes.) And Mr. Martinez spends all of his money on drinking binges and disappears from home for days.

In Chapter 4 we described the interaction between George La Salle and his mother and its relevance for the development of undifferentiated affect. Here we will remind the reader of one small incident (see sequence 11):

George goes to his mother and says, "Mommy, I got a sore on my finger." Mrs. La Salle responds with, "That's not the only place you're going to have one." After a few minutes, she calls to George and asks him to sit near her. To the request for specific nurturance, the response is unspecific threat. This does not indicate to the child why he will be punished; and it does not tell him in what way. Mrs. La Salle's attempt to make reparation for her undifferentiated aggression is an undifferentiated affectionate movement.

The children's affective response to a socialization pattern which is characterized by gross, unpredictable clues pitched at an extreme of intensity or at a deficit of contact is heightened anxiety in any new situation and an adherence to primitive, clear-cut patterns of experience. Since the child cannot relate his experience meaningfully to his own behavior, his sense of participation *in* the event or *with* the other is impaired. The experience of being angry, for example, is articulated not as "I am angry," but as "You are hurting me." Feelings become externalized, and this militates against any clearly delineated grasp of the affective experience. Inability to learn from experience, a characteristic of many of these children, may be a result of the fact that they do not fully experience many situations as happening to themselves. These children tend therefore to search for extreme and dramatic stimulation. It is as if the stimulation must be considerably amplified before it is intense enough to make the child perceive that "this is happening to me" rather than "around me." This may add another explanation of their need for danger and adventure and of much of the senseless cruelty often displayed in delinquent activity.

At times, what seems to be a family member's inability to verbalize feelings is actually the result of a special modality of experiencing. When a therapist, for example, attempting to explore situations raised by a family member, asks another member what he perceived, thought, or felt about the event under discussion, the answer is frequently, "I don't know." When one member is viciously teased by another and the therapist successively asks, "Are you bored by him? bothered? annoyed? angry? enraged?" in an attempt to explore possible gradients in intensity of aggressive affect, the answer remains, "I don't know."

The global and undifferentiated quality of the children's experiences, which gives them no chance to estimate themselves and their behavior accurately, prevents the child from being in contact with or knowing his feelings. Like cognition, affective life requires the organization of experience into discrete manageable units which can be discriminated against the background of other experiences. This, it would seem, is contrary to the way in which experience has been integrated by the members of our families.

Anger and Nurturance as Interchangeable Forms of Contact

On his arrival at Floyd Patterson House,[9] a child greeted a therapist in a rather aggressive tone of voice, saying, "You are always using the same lousy jacket." Without hesitation the therapist responded, "Yes, I use it because I like it. It seems to me a rather nice jacket, don't you think so?" At this point the child's face opened into a broad smile, and in a friendly voice he said, "Yes, I like it too." We would like to focus on the change of affect accompanying the child's responses, ignoring the purposefully elaborated response of the therapist. It seems as if the shift in affect from an aggressive to an affectionate modality was quite easily achieved.

In the second stage of a session with the McCallister family, Daniel, 13 years old, was engaged in a job that he executes with great skill—organizing the therapist as a controller. He played dangerously with a table lamp, teased his sister, and verbally attacked the therapist. The therapist responded first in a restricting, controlling fashion similar to the way Daniel's mother responds. At one point, however, he began to caress Daniel. The response of the child was an immediate melting into a little boy, and during the rest of the session the therapist was able to "control" the child by holding his hand in an affectionate way.[10]

These clinical examples, as well as observations of other family interactions in which the mood shifts from aggression to affection are swift, lead us to think that if the child's primary motivation for acting in a

---

[9] This is a "Half-Way House" between the Wiltwyck School and the community.
[10] Although this is not generally regarded as "usual" therapeutic procedure, we have found this measure to be at times effective, especially with children who need strong external controls over disruptive behavior so that the session does not become altogether chaotic.

particular way is the need for contact with the adult, he responds first in an aggressive modality, the modality more familiar to him because it yields more notice and response from his mother. He will easily exchange the aggressive for the affectionate mode of contact, however, if this will assure him of continuing contact.

This model is similar to the early mother-child interaction, in which we find at one extreme contact through nurturance and its opposite, fear of abandonment, and at the other, contact through aggression with its variations of power operations. If the child's goals are oriented toward adult contact, the alternatives could, therefore, be interchangeable.

Modalities of Contact

Our families can be seen at either extreme of the enmeshed-disengaged axis or as alternating in time between the two poles. These qualities of interpersonal contact seem to be significant in the development of cognitive-affective characteristics in the family members.

Enmeshment

An outstanding characteristic of "enmeshed" families is the quantity of maternal response to the children's behavior. Mrs. McCallister, for instance, centralizes control in the family in such a way that she is most often responding to the children's behavior with some form of control response. These control signals (like traffic signals) carry only the instruction of, "Don't do that now!" They do not carry instruction as to ways of behaving in the future, and they do not help the child determine what part of his behavior is inappropriate. The child is organized to search for the limits of permissible behavior with reference to his mother, rather than to internalized codes.

The lack of predictability of the controlling signals, however, imposes serious limitations on the development of rules. The existence and subsequent internalization of rules result in separation or differentiation of people through the intermediate step of relating to the rules. It therefore frees the participants in an interaction from the need for continuous investment in interpersonal control. This individuation, separation, and freedom are lacking in our families. Rules are continuously stated only in terms of *immediate interpersonal control*.

Regardless of the effectiveness of "presence-control," the mother seems rather hopeless about effecting change in controlling the child's behavior when it occurs outside the immediacy of her presence. The child learns that the range of mother-effectiveness extends to the limits, at most, of her visual or auditory field.

Illustrations of this limitation in the mother's function are her ignorance and bewilderment in describing her child's activities outside the home: "I do not know if he goes to school. He leaves the house, that I know"; or, "I learned of his stealing in court, but I do not know if he really did it because I wasn't there"; or, "I couldn't say for certain that it happened even if he (the child) says it did because I didn't see it." These responses, of course, emphasize the intrafamilial world of contact and the danger and distrust of the world outside, and they encourage the acceptance of two different types of behavior: "What may be valid at home is not necessarily valid outside."

What are some conditions that determine the development of this reliance on undifferentiated contact as a prevalent modality of relating?

The mothers in our population *themselves* come from deprived families. They are people with very low self-esteem, who are extremely dependent on outside anchorings for definition of self. They see themselves as helpless, incompetent, and hopelessly exploited by men. They tend, in situations of stress, to become depressed or ill, and they search for solutions in drinking or in the transitory love of a lonely and incompetent male. In their functioning as mothers they find a sense of worth in being needed that validates their being. They validate themselves through their mothering role, and even in their relationship with men they see themselves mostly as mother (see the subsequent section on *Family Structure*). The sense of self depends on fulfilling the mothering role.

Many of our mothers explicitly express or implicitly convey the concept of availability as the central value in mothering. The mothers become the pathway, as noted in the previous section, through which family transactions are conducted. The mothers are not, however, child-oriented, nor are these child-oriented families. These mothers are centered in "being mother": "I am a mother" is a *generic* statement, it should be stressed, which bears little relationship to a sense of being the mother of a particular child who is seen in a differentiated way and related to according to his individualized needs.

Highlighting this difference between the "mother's role" and the function of mothering is the interchangeability of children. These mothers can describe their children with awareness of their idiosyncratic characteristics if they are requested to do so. Nonetheless, when they are in the family group, their response to the children is often to treat them globally, as a group of interchangeable parts. As previously stated, a mother angered by the behavior of a child out of reach may spank a child that is near her.[11] Mrs. Smith labels the behavior of two siblings arguing, or one child stealing, as the "ways of the Smiths," thus labeling *all* of the children for the behavior of one. We hear many statements by our mothers such as: "You inflame my varicose veins," or "You'll give me a heart attack," wherein the behavior of one child is generalized to the group. Mrs. Montgomery (Chapter 3) accuses all the children of stealing from her. In the course of the discussion, the possibility of discovering the real culprit occurs: she now engages in distracting operations that "save" that child; and the accusation remains general toward all the children. Transactions of this sort, in which the children become an undifferentiated "mass of children," are related to the undifferentiated role of mother.

The lack of differentiation in the mother's role demands complementarity in the child's response. "If I am mostly a mother then you must be mostly a son (daughter)." Together they function as a system in which the responsibility for one's action becomes the responsibility of the other member of the system, limiting the development of autonomy within the family world.

Mothers at the engagement or enmeshment pole of the axis feel absolute responsibility for their children's behavior. If a child steals, the mother reacts as if to say: "I am a failure." This makes for a complementary experience on the part of the child: "If I steal, I hurt my mother," rather than, "If I steal, I am a thief." In the child, the sense of responsibility for his own action wanes due to the lack of demarcation between his own and his mother's behavior. The child's stealing becomes the mother's mistake. Transactions of this nature, as noted, discourage autonomous exploration and mastery of problems.

Disengagement

Since the basis for cognitive and interpersonal relationships develops around intense contacts in the areas of nurturance and aggression, when the mother (or child) behaves *outside* the modality of "engagement," she experiences complete lack of connection and functions at the disengaged pole of the axis.

The same mothers who are constantly engaged in interaction with their

---

[11] Similar observations have been made by Pavenstedt (1965).

children may suddenly declare themselves fully disengaged from any responsibility for, say, their children's breaking windows, simply because *they were not there*. The "being there" becomes essential for the "reality" of the event. Many therapists automatically assume that on some level these mothers *must* be aware and participating in terms of full responsibility. They tend to see the denial as a conventional cover-up device. This orientation does not do justice to the inner organization of many of these mothers. When they say, "That's what the teacher says, but I don't know if it is true because that's what she says," they are stating the narrow limits of their cognitive reach and their role organization as well as their mistrust of the outside world. They seem to have lost sight of the child as a learner and doer apart from and outside of their physical presence.

Other missing interactions between mother and child are reflections of the same phenomena. We refer to those intermediate operations which help children to apply rules, learned in the adult's presence, to behavior outside the adult's presence—the rituals through which parents link themselves with the child's life outside the home. For instance, the commonplace question, "What did you do today?" asked by parents when the child comes home from school, seems to be missing in our families. No inquiry into his day, into "What happened?" or "What's going to happen tomorrow?" ever has a chance of becoming articulated. Such concerns seem to have no place within the busy here-and-now of the overburdened lives of our mothers. They seldom ask any of those simple and somewhat supervisory questions through which the child may progressively draw for himself and for his parents a vivid picture of his existence away from the immediate moment. It is not at all uncommon to see a child wandering in and out of a session without being asked to reconstruct or describe what he did outside or why he left. In a reciprocal vein, it is uncommon to see the children stimulated enough to explore what happened with their siblings and with their parents when they were not present. Their questions usually narrow down to "Where is my mother or brother?" Obviously, the absence of communications which repeat and review the past or attempt to anticipate the future leaves the child little material with which to develop the idea of a world that remains real even when he is not there.

We must examine more carefully the underlying fact that to the degree to which these mothers do not transcend the role of mother as a "source" of knowledge and rules, they are burdened by constant intervention in their children's lives in the immediate present. The particular processes through which they move from being a "source" to being a "vehicle" or "carrier" of outside knowledge and rules are still to be understood. We only observe that an attitude of shared respect for a third system—whether rules, content, or knowledge—gradually emerges when the family begins to change. The nature of whatever is to be learned seems to become sufficiently depersonalized or objectified so that instead of a constant interactional dialogue between mother and child we have a trilogue—mother, children, and "what's to be learned."

Such a trilogue is far removed from the natural state of affairs in these families. Usually the mother has been exhausted into despair and helplessness by her need to respond continually in terms of "presence control." She has been so overburdened that by the time the family comes to the community's attention, all one can witness is an overwhelming interactional system in which the mother attempts to resolve her plight by fleeing into absolute abandonment or disengagement from her children. One sees, then, no middle ground as part of the model of observable transactions between mother and child. It was this gap that impressed us during our first observations of these families. Unaware that this state of affairs was part of a natural process, we centered our attention primarily on the apparent disengagement, the relinquishment of executive functions, until we fully realized the other strains, reflected in the enmeshment processes discussed previously.

Figure 1 is a visual model of the family system processes which we have been describing. The experiential sequence depicted in the lower half of the scheme describes, as in an iceberg, some of the stress phenomena in our families. These processes fall on the *enmeshment pole*, and have usually occurred before the family reaches the attention of social work agencies and other mental health facilities; the visible part of the "iceberg," with the relinquishment of parental authority, is seen in the upper half of the experiential sequence as shown in Figure 1—the *disengagement pole*.

At the enmeshment pole, family transactions are characterized by a fast tempo of interpersonal exchange because multi-problem families tend to resolve tensions by action and because of their paucity of mediating processes between impulse and action. The resulting style of interpersonal relationship has a high degree of mutual enmeshment and fast shifts in both focus of transaction and affective tone. At the disengagement pole, family members seem oblivious to the effects of their actions on one another. Monologues, parallel play, and a variety of maneuvers of psychological and physical abandonment characterize this modality.

Neither extreme of interaction facilitates a differentiated experience of family transactions. Both leave family members relatively helpless in the face of interpersonal tension, with very few tools for conflict resolution. Awareness of personal impingement and interpersonal causality remain global.

The child's intensive training, as charted in the lower half of the schema, has a strong influence on his cognitive-learning style. The unpredictable, global presentation of stimuli to which he has been exposed produces a built-in attentional disturbance. He tends to be overdeveloped in making quick maneuvers and in fastening his attention on the changing, immediate physical aspects of adult cues. He is underdeveloped in making sustained explorations, and his capacities to use focal attention for conceptual problem-solving are unexercised.

This system prepares the child to clash with the demands of the school. The school's emphasis on recruiting focal attention to the service of abstract content and on the use of this content for symbolic exploration of the world does not coincide with the child's orientation. The child copes with the anxiety aroused by such school demands by attempting to elicit from the teacher that which is most familiar to him—proximal control. This attempt to resolve conflict is often perceived by the teacher as an aggressive act and responded to either with insistent attempts to control the child or by removing him from the classroom situation. Thus, the child's development of a special coping repertoire within the family is, in effect, preparation for failure in school and for a life of underachievement by the standards prevailing in American middle-class culture.

Family Structure

Cursory observation of the bone structure of the arm can reveal the limits of the arm's movement. But observation of the bones alone will not tell us the strength, the speed of the movement, or the style and grace with which the arm once held a fragile object or embraced a loved one. Analysis of family structure often has the same quality of quick, gross assessment of the *range* of interactional possibilities without telling us much about the quality of the interactions.

But structure can also be expressed through action, and family structure can be observed through interactional patterns. It is through inter-

FIGURE 1

THE ENMESHMENT-DISENGAGEMENT SYSTEM

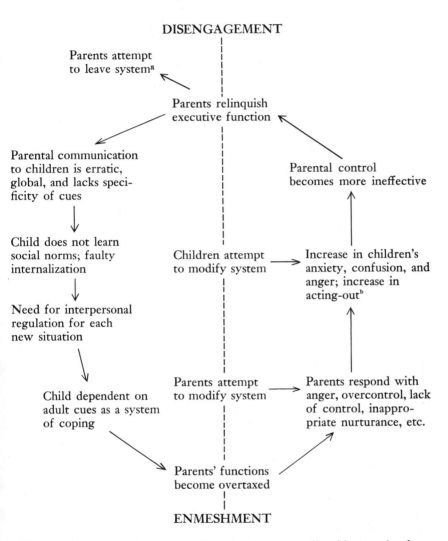

DISENGAGEMENT

Parents attempt
to leave system[a]

Parents relinquish
executive function

Parental communication
to children is erratic,
global, and lacks speci-
ficity of cues

Parental control
becomes more ineffective

Child does not learn
social norms; faulty
internalization

Children attempt
to modify system

Increase in children's
anxiety, confusion, and
anger; increase in
acting-out[b]

Need for interpersonal
regulation for each
new situation

Child dependent on
adult cues as a system
of coping

Parents attempt
to modify system

Parents respond with
anger, overcontrol, lack
of control, inappro-
priate nurturance, etc.

Parents' functions
become overtaxed

ENMESHMENT

[a] When parental control becomes ineffective and parents relinquish executive functions, they may abandon the family altogether, but most of the time they segment the
family by institutionalizing a child or children, acting-out (in illness, promiscuity,
alcoholism, etc.), or allowing a sibling substructure to take over parental functions
(see next section of this chapter).

[b] At the point of increase in the children's anxiety and acting-out as an attempt to
modify the system, children may turn to the siblings for control, guidance, or
identification (delinquent or not); they may abandon the family, e.g., run away; or
they may join a delinquent gang.

action that family members define themselves. When a mother sends a message to her child, she is defining who she is in relation to him and who he is in relation to her. Family structure builds and expresses itself through this transactional definition of selves. Recurrent transactions establish individual roles which lead to the family system of how, when, and through whom to relate as the habitual becomes the norm.

In the initial contacts with a family, it is possible to assess a particular type of structural arrangement from observation of patterned transactions among its members. One looks for: (1) the lines of power and leadership; (2) the labeling of the members and their assignment to particular roles; (3) subgrouping alliances and shifts around different significant themes; and (4) the fluidity of assigned labels when there is a change in family composition or in family themes, and the way in which language is used to support this structural balance.

Talcott Parsons (1955) stated that:

> . . . the structure of the nuclear family can be treated as a consequence of differentiation on two axes, that of hierarchy or power and that of instrumental vs. expressive function. . . . these two axes of differentiation as symbolized by the two great differentiations of generation . . . and sex, overshadow other bases of differentiation within . . . a "typical" nuclear family (p. 45).

He went on to say that there are four role types which have a "primary" order of structural differentiation from each other in the nuclear family:

> The father role is, *relative to the others*, high both on power and on "instrumentality"—hence low on "expressiveness." The mother role is high on power and on "expressiveness," thus low in instrumentality, the daughter role low on power but high on expressiveness—hence low on instrumentality (p. 45).

Later, Parsons called the father the instrumental leader, the mother the expressive leader, the son the cooperator, and the daughter the loyal member. He suggested that the model of the healthy family is one in which the roles determined by the two axes are maintained. Disequilibrium results, for instance, when the son assumes instrumental executive functioning, or the mother assumes a daughter's role, or there are expectations for individual family members that are different from the universal, functional family roles.

We have quoted an early work of Parsons' because this picture of the structure of the nuclear family is valuable as a background against which the structure of the families in our population can be delineated.

It has become apparent that the families with which we worked have characteristics in structure and function which have been inadequately studied thus far. The conceptual models in the growing literature on family systems are not fully applicable to our group. These are models of the American middle-class family (or sometimes of the stable working-class family); they focus on intimate interspouse communication and on the socialization process of the child in a child-centered family. Family structure is regulated by clearly defined patterns of interaction between mother and child from birth until the resolution of the Oedipus complex, and by a continuous relationship of child and parents through adolescence until young adulthood.

Some characteristics of family structure that seem basic for *our* population, however, are:

1. They are largely a one-parent family; the mother provides continuity through a succession of unstable father-figures.

2. In an "intact" family, the spouse subsystem functions mostly as a *parent* subsystem.

3. The nature of the parents' power is confusing. The parents are at times in absolute, autocratic power and control; at other times, they feel completely helpless.

4. The parent(s) relinquishes executive functions by: (a) delegation of instrumental roles to a "parental child" (or children); or (b) by total abandonment of the family (psychologically and/or physically).

5. The sibling subsystem acquires significance as a socializing agent far beyond that which has been recognized heretofore.

6. There is a breakdown in communication between parents and children, and the sibling subsystem tends to encourage expression of opposition to parental control.

We turn our attention now to the nature and function of our families' subsystems and to some of the roles which seem to us of such significance as to warrant special consideration.

Husband-Wife Subsystem

The "husband-wife" system is a vaguely delineated and underemployed subsystem. Husband-wife transactions, when rendered explicit, usually betray an impressive array of unfinished, vague, unresolved interpersonal-definition tasks. These revolve around considerations such as: "who am I in relation to you"; "you and I around money"; you and I around sex"; "you and I around companionship," etc. Communications between husband and wife in these task areas usually are not sharply delineated, but vaguely organized and obfuscated. Problems about role dissatisfaction do not seem to be experienced as sharply as we presume is the case in the classic neurotic family.

Problem areas are not usually anxiously concealed as a defense against diagnostic examination, but the lack of specificity and stability in areas of conflict makes diagnosis difficult. The conflictual issues are so fluid that the couple, as a couple, is almost unavailable to exploration, negotiation, and modification in these areas. Though the level and variety of problems can be simple and limited, the transitions, as already noted, from aggressive to affectionate interactions seem to be quick, with moods which ignite and defuse with extraordinary ease. The "binding" of tension, the holding of a particular issue or a problem, remains unsustained. This makes for a special situation: only the parenting roles seem to offer stable channels for potentializing marital conflict. Difficulties in mapping out husband-wife roles find camouflaged expression only in terms of father-mother role conflicts—"you and I around parenting the children." The father and mother find it almost impossible to experience and report on themselves as husband and wife. The father-mother conflicts seem to emerge from a host of unfinished definitional efforts in a hazy husband-wife sphere; such definitional failures and gaps are found in all previous developmental stages of these parents as a reflection of their own impoverished interpersonal and emotional histories. Previous failure to define the self competently as child, sibling, friend, learner, etc., results in an intense need to overemploy the role of "parent," especially the role of the nurturant parent. This becomes *the* role for experiencing some kind of reflected identity. These parents, however, are not actually *child*-centered; they are centered in the parent role. A child-centered parent is generically defined as "person" before becoming defined as "parent." He or she is sufficiently differentiated as a separate and self-sufficient entity to acknowledge the distinctiveness of children and to concentrate on their growth.

This growth process apparently did not take place in the adults in our families. As noted, they attempt to resolve the primary problem of defining a basic self-identity through the role of parent. Their children thus become absolutely necessary for adult interpersonal orientation and self-definition. The usefulness of children as sources of feedback and as extensions and reflections of self overrides any parental ability to perceive them as potential persons (see foregoing discussion of *enmeshment*). In sum, it is the children who organize intense interpersonal contact and offer some justification for parental existence, as well as some basis for discovery of a fundamental role.

The role-organization around socialization of the children can be so important an axis of self-esteem and of interpersonal feedback and definition that a therapist-communication criticizing a *specific* parent-child transaction or the "hows" of the interaction runs the risk of being felt as a massive, global, frontal attack on the central aspects of the self, verbalized in the form of: "He [therapist] is calling me a very bad person."

Sibling Subsystem

Let us begin with some general theoretical considerations concerning siblings and the sibling subsystem, since this aspect of family structure has not been given sufficient attention in the psychiatric field. One could start by questioning how much of a child's life in the family actually falls within the area of parental observation and responsibility. It is obvious that answers to this question would vary in different cultures. There would be some agreement, however, that a great part of the child's activities transcends parental contact and is carried on in the midst of his siblings. Clinicians have recognized this fact only indirectly in the concept of sibling rivalry, the focus being on the need of the child for parental attention.

We consider the influence of siblings in general, but particularly in our families, to be directly significant in the development of the self-concept.[12] We agree with Sullivan that self-esteem and the concept of self are dependent on reflected appraisal. Our sense of identity depends in great measure on the validation by our immediate world that "I am I." The family world is not limited to the interaction of mother-child, father-child, or parents-child as a reflection of complementarity. Siblings are

---

[12] Note an example from animal behavior. Scott (1958, pp. 182–184) noted that in dogs and wolves there is a close association between mother and puppies during the first three weeks of life. After this period and at a time when the mother leaves the litter for long periods, the strongest relationships are formed with litter mates (peers). This is the basis of pack organization of adult dogs and wolves. Sometimes trappers steal a wolf before the litter has reached three weeks of life, fully aware that this is their best chance to develop an unwolflike wolf by offering it what is in many ways similar to the human parent-child relationship.

also significantly involved in the process of appraising and confirming aspects of the child's personality.

It is significant to note that although studies of group behavior, peer groups, gang influence, etc., have been multiplying in number, consistent exploration has not been conducted in the area of the sibling group and its influence as a primary socializing agent. This may be explained in part by the fact that mostly middle-class families have been selected for psychiatric exploration. Emphasis on the family may also have over-shadowed the importance of siblings as crucial mediators, reinforcers, modifiers, or resistors of parental socializing.

In our study population there is a definite hiatus between parents or parent-surrogates and siblings. It is as if parents and siblings, although living under the same roof, are autonomous entities in many vital aspects of living. The siblings frequently operate outside of the awareness and out of the control of the parents. We have already described how many of our parents deny responsibility for a child's unacceptable behavior on the grounds that they were entirely unaware of it and/or that it occurred only in the community outside the home. They clearly state that because their child's behavior was outside of their cognizance, it was, therefore, outside the boundaries of their ability to cope with it. It is this inability of the parents to respond to the children's needs with proper guiding actions that pushes the children in our families toward their siblings in order to achieve some "anchoring."

We have also previously noted that in the course of ego-development the child requires adequate parental response to his actions as a signpost for an adequate evaluation of self. His evaluation of the correctness of his opinion or the adequacy of his performance requires an experience of "bouncing" against discrete, interpersonal boundaries. The child's self-evaluation develops through the confrontation of an "I" and a "you" in different situations in which the "I" experiences his impingement on the other and can correct, modify, or reinforce certain aspects of self-behavior accordingly. Lack of individual response on the part of the parent to the child's behavior creates a deficit in the child's awareness of his impingement on others.

In our families, the child's behavior, verbal and nonverbal, is frequently responded to by the parent in ways that do not permit the child a clear evaluation of himself or his performance. As a consequence, the child experiences uncertainty and confusion about his behavior and sometimes turns to apathetic withdrawal as a security measure. The quality of parental response or lack of response pushes the child to his siblings for reflected appraisal, guidance, control, and direction as to how to cope with the familial and outside world. "Parental children" are those children to whom authority is implicitly or sometimes explicitly allocated by the parent and/or siblings. In the absence of parental responsiveness, these children become the source of reference for executive guidance, control, and decision.

The parental child (or children) is certainly not equipped for the job of parenting, though at times he can do an adequate job with regard to concrete nurturing and support and become even more exploratory, guiding, and predictable than his parents. More often, the demands put on him clash with his own childhood needs. We see, then, the development in the sibling subgroup of two types of interaction:

1. (a) The siblings can form a cohesive, defensive group if one of them is evidently in need; they can play together or join in a delinquent gang in which they can cooperate on a job.

(b) They are usually structured in hierarchical linearity, and are frequently involved in power operations designed to test the lines of power.[13]

2. The parental child's functions, especially his "power" functions, seem to be necessary for the total family equilibrium. Although role shifts are generally a difficult feat for family members, when the parental child is removed from the sibling subgroup, this role tends to be reallocated to another sibling. In families in which the role of the parental child is clearly allocated to and sustained in only one member, the position of this child in the group is one of added stress. He is caught between the concentrated challenge of his siblings, who displace onto him their anger against their mother, and the rewards of his position—power and alliance with the mother. When the parental child is a daughter, the possibility of escaping from the conflict situation by conceiving a child of her own becomes an overwhelming push into early unwed motherhood.

Sibling subgroups frequently become organized into structures which sometimes function with a predominating cohesive theme. We will illustrate by presenting clinical examples of such themes: the *socializers*, the *interpreters*, the *moralistic pack*, and the *rescue squad*.

1. The Brancusis, an Italian family,[14] provide an example of siblings acting predominantly as *socializers*: The siblings are Carl, 14; Helen, 13;

---

[13] J. P. Spiegel (personal communication) has noted that in the Greek-American family, the power is allocated to the first-born.
[14] This family and the next two are not research families.

Joseph, 12; Kenneth, 9 (the Wiltwyck child); and Daryl, 8, who is at Childville.[15] Carl has already been in two reformatories and has spent six months in jail. Mr. Brancusi presents his parental role as follows: "My wife takes care of the children. I don't bother with them unless there is a real emergency." He doesn't know why his son, Daryl, is at Childville or why his son, Kenneth, has been referred by the court to Wiltwyck. "I don't know, I never take much time to find out. I have enough trouble trying to keep myself working. Besides, when I talk, they don't pay me any attention so I don't spend much time with them." The children talk about the parents in terms of their drinking and fighting and assume protective roles toward them.

In the second stage of one family session, Helen talks about Kenneth's stealing: "He hangs around and they go stealing [laughs] and then they got caught." Gradually she says, "My girlfriend goes with him. They both . . . sometimes we all go stealing."
Kenneth: She tried to open the lady's pocketbook.
Helen: And he's gonna snatch it.
Joseph: She is the one who taught me how to do it.
Helen: I didn't teach you, you still don't know, Joseph.
Kenneth: She teached me.
Therapist: (*Asks about Carl.*)
Helen: Carl follows us, must feel foolish following us.
Therapist: Why does he follow you?
Helen: When we take the money, he wants part.
Joseph: He is the one that learned them how to do it.

We see in the above the disinterested (or possibly hopeless) father and the development of a sibling gang with status hierarchies, a certain pride in its skills, and a semblance of guidance (although antisocial) provided by the two older siblings.

2. An example of a family in which some of the siblings act predominantly as *interpreters* are the Garotas, an Italian family. Besides Mr. and Mrs. Garota, there are Allen, 11; Anthony, 9; and Gloria, 7. Mr. Garota describes Anthony, the Wiltwyck child, thus:

> The boy hasn't been disciplined enough. She hasn't disciplined the child since he was three years old. I had to show him something, put some fear in him, but he's been out of my hands for the last couple of years because I am afraid to touch him. She'll

---

[15] Childville is a private child-care agency for disturbed youngsters in New York City.

[Mrs. Garota] have me locked up. In fact, she brought me to court because I hit the child.

Mrs. Garota says about the same child:

> I took him to a psychiatrist and the psychiatric doctor is the one that recommended . . . he says he's a very disturbed, very nervous child. Like lately he's getting the idea into his head that he has no friends or nothing, that nobody loves him and the world is against him . . . but I keep telling him, "Mama loves you."

It had become clear in the family sessions that the parents had chosen this child as the battleground for their conflicts.

In the second stage of one of the family sessions, we get a sibling's view of Anthony. Gloria describes her understanding of him:

> I think Anthony is frightened because he thinks people are going to hit him, that people hit him because he is bad, and he's scared they are going to hit him . . . He thinks that he is sometimes bad, like when he does something bad he thinks it's not so bad and if he does just a little good . . . but when he does something good he thinks that's bad. He's all mixed up.

Allen gives his image of Anthony in these terms:

> Like if my father hits him he thinks nobody likes him. Sometimes when my mother hits him he says the same thing . . . my parents fight, you know, and somebody will get hurt but who will be the guilty one? Like, Anthony comes home one night and my father says to my mother, "You didn't punish him, you didn't hit him or do this," and they start a fight, and who will be the guilty one, who will? Anthony. Because they fight over him.

Gloria, and sometimes Allen, both in and out of the therapy sessions, often seemed to fill the role of "interpreter" or "explainer" of reality. Gloria was in charge of seeking the reasons, the "why's" for interpersonal and extrapersonal events concerning her family. Frequently she corrected the misunderstandings of her parents with regard to letters from the Department of Welfare or the court. She explained the outside world to the family, and often, the family to the outside world, in the same way in which she explained to Mrs. Garota and the therapist the behavior of Anthony. The function of interpreting, which is ordinarily performed by the adults of a family because they are capable of filtering reality for the children, is often so impaired in disorganized, under-privileged families that the only compensation possible is in enlisting the capabilities of the most intellectually equipped sibling. In this family, both Gloria and Allen often became the ones who translated the experiences of childhood and the inner life of other siblings to the first generation—the adults—who seldom understood the children's point of view.

3. The siblings in the Peters family, a Negro family, often behave as a *moralistic pack*. This family is composed of a mother and seven children—six boys and one girl, Maria. The cause of referral was Richard's truancy and breaking into parking meters. Mrs. Peters is an extremely ineffectual woman of dull-normal intelligence who had been institutionalized in her youth at Letchworth Village, a New York State Training School for the feebleminded. A year prior to our treatment sessions with this family two of the boys, James and Lucas, returned home from prison, where they had served sentences for drug addiction, drug peddling, and robbery.

One of the family sessions centered around the demand, addressed to Mrs. Peters by the four younger children led by John, for the eviction of the older brothers, James and Lucas. The mother implicitly agrees with her younger children and encourages John. Nevertheless, she overtly adheres to her concept of maternal availability toward her misguided older children. As the session proceeds, the siblings' attack on James, the drug addict, assumes the ferocity of a lynch mob.

In the second stage of this family session, James and Mrs. Peters go to another office with a therapist. The moralistic pack now picks the younger brother, Craig, as a scapegoat, because "he is crazy."

It became clear in the course of therapy with this family that the sibling group, operating on the basis of displaced anger at the mother, required someone to fill a scapegoat role, that person shifting according to availability. The *content* of the moralistic tirade (addiction and drug peddling, for example) was less important than the needed *process* in this family system. The mother's relinquishment of executive function to Maria, the "parental child," and to John, the "man," was a covert operation, resulting in the children's use of James, Lucas, and Craig as displaced targets for their anger at their mother.

4. Finally, the McCallister siblings impress us as a *rescue squad*. Since we think of this family as a prototype of the "*primitive family*," we will not only describe this particular sibling substructure in some detail, but

will also use this opportunity to spell out at some length the *entire* family system as a backdrop to the understanding of the sibling processes.

Mrs. McCallister is a bright, sensitive, agitated, small woman. Mr. McCallister is young, dull, and concretistic (there is some possibility of brain damage). He is an illiterate man with extremely poor verbal defenses beyond, "That's a lie." He drinks frequently and "relives the past," as his wife often says.

Mrs. McCallister appears to be the warm, effusive, emotional center of the family, and the exclusive pivot from which any semblance of executive function emerges. She is constantly, although erratically, directing the family, mostly in terms of control: "no's" and "don'ts" seem to be always present in her speech. In the fashion of a confused traffic officer, she signals mostly with her hands, yells at one child to stop poking his nose, grabs another who is playing with the microphone, etc. She stays with an activity only briefly, however, seldom following through, and she almost always has to go back to the child with whom she began. She is overwhelmed, but when she is dealing with the children, her bright face seldom shows it. Physical hand signs and actual grabbing are of undue importance in her means of communication and control.

Chaotic or misdirected activity is a strong general characteristic of this family. The parental picture appears completely skewed. Mr. McCallister, who sits quietly throughout these interactions, at times with a bored manner, sometimes makes a weak admonition to one of the children. When he is addressed, he smiles with embarrassment, and pleads, "Let her answer 'cause I ain't got no education." Mrs. McCallister accepts, and actively protects his passivity with a clear show of genuine pity. She acts as the filter for whatever he has to say and as translator for whatever we have to say if Margaret, the "parental child," does not do it first. Mrs. McCallister's entire existence, it would seem, is predicated on being a busy nurturer to her husband and children. She seems to ask little or nothing in exchange (in terms of socialized or responsible behavior), as long as she is needed and can cover her fear of being abandoned. She talks hurriedly and confusingly about "little Daniel" and "big Daniel" in the same breath, showing that she does not clearly demarcate her husband from her children.

The McCallister family often organizes into a "queen bee" structure. Mrs. McCallister emerges with some strength, attempting rudimentary (although always insufficient) efforts at organization which give way under the strain of fights with her husband. These fights, despite the therapist's intervention, leave Mr. McCallister squirming at the verge of physical acting-out. At home he actually attacks her. At such times he is almost like a replica of his son Daniel: he is easily out-argued, and at the same time is completely ineffectual in attempts to control impulsive motor discharge. This is not to imply that Mrs. McCallister has much better control. She once stabbed him, and she is quite impulsive with dishes. During fights that occur in the therapist's office we see a second organization. While previously quiet but "in" the family, Mr. McCallister is now isolated. The children marshal themselves around their mother to protect her and be protected.

At home, the family arrangement and its behavioral expression take more dramatic form. Margaret and Daniel literally attempt to pull their parents apart. In the ensuing panic, Tessa, a frail younger daughter, clutches the baby and takes her into hiding in a closet. Bonnie, if Margaret and Daniel are still struggling, runs to the police. Herbert flees to the bathroom with some of the other children. At such times, the older siblings organize themselves as an independent structure, a "rescue squad," to protect the parents from themselves and the younger children from the possibility of accidental harm. There are substitute but relatively stable role assignments for these constant emergencies, which demonstrate that the children have learned their survival routines well.

Along with Bonnie and Daniel, Margaret is concerned not just for her mother, but more basically with keeping the family together. Within the sibling subgroup these three children represent the strongest pro-unity forces in the family. They float between the parental and sibling camps to mend and umpire splits and gaps. Though essentially in her mother's camp, Margaret, who is the loyal, first "parental child," appears to be the most "torn apart" or neurotic. Overburdened to extremes, Margaret often supersedes her mother. She can become so "maternally worried" that she escorts Daniel from the bus station despite a parental decision that he is old enough to try it alone. Margaret is understandably phobic about seeking life or relationships outside the home; she has trouble making friends and is obsessed about getting a job to "fix" the family. During the sessions, any allusion to the parental conflict makes her cry profusely. She becomes mute, and looks very pained and distant. During the office fights, while she cries, the rest of the children usually appear unrelated, indifferent-looking, or busy as a tight, playful, affectionate subsystem.

The boys, Daniel and Herbert, are both very infantile. Daniel is easily frustrated and becomes uncontrollably demanding and violently angry and tearful. Mrs. McCallister immediately feels guilty and agitated. She showers him with physical caresses and consolation, and promises that he will get whatever toy he wants. Daniel, like his concretistic father, has tremendous problems with taking statements literally. He is quick to hit his siblings because of any misunderstanding. Herbert often peeps unintelligibly when trying to communicate something, and everybody laughs. He is very shy, and also given to acting-out, which, along with his poor verbalization, is causing problems for him in school.

All the boys in this family seem to have problems in differentiating signals and grasping or resolving interpersonal communications. Anger is so accepted by all the siblings that to play house (observation in second-stage sibling subgroup) is for them to drink "liquor" (water) and then to beat the girls. Margaret and Bonnie joyfully act out their roles by throwing bottles at the boys. The game is played with all the laughter and spontaneity of "ordinary" children everywhere "playing house."

Perhaps families with unmanageable, raw, and consistent aggression at the parental level force the children to attempt to render harmless the anxiety thus engendered by accepting the aggression and incorporating it into everyday play. There is so much violence in the family that repressive or disassociative defenses would be insufficient for handling their problems, even if the children had the equipment to employ them. None of the siblings wants to get married. All of the girls treat the boys as if they were inherently helpless, and all of the boys feel the girls "know" more. Nonetheless, there is affection between them, and when Daniel has to stay at Wiltwyck rather than returning home, they frequently show their pain by crying.

In sum, then, as a prerequisite for survival, a child growing up in a family requires the satisfaction of certain needs. It is obvious that the nurturance needs of the infant can be satisfied only by the mother or mother-substitute, and it is culturally prescribed that needs like control and guidance will be supplied mainly by the parents. In extended families, however, it is also acceptable for grandparents or aunts to support, supplement, or take over such functions. It has been studied less, but is nonetheless equally true, that siblings support, supplement, or resist these parental functions in many significant areas of socialization. In disorganized families, in which parents relinquish executive functions, the unsatisfied needs of the child exert a pull that is responded to by the siblings as a separate subsystem.

A Significant Feature of Our Negro Families: The Nonexistent Grandmother

The significance of the grandmother's role as a cohesive, central force in low socioeconomic extended families has been given some attention by a number of workers. Our own observations of grandmothers in unstable "extended" families, however, indicate the necessity of re-evaluating the significance of their role.[16]

Many of our families have a composition which includes the mother, her children, and an older daughter with an out-of-wedlock child. This organization might seem to resemble a three-generational structure: a grandmother, a mother, and her children. Such structural arrangements are seldom found, however.

Generally when a new child is born to a family, there are changes which must occur beyond introducing the biological labels, "mother" and "grandmother"—changes in the functional organization of the family. The daughter must learn a new role as a mother, and her mother must learn a new role as a grandmother. For a daughter to become a mother and to achieve the cognitive-affective reorganization entailed by this new role, a change needs to occur in her basic role as daughter. For the grandmother's role to emerge, a change in her fundamental role concept as *mother* needs to occur.[17] New roles emerge from a concomitant restructuring of interactions occurring through the two accustomed roles. The daughter moving into a mother's role needs to experience a growing sense of autonomy from her own mother in order to take jurisdiction over her growing child.

This process, which is preceded by moves from a child-daughter role to an adult-daughter role, is not clearly established in our families. The child-daughter does not grow to become a *mature* daughter potentially capable of mothering her own child without needing to completely relin-

---

[16] Age differentials do not enter into the designation of grandmother role. For "grandmother" could be 50 or 30 years old. "Mother" could be 50, 32, or 15 years old.
[17] The apparent motivation (sometimes expressed) for refusing to move from the mother to the grandmother role may vary considerably. In one instance, the grandmother's role was rejected because the mother wished to remain, as in her own family, the "older daughter who takes care of the rest of the kids." In another family, the mother firmly held on to her old role because of verbalized fears: "My daughter don't know how to do things for the baby." The individual's conscious and unconscious urges supporting the family's structural problem (not allowing the grandmother role to emerge) can be manifold. Our main observation, however, is a system-fact: grandmothering functions are blocked whatever the idiosyncrasies in the inner dynamics of family members.

quish her role as daughter. Abrupt and frictional leaps rather than gradual and negotiated transitions become, then, the *only* possibility for role development in our families. For a daughter to become a mother is for her to assume all the functions of mothering, identifying with the mother and simultaneously (physically) eliminating her.

Sometimes her inability to separate the two roles as daughter and mother is "resolved" in a different fashion—the daughter fully relinquishes the mother role to the grandmother, who takes over the maternal functions for the new child, now treated as one of her own children.

These failures of gradual and synchronized role growth are even more significant in families with a scarcity of socializing influence from an adult male. The blocked self-corrective processes create for the child difficulties in learning to be his mother's child because he experiences his mother mostly as his grandmother's daughter, or, at best, as an older sister. Reflecting this static system are transactions like those between Mrs. Montgomery and Phyllis, previously discussed in Chapter 3 (see sequence 9):

Phyllis: I will do it. I know what I do.

Mrs. M.: You do not. I ask you to get up and dry the baby. You lay up there on the bed until 12 or 1 o'clock and refuse to get up and dry the baby. Well, I can't see the baby neglected so I go on and do it, that's why. 'Cause if you mean right, you'd go and do it without me asking you. . . . To keep from my asking I go and do it. . . . I have to go out and fix breakfast. You won't even get up to fix the baby's breakfast. The baby goes to sleep starved, and it's wrong to let the baby be neglected like that, so I just go and do it . . . and you don't do these things that I ask you to do. I ask you to come in the house and do something in the house, or help me do something in the house . . .

Phyllis: (*Interrupting.*) You don't ask me nothing. You don't ask me nothing.

Mrs. M.: I ask you.

And so on.

A little later, Phyllis says:

When I get ready to do something for her, you always holler, "I am taking care of this baby. Don't holler at her. Don't do this. Don't do that." So I don't say nothing to her. You are taking care of her. Take care of her! *Do everything for her. Everything!*

Mrs. Montgomery's attempts to help her daughter be a mother are couched in terms of keeping her in the obedient daughter role; the emphasis is "Do as I tell you so that you will fulfill the mother role." Phyllis' autonomy is sabotaged, and her attempts at differentiation consist of giving up responsibility for her own child. In her rebellion as a daughter, she forfeits her role as mother. The structure of the family remains frozen. Mrs. Montgomery stays central as *mother*, with Phyllis' infant becoming an "addition" to the hierarchy of siblings.

Blocked emergence of roles of new grandmother and new mother is illustrated also by the La Salle family (see Chapter 4, sequence 7). Mrs. La Salle stated that her children were taught (by *her* mother) to see her as incapable of mothering. She complains somewhat competitively that her children were allowed more freedom than she herself had, and that she had difficulties in establishing her basic right as a mother to be in charge of her own children.

At other times, we find Mrs. La Salle saying that if she left the house, her mother would send the children after her to bring her back. Mrs. La Salle points at her attempts at identification with the mother's role and her effort to correct her own role to create a new family organization in which she would as act a different, alternative model to her mother. This attempt was possible only when her mother died.

Failures in moving toward the development of a three-generation extended family away from a two-generation pseudo-extended family are typical in many of our families. The inability of family members to negotiate and achieve reciprocal changes reinforces and transmits the inflexibility of family roles to the third generation, precluding the possibility of growth in the family system.

The Peripheral Male[18]

In the unstable Negro family there are a number of possible roles the male can assume. The male's role may be that of a husband-father in an intact family;[19] a stable but "sporadic" entity; or an almost undelineated

---

[18] This characteristic of lower-class family organization (and especially of some lower-class minority groups) has received some attention with regard to the impact, emotional and otherwise, on family members. Parsons and Bales (1955), in their exhaustive treatise on family structure and the socialization process, base their theoretical orientation on a *two*-parent nuclear family. Most psychoanalytically oriented workers similarly believe that the stable presence of a father-figure, especially in the early years, is essential, or at least of major importance in the healthy psychosexual development of the child. Detailed examination of the problems of the one-parent family can be found in Pettigrew (1964), and Glasser and Navarre (1965).

[19] "Intact" is used here to indicate a family with a male and female living together with their children, regardless of the legal status of the marriage.

image, shifting continuously and unpredictably. The last is a rather common situation, consisting of a variety of rotating paramours "floating" through the household. In many of our families, children have different fathers who are accepted only peripherally in the family structure.

Even in the intact Negro family (or one in which separation from father-husband has occurred after a period of family intactness), however, the male remains somewhat peripheral. He contributes to the financial support of the family (when he is gainfully employed), engages in sexual and procreative activities with his wife; but he leaves the handling and rearing of the children completely to the mother, although he demands immediate obedience from the children. Like the Puerto Rican male, he often maintains an extrafamilial life that includes a group of drinking pals and occasional extramarital affairs.

In the Lewis family, for example, the mother and the children formed an extremely cohesive alliance to keep Mr. Lewis ignorant of the problems in the children's lives. (This family contains seven children and an out-of-wedlock child, four years old, of one of the older daughters.) Mr. Lewis, a truckdriver, would not know that Dorothy had not come home to sleep or that she returned at 3 A.M. from a party supposedly at the "Y." When Leonard went for a joy ride in a stolen car, his father was similarly ignorant and uninformed. The family myth was that he was so authoritarian and violent that they (Mrs. Lewis and the children) could protect themselves only by keeping him isolated from family affairs. Yet they illogically complained when Mr. Lewis not only accepted, but plunged into his family isolation and spent weekends drinking with his friends.

In families in which there is a "sporadic" but "stable" male figure, it is the mother who determines the boundaries of his engagement with and participation in the family. Mrs. La Salle, for example, clearly delineated her paramour's role: he could come to the house and be with her, but he was not permitted under any circumstances to meddle in the parenting of the children. When he stayed at night to share Mrs. La Salle's bed, the children's jurisdiction and pre-emption of her bed would be restricted (see Chapter 4).

The Jefferson family[20] is another example of a stable relationship between the mother and a paramour. The three children, aged three to seven, are all offspring of the paramour, Mr. Watson. Mrs. Jefferson and

---

[20] Not one of our research families.

Mr. Watson have never lived together. Each maintains a separate household; neither is interested in marriage. Mrs. Jefferson states that she would never marry him because he is an "unreliable person." In this instance, the male never fully assumes either a husband or a parental role.[21]

As these examples suggest, even when there is a male figure in the family, his parental role is restricted either by mutual agreement of husband and wife or by jurisdictional delineation in the mother's paramour relationship. These male-female relationships are fraught with stress and power operations, and are almost invariably resolved by some form of eviction or escape of the male.

An illustration of a "floating" male figure in a household is provided by the Jones family. Mrs. Jones shares her apartment with two female relatives. Various men enter the family for short periods. Sometimes the man is one of Mrs. Jones' paramours; at other times, he is an aunt's lover. These men sometimes contribute, and sometimes not, to the financial support of the family. From the child's vantage point, the mother's paramour is often just another depleter of the mother's less-than-bountiful resources.

In "richer" situations, the tangential male, "the man who likes my aunt" (see Montgomery family, Chapter 3), appears as the unpredictable giver. He takes the children to shows and showers them with money. At other times, however, he takes money from them, abandons them, and leaves them "holding the bag" for cabfare.

What are the available models for male identification for children growing up in these families? The child's opportunities for selecting models for male identification are reduced to the older brother(s); the relationship between brothers and sisters; and the differential ways in which the mother treats her sons and daughters. The mother also offers the child two other sources of orientation to the male image: her own views and attitudes toward men, which mediate an image of an irresponsible, exploitative, and sometimes violent male; and most significantly, mother-son transactions. These transactions revolve primarily around

---

[21] The Department of Welfare policy of withholding aid for dependent children when an able-bodied male is present in the family could be considered a cultural determinant which discourages legal marital stabilization and reinforces this kind of relationship. The practice of occasional "midnight raids," sometimes employed by social investigators to catch the transgressing male, is an additional strong reinforcer of this type of transient, "unstable" structure.

areas of control-obedience. She addresses herself to the child in terms of "do something *now*." If the child can avoid the "now" he can usually avoid the "do something," since most of these maternal commands do not carry temporal components. The conditional, "you *should* do," or "you *should have* done" (with an emphasis on "should" that implies maternal expectations for internalization), is rare. In this type of interaction, the learning of masculinity is derived predominantly from the son's role—obedience, avoidance, and a rebellious pattern toward the female.

In manifold ways, then, the man's participation in these families is structured away from any direct, active, and guiding role in the parenting of the children. For example, Mrs. La Salle states about her paramour: "He's not supposed to become involved in my business" (the children). Under these circumstances, the mother's role (centrality) does not complement but almost fully supplants the male's, and he functions as an almost unneeded and insignificant satellite. Frequently, no verbalized or conscious sense of pain or disturbance about his remoteness seems to be present. The children accept the family's structural deficit as well as the mother does. They incorporate the idea of the male's role as one of uselessness, or at least of unknown usefulness. They fail to sense or develop feelings of tenderness toward him or to perceive guidance attempts (feeble as they may be) on his part. The children are further impoverished by rarely witnessing adult male-female transactions of cooperation and mutuality.

A boy's readiness to learn from extrafamilial males is handicapped by his derogated self-concept of the *meaning* of maleness and by his lack of ability to visualize his future role in the family. Identification needs are often met by only an incorporation of those outstanding role-fragments of extrafamilial males that are valued in the collective and oppressed life of the slum community. These fragments often have to do with an antisocial cleverness and aggressiveness which give status as "copers" to figures such as the corner pimp or the important "numbers man." It is from contact with the narrow, glamorous, surface material projected by these figures that many a child from our unstable families derives a kind of one-sided and distorted male model. These fragmentary identifications have the effect of creating further confusion in the child by equating irresponsibility and violence with masculinity.

The child's opportunities (and ability) to forge the "fortunate circumstance"—to elicit, perhaps, the hidden benevolence of the corner pimp, or the "pusher," or the guiding and knowledgeable concern of the numbers man—are extremely limited. He encounters, in general, few occasions to enter into well-sustained and, more significantly, multi-dimensional contacts of proximity with these figures. Even if these extra-familial males should happen to be equipped with affective characteristics which might possibly correct the child's growth, these characteristics are seldom presented through a sufficient variety of situations and with enough of a behavioral repertoire for the child to select positive features. This complicates the problem for the child, who is, in effect, more prepared to be attuned selectively to salient negative characteristics than to seek exposure to the possible depth and variety of affective-behavioral nuances of which this male may be capable.

In our unstable Puerto Rican families, we have observed that the males generally seem to be less transient and more definable, even if negatively, by the family than in the unstable Negro families. The male seems to have more of a full-bodied connection with and role in the family. He may be alienated, but he remains within the family structure for the most part. His absence is felt. He remains a possibility in fantasy and in conversation. Even the acts of derogation and attacks on the "missing," "weak," or "bad" father seem to play an active organizing role in the family structure. People rally around him or against him. Sometimes he is talked about, kept around, as it were, to be rebelled against.

The mother's relatedness to and incompleteness without the adult male seems to come across to the Puerto Rican child much more clearly than it does to the Negro child. This is understandable, as our Puerto Rican group, even under acute pathological circumstances, has not apparently accrued the extreme degree of intergenerational impoverishment around the male role that our Negro group has. The Puerto Rican families can still draw from the vestiges of a patriarchical tradition. The father's inadequacy still tends to be measured through the patriarchical myth of what a "father should be like." If the myth fails, the family can often turn to other male models—uncles, cousins, godfathers, etc.—with more likelihood of finding compensatory figures than most of our Negro families, who tend to rely on female relatives for "solutions."

With this general background, we can now turn to a brief presentation of certain composite, salient characteristics of our Puerto Rican families.

Some Features of Our Puerto Rican Families

Negro and Puerto Rican slum families share many characteristics of the culture of poverty, but they differ in certain aspects, many of which are culturally determined.[22] Cautioning the reader about the artificiality and oversimplification of abstract descriptions of "typical" family organization, we nonetheless venture to point out certain features of the Puerto Rican families in our population.

In very disorganized Puerto Rican families the bulk of interaction is built upon enmeshed exchanges revolving around violence, sex, and money. For most Puerto Rican families, however, extensive work in disentangling positives (see Chapter 6) modifies the stereotyped thematic flow and yields a family picture that looks less dramatically pathological. This is probably because the disorganized families of this ethnic group still seem to have some access, however tenuous, to a stabilizing cultural tradition. Family interactions seem to be underlaid with a certain stability of roles—those of favorite and scapegoat, for instance—which is in sharp contrast to the paucity of differentiation found in other disorganized families (see the Montgomerys, Chapter 3).

Concurrently, patterns of affective expression seem to be less ephemeral and shifting than is the case in many families from the disorganized group. Family members can, for example, bind and store anger (*guardar rencor*) against each other; the framework of affective interplay, though tumultuous, displays some constancy which allows for thematic development. Breaches of confidence between mother and son or husband and wife, betrayal, jealousy, fear of deception, debts of gratitude, etc., can almost always be elicited and retained as significant themes to be played out.

These themes are often expressed by the use, in English, of Spanish reflexive verbs, which seems to buttress these families' orientation toward externalization. The reflexive is a form in which the subject and object of an action coexist in the same person, so that the subject seems to manipulate himself as a member of an interactive field. "I put myself to cry and suffer." "I put myself contented." "He puts himself jealous." Of course, allowances must be made for the natural tendency to carry forms

---

[22] The plight of the Puerto Rican Negro family is not discussed here because it presents special problems which would require separate and extensive elaboration.

acceptable in one's native language into a new one. The same form can come to be experienced with a sense of the self's possessing the feeling, rather than having the feeling imposed upon it, as if from an external source. But only intimate acquaintance with a specific family can clarify the degree to which intrapsychism is present in the themes to which the family adheres when they are couched in this fashion.

Many of these themes are, of course, vestiges of the cultural tradition of Puerto Rico. In Puerto Rico, the old myths of the family, with their blueprint for family organization, coexist with emergent forms being created by socioeconomic changes, with their implicit requirements for modification in pivotal areas, particularly the role of women. The clash of the traditional and the new is even more sharply experienced by the Puerto Rican family living in the more complicated culture of the large American slum, where the gap between cultural values and the actual manner of living may widen, or the old concepts be retained in name but in practice turned into something quite different.

For example, the Puerto Rican family adheres, on a manifest level, to a patriarchal structure with strong authority supposedly invested in the father, the *macho*. He is expected to show strength and authority in aggressive and physical ways that illustrate lack of fear and, through the sexual conquest of women, virility. The Puerto Rican woman, in turn, is expected to be submissive and loyal. She has no right to question her husband's activities, although she has authority in her home and in regard to the children's well-being. Children are expected to respect their parents and to be generally obedient.

In fact, on a surface level, the theme of *respeto*—respect—is the cornerstone of Puerto Rican child rearing. But one frequently finds this concept entangled with demands for sheer obedience, so that it is used to sabotage a child's autonomy. In its name, a great capacity for tenderness is subordinated to an undue emphasis on producing a docile child. Consequently, a half-formed longing for tenderness seems to be submerged under a prominent fear of the consequences of seeking it. Many members of our Puerto Rican population could give variations of the following quote: "I don't dare to touch my father's face. If they gave me $1,000 to shave my father, I wouldn't take it. We are eleven brothers and we don't dare to kiss him." Under the aegis of respect for the parents, the child is subjected to great disrespect. A boy's first efforts to demonstrate his autonomy or masculinity may elicit praise and almost assaultive tenderness from his family, but in the next moment he is mocked almost into insignificance. It is not surprising that a boy, caught in this conflict, may go to great lengths, even adducing delinquent activities, to avoid ridicule and prove that he is a *macho*, or at least not a *pendejo*, an *añoñao*, or, worst of all, a *maricón*.[23]

Even as a grown man, the Puerto Rican male, in an attempt to bolster his self-image, involves himself in extramarital sexual conquests and adolescent-type activities directed against his wife (and women in general): excessive drinking; domino and card playing with friends; avoidance (in social, party-like gatherings) of conversations with females while concentrating on peers, etc. His relationship with his wife involves an ambiguous son-husband role. He is dependent and demanding; he leaves most practical matters at home to be handled by his wife; he feels that his duty ends with being the provider. At the same time, he feels displaced by his children and has difficulty in finding a way to become integrated into the family.

If the Puerto Rican man feels defeated by an alliance of his wife and children, his wife feels enslaved, exploited, and deserted by her husband, though she relates to him intensely. She talks about him a great deal, in contrast to his almost total silence concerning her.

From different interview materials a composite image of the Puerto Rican male as seen by his wife might be drawn as follows:

> The Puerto Ricans don't know how to help their wives. I don't believe there are fifty Puerto Ricans who are good husbands. Marriage is slavery for the woman. A Puerto Rican man flirts with a woman, hugs her, fights with her, and makes love to her. And then he leaves her with three or four children as though it were just a joke. The American husband—if the wife is in the kitchen, he goes and he helps her. He helps her to clean the house. If he needs to clean, he *does*. If he needs to cook, he *does*. If the wife needs to go out, when she comes back he doesn't ask her where she went. She came, and that's enough.

---

[23] Among various self-description slang terms we have chosen these four because they seem to operate almost as a gradient of emotional states revolving around the experience of self-sufficiency and masculinity. *Macho* is the height of masculinity— aggressiveness and virility. *Pendejo* means "pubic hair," interpreted as a minor early sign of puberty, unessential to the sexual act or the real "genital stance." A *pendejo*, then, is an incompetent—a person prone to being made insignificant or ridiculous. An *añoñao* is a very dependent, childish person. A *maricón* is a homosexual.

The woman's self-picture is one of being exploited by the man and powerless to defend herself. The only alternative to this exploitation, she feels, is separation from her husband, and she wavers between the alternatives of resignation and self-assertion, the latter implying the destruction of her family. Caught in this dilemma, one of her most palpable reactions is resignation and depression. She seems to deny her real strength, actually manifested quite clearly in her practical adaptation to the new culture, her management of the new household, her relationship to her children, and her ability to press for role revision on the part of her man.

The consequences of this interlocking picture of the Puerto Rican man and woman trap the child in some of the same perceptions. His parents seem to demand from him a pledge of allegiance which implies choosing between his father and mother. He sees his father as generally inadequate (though at least he *sees* him). There is a mythology about the father, even when he is not present. The mythology portrays him as inadequate and irresponsible, but at the same time important, powerful, and dictatorial. He perceives his mother as loving toward him and helpless in relation to his father, who tends to betray her.

The classic fantasy of a positive Oedipal solution with displacement of the father is quite common. Faced with the contradictory demands put upon him by this family arrangement, the child uses the solution of dichotomizing his responses: there is "good" behavior at home, involving a submissive attitude with repression of resentment; and expressions of aggression and antisocial acting-out in the school and on the street.

To deal with the pressures produced by problems of child rearing, husband-wife problems, and other troubled areas of family life, families from certain sectors of the Puerto Rican population reach out to "significant others," notably the evangelical churches[24] and the *espiritistas* (spiritualists)—indigenous resources which can enter the family and work within it as an integral part of the system.

These agents, who "speak" the inner language, a kind of "spiritualese" reserved for describing psychological stress (which is often interpreted supernaturally, upholding the orientation toward externalization) can be looked upon as social creations designed to deal with stress in the particular terms in which the culture expresses it.

The linkage with these resources can be particularly important for

---

[24] See Chapter 3, the Garcias, for an example of the ego-buttressing significance of the church.

Puerto Rican families in large American cities because they are ties with the old ways and can be employed to maintain family intactness. For example, a very religious family turned even more intensely to their church when distressed by their stubborn thirteen-year-old daughter, who was experimenting with lipstick and auditioning for a dancing role in a school play—actions which were interpreted as dangerous signs of en-croaching Americanism, sure to end in delinquency and disgrace. The day before the play, without having openly "given in" to family pressure, the girl was suddenly "visited by God"—a socially endorsed hallucinatory experience through which she was instantly pulled back to the church, and, simultaneously, her family. The same "solution" was repeated by her sisters as they reached the age where they were beginning to seek autonomy from the family. Such uses of peak religious experiences as a centripetal force, as it were, are not uncommon in the Puerto Rican family.[25] They show how the indigenous resources to which the family turns can act as an integral part of the family system.

Or in another family, the wife's infidelity was couched by both spouses in terms of her having been possessed by the spirit of a prostitute. When their problem was expressed in this way they could both, of course, be free of responsibility and could join together, at least temporarily, in going to an *espiritista*. The spiritualist, working within the protective framework of externalization, accepted their explanation. He compelled them to go on a long trip together to dispose of a chicken leg stuck with a nail in order to exorcise the spirit. In other words, he assigned a "family task" designed to bring the isolated husband and wife together in a co-operative undertaking over a long period of time, producing some amelioration. A middle-class professional trying to help this couple prob-ably would have attempted to reinternalize and personalize their problem gradually. But in the attempt to couch it in a modality of experience accessible to him, he might have rendered the problem unmanageable for the couple. The spiritualist, by keeping within their culturally endorsed protective framework, avoided this risk.

The point is, of course, that to understand the dynamics of families, particularly those from the disorganized population, the professional must acquaint himself with whatever supportive systems exist in those families' immediate surroundings. If he can come to understand, and

---

[25] We have seen much less of this phenomenon in the urban, disorganized Negro family.

perhaps even learn from the techniques used by a family's indigenous resources, he may be able to develop approaches which are compatible with the population he wants to help.

In sum, in the extended, unstable family, whether Italian, Negro, Puerto Rican, etc., there are certain features of structure and process which constitute a unique format of socialization, displaying the phenomena of disorganization. The pattern of the extended family as a relatively organized large collective body in which members have clearly delineated, yet flexible functions and are attuned to the protection and sharing of each other's individual resources is rare in our population. Beyond the availability of people's presence and a place to go when meeting difficulties in coping with the outside world, the family's resources are scarce. Involvement with the subtle issues of structuring psychological growth (in affective, cognitive, and communicational areas)—with actively comprehending the child's viewpoint and with the deliberate formation of the child's fundamental attitudes and thinking habits—is tenuous. The child seldom finds enough moments of a "cooperative collective," and must, in general, settle for whatever sense of protection he can derive from people generally absorbed in the intrusive and conflicting aspects of living collectively. It is precisely the failure of this collective to evolve sufficient regulatory principles for sustaining and revising interpersonal transactions that distinguishes our variety of extended family from its equally underprivileged but somewhat more stable peers and challenges our therapeutic skills.

REFERENCES

Bernstein, B. Social class and linguistic development: a theory of social learning. In A. H. Halsey, Jean Floud, and C. A. Anderson (Eds.), *Education, economy, and society*. Glencoe, Ill.: The Free Press, 1961. Pp. 288–314.

Bernstein, B. Linguistic codes, hesitation phenomena and intelligence. *Lang. speech*, 1962, 5, 31–46.

Deutsch, M. The disadvantaged child and the learning process. In A. H. Passow (Ed.), *Education in depressed areas*. New York: Bureau of Publications, Teachers College, Columbia University, 1963. Pp. 163–179. Quotation used by permission of the publisher; © 1963 by Teachers College, Columbia University.

Glasser, P., and Navarre, Elizabeth. Structural problems of the one-parent family. *J. soc. issues*, 1965, 21, 98–109.

Hess, R. D., and Shipman, Virginia C. Early experience and the socialization of cognitive modes in children. *Child Develpm.*, 1965, 36, 869–886.

Kagan, J., Moss, H. A., and Sigel, I. E. Psychological significance of styles of conceptualization. *Monogr. Soc. Res. child Develpm.*, 1963, 28, No. 2, 73–112.

Minuchin, S. Conflict-resolution family therapy. *Psychiat.*, 1965, 28, 278–286.

Minuchin, S. Psychoanalytic therapies and the low socio-economic population. In J. Marmor (Ed.), *Modern psychoanalysis.* New York: Basic Books, Inc., 1968 (in press).

Minuchin, S., Auerswald, E., King, C. H., and Rabinowitz, Clara. The study and treatment of families who produce multiple acting-out boys. *Amer. J. Orthopsychiat.*, 1964, 34, 125–133.

Minuchin, S., and Montalvo, B. An approach for diagnosis of the low socio-economic family. Psychiatric Research Report 20, American Psychiatric Association, February, 1966.

Parsons, T., and Bales, R. F. *Family, socialization and interaction process.* Glencoe, Ill.: The Free Press, 1955. Quotations used by permission of The Macmillan Co., Copyright 1955 by The Free Press.

Pavenstedt, Eleanor. A comparison of the child-rearing environment of upper-lower and very low-lower class families. *Amer. J. Orthopsychiat.*, 1965, 35, 89–98.

Pettigrew, T. F. *A profile of the Negro American.* Princeton, N.J.: D. Van Nostrand, Co., 1964.

Schachtel, E. G. *Metamorphosis: on the development of affect, perception, attention, and memory.* New York: Basic Books, Inc., 1959.

Scott, J. P. *Animal behavior.* Chicago: The University of Chicago Press, 1958.

Smilansky, Sarah. Promotion of preschool, "culturally deprived" children through "dramatic play." *Amer. J. Orthopsychiat.*, 1965, 35, 201–202.

Sullivan, H. S. *Schizophrenia as a human process.* New York: W. W. Norton and Co., 1962.

White, R. W. Ego and reality in psychoanalytic theory; a proposal regarding independent ego energies. *Psychol. issues*, 1963, 3, No. 3, Monograph 11.

White, R. W. The experience of efficacy in schizophrenia. *Psychiat.*, 1965, 28, 199–211.

Wolff, P H. The development of attention in young infants. *Ann. N. Y. Acad. Sci.*, 1965, 118, 815–830.

Wolff, P. H., and White, B. L. Visual pursuit and attention in young infants. *J. Amer. Acad. child Psychiat.*, 1965, 4, 473–484.

Intervention

*D*uring the course of our research project, and subsequently in the treatment of disadvantaged families for a period of years following the termination of therapy with our research families, we developed a number of interventive techniques designed to make inroads into certain aspects of the family systems described in the preceding chapter. The current chapter deals with various technical and professional aspects of these interventions.

Although throughout our research there was a continuous discussion of cases as well as peer observation and supervision of the treatment sessions, each therapist tended to develop his own therapeutic style, as might be expected. Only toward the end of the project could we identify and clarify various concepts of intervention; at this time we felt we were in a position to begin to delineate and formulate more precisely some over-all therapeutic strategies.

Opportunities to explore these concepts of intervention in a more focused way became available to us as a result of detailed analyses of transcripts of the sessions in the study of: (1) therapist behavior; (2) responses of family members to therapist interventions; (3) interactions between the therapists; and (4) responses of family members to each other. In addition, we were able to review the therapists' interpretations of these events in an examination of transcripts of the fourth stage, in which the dynamics of the sessions and strategies for the future were discussed. We began to test some of our newer ideas about therapeutic interventions toward the end of the project, and we are continuing to do so in our current work.

For the most part, we are unable to separate the concepts that were implicitly used by the therapists during the research project from the more crystallized formulations that emerged later on. We will, therefore, present the strategies and techniques we are currently employing in our work with families whose background and degree and quality of disorganization are similar to those of our research families. We might note that the use of alternating roles of participant and observer with family members, active and varied manipulation of the composition of the family group in the sessions, and various tasks to potentialize conflicts (see later sections of this chapter) are relatively recent arrivals to our therapeutic strategies.

The material presented in the preceding chapter concerning the structure and dynamics of our families was arbitrarily organized into three sections. We will continue this organization (although not in the same sequence), for we discuss our therapeutic interventions in the context of principles and techniques which challenge: (1) the communicational system; (2) the structure of the family; and (3) the affective system. We will, in addition, present a section specifically concerned with the pulls, stresses, and strains on the therapist. We might note, however, that the problems, pitfalls, and experiences of the therapist are touched on in other sections of this chapter, too. The final section recapitulates and discusses some general principles of our therapeutic endeavors.

The organization of this chapter is, of course, artificial and oversimplified; it does not reflect the interconnections of these operations or the way in which they actually present themselves during the therapeutic hour. It does reflect our bias for active participation on the part of the therapist.

Challenges to the Communicational System

Enactive Formulations[1]

As already noted, our family members are generally action-prone, concretistic, and restricted in the use of verbal symbols. They have difficulty in producing and sustaining rational and coherent dialogue; their modality of talking is more informative when one "reads" behavior rather than verbal content. Understandably, they are not readily reachable by abstract, conceptual, or symbolic interventions. Therapists' styles of cognition and communication tend to be abstract, symbolic, and oriented toward highly differentiated nuances of verbal transaction. Unless there is specific and concrete focus, gaps develop between the therapists' cognitive and communicational styles and those of the family members. An overt manifestation of such incongruency is the "pseudo-dialogue," in which the therapist and family members talk in parallel monologues while assuming they are relating to and communicating with each other. At other times, family members may attempt to decipher the therapist's communications but fail, eventually escaping through disruptive actions, mutism, or direct statements such as, "I don't understand you," or, "I don't know." Some therapists tend to interpret such behavior as resistance. Others label the family members' communication styles as "noise," while

---

[1] We have found Bruner's (1964) early classification of three modes of coding and processing experience (enactive, iconic, and symbolic) very useful for the therapist in his attempts to couch his messages in ways that will be most accessible for family members. He said: "It is fruitful, I think, to distinguish three systems of processing information by which human beings construct models of their world: through action, through imagery, and through language. . . . I shall call the three modes of representation mentioned earlier enactive representation, iconic representation, and symbolic representation. Their appearance in the life of the child is in that order, each depending upon the previous one for its development, yet all of them remaining more or less intact throughout life—barring such early accidents as blindness or deafness or cortical injury. By enactive representation I mean a mode of representing past events through appropriate motor response. We cannot, for example, give an adequate description of familiar sidewalks or floors over which we habitually walk, nor do we have much of an image of what they are like. Yet we get about them without tripping or even looking much. Such segments of our environment—bicycle riding, tying knots, aspects of driving—get represented in our muscles, so to speak. Iconic representation summarizes events by the selective organization of percepts and of images, by the spatial, temporal, and qualitative structures of the perceptual field and their transformed images. Images 'stand for' perceptual events in the close but conventionally selective way that a picture stands for the object pictured. Finally, a symbol system represents things by design features that include remoteness and arbitrariness. A word neither points directly to its referent here and now, nor does it resemble it as a picture" (pp. 1–2).

reciprocally, some family members refer to the therapists' communications as "social worker talk." Family members and therapists alike, at times, derogate each other's communication styles.

Awareness of this gap and skill in transforming messages into a communicational modality which is similar to that of the family are requisites for therapists with this population. To understand what we mean by "communicational modality," it must be remembered that a message can be coded in a symbolic, verbal manner or in action. The therapist can *say* something or *do* something that expresses the same meaning, or preferably, he can do both. For instance, in one family session a therapist found himself under heavy attack. He then changed his seat and sat among the family members. Pointing to the empty chair, he said, "It was very difficult to be there being attacked by you. It makes me feel left out." The therapist might have described in words alone that he felt left out of the family; instead, he changed his seat to be among the family members and then commented on his feelings. He sensed that although his verbal statement would pass unnoticed by all but the most verbal members of the family, his "movement language" would be attended to by everyone.

Families that experience chronic frustration and impotence and that do not see how they can affect their own environment either remain immobile in situations in which directed differentiated movement is indicated or else respond with fast, directionless activity which serves only as a crude way of alleviating stress. They need from the therapist instances of well-timed responses that can use the same motoric modality, but in differentiated fashion—in pursuit of a focus—rather than for active but purposeless acts. The immediate result of the use of this modality of communication is that it makes available possibilities for further therapeutic interventions.

Communications to our families which are congruent with or attuned to the enactive modality seem to make accessible avenues of direct communication that were previously unavailable. When, for example, instead of asking a family member, "How come your mother doesn't talk with you?" the therapist challenges, "Could you make your mother talk to you?" the family members seem to become generally more capable of exploring interpersonal conflicts in this area. Stimulation toward the actual "enactment" of problems, let us note, does not preclude the over-all goal of assisting family members to curb their tendency to constant action. It simply implies that the participants are moved *gradually* rather than *abruptly* toward more representational and symbolic levels.

Enactive formulations on the part of the therapist are especially relevant during the initial periods of therapy. They actualize the working grounds around which to intervene usefully. For example, in one family[2] composed of Mrs. Wilson, her mother, and three children, the therapist's interpretations were directed toward pointing out the grandmother's domination of the mother. Interpretations to the grandmother in terms of her domination and to the mother in terms of her passivity and acceptance of the grandmother's control were experienced by them as criticism of their ways; both responded with resistance. Another interpretation, which remained closer to the observed phenomena, was successfully tried later on. The grandmother was asked to observe the interaction between her daughter and her grandson behind the one-way mirror. She reacted to her daughter's passivity toward her grandson's disruptive behavior (loud banging on chairs) with, "I would have stopped him right there." Two minutes later, her daughter did stop the boy in a calm, nonaggressive fashion by questioning him about his day at school. The therapist stated descriptively to the grandmother, "You are always two minutes ahead of your daughter."

This temporal emphasis captured the specific way in which the grandmother was dominating her daughter. "Domination," as an interpretation, required from the family members skills in inference and introspection which differed from those involved in responding to "two minutes ahead." The latter reflected the manifestations of the problem almost as observed; the level of abstraction required here was closer to the actual occurrence, involving mostly an "iconic" exertion, perhaps a remembering of what was seen (see footnote 1, page 246).

In general, we have found that interpretations which employ an almost physical or "territorial" language and which are grounded on more primitive cognitive and communicational systems seem to be more in harmony with the way in which our families communicate among themselves and, therefore, more likely to be effective.

The above considerations are applicable to all therapeutic interventions with these families. We employ this communicational orientation when we introduce structured tasks, changes in family subgroups, and one-way mirrors in our attempts to deal with specific indications of problems rather than their symbolic representation. Although these maneuvers might be interpreted as merely supportive, noninsight interventions, we

---

[2] Not a research family.

contend that they help to induce changes in the families' communicative modality which are precursors to other types of change because they use such moments of contact *within* the family's patterns of communication to induce moments of manageable distance from which the evaluation and correction of these communicational patterns can be attempted.

Beginning Phases of Therapy: Reducing "Noise," Focusing on Rules of Talking, Disengaging Content from Relationship Messages

The amount of disruption that characterizes the communication among family members requires that beginning phases of therapy be oriented toward diminishing "noise." We point out to the members of the family that because of verbal and paraverbal noise it is difficult to hear what people are telling each other and that in this atmosphere it seems as if the person who talks expects neither to be heard nor to receive a response if heard. Members of the family are required to single out the person to whom they are talking and demand that that person respond to them. The therapist frequently repeats what the members of the family have said or asks the other members if they have heard what the person said. He becomes a decoding center for communication. In this role, he protects the individual by centering his interpretation on the communication itself and on the rules that allow for coherent communication rather than on the person producing the communication.

In effect, we are saying that the early phases of therapy with this population focus on being a "primer" for talking. The therapist attempts to induct the family into a system of communication in which content and relationship messages are more clearly discriminated from each other. He becomes not only a guider but also a controller: he stops interruptions that cut across a family member's communication; he points out the need to wait till the other member closes his statement before he can be answered; and he indicates that the answer must be relevant to the previous theme. He focuses the dialogue on a single theme and helps the family members carry this theme to some kind of completion.

The difficulties for the therapist in the foregoing role should be obvious. He wants to derive a picture of the family communication process, but at the same time he attempts to intervene in ways that would modify it in the direction of a system of communication that allows for interpersonal negotiations. Our family members usually interact with each other in a context of jumbled messages, with resultant difficulties in understanding one another. If at this stage the therapist is unsuccessful in making his operations rewarding, he will soon be trapped into accepting the family's system of communication and into attempting to do therapy within a field of noise. He will find himself having to talk across and around other people who are talking. He will, in a sense, be rewarding a basic feature of the family system which accounts for its striking inability to resolve interpersonal problems.

Another pitfall in this phase of therapy is the therapist's unwitting tendency to communicate only with those members of the family more likely to use the logical language he uses. The result is that the most disruptive children, or the ones who use verbal messages only when they want to establish their presence, disappear from the field of verbal interchange. They are soon left only with the recourse of making personal impact through disruptive interaction.

Summing up, then, initial phases of therapy center on focusing the family's attention on the rhythm and rules of communication, on establishing a minimum of structure for communication traffic which makes the reception of signals possible, and on rewarding the use of verbal modalities for problem-solving.[3] The therapist is concerned with showing the family members how they can question each other in such a way as to elicit information instead of just establishing contact. Since family members are so concerned with sheer interrelationship, with proximity to each other, the *content* of many messages remains obscure. The therapist points out the discrepancies between relationship and content messages and how the former can completely override the latter. For the family members this introduces a shift of focus—a modification of the automatic response to relationship aspects of messages with a corresponding deployment of attention to content aspects. The problem in our families lies not in the contradictions between the two levels of a communication as much as in their lack of acknowledgment and recognition of the content aspects of messages.

Family members must be shown that frequently there are at least two levels, simultaneously expressed, in a given message and that it is perfectly reasonable to respond to one level or the other; they need to be aware of the level to which they are addressing themselves, however, so

---

[3] Note that with the La Salle family (see Chapter 4), the therapists were concerned with these considerations throughout the therapy sessions, with some degree of success.

that possibilities of real communication can exist. As a matter of fact, an indication of incipient change in our families is when a member can actually differentiate these two types of communication. Members of the family need not become sophisticated analysts of their own communications, but they should be able to eventually produce some statements which reflect upon their communicational methods. An example of a simple statement which displays growing observational awareness is that of Phyllis Montgomery to her mother, which says, in effect, "I cannot hear you because you always holler at me, so I stop listening" (see Chapter 3).

Enlarging the Focal Theme

Besides guiding the family members into an acceptance of rules for communication traffic and for separation of content from relationship aspects of messages, the therapist's efforts to change communication processes also hinge on providing the family members with new and more differentiated labels for framing their experiences. The evaluational labeling that a family member employs in a particular situation can sometimes be modified in ways that help exploration around new dimensions. For example, a mother discussed her child's failure to do homework in terms of, "This no good so-and-so; I told him yesterday that he would have to do his homework at four o'clock." The therapist selected from the mother's statement content which might be useful for both child and the mother. For the child, he stressed that aspect of the mother's communication which showed her "concern" with his improving in school; for the mother, he reinforced the fact that she was showing positive "interest" in her child's competence in the school situation.

This kind of feedback, which is centered on positives, can be given in the context of many situations. The same child later said, "I conned the teacher about getting back into school. He kicked me out, but I got back." The therapist again selectively focused on those aspects of the child's communication which reflected successful coping attempts—the return to school after being "kicked out." He accepted the label "con," but helped the child to realize that this instance of "conning" was, in actuality, competent convincing of the teacher and competent coping with the world.

These interventions, which depend on retaining an old label which has become embedded in the communicational system of the participants but adding a new way to perceive it, tend to increase the coping capacities of our family members. New word nuances become incorporated into the communication system, helping to induce a different perception of certain interactions. This therapeutic technique provides other contexts for words that previously only had one. In a field of cognitive and affective impoverishment, it allows for an expansion of the understanding of reality and a search for more effective coping devices.

Finally, communication in most of our families usually relates to a few important central issues only. One could even try to develop a typology of families in terms of the issues around which most of the communications revolve. In the Montgomery family, for instance, we could say that the area of stealing has a shared, overriding significance. Multiple, seemingly unrelated events in the family are organized through the affective meaning of "stealing." Circumstances which to an outsider are not necessarily related to stealing become overencompassed or contaminated by the prevalence of stealing as an interpretative theme. From the standpoint of the participants, the stealing by one child from another becomes fluidly associated with the stealing from a third child by a fourth one, all of them from their mother, and their mother from their father. Because of the insistent chronicity of these operations, even neutral messages are decoded within a "stealing" framework.

In this family, consequently, central themes are blaming and nonblaming. These issues, intimately related to the nuclear issue of stealing, often seem to regulate even the most fundamental affective thresholds, for instance, the lowering or raising of self-esteem in all family members. To be a good mother is to be a mother who "doesn't blame anyone"; to be a bad mother is to dare to "blame." Blaming and nonblaming act, in effect, as powerful frames of reference through which the participants interpret many inner and outer experiences.

The therapist's interpretations in therapy sessions with this family centered on conveying to Mrs. Montgomery her need to be self-assertive; these were decoded as, "You blame me because I am incompetent." It would have been more helpful, perhaps, if the therapist had relabeled some of her blame operations toward the children as "concern" for their well-being and as evidence of competence in her role as a mother. Similarly (see Chapter 3), when Mrs. Montgomery and the therapist were in collusion to avoid blaming the child, it would have been more appropriate to relabel her attitude as an indication that although she was trying to be a "good" mother, "this doesn't work." Even though this might have been interpreted by Mrs. Montgomery as still another instance of being blamed by the therapist, consistent relabeling would have undoubtedly enlarged the theme.

In work with these families, then, the therapist has to learn how to open, reformulate, and enlarge narrow sets of overinclusive categories into more differentiated realities. Such operations, which are taken somewhat for granted in most therapies, are essential when working with populations characterized by cognitive-affective scarcity.

Operations concerned with the relabeling of specific affects or transactions (see previous example of child saying, "I conned the teacher") are qualitatively different from those concerned with relabeling in the context of nuclear themes. The latter have a generative impact in that they revolve around core dynamics, thus allowing for repercussive changes in many areas of family life.[4]

With the Smith family, in which the mother defined herself as a "controlling" mother while the children "rebelled" against her control, the therapists rephrased the issue to, "Look how the children's inability for self-control is making you overburdened and helpless. Let's try to help the children increase their self-control." The mother was relabeled as overburdened instead of controlling; the children were relabeled as lacking in self-control instead of overly rebellious. For the mother, this was an ego-enlarging experience. Her initial expectations of the therapist had been in terms of the family's general thematic framework ("In order to gain some acceptance from him, I must control my children"). The relabeling of these phenomena allowed her to relate the therapists to her most submerged and unarticulated wishes—to get help from her children in assuming control. Positive expectations of the therapists followed, and with them a quickened pace of interpersonal learning.

Therapeutic operations in the family involve, then, the transformation of old themes and the introduction of new themes around which transactions and negotiations can occur among family members. This can be done sometimes by just calling attention to issues that are considered nonsignificant and unfocused in the usual family transactions.

---

[4] One could stress that the importance of similar operations resides in the fact that they reorganize the transactional field in ways which retain therapeutic leverage and "one-upness" for the therapist (see Haley, 1963). Our emphasis, however, is on the way these operations facilitate family growth, on their generative effects within the intrafamilial field.

Interventions That Challenge Structure

The Use of "Stages"; the Emergence of Multiple Roles

Various personality organizations become salient and more differentiated when members of the family have the opportunity to function in different roles. With our research families, the strategy of the three stages allowed the therapist to interact with family members in a number of different "real life" situations. This strategy also allowed the family members to experience and to discriminate a number of characteristic differences among the roles within the family and to pay attention to the fact that there are generational axes with differences in roles and functions.

We have seen in the Garcia family (see Chapter 3) that the strategy of the therapist when he was seeing the spouses alone was one of structuring the situation to determine the nature of their interaction in the husband-wife roles; he made it clear that in this stage, "You are spouses and not parents." In the first and third stages, and only there, their role as *parents* was considered. The significance of this therapeutic strategy was the opportunity for the evolvement of husband and wife roles which had heretofore been hidden behind parental roles.

We have also seen in the La Salle family (see Chapter 4) that sibling operations when the children were alone were different from what they were when the children were with their mother. In sequence 16, when Mrs. La Salle left the room, George and Tim tried to organize the sibling interaction as though their mother were present by reintroducing control with attempts either to make the therapist a controller or to provoke the siblings into controlling roles. When this failed, George slapped himself in order to introduce control, as if from an external force (sequence 17). This session, without the mother's controlling presence, eventually allowed the appearance of a certain type of "rational" leadership in Meredith, who was completely subordinated when the mother was available.

The possibility of performance within certain roles by family members, then, seems incumbent on certain structural arrangements or rearrangements of the family. When we group the spouses alone and artificially block communication between them as parents, we are working toward the ultimate goal of having them operate as spouses within the context of the total family. The same thing, of course, is true for the siblings. The appearance of leadership in one of the children in the sibling substage should later contribute to the development of autonomy and independence from the mother in that child. This became evident in the La Salle family, when Meredith was able to challenge the irrational authority which his mother employed in the name of "therapy."

The therapist, thus, helps to mediate the transfer of behavior that was possible under one configuration into another configuration. His goal is to help the family members function within the context of the total family in multiple roles. He supports various features of personality organization that sometimes exist but are not clearly focused, and he helps to frame interactions in such a way that new roles will be experienced and performed by family members.

Alliances and splits may or may not shift according to the nature of the participants and the nature of the issue they are using as a transactional center. Alliances among siblings that appear when the total family is participating can remain the same or shift when they meet in the second stage as siblings. For example, a child scapegoated in the first stage when the parents are present can function in the same role in the second stage; or another sibling can take this role; or scapegoating can disappear altogether in the sibling subgroup. We believe that a family system in which a child is scapegoated when the total family is together as well as when he is alone with his siblings is a particularly rigid one and that its rigidity will be reflected in the child's internalization of a consistently pathological self-image.

The influence of the family structure on the therapist's behavior can be seen in his behavioral change when the first and second stages are compared. For example, with the La Salles the therapist's participation in the sibling stage seemed to be in the role of a benevolent older sibling, but he was an adult in the first and third stages. As a matter of fact, when Mrs. La Salle was present, he assumed controlling ways of interacting rather similar to hers. The therapist's supportive behavior with regard to the children was displayed only when Mrs. La Salle was not present.

Not only do the children, then, produce certain behaviors only within specific contexts, fragmenting their experiences in such a way that they are unable to carry over behavior which was appropriate in the sibling interaction to their dealings with adults, but the therapist, too, can become trapped by the phenomena occurring in a family, behaving in roles which do not cut across from one family subsystem to another. The rigidity of the family system is so great that it frequently robs the therapist of the freedom to operate along dimensions which are different from those the family uses. To the degree that the therapist rigidly adheres to context-specific responses and is unable to transfer his behavioral roles from one therapy stage to another, he will reinforce segmented perceptions of the world in the family members.

Challenging the Pathways

The family coming for therapy has its own view of the problems that affect it and the ways in which it needs to be helped. The members demand that the therapist produce change without upsetting the old, familiar ways of transacting; that is, he must change them within their usual pathways of dealing with each other. The family members say, in essence, "Change should conform to the direction and organization we are already in." The family thus structures the pathways of possible change in ways that make change impossible to occur. They demand, in effect, that the therapist not challenge their ways of interacting but follow the habitual channels of transaction. The therapist is often pulled into these transactional pathways. Although he may be sending interpretations that are correct in content, he may be responding unwittingly to the structural demands of the family by addressing himself to the family members in such a way as to fortify and crystallize the ongoing structural arrangement.

The therapist can challenge the family structure by concretely modifying the direction of transactional pathways: he can turn to or address the silent member; he can actively interrupt pathways, telling the wife to stop "taking over"; or he can initiate dialogue from father to son in order to circumvent a regularized father-to-mother-to-son interaction. For instance, in the Garcia family, in which the problem was presented as one of conflict between the oldest boy and the father, the family demanded that the therapist follow the lines of "helping the mother to help the father in his interaction with the son." In this family it was therapeutically indicated to *shrink* the mother's function, yet the family's demand was that change should go through the mother. The Oedipal situation in this family can be expressed, then, in pathways terms. For instance, Felipe could approach or contact his mother only when his father was absent. If Mr. Garcia approached Felipe individually, Mrs. Garcia would intercept the beginnings of a relationship before it could develop into cooperation. Whenever Mr. Garcia was aggressive toward Mrs. Garcia,

Felipe was allowed to be present. Whenever Mrs. Garcia was aggressive toward Felipe, the father could be present. All these different configurations reflected one core dynamic—the difficulty of having positive access to one parent if the other parent was available. A triadic configuration was possible only in an aggressive modality. As a result, Felipe had no access to a variety of positive, interactional configurations which were indispensable to his growth.

In this family neither the husband nor the wife suggested that the change should be one of increasing the possibility of effective communication between the father and son. The members were requesting that the profile of the pathways should remain intact, but that family effectiveness should increase. The therapist challenged the possibility of change through this particular set of operations. He felt that an increase in Mrs. Garcia's effectiveness would only increase the gap between the father and son, depriving the son of a model for male identification. The therapist's task became one of decreasing Mrs. Garcia's centrality as a pathway of communication among the family members, increasing her communication with her husband as *husband*, and demanding that Mr. Garcia should become more available for communication with his son.

The therapist's challenges to the familiar pathways of transaction in the Garcia family increased family resistance. Contact between father and son had always been through a language of aggression: father demanding immediate obedience; son responding with rebelliousness. The possibility of communication in a language that could include mutual exploratory themes or themes of respect and affection was resisted by both father and son as well as by the mother, who felt that if father and son developed a language of cooperative communication, she would become isolated and abandoned. So we see that any attempt to challenge the pathways of transaction reactivates and makes available for therapeutic intervention the hidden dynamics of the family.

Another example comes from the Menotti family,[5] composed of eleven-year-old twins (a boy and a girl) and Mr. and Mrs. Menotti. The son, who was having school difficulties, was clearly being scapegoated in this family. Throughout the interview, the therapist saw that whenever Mrs. Menotti challenged her husband for his lack of competence or effectiveness in his job, he immediately directed his attention to the boy, "correcting" his disruptive behavior and thereby reinstating his competence,

---

[5] Not a research family.

at least in his relationship with his son. The same process prevailed when Mr. Menotti challenged his wife for her ineffectiveness as a housewife. She would then immediately begin to talk about the child's truancy and misbehavior in school. The therapist focused on this pattern of transaction, closing the pathways of interaction between father and son and prohibiting the mother from talking about the child in situations of interspouse stress. These maneuvers increased the tension between the spouses in the therapy sessions and actualized their aggressive interaction, which had been hidden and unavailable for therapeutic intervention.

One might wish to explain the child's acting-out as a result of the projection of parental intrapsychic problems and their actualization through the child's behavior;[6] nonetheless, the resolution of the problem as we see it is not achieved by helping the parents to contain and resolve the problem within their own intrapsychic spheres but rather by actualizing the family problem in the appropriate interpersonal sphere—the husband-and-wife sphere.

When the therapist prevents the child from being used as an avenue of projection, the inappropriate channel of discharge is made unavailable, and the interspouse sense of dissatisfaction becomes manifest. In traditional therapies, interpretation of the particular projective mechanism is employed by indicating the scapegoating function of the child in the family. What the therapist does when he challenges the transactional pathways, however, is to create a new experience, the *interpretation* eventually becoming available through the process of blocking or curtailing the habitual pathways of interaction. This approach is derived from the notion that the problem of the child is a result of certain ongoing organizational pathway arrangements in the family and that the child, in collusion with the parents, maintains a predetermined role which serves to freeze the current homeostasis. Resolution is found, then, through pathway modifications.

As already noted, the compelling nature of family structure and its resistance to change can be seen in the way in which it organizes the therapist's behavior into unwittingly supporting the very arrangements he is out to change. A therapist will talk with the most verbal member of a family without recognizing that by doing so he is making this person central; or he may interpret the behavior of the weaker member of the

---

[6] Johnson (1947, 1959), Johnson and Szurek (1952).

family to a more central member and by eliciting the help of the stronger member render the weak weaker. The therapeutic problem, then, is how to enter into a family system in order to challenge it while avoiding, at the same time, the power of that system to induct the therapist into the patterns of interaction that maintain current homeostasis. An example will clarify the meaning of this.

In the Wilson family, previously discussed, a suicidal mother presents the family problem: "Yes, the problem is my helplessness." The line of therapy she implicitly demands is, "In order to change me, help my mother to support and sustain my helplessness." This family, at intake, was composed of a mother, a grandmother, and three children. The grandmother, assuming the executive role in the family, had immediately informed the therapist that her daughter had been ill and needed to be treated in a special way. Both intake therapists responded to this verbalization by indicating to the grandmother the pathological component in her control of her daughter as well as the fact that her concern restricted her daughter in her role as a mother to her acting-out children. Although the interpretations dealt with family pathology and family structure, both therapists directed their communications to the grandmother. The therapists had become inducted into a role similar to that of the grandmother. By attacking the family's pathology, they were presenting themselves as the "protectors" of the mother. By addressing themselves predominantly to the grandmother and not to the mother, they accepted and reinforced the grandmother's centrality and power and supported the mother's dependency on her.

The therapist generally has four choices with regard to his conduct toward existing pathways:

1. Obey the pathways, yet attempt to change the nature of the interaction channeled through them.

2. Disobey the pathways without explicitly pressing for or pointing to the possibility of different ones.

3. Disobey the pathways while explicitly requesting the use of new, counteracting pathways.

4. Eliminate the pathways.

The first choice is necessary when the possibility of new pathways is limited and the therapist's opportunities for intervention are scarce (for example, in a family with a "strong" mother, many small children, and a brain-injured, extremely limited father). The therapist may be confined to keeping the existing pathways intact while attempting to change the interactions channeled through them.

A mother complained that her three older children, aged six, seven, and eight, "are okay, real quiet at home, but act up like hell in school."[7] The therapist, observing her overpowering the children in the session, soon suspected that her rigid control of them prevented them from behaving independently at home. At school, where the mother's inhibitory control was missing, they were prone to recurrent explosions. He decided to help the mother change her behavior toward the children at home without challenging her style of mothering. To challenge her controlling functions, the therapist sensed, would imply an attack on the core of her identity—being a mother. The existing pathway was clear but limited. He could only go to the children through their mother's control.

The therapist decided on the following strategy. For several sessions he concentrated on the mother, praising her for her clear success with the children at home—"where you keep them behaving good all the time." After designating this area as one of unquestionable success, he moved toward discussing with her whether "we could find someone like you in school." Since they agreed this was impossible, could she use her good control to prepare her children for school? Yes, she could teach them to listen, to question, to express their ideas—always, of course, keeping "the good control you've got over them." Eventually, through trying to change them for school, she changed her own behavior at home. But the strategy was successful only insofar as she never experienced herself under any obligation to change her mothering at home; the experience was mainly that of being guided to "do more of a good thing."

For the second choice, through simple, nonverbal, nonthematic maneuvers the therapist can disobey pathways without pressing openly for the use of new ones. For example, in a family with an able but submerged, peripheral man and an overcentralized woman who constantly displaces her husband in his attempts to engage the children, the therapist can deliberately distribute his concern toward the neglected side, the man, rather than the expected side, the mother. She will constantly try to recruit his attention and responses, but the therapist disobeys; he looks and talks more to the man, activating paternal contact with the children. Just this nonverbal conduct on the part of the therapist may be sufficient

---

[7] Not a research family.

to reopen tensions in a conflict presumably already closed—the female ascendance-male submission balance that is robbing the children of their father.

The therapist must often choose the third way, going beyond non-verbal and distributional maneuvers in order to disobey the roles that have been complementarily assigned to him to maintain the family system intact. He can forcefully attempt reversals in the usual pathway directions. For example, when he frontally silences the wife and guides the husband, urging him to take on such unfamiliar functions as talking with the children, he upsets the family equilibrium to a higher degree.

Finally, when the tenacity of a system is such that the family quickly reorganizes itself along its usual pathways, the therapist cannot modify the process with all the participants present. He must short-circuit the pathways by using strategic removals. The wife can simply be removed to the observation room until the husband has developed enough of a relationship with the children and the therapist to cope more effectively with his wife when she is reintegrated to the group.

Interpersonal Tasks

The need to assist family members to become aware of the rigidity and automaticity of their pathways eventually compelled us to search for interventions that would highlight pathway issues as the core problem in need of modification. The possibility of challenging pathway phenomena gradually yielded a technique of *task-oriented family therapy*, which directs family members to participate in familiar tasks under conditions that are different from, and sometimes the opposite of, their usual familiar patterns of interaction.

The procedure we developed is as follows. The therapist first meets with the total family. During this initial period, he observes the free development of interaction among family members, deriving from this a diagnostic picture of transactional patterns. He then makes explicit the unstated forces governing the transactions. He selects one area of conflict between some members of the family and addresses himself to these members, indicating the nature of the conflict and their usual pattern in dealing with it. He points also to the pain-producing characteristics of this pattern and its unsatisfactory consequences. The therapist then instructs the family members involved to continue dealing with this conflict, but now he suggests that the interaction should occur within a different emotional context. For example, if the family members are involved in competitive interaction, he suggests cooperation. He may also suggest different "directions of response." If the sons usually go to the father through the mother, for example, he suggests that they go to the mother through the father, or go to the father directly.

The therapist then asks the other members of the family to join him behind a one-way mirror from where they can act as observers of the family subgroup transaction. The members of the family involved in the conflict remain alone in the original room while the therapist directs and assists the rest of the family in their observations so that they become more discriminating in their perception of a familiar transaction. Usually, the participant (task-assigned) family members begin, at some point, to relate according to their former patterns in opposition to the instructions of the therapist. The therapist may then instruct one of the observing family members to enter the room in order to attempt to redirect the situation toward the growth-encouraging pattern of interaction that had previously been discussed.

If this new transaction follows the usual pattern, the therapist allows the process to develop, but then he may send still another family member back into the room or enter himself to help the family members consolidate their understanding of what has happened. He points out the ways in which the process has developed and how the members' usual patterns of transaction inhibit the development of new patterns of interaction that can bring more satisfaction to the members. In this way, in a session lasting one hour, the exploration of one area of conflict may involve four or five different subgroupings within the family, the various members alternating (but not in a fixed pattern) between the roles of participant and observer. By arranging group composition according to clinical needs, any one of a variety of subgroupings and/or interpersonal tasks can be introduced in order to determine and expand the boundaries of the family's structure and function. The compositional arrangements and task-demands strain and test the limits of undifferentiated and/or stereotyped interpersonal patterns. The emerging interchanges expose the degree of flexibility and resiliency of the roles of family members when they are dealing with conflicts as well as the processes through which "new" behavioral patterns dissolve and reorganize into the old, familiar ways.

Tasks can be introduced to tap data on three levels:

1. *Natural units*: Tasks can be given to the subgroups which are formed as a result of inherent structural family characteristics—male and female,

parent and child. In this case, the therapist arranges subgroup composition by dividing the family along sex or generational lines.

2. *Idiosyncratic units*: These units are specific and distinctive for each family. They are groupings which reflect adaptive or maladaptive alliances and splits among family members. They are recognized only through a detailed knowledge of ongoing intrafamilial dynamics. In this case, the therapist may divide the family according to their own spontaneously formed groups. Or he may alter their composition, selecting subgroup membership in such a way as to arrange artificial units which challenge the underlying alliances and splits. For example, if A, B, and C are family members in a particularly hostile coalition toward D, E, and F, then units of C, D, and F, and A, B, and E may be organized for task performance.

3. *Disabling generic characteristics*: These are general features, usually of communication and affect, which the family shares to a lesser or greater degree with its particular subculture, for example, difficulties in focusing, listening to each other, engaging in dialogues which really exchange information, sharing in sustained cooperative problem-solving, delayed affective discharge, exploring positives in each other, etc. In this case, the therapist observes the interactions of members in "natural," "idiosyncratic," or "artificial" units under task conditions that may help determine the extent to which these generic features curtail the effective resolution of interpersonal problems.

As an example of this process, let us consider a family[8] composed of a man whose derogatory self-image and feelings of isolation are expressed in an autocratic, critical relationship with his spouse and children; a woman whose dependency and helplessness are reflected in an explicit acceptance of her husband's dominance and an implicit coalition with her older son, encouraging him in a continuous rebellion against his father; and their two sons, aged fourteen and twelve, who, caught between their mother's overprotectiveness and their father's consistently negative perception of them, project their confused identity into the home arena as well as school through blind attacks on their "pursuers."

During one session with this family, the therapist pointed out to the father that his attack on the older son was accompanied by an explicit statement that he was trying to help his son as well as by a less audible and more jumbled message which indicated his pain about his own helplessness. The therapist indicated to the fourteen-year-old son that al-

---

[8] Not a research family.

though he seemed to want parental acceptance, he did not trust that it would be forthcoming, so he was continuously engaged in provoking his father and rendering him helpless, thus intensifying his father's negative and critical response toward him, since that was his father's only way of remaining a worthwhile adult. The therapist then directed the father and son to continue dealing with the specific conflict, but gave them instructions as to the ways in which the interaction should occur. He suggested that the father find positive areas in his son that he could highlight, and that the son talk in such a way as to elicit his father's support.

In the observation room, the therapist, the wife, and the younger son observed how the father and older son, after a feeble attempt to become engaged along the lines suggested by the therapist, again became involved in a power operation. The mother expressed her impatience with her husband's "preaching" and his rigid behavior, while the younger son pointed out that the father wanted to teach his brother something worthwhile. The wife expressed her feeling of wanting to be in the other room to stop the onslaught, her pathway being, of course, to help the son by stopping the father. The therapist then pointed out to the wife how she and her husband were fighting through their son, leaving the father and son isolated from each other and robbing them of any chance to develop a mutually satisfactory relationship. He further noted that her tendency was to empathize with the attacked child, label her husband the aggressor, and intervene in such a way that she and her husband soon became involved in a heated argument which "freed," and at the same time isolated, the son. The therapist suggested to the wife that she should now go into the other room and try to help the husband support the son.[9] His suggestion clearly challenged the automatic pathway of mother-to-son-to-father, calling into play the heretofore nonexistent cooperative pathway of wife-to-husband-to-son.

Some minutes later, the husband and wife were blaming each other, and the son had again become isolated. After this process developed, the therapist intervened and helped the family members re-examine their interactional patterns. In the next session, under similar conditions, the wife left the room, saying that since she could not remain without intervening

---

[9] This description of an active interventive technique creates the impression of a controlling therapist dictating the movements of the patients as though they were puppets. In the actual setting, however, there is the same emotional commitment and human contact between the family members and the therapist that characterize other forms of therapy.

between father and son, at least she could remove herself and go to the observation room, where she would be unable to interfere.

The therapist's work in a task session entails the following:

1. Diagnosing family structure in relation to the salient conflicts and recurrent interactions that impede the observational and problem-solving capacities of the participants.

2. Assigning participant roles to the family members who are centrally involved in the conflict and removing other family members from the situation.

3. Instructing the participant members in new and unfamiliar ways of dealing with the conflict.

4. Actively guiding the removed members into the observer's role.

5. Identifying the kinds and forms of interpersonal and intrapersonal obstacles that emerge as the new problem-solving participation is attempted, and making inferences as to the defensive systems, both inter- and intrapersonal, which block new growth.

6. Helping family members to progressively integrate their observing roles with roles involving their active participation in the conflictual interaction.

What is the rationale for this type of therapeutic intervention? To become aware of one's manner of functioning, one must observe one's own actions. The ability to introspect (reflexive observation) is developed in the child through his incorporation of vigilant parental control and his need to tell the parenting figures what happens to him. This subjective process of observing one's self and what one is doing creates, in effect, a paradox: to become an observer, one must stop participating; yet while one is participating, one cannot observe one's own participation because of the process of commitment. This paradox generates a problem for effective psychotherapy. Existential therapists try to help the patient *experience* without concerning himself with observing the new experience; other therapists generally try to bring about an intellectually integrated interpretation while at the same time maximizing the affective experience of the process. Ackerman (1961) has experimented with showing family members films of their own sessions. Other workers have family members listen to tape recordings of their sessions. All such therapeutic devices attempt to maximize an individual's ability to observe without limiting his ability to participate.

Our use of tasks also capitalizes on this principle and, in addition, provides an artificial barrier against the strong habitual reactions of our patients. Although the one-way mirror maintains the emotional impact of direct interpersonal experience, it contains and controls impulsive discharge. The latter, it might be noted, is the most serious problem with our acting-out families. Moreover, our family members are unskilled in introspection—in observing and evaluating their own actions—and require a therapeutic approach that centers on ways of making this process more available to them.

The questions, then, are these: How can we help the family member observe his own actions without at the same time blocking his participation or devitalizing his experience? How can we introduce introspection at the moment of interaction? The answers to these questions may best be provided by considering first, what happens to the observing members of the family, then, what happens to the participating members, and finally, the role of the therapist.

Observer

The observer is able to look at the family conflict while he has no responsibility to participate, yet he is still very much caught in the interaction. The one-way mirror acts as a semiporous membrane. He is, as it were, still sitting in the other room in the empty chair, but he is simultaneously aware that his role has changed. Although he cannot influence what is happening to the participating members, he continues to be impinged upon by their behavior. His impulse to react with *action*, which is characteristic of our family members, can be said to bounce against the mirror; thus, it is delayed, and with the help of the therapist is channeled into verbal forms. The therapist, sitting near the family member, now engages him in a completely new function: he is invited to join the therapist in the observation of the participating members' interaction. His role has changed from that of participant to that of observer, although he continues to feel involved in the interaction. With this change in role, there is a change in his relationship to the therapist, with whom he has become, in a sense, a peer in the observation.

The shift from participant to observer is certainly not easily achieved. Parents and children of multi-problem families frequently respond to cognitive-affective stress by defensive maneuvers of fast engagement. Interpersonal, crude proximity is a characteristic way of escaping from conflict. A child caught stealing, for example, refuses exploration in this area by attacking his sibling for "not minding his own business"; a mother's awareness of her helplessness is usually blocked by her multiple and erratic control maneuvers. Some mothers, when asked to observe the therapy of their children for a number of sessions, respond with increased anxiety in the observation room. The level of noise, the inability of the children to keep to the subject, the power operations that characterize their daily behavior—all have a powerful impact on the mothers *as if they were perceiving them for the first time.* "It's too emotional to observe," said Mrs. Smith, who had spent two years in conventional family therapy.

To counter the use of fast engagement as a defensive maneuver that blocks differentiated perception of family interaction, we have made it part of our procedure that the parents, at some point in therapy, remain in the observation room with a therapist for a number of sessions.[10] This eventually entails a shifting of observational sets for the parent, for their usual mode of response involves little or no "hesitation," is frequently a controlling one with respect to the children, and reflects an overfocus on the children's negative behavior. When we put a mother, say, behind the one-way mirror, we initially attempt to orient her observations away from her offspring (whom she immediately latches onto) by shifting her attention onto the behavior of the therapist in the room. We consider this to be a significant intermediate experience which permits certain changes in affective-cognitive thresholds. Such changes are essential before the observer can attend to learning to identify the behaviors of the children that are blocked by her presence or to tackle the question of changing her unrewarding patterns of relating to them.

Thus, the co-therapist working with the mother in the observation room initially orients her to focus on co-therapist operations. We have also found that the mother experiences a certain kinship with the *children's* therapist because "he becomes like me." The sense of "equality" with the adult in the room occurs almost inevitably, for at times the therapists also fall prey to the children's system—a result of the children's capacity to organize adults into either authoritarian or helpless positions. The experience behind the one-way mirror thus increases her self-esteem. There is a sufficient drop in the level of her anxiety and tension so that she can begin to focus her attention on events among her children which express interactions other than anger, power-conflicts, rebelliousness, etc. She is helped in this process by the co-therapist sitting next to her, who by design treats her more as a peer, or co-observer, than a "patient."

---

[10] This maneuver is essential in the "enmeshed" family (see final chapter).

At the same time the mother is learning the value of breaking up the family group, of deliberately manipulating group composition. Now she may be able to do this herself instead of always trying to deal with the whole group and being swamped by the sheer amount of noise and demands on her.

Finally, we might note that when members of the family respond along growth-encouraging lines, it is important that the therapist reward or support these changes. However, the observing family members also reward the participants, and their reward is more significant for the crystallization of the change than is the therapist's support. When a change occurs, and the family members solve a conflict in a new and different way, the reward lies in the actual resolution of the conflict, the mastering of the new pattern of interaction (although it may be temporary), and the emotional support of the family as a group.

Participants

In considering what happens to the participating members, it is well to remember that many transactions among the family members have become routinized and automatic. For example, a wife's request for help from her husband may characteristically elicit a response of resentful help. Perceiving this as control, she responds with refusal to accept help. This, in turn, produces in her husband a sense of helplessness about contacting her, which is followed by controlling anger. Such behavior can occur repeatedly in an automatically triggered response sequence. The verbal interchange seems altogether unrelated to what is being transacted nonverbally. Though help is asked for and offered, the tension lies in the pitch of the voice, the posture of the body, the muscles of the face. This transaction becomes automatic, and the participants find themselves in their usual conflicting positions, unaware of how they got there. When we suggest in the task situation that the wife ask for help in a direct form and that the husband respond to her request without his usual controlling attitude, we are demanding, in effect, that they participate in new roles. We are demanding participation in a new way of acting that minimizes the possibility of automatic responses and increases their awareness and sense of participation.

The couple's task assignment is being conducted in a situation of induced stress because the participants are aware that the rest of the family is observing them. The consciousness of being observed is an intermediate step in the process of introspection. *The participant observes in himself what he assumes the unseen observer is focusing on.* This sense of being observed indirectly brings the observer's role to the participating members as well.

When participants are unable to operate along the lines of the task assignment, we have found that they experience a heightened awareness of the disabling nature of their usual patterns of interaction: certain patterns that have been ego-syntonic are now seen as ego-dystonic. For example, in one family the children were assigned the tasks of "talking to each other, one at a time, and looking for positives in each other, without 'ranking.' " After the initial increase in noise that always accompanies this task, some of the siblings took the lead in organizing the assigned interaction; when there was disruptive behavior or when a sibling was derogatorily labeled (and this was very frequent), some of the children attempted to reinstate the task by pointing to the mirror and stating that they should do better because their mother and the therapist were observing them.

We have thus established distance from an automatic process by increasing the awareness of the process itself. When we work with the multi-problem family, we introduce a virtually unused psychological function: the observer becomes, as it were, internalized, and the process of reflection and introspection is fostered.

The Role of the Therapist

Devising the strategies of task assignment in what we have now come to call *conflict-resolution family therapy* requires a clear understanding of individual dynamics and how these are manifested in family transactions as well as in the family's patterns of communication. These strategies must be flexible and continuously sensitive to the changes the family is undergoing. At this point, it should be emphasized that when we ask for an interaction in an unfamiliar way we are not attempting to break a habit by the simple formula of creating another; we are hoping to induce a vivid awareness of hidden patterns and underlying motivations while at the same time providing an opportunity for experiencing new ways of attacking a problem.

There are many ways to describe the unusual role of the therapist in this technique. In some respects, his role is more central than in traditional family therapy; in other respects, he is less central. At times he is like the director of a play, suggesting that the family members try to comply, pressuring them into seeking new methods of interacting, and demanding that they fulfill his expectations. He also plays a traditional role, interpreting underlying dynamics and teaching the family a new experiential language. In the observation room, he gives direction to the perceptions and observations of the observing members; he also acts as the connecting link when a new member comes to the observation room, informing him as to what has been going on. At the same time, because the family members themselves are participants as well as observers, and even in a sense "therapists" (when they attempt to help family members correct their faulty transactions), the therapist's role is partially decentralized. When the therapist is in the observation room, the participating family members are alone in the other room tackling the conflicting transactions by themselves; they are actually trying out new ways of mutual interaction without the help of the therapist.[11]

Operationally, this process hinges largely on the therapist's attitudinal equipment and his ability to convey the notion that areas of conflict are being intensified—not arbitrarily, but as a springboard for developing exploratory and cooperative interaction in these same areas. The search is clearly for cooperative outcomes in areas in which participants usually emerge only as antagonists; the bias is for reallocating positive resources in the family system. For example, to suggest to a wife that she should now go into the other room and try to help her husband support their son is to call upon the "cooperative" capacity by which she enters into collusion with her son against his father as a resource for collaboration with her husband. This affirmative, exploratory bias is consistent with our general search for ego-enhancing material in our population, and it helps change perspective toward the experiential material which emerges during a task assignment: feelings and behaviors can be analyzed not only as "expressions of conflict" but also as "obstacles to cooperation."

One final word of caution: conflict-resolution family therapy in the hands of an inexperienced therapist can lend itself to an authoritarian display of power and an artificial manipulation of people. The only road to the development of meaningful tasks is deep understanding of family dynamics. Whatever the nature of an interpersonal task, it must be well timed and fashioned out of sound preliminary clinical hunches. The new

---

[11] We might note that at this point the significance of power maneuvers between family members and the therapist is diminished, permitting many family members a desirable concentration on learning from each other.

experience must be carefully chosen for the level of incongruity which it presents to all family members—to those who are directly called upon to attempt a restructuring of relationship as well as to those who are positioned in more peripheral roles.

The significance of conflict-resolution family therapy for the low socioeconomic population lies in the following:

1. It presents usual interactions framed as interpersonal problems and suggests that these problems have concrete solutions in the interpersonal realm.

2. The tasks are clearly structured, deal with familiar situations, are focused on the here-and-now, and compel family members to search for solutions through interaction among themselves.

3. When working with large families, the division of the family into subgroups—participants and observers—facilitates the definition and differentiation of the kinds of transactions extant in the family; these are usually hidden in the erratic and multiple stimulation of the larger group. Having the nonparticipating members observe the interaction keeps the total family involved, however.

4. Observation through the one-way mirror emphasizes inspection rather than introspection, maintains the impact of the familiar impingement, delays or eliminates the discharge of the habitual response, and channels the impulse into verbal forms.

5. The use of subsystems seems to be characterized by qualities that correspond point for point with the family members' capacities for experience. Small subgroupings present interpersonal stimuli through a narrower interpersonal field; these stimuli are more manageable by our family members because of their limited skills in encompassing a larger field and in sustaining attention.

6. Smaller groups buffer, somewhat, the impulsive nature of the responses of individuals in them—namely, the lack of hesitation and reflection when the family members are impinged upon by multiple stimuli.

7. The use of variations in subgroup memberships enhances the possibility that discrete rather than diffuse affects will be the prevailing experience. Changes in the composition of subgroups are very noticeable interpersonal events (member inclusion or exclusion) which permit the emergence of distinct affective reactions. These group changes directly challenge the family members' global and undifferentiated observations

of self and others, providing an opportunity for developing more differentiated concepts of interpersonal causality.

8. The active manipulation of subgroup composition (the use of selective removals and inclusions) introduces new roles and exerts a direct pull on one of the most prominent mechanisms characterizing our family members—*externalization*. Their tenacious reliance on the behavior of others as a projective target and as a means for organizing their own behavior is powerfully tested. Members cannot anchor their attention on the surrounding cues on which they automatically rely; they are compelled to consider alternative responses toward the others who are actually present.

Developing Complex Structural Profiles: Social Networks

As a logical evolvement of our concern with significant subgroupings within the family, we began to explore the dynamic social surroundings of the family.

In working with families that lack specialization of function and differentiated positions around conflict, the therapist, together with the family, must explore its immediate surroundings, recruiting (and experimenting with) "significant others" who may support, maintain, or challenge certain crystallized ways of interaction among family members.

There are situations where natural and steady networks exist, particularly in the enmeshed-extended family. Here we often have, besides relatives, well-defined "significant others" who may be employed to counterbalance and pull the family toward change. In our experience this is especially common in our Puerto Rican families, where there is almost always at hand some significant extrafamilial sustainer or modifier of family behavior. In such extended groups, the therapist feels some of the cohesion and power of what has been called an "asset" of the "culture of poverty";[12] he can arrange varied and changing group compositions, making use of selected members of the surrounding social network and shaping different units for therapeutic intervention at different stages of family development. That is, among the surrounding "others" he selects with the family only those relevant to immediate or emerging therapeutic goals. For example, in working with an adolescent girl who is harassed by her mother, he may compose a subgroup of the girl's friends and

---

[12] See Chapter 2.

family. After work with this subgroup has facilitated the emergence of the mother's ability to respect her daughter's autonomy, he may create a different network, perhaps including some of the mother's friends, who can support the mother's gains. Other combinations may be possible later as the dynamic focus shifts.

In disengaged families (especially those who besides being internally handicapped live isolated from even a "culture of poverty"), experimentation of this sort is difficult, but it is imperative. The scarcity and superficiality of contacts, not only from family members to the outside but also from the outside to family members, leaves them stagnant and frozen in chronic isolation. To strengthen such a frail social fabric, peripheral persons must be sought out and linked into workable social networks which can surround and support the family.

The neighbor, the man at the grocery store, or the truant officer may converge on a family without constituting a change-producing configuration. To select well among a few "casual others" those who may eventually become "significant others," the therapist and family members must learn together how to value and examine a forgotten fleeting acquaintance or how to track a particular "someone" met through the geographic accident of the laundry, subway, or bar. Family members must be helped to move beyond exclusive reliance on the social worker, minister, guidance counselor, and other agency representatives who tend to remain "formal others." It is usually in the world of "informal others" that some relevant positions toward specific family problems develop and from which a small and transient but change-inducing community may emerge.

Mrs. La Salle, for instance, commented on one potential "significant other" when she discovered a woman who, like her, had a delinquent son. In other families the discovery may come through a remark about a "neighbor upstairs." Though initially presented only as a "nosy neighbor" and as "fussing about my way of handling the kids," under probing she may turn out to be the resource who occasionally or frequently babysits. If the family recruits her for just enough sessions, a "simulated system" of grandmother-mother-children may be constructed, allowing enough of a balance of forces to at least start the mobilization of change.

The dynamic idiosyncrasies of each family dictate how and when some members of "natural surrounding groups" may be constructively linked with the family into a new system. The new group, comprised of the family and the new aggregates, represents a much more complex social unit, with increased areas of specialization, compared to the family unit; this makes it possible for the therapist, as part of the group, to play upon the different structural combinations, mobilizing tension in the direction of change. The development of complex profiles of "simulated family systems" demands further exploration, but as a therapeutic strategy, it seems to bridge the conceptual gap between working at the family level only and the societal level only.[13]

Challenges to the Affective System

Toward Modifying Mood and Affect

Many of our families are characterized by a prevailing mood that accompanies, dominates, and lends a particular affective tinge to almost all of the transactions among family members. These families display a mono-affective quality in their interactions, generally adhering to a narrowly defined, restricted mood level, despite the content of the issues to which they might be attending. Thus, in some families, a bantering, joking quality in the interactions among the family members seems to deny the very reality of even the most dramatic, significant, or tragic situations confronting them. In other families the domination of aggressive affect in the members' transactions may mask the tenderest of relationships which might be implicitly present. In still other families, apathy and depression reign, putting a damper on and blocking any peaks or heightened intensities in mood and emotionality in their interactions. In such families, emotionality seems flat; subjective experiences are apparently lacking in range and intensity, and seemingly without personal significance.

When the predominance of one mood or characteristic family affect envelops most of the family's transactions, therapeutic attempts to deal only with the *content* of the transactions seem to have little or no effectiveness. The therapist's interventions must of necessity become primarily oriented toward modifying, modulating, or manipulating the central family affect, and to this end he employs many of the techniques previously described. That is, in families which interact within the confines of a tight, rigid framework of a restricted, mono-affective system, interventions which challenge pathways, expand the content of communications, etc., may further the primary goal of producing changes in the affective system.

---

[13] For other therapeutic uses of the social network see the work of Speck (1966).

Some of the operations we have used which address themselves to changing the family's affective-mood system are the following.[14]

Joining the Affective Axis of the Family as a Precursor to Changing It

The therapist can adopt the pace and the tempo of the particular family member who seems to be playing a crucial role in shaping and sustaining the central family mood: he can become a more flamboyant "joker" in the joking family, a more skillful polemicist in the argumentative family, or a more effective "fighter" in the aggressive family than the member who appears to be the prototype of these roles. By such a maneuver, the therapist achieves a certain salience in the particular family, for he has displayed mastery over the others within the confines of their affective system. He has, in effect, asserted himself as one of the more powerful members of the group.

After he has thus become part of the family system, he can initiate the second phase of his strategy—that of modifying, monitoring, accelerating, or decelerating the particular affective texture and tempo that characterize the family.

In the Parrington family,[15] for example, the therapist initially followed Mrs. Parrington's upward swing of mood, fast tempo, and intrusive, staccato style of response; he thus allowed himself to be pulled into the family's power operations. His induction line into the family's affective system soon gave him an "edge" in their power transactions, for he became accepted by the family members as one of the most influential and powerful members of the group.

After the therapist had stabilized his position within the Parringtons' affective system, he began to go beyond Mrs. Parrington's affective style. He exaggerated her responses, becoming even more controlling than she; and he displayed intense peaks of aggressiveness. Mrs. Parrington reacted sharply to the therapist's "caricature," saying to him at one point, "You're getting too upset; take it easy." She was beginning to display some skills in controlling her "alter ego" as performed by the therapist, and was gradually developing a responsiveness to cues which might signal a mounting lack of control on either her part or the therapist's. She gradually began to modulate her own interactions of anger, knowing that they

---

[14] These operations are listed separately for ease of presentation; they are, of course, neither mutually exclusive nor distinctly differentiated from each other when we employ them in actual sessions.

[15] Not a research family.

would be met by counter-anger responses of the therapist. At this point, the therapist gradually decelerated his own tempo by means of soft inflections, sluggish verbalizations, and a deliberately relaxed or "tired" posture; he spaced and performed these responses in a way that would make them clearly perceivable to Mrs. Parrington.

Once this new phase had achieved some stability, the therapist tested its strength by occasionally reintroducing or fostering renewed power operations between Mrs. Parrington and himself or her daughters.[16] She responded by defending her gains, thus reinforcing a new affective flexibility in the family system. In this way Mrs. Parrington became a leader in monitoring the therapist and her daughters into a new, middle range of flexible, affective responses.

The Therapist's Affective Participation as a Model

With some families, the strategy of the therapist involves challenging the affective system by introducing a missing family affect, using himself as a model. This has been a particularly effective operation with our flat or depressed families, in which the therapist becomes a model for excitation or some sharpening of experiential awareness. In one family, for example, a son was in danger of being put in jail, but the family members did not respond with affect which was appropriate to or commensurate with the critical event imminently confronting them. The therapist's exaggerated response of deep concern and "danger" stimulated some new and appropriate affective responses among the family members.

In a session with the Martinez family, one of the sons, Arturo, insinuatingly teased his father about the way in which he combed his hair, implying that he was a "fairy." Soon the whole family, including Mrs. Martinez, joined forces in the general teasing, with the father himself eventually entering this "teasing alliance." The teasing was presented as a joke, and was in the context of a mood that masked the actualization

---

[16] Of interest here is the shift in strategy employed to stabilize the new, uncustomary system. Temporarily, the family members were encouraged to organize themselves around conflict in their accustomed ways. When the old ways (now becoming unfamiliar) were reintroduced, the family members were forced to experience their new patterns more vividly, and to attempt to protect them. We suspect that in most middle-class families and in the well-differentiated, organized, low socioeconomic family this strategy is possible earlier in therapy. But in most of our disorganized families, it seems possible only late in therapy, after interpersonal tasks organizing family members around conflicts in unaccustomed ways have helped them sense their power to withstand or obstruct change or to rush back to the familiar. Once this power has been sufficiently discovered or experienced, it can be employed to defend gains (see Haley, 1963).

of other affects. Mr. Martinez' participation in the "jokes" derogated his position in the family and left him bewildered and confused.

At this point the therapist could have intervened in a number of different ways. He could have adopted a traditional intrapsychic approach, and dealt with the possible latent homosexuality of Mr. Martinez or with the unconscious homosexual tinge in the relationship between father and son. He chose, however, to respond with intense and visible indignation. He got up from his chair, faced the father and then "attacked" the mother for joining the children in the derogation of her husband, explaining that by doing so she was increasing the prevailing disrespect for their executive positions as parents.

Two sessions later, Mr. Martinez aligned himself with the therapist, actually producing a response of indignation when a similar incident occurred. Following his indignant response, a frail, tentative complementary response of shame was evinced by Arturo. "Shame," as a new transactional product, thus emerged from circumstances in which the therapist's affective participation served as a model.

Mood Allocation

In attempting to modify the affective system in some families, the therapist must be responsive to the "spatial" distribution of moods; that is, their absence, presence, and general characteristics within relatively circumscribed situations and subgroupings within the family.

In one family,[17] for example, a feeling-tone of separation and aloneness dominated the relationship between the spouses, who compensated for their plight by a suffocating closeness to their children. In this family, the therapist deliberately employed rather lengthy sessions when he was alone with the couple, in which he strove to allocate moods of intimacy and closeness, in sharp contrast to the gentle but distant feelings which characterized his responses to them in the relatively short sessions he held with the couple when the children were present.

Another family was characterized by a stiff, "pseudo-intellectual" religious tinge in the relationship between the spouses, as in many disadvantaged families, for whom life in the church is all-encompassing. They were always together, and they generally excluded the children, whom they involved only for brief, fleeting periods, and even then tended to talk "over their heads" with constant use of biblical language. To this

---

[17] A lower middle-class Negro family, not in our research sample.

"spatial" distribution of affect, the therapist responded with the use of only brief sessions when they were alone, in which he employed concrete, simple, plain, and somewhat seductive language. He held relatively longer sessions with them when the children were present, however; in the sessions with the total family, he was both playful and reflective, relating quite openly and directly to the children.

These general maneuvers of mood allocation that are comprised of various combinations of session *length*, subgroup *composition*, and the *therapist's own affective mood and language* can become a significant means by which to help the family members redefine their usual associations (and substitute new ones, perhaps) between moods and interpersonal contexts.

The therapist may also relate to temporal aspects of the flow or affect within any given session. With families that tend to hold on to and maintain a specific mood, the therapist, if he feels it to be desirable, attempts to shorten the duration of that particular affective sequence. For example, in a family in which the members repeatedly become involved in competitive interactions or power operations, the mere process of avoiding or curtailing a mounting escalation by shortening the length of the sequence is an important maneuver, since it automatically increases the length of sequences involving interactions in more neutral areas.

The therapist can also focus the attention of the family members on certain positive and rewarding sequences, for example, affectionate interactions which he wishes to encourage. In this instance, he "pushes" the family members in a direction which focuses their attention on this particular interaction, for he has decided that experiences in this area should be reinforced and strengthened as a way of providing the family with a wider choice of affective responses. This particular operation of extending or shortening certain sequential moods can be extremely significant in inducing changes in habitual affective patterns.

Modifying Affective Valences

Many of our disorganized families display an equal or inappropriate allocation of affective valences to events and areas of life which ordinarily require and elicit differential or hierarchical weighting. These are the families that respond with equal distress, or lack of it, to a broken faucet or a child's broken arm, as if both events were of the same significance; or who treat lightly a child's chronic stealing, yet get immensely upset because "he doesn't move when I say so."

This style of functioning, with its lack of or inappropriate affective priorities, reflects a fundamental disorder in "emotional perspective." With these families, the therapist must, in effect, evaluate the affective import of many events and directly communicate to the members his own feeling as to what is significant or pertinent. He is engaged in a process which involves a recharting or reweighting of many areas of the family's experience.

For example, a young child behaves in a family session in a number of ways which suggest that he is often generous, curious, inventive, and observing. Yet other members of his family, who seem generally depressed and depleted of energy, insist that he is always "dull." The child's positive behavior in the session is not only undervalued and regarded as inconsequential, but for the most part is essentially unnoticed. The therapist's task is to help the family members *value* the child. By responding to the child differentially, endorsing his production, reacting enthusiastically to his creative curiosity, the therapist creates affective space for the child in the family and helps the family members too.

It goes without saying that if the family, as is more frequently the case, has allocated to these areas some affect, even if negative ("time-wasting," "bad," etc.), the therapist's job becomes more straightforward, for at least the members are relating to these areas as existing or real; that is, the areas possess some "figure" properties.

Tasks, Subgroup Changes, and Labeling Revisited

Traditional therapeutic emphasis, predicated on the basis of reclaiming repressed feelings, was developed with regard to a patient population with a relatively differentiated psychological inner organization. With the families discussed here, however, it should be evident by now that the therapist must attempt to dislodge affect from amorphous experience and to modulate and expand the range of subjective emotional events. To achieve this aim, the therapist must engage in a variety of maneuvers, some of which have just been presented.

In earlier sections of this chapter we discussed the importance of enlarging the focal theme by relabeling and expanding labels; we have also described how we employ the varying of subsystems under different task conditions and how we use alternating roles of participant and observer in work with our family members. These techniques are also quite useful for sharpening and differentiating nuances of affective experience. For example, a seemingly artificial task assigned to family members who are constantly involved in competitive interaction, such as spending five minutes looking only at positives in each other and then pointing out the difficulty they are experiencing with this very simple assignment, can serve to increase their awareness of the narrowness of their affective interaction and hopefully heighten their need to change it.

In other families, the possibility of inducing changes in mood may be increased by the strategic alteration of the composition of groups and subgroups. The therapist, for example, can remove certain members from a group because the roles they perform prevent the emergence of certain moods or affective interactions; or he can bring into a subgroup members whose roles may short-circuit the development of other moods. In other situations, the therapist can "bring in" or make more central the more composed, reasonable member of a group, thus setting the stage for this particular mood-level to prevail.

The following example illustrates the interrelationship among the above maneuvers and how they facilitate the process of affective expansion. In addition, our illustration highlights the use that the therapist makes of himself to achieve this aim.

The Parrington family (mentioned earlier) is composed of the mother, paramour, and eight children. The children cluster into two age subgroups: three adolescent girls, who are 13 to 17 years old, and five smaller children, who are between 2 and 8 years old. Mrs. Parrington is a heavy-set, bright Negro woman in her late thirties.

After several sessions with the total group, it was clear that two different dynamic centers prevailed in this family. One revolved around the three older daughters' need for autonomy, the other around the younger children's nurturance and guidance needs. Mrs. Parrington was better able to deal with the younger group, in which her control was not challenged, than with the increasing need for autonomy and independence in the older daughters.

We divided the family along its own gross outlines, holding sessions alternately with the mother and the older girls, and with the mother and the younger children; later on, we had sessions with the whole family. Sessions with Mrs. Parrington and her paramour were also held to begin the task of assimilating him into the family group. He was the father of only the youngest child and was restricted by Mrs. Parrington to the role of "peripheral" male, with only narrow parenting functions toward the rest of the children.

In working with Mrs. Parrington and the adolescent daughters the therapists found themselves in the midst of constant power interactions. The daughters would repeatedly challenge their mother's authority but were constantly squelched by her ability to out-shout and out-intimidate them. For several sessions it was impossible to disentangle any thematic material beyond loud claims and counterclaims as to who was "right." Interactions among the siblings could never develop far enough; the mother would immediately become embroiled with the daughters, and she would automatically be triggered into authoritarian behavior. The rigidity and persuasiveness of this operation robbed the therapists of freedom in therapeutic maneuvering.

The therapists responded first within the family's affective range, finding themselves brought into power operations despite their attempts at benevolent neutrality. When it then became imperative to organize a new interpersonal situation to diminish reliance on others as triggers for impulsive reaction, one therapist engaged the daughters in a "sibling stage" session, seeing them alone, while the mother joined the co-therapist behind a one-way mirror for "co-observation."

In the first session with the three adolescent girls, the two oldest, Shirley and Anne, engaged in an argument as to who had started most of the beatings the week before. After a variety of escalating attacks and counter-attacks, consisting largely of assertions as to who was the most stupid, Shirley said despairingly, "I wish you could learn to beat me back so I don't always wind up beating you so bad." In this family, the language of aggression was a focal theme, contaminating and blocking the experience of positive affect. The therapist seized this fleeting occurrence of a hazily expressed but "new" affect, labeled it "concern," and made it a central issue. He froze the interaction by dramatically showing his surprise at Shirley's "protection" of her sister, and then led the girls to look for other instances in which "Shirley shows concern for Anne." This snatching, labeling, and expansion of a transitory affective nuance were crucial to the dislodging of affect in this family. The active pursuit of strategic moments to introduce a more subtle experiencing of feelings was essential for exploration of new affective dimensions.

The new issue fostered reorganization of several inner and outer events (memories and feelings about past incidents). The focal experience of "concern" framed different perceptions; the girls and the mother behind the mirror began to detect some positive affect in what had formerly seemed only familiar incidents of power interactions. Though the incorporation of "concern" was tenuous at the beginning, it established a frame of reference for later exploration of confusion between "tenderness" and "being a sucker" which plagued the family.

The emergence among the siblings of a new affective cluster—concern —hinged on a fundamental subgroup rearrangement. Had the mother been with the girls, the transaction between Shirley and Anne would have been short-circuited long before the embedded affect could appear. The sister-to-sister sequence would have been quickly transformed into the usual transactions of control from mother to daughters.

Concomitant with this expansion of affective range, the therapists began to use their own affective flexibility more actively to modulate and control the family's level of intensity. At certain points in family interaction, when the possibility of escalation was imminent, the therapists decelerated their tempo of verbalization, softened their tone of voice, and displayed depressive features in their gestures, producing a flattening of mood which helped to block the family members from entering another stereotyped power sequence. Clearly, this response to the therapists' affective shifts was possible because they constituted by now an integral part of the family group. The well-timed exaggeration or diminution of the therapist's own affective responses was apparently essential in promoting cognitive-affective reorganization and expansion, in dislodging affects, and in encouraging the articulation and expression of new affective patterns in this family.

Beginnings of Change in the Affective System: Challenges to Therapeutic Skill

Transitional Labeling

Changes in affective patterns of response do not manifest themselves too often or too easily; new moods rarely appear as complete and finished products. As a result, the therapist must be alert to any manifestations of intermediate developments toward the growth of a new affective pattern. This often requires the labeling of transitional experiences at a point in which family members themselves do not and cannot recognize change.

In the Parrington family, for example, the customary reaction to one of the adolescent daughters' defiance entailed long sequences of stereotyped, unending, aggressive onslaughts from all members of the family. At a particular point in therapy she was again seen as defiant by the family members, when she was rather late for one of the sessions. This time, however, she was received with a sequence of tense, prolonged silence. The therapist labeled this event as change, as a transitional positive sequence in which silence replaced the bitter onslaughts. His intervention provided a transitional link between an old and a new mood, and was particularly effective because the family had not experienced their new behavior as any indication of change. The Parrington family, like our other families, had predefined the ways in which change should occur, and the area in which it must occur;[18] they would have perceived change only in the context of a full disappearance of the daughter's defiance. The cessation of the open hostility and aggressive onslaughts which had complemented and sustained the girl's defiance had been viewed only as a spontaneous reaction, and was disqualified as change.

Handling Dislocation and Oscillation

In most of our families, initial changes on one side of an affective pole are rarely perceived, and, if perceived, are seldom viewed as capable of eventually inducing complementary changes on the other side. Generally, complementary changes are impatiently awaited by family members as being too slow or too late in emerging. The consequent frustration for family members because of the absence of change "on the other side" ushers in a period of dislocation—a situation in which the "changed side" impatiently looks for but does not find affective changes on the other side. The therapist must actively intervene, at this point, to attenuate expectations for a dramatic, concurrent, complementary change. Dislocation phenomena are natural developments in work with these families, and elicit a variety of feelings, prominent among which are despair, discouragement, and anger. Such feelings may impede the progress of therapy unless well managed.

Periods of dislocation are especially taxing for the family and the therapist if they involve prolonged and continuous oscillations. Oscillations are seen when the "unchanged side" reciprocates, only to find that the "changed side" now seems to resist, retreating to previous patterns of response. Both sides are now capable of producing change, but seem to avoid simultaneous encounters with each other as "modified sides."

---

18 We have previously discussed this interpretative framework in terms of family expectations that change must go through predetermined pathways, thus negating the possibility of change.

This process may be so anxiety-producing as to compel the therapist erroneously to revert to an intrapsychic orientation, dismembering the family in order to deal individually with what he sees as "regressions" on the part of some members, and disrupting the natural flow of a system in search for a new equilibrium. Some oscillations are inherent to the process of family change. They seem to require a good deal from the therapist's affective repertoire (e.g., patience, calmness, and persistence).

Several common maintenance operations employed by therapists during the trials of dislocation and oscillation are the following:

1. Conveying a temporal perspective, that is, anticipating that a difficult period lies ahead and pointing out with examples that "when and if" positive feedback (change in the other side) comes, it is usually of a delayed nature.

2. Labeling as "to be expected" the pressure felt by the "changed side" to drop its gains and succumb to the power of the system to force reorganization along old lines; labeling the pressure which is usually seen as coming only from the "unchanged side" as a challenge.

3. Shifting the focus of attention and discussion away from the "unchanged side" to other members. This is simply a shift in the source of feedback, and is usually done by pointing to any evidence of how other members, say, the younger children, are gaining or likely to gain in the long run. This intervention is most useful in that it dissipates the tension experienced by the "unchanged side"; it improves the possibility that it will not experience its own change as "giving in," which might intensify and prolong the period of dislocation. As already noted, whatever the devices the therapist uses in this period, they call for the most supportive and encouraging resources in his own affective life.

The Therapist as Part of the Therapeutic System: Stresses and Strains

Clinicians have often observed and described their patients as if there were a sustained cleavage between patients and themselves. This illusion is easily shattered in work with families in which the ways the therapists and patients impinge on each other seem to be regulated by their (therapists' and patients') induction into a new system.

Induction processes have been studied in individual therapy in terms of the assimilations and accommodations of the patient and therapist to each other's language and style.[19] Such processes include even the production of dreams, which are fashioned along the theoretical lines that the therapist endorses. In general, the induction of a therapist into a family group entails adjustments on his part to the particular subculture that the family represents, with the consequent development of a new group. This new group is organized with different rules, "the rules of therapy," and requires adaptation on the part of all members.

Small groups like our families, however, with extremely inflexible and stereotyped patterns of disordered interaction, place the new member, the therapist, under considerable pressure to respond only along lines that are in harmony with the family's prevailing organization. Restricted roles are provided for the therapist by means of a series of implicit and explicit demands presented in a structural or communicational way; these tend to rob the therapist of maneuverability and flexibility.

In our families roles are scarce, interactional patterns rigid, and the language of accommodation and negotiation so limited that the therapist's freedom of action diminishes. The sense of enmeshment and frustration that characterizes the emotional state of the therapist in the postsession discussions is directly related to the reduction of possibilities for intervening in a variety of modalities. The therapist's functions of clarifying and reflecting feelings and strengthening and sustaining skills in symbolic problem-solving are curtailed by the excessive demands placed on him to behave with only a few variations in the restricted role of either nurturer or controller.

Despite these demands, he can still be well in command and planful in his interventions. Planned intervention by the therapist we call *"accommodation"* to the family system; the unplanned induction we call *"suction"* into the family system. These processes will be spelled out in further detail below.

Accommodation

In *accommodation* to the family system, the therapist chooses his areas of intervention rather deliberately but assumes communicational styles that are congruent with the styles that the family uses. For instance, with

---

[19] J. Jaffe (personal communication) reported some experiments on the ability of the therapist and patient to predict deleted words of samples taken from early and late sessions. He found increased ability on the part of both therapist and patient to guess each other's communicational pattern.

the Garcia family, the communicational style that the therapist adopted involved the use of a romantic language with many words like heart, soul, love, and others which the Puerto Rican culture encourages. The fact that the therapist for this particular family came from a Latin culture which uses this language and style facilitated accommodation.

The accommodation of the therapist is sometimes manifested in ways which are not apparent in the typed transcript. Observations of actual sessions, however, disclose a certain behavioral "fit" between the therapist and the family through which the therapist carries the family to appropriate moments of gravity and solemnity indispensable for the assimilation and definition of certain problems. This use of the family tempo increases the ability of family members to capture the significance of certain interpretations. In the Garcia family, for example, a mood of intimacy was encouraged. The inflections of the therapist's voice when he spoke with Mr. Garcia made him seem an intimate friend, concerned for his well-being; the therapist used language containing nuances which Mr. Garcia recognized as the language of concern in his own subculture. The long "speeches" made by the intimate therapist were congruent with the family's culturally induced expectations for a friendly advisor. Such therapist-operations, which revolve around subtle and appropriate manipulations of mood rhythms, are essential to the reception of certain content. This particular communicational style would have been contraindicated with the Montgomerys or the La Salles, where it became appropriate to adopt a more percussive, staccato style which addressed itself to the need for abrupt recoveries of shifting attention. The therapists for the Garcia family needed to employ slow, melodious violin touches; work with the La Salles required the more pointed, thumping rhythms of jazz.

We consider it extremely important for the therapist to be able to gauge the threshold of attention in a family in order to calibrate the intensity of his messages to the family's affective requirements at any particular moment. At certain times the therapist must yell more vigorously than the family members; dramatize his affect by making his silence audible; change his seat to increase or decrease proximity; introduce examples from his personal life; or use audibly the four-letter words that the family members use secretively among themselves. It is in the artistry of appropriate selection and timing in the use of such maneuvers of mood control that the therapist's messages achieve a palpable reality for family members.

Suction

Suction refers to a process, in some situations, by which the therapist's choice of roles becomes restricted. He is compelled to behave in ways that he would not generally choose. This can occur even when he senses that his behavior is being shaped to protect the family's equilibrium.[20]

In the McCallister family, for example, composed of a mother and eight children, the dominant family pattern revolved around the mother's role as the central relay station for all communications to the children. Any message to a child from an outsider generally went *through* the mother to the child, robbing the children of individual acknowledgment. On one occasion, the therapist responded to an attack by a child by avoiding direct answers to him and engaging Mrs. McCallister in a dialogue "about" the child's behavior, thus reinforcing the very centrality of the mother he was trying to discourage.

In the Martinez family, the therapist could have been recruited into the family's style of communication had he smiled when the family began to ridicule the father (see earlier illustration). He also could have been trapped by the Martinez family structure, protecting its homeostasis, had he directed his communications only to Mrs. Martinez. Instead, he carefully "spread" his response by first making Mr. Martinez central, insuring his attention, and then confronting his wife. This "spread" helped the therapist avoid assuming the role of protector of the father, which could have implicitly reinforced the father's weak position in the family.

The process involving the therapist's entering into a family system in order to challenge it, while at the same time resisting the power of the system to induce him to reinforce family pathology, produces special strain in working with these families. The requirements for immediate proximal involvement shift so suddenly that the therapist must be capable of being completely "in" one second and "pulling out" the next in order to question the very basis of the relationship in which he has just been involved.

To compensate for the effects of suction, we rely mostly on the therapist's experience in working with these families; he becomes alert to the manifold ways in which he is pulled, and if his own anticipatory processes cannot rescue him from suction, he can rely on the co-

---

[20] Suction is not necessarily countertransference. The pull of the family system may be so strong that different therapists, despite different childhood histories, come to behave in remarkably similar ways.

therapist. Co-therapists can be trained in specific ways of buffering the effects of suction. Whenever one therapist is involved in interaction with a family, the co-therapist's field of observation includes the therapist, not just the family alone. He learns to watch specifically for the ways in which the family organizes his partner into behaving along lines which do not permit family change. When it is his turn to be active, the other therapist becomes engaged in recovering distance and looking anew at the system.

Even when the therapists are skilled in these techniques some instances of suction are an inevitable aspect of the development of the therapist-family system.[21] These, however, can frequently be used to the family's advantage.

In some cases, a therapist systematically observes the session behind the one-way mirror and can readily enter the therapy room in order to disengage the participating therapists from unwitting adaptations to negative family patterns. He enters the session free of conformity to the prevailing group norms, organizing the "working" therapists and sharing his observations with the group. Sometimes we have found it effective for this "third therapist" to operate as an additional member of the group, becoming more part of the process, part of an "extended family" of therapists. This move seems effective because subjects in such cases are accustomed to living in an extended family system. (We will not go into the details of the complications this raises other than to state that as a therapeutic arrangement this requires further exploration.)

The third therapist has the particular advantage of not being involved in the thematic thread being pursued at the moment; his comments center, of necessity, on over-all aspects of the session and help free the therapists from "entrapments" with regard to the family system. The surprise elicited by his entrance and the "magical" abrupt quality of his sudden appearance usually force the family to fix and sustain special attention to his message. This increases the chances of family members' remembering the significance of the event and the implied interpersonal lesson he brings. For the therapists in the room, this technique not only makes possible a recovery of maneuverability but also often permits them to reorient their roles to elicit here-and-now therapeutic tensions in the direction of family change. The fact that the observer is not caught in

---

[21] It might be noted that some degree of suction is involved in the process of eventual accommodation.

the group process often allows him to sense more clearly the paths which the refashioning of therapists' responses must take.

Therapist's Affective Experiences

In the early sessions the therapists and family members, through accommodation and suction, try to find some way of communicating with one another. Clashes between their different communicational cultures result in stresses that tax the psychological well-being of the participants. But these tense experiences tend to diminish later on in therapy. The therapist gradually assimilates some of the ways in which the family members talk, understands more of the tempo necessary for contact with them, and learns to borrow from them certain key affective phrases indispensable to communicational exchange. This process finds its counterpart in the family, which begins to make sense of that "peculiar talking arrangement" which is the therapeutic session.

Therapists who work with these families should be alerted to certain processes that are inherent in this clash of cultures. The affective entrapments on the part of the therapist can lower his self-esteem and cause him to feel superfluous and impotent. He can respond with a series of reparative acts unrelated to the psychological growth of the family. These experiences are especially burdensome in early phases of therapy.

The therapist can also find himself exhausted when a session ends. He has gone through the stress of trying to talk through and over an unaccustomed level of noise. He has tried to maintain a theme and make himself heard by either overactive or listless family members. He has had to awaken members of the family, or to physically control a child's acting-out during the session, and has had to do all of this while being bombarded by multiple stimulation. A variety of transactions have occurred at the same time, seemingly without any connection to each other, and he has tried to weave what was being transacted into some unity, hoping to maintain a theme with some family members while keeping others engaged in active listening. And he has been continuously thwarted in the process.

He increases the intensity of his voice and the tempo of his messages to make some communicational impact. He gets up from his chair and moves closer to the family members, trying to shorten at least the *physical* distance between himself and the addressee. But he finds that even this frequently fails to focus the attention of family members on his communications. His own attentive set, at the same time, is constantly interrupted; he is repeatedly distracted by the multiple teasing and the aggressive operations in which the children in these families are continually engaged.

These difficulties pressure him into accepting unfocused discussion and into lowering his expectations of his ability to communicate with the family or the ability of family members to communicate among themselves. In some cases he may even behave as the members of the family do, as if communication for "contact-purposes" alone is in itself sufficient; he replaces an orientation to content with a kind of active but unexamined relatedness. The feeling of superfluousness and ineffectiveness intensifies his need for some evidence of impact. He multiplies his interventions without regard for their real import or therapeutic value, and repeatedly experiences a sense of having tried in vain to make some impact.

But at other times he can feel elated because of some evidence of "registering"; these are usually moments of "stability" or "affiliation" in the family. His feeling of superfluousness, at this point, is replaced by a keen sense of potency and centrality in the family, as if it were in him and in him only that any possibility of family organization resides.

Clashes between the therapist and family members with regard to the value of talking also challenge the therapist's affective endurance. Talking has very little usefulness and prestige in these families. Talking has not been tested as a way of coping with interpersonal and social problems, or if tested it did not help much to change the unyielding realities of poverty. The resultant devaluation of thinking in words threatens the therapist precisely at the core of his clinical armamentarium—his ability to talk in a special way. He may cope with this feeling by overemphasizing his concrete "giving."

Material aid can then become his answer to his wish to be useful to the family. He may unwittingly encourage enormous collective dependency; in addition, he becomes identified with resented authorities, such as Welfare, the courts, and the schools, which are seen alternately as "givers" and "deprivers." Therapy may then be seen by the family as depending exclusively on whether or not one can get material supplies, rather than as a process which helps in altering those fundamentals of communication which may be blocking a move into autonomous behavior.[22]

The "power" in the family system must be met, then, with certain

---

[22] Helping the family by giving them money for babysitting or carfare or even loans to buy a coat or install a heater has been used frequently and successfully, however.

characteristics in the therapist. He must have a capacity for trying fast engagements and disengagements, not being afraid of proximity or distance, and responding with his own affect and total personality while at the same time being able to withstand the considerable pressures of proximity.

Recapitulation and Discussion: Principles Underlying Therapeutic Intervention

The foregoing discussion of therapeutic interventions was perforce oversimplified and schematic. It does not reveal the conceptual and attitudinal framework that guides and gives meaning to our therapeutic endeavors in our day-to-day clinical work. We would like to present some aspects of this framework now and at the same time review some of the general principles we have already discussed.

Family Systems Require Active Change-Agents

Throughout their prolonged experiences with each other, family members have evolved a system of mechanisms for exchanging and negotiating around areas of conflict. As a result of years of accommodation to areas in which there is tension, they have developed systematized ways of organizing, avoiding, manipulating, or detouring in situations of stress.

The first goal of the therapist in his attempt to break down these systematized patterns is to watch the family system as it stands so he can roughly identify some areas of stress and the ways family members customarily negotiate around them. However, in our view, unobstructed exposure is insufficient for learning about these family systems. Particularly with the disorganized, low socioeconomic family (though not exclusively), it is necessary for the therapist to activate conflict and increase tension as a means of studying the systems. This is necessary because the family's use of accustomed ways of resolving conflicts is not well demarcated.

The therapist activates conflict and increases tension by "testing the limits" and "rocking the system." To test the limits, he challenges the customary direction of pathways, the usual flow of communication along these pathways, the concurrent stereotyped mood levels, etc. This brings out the mechanisms through which tension and conflict are usually mastered in the family. To rock the system, the therapist *overexposes* conflict. He deliberately sides at different moments with different participants. And he tugs and pulls at the positions the members customarily take around areas of conflict.

While he is studying the family system by these means, he is also changing it. By unbalancing and loosening the family's customary patterns, forcing them to organize around conflicts in new ways, the therapist helps them perceive how their usual ways of interacting resist change. That is, by going beyond the threshold of anxiety or tension that the family system usually allows, he induces the family to use its customary ways of bringing the "tension-intensity" back to its usual level. When this happens, the family can begin to perceive its powerful capacity to regulate, resist, or modify attempts to change and to experience the natural pull and resilience of its customary behavior as an obstacle to the change they are presumably seeking.

The problem with this procedure, of course, is determining how far the family can move beyond its customary limits. In our view, this is best solved by observing the family's own processes and its own capacity for flexibility. Although clinical experience with similar families may guide the therapist's judgments of a family's capacity for change, we prefer to rely on observing the family's own performance rather than measuring it against some average or norm. We stress the obtaining of impressions of the family's elasticity within its own internal framework.

Priorities of Intervention

After working with many families, the therapist becomes familiar with certain family syndromes that seem to present similar priority areas of stress. For each form he develops a sense of the particular ways to enter the system which are most likely to unbalance it.

In order to detect the over-all contours of a family form and some of the priorities of interventions which it seems to suggest, the therapist must learn to dismiss certain specific features of different interactions and to be involved with the more inclusive balance of forces and patterns of transacting that are similar in certain groups of families. By observing a variety of discrete interpersonal events, he senses a limited set of stereotyped familial patterns; he assumes that changes in these larger, more inclusive, and recurrent patterns will generate repercussive changes which can affect the discrete interactions.

Within the family as a total system, the subsystems can sometimes achieve a dynamic significance that renders them impervious to interventions directed toward the total family. Also, certain dynamic organizations within the family are more easily accessible if one works with significant subgroups.

The therapist planning interventions according to dynamic priorities thus takes into account the shifting structures that appear as he works with the family. For instance, with the Garcias, the therapists, by delineating and giving priority to the spouse subsystem, eventually facilitated effective interventions in the parents-children structure. Similarly, in the Parrington family, the patterned transactions between mother and daughters rendered the sister-to-sister pathway inaccessible; only a change in structure (the withdrawal of the mother) made it possible for the therapists to work with the sisters.

The priority of interventions, then, depends on the family form at hand. In the final chapter we will discuss some generic family forms (profiles) familiar to our therapists and the priorities of intervention which these forms seem to suggest.

An Atemporal, Experiential, and Affect-Centered Therapy

A bias for creating and seizing upon the optimal tension levels among the participants in therapy in order to foster therapeutic movement is strongly implied in our orientation. To achieve the optimal tension levels, we try whenever possible to transform a conflict that is talked about into a conflict that is happening now and to shift the level of intervention from talking about past events toward resolving a felt tension in the present conflict.

This emphasis seems particularly effective for some of our families, who function with such a global affective style that they constantly blunt the meaning of conflict. The sharper experience of conflict brought about by this emphasis on the here-and-now elicits new differentiations of experience which can facilitate the monitoring of emerging tensions into a search for new coping devices.

Minimizing the use of the "mediated" conflict—the "talked about" conflict—and using it mainly as a springboard for eliciting typical ways of resolving differences in the immediate arena is also effective with these families because many of them have difficulty in describing events verbally. When the family is describing a conflictual situation that happened yesterday or a year ago, it may or may not behaviorally indicate its specific patterns of resolving conflict in ways that allow for corrective intervention. If such families are to assess and modify their behavioral-affective states, we must help them by valuing what they value—their immediate experience—using it as a vehicle for change.

However, these families are bound to have multiple crises outside of the therapy room, and it would be artificial not to consider these as part of their experience. To reconcile our concern for an affect-centered experiential therapy and the inclusion of the total life of the family in and out of the session as data for exploration, the therapist working with this group will need to go out of his office and develop an intimate knowledge of the life-space of his family-patient.

A Bias for an Exploratory Attitude

In our view, a new family organization comes as a by-product of the family members' exploration of ways of mastering their interpersonal tensions. Thus, in our therapy, we focus on the search for ways of resolving interpersonal conflicts.

When the family uses its old pathways, it is resisting change even while presumably seeking it. Only when the familiar pathways are disrupted can the family realize how their accustomed ways of interacting have frozen the family system. Most of the therapist's interventions, especially those involving the use of interpersonal tasks, are directed toward helping the family perceive this.

These tasks are assigned because these families are seldom task-oriented and are accustomed to unstructured interactions. We have found that experiences of structured attention apparently induce a new use and a new appreciation of unstructured attention. That is, when tasks bring out a legitimate exploratory attitude and harness resources for an organized instead of a vague focus, they foster a better use of unharnessed, flexible exploration at the same time. This becomes noticeable particularly between task assignments, when qualitative changes in the way members comment on their observer or participant roles seem to take place. The family members display increased ability for unfocused but somehow productive reflection upon the events they have just experienced.

When this unfocused attention is transformed into open-ended problem-solving, new and subtle searches on the part of family members become possible. Familiar events are scanned for different information, and areas previously considered irrelevant become relevant. This is why we emphasize interventions couched in such a way that they highlight *curiosity*, not just competence, as a main source of and impetus for problem-solving attempts.

The Therapist as Part of the System

The therapist's choices of intervention are decidedly limited because he must operate under the organizational demands of the family system. But this has the advantage that awareness of himself in the midst of these "system pulls" allows him to identify the areas of interaction which require modification and the ways in which he may participate in them to change their outcome.

To induce change, the therapist generally relies on multiple strategies which can be subsumed under two central ones—the selective and alternating use of two kinds of participation: (1) interventions in the system within the *usual* family organization; and (2) operations directed to induce *new* organizations, roles, and functions.

1. The therapist loses distance and is fully "in" when he enters the role of complementing the family members with counterresponses which tend to duplicate those that they usually elicit from each other. Our orientation encourages the assumption of this role. By this means, the therapist can teach the family members the generic lesson that behavior is modifiable, and also give them specific and imitable cues as to how and when counterresponses are needed in the family system. The reconciliation of differences between the therapist's style and the family's achieved at these times can be deliberately employed to foster the reshaping of family behavior, to teach from within, as it were. This is most evident when the therapist calibrates the enactment of his complementary roles so that although they are similar to those commonly employed in the family, they are different enough to unbalance the system and move it toward a better structure.

For example, in one family, he may be required to appropriate the role of an emerging but still passive father to become an assertive father. In another family, he may need to appropriate temporarily the parental functions of an ineffectual mother who tries but fails to be competent, in order to show her ways of gaining effectiveness.

Frequently, if the therapist is reluctant to leave the role of distant participant, he may not only support the role stereotypes prevailing in the family's system but even fail to detect the pulls of the system. In contrast, the therapist who risks losing distance and who spontaneously acts out some of the family ways of interaction can then regain distance and more effectively present directive cues as to how and when family members should try to reach a new organization. His effectiveness at the moment of regained distance is enhanced because he has been able to explore the roles of the family members, not just by questioning them or imagining himself in their positions but actually by daring to be placed in those positions.

Allegiance to the welfare of the total family and commitment to a problem-solving attitude rather than to particular members of the family are enhanced rather than endangered by the therapist's ability to alternate distance and proximity.   •

2. The therapist is also that part of the system which can move out not only to interpret, or mediate, but also actively to change or organize interpersonal situations and bring into play hitherto unexercised skills in observing and reflecting on the part of the family members. During this process, he facilitates certain transitions and integrations between actional and ideational exploration. He also encourages the family members to develop the capacity to manipulate group composition in the family in order to change the nature of their own interpersonal transactions and foster interpersonal competence.

Clearly, when the therapist is working with families that have had insufficient models for effective interpersonal response, the demands on his ability to expose and share his methods of intervention so that they become graspable and transferable to the family members are greater than they would be in work with less disorganized families. He must carefully monitor his participation so as to teach the family to employ his means of mediation, interpretation, and changing composition, and he must make sure that this is a tangible process by taking himself out of the interaction and making the family members continue it. In other words, in the same fashion that the family allows or structures him to use their methods, to appropriate certain of their roles, he must provide opportunities for them to use his methods and appropriate his role, helping them to initiate the processes which they have seen him employ.

The next chapter presents material concerning our specially developed instruments, the Wiltwyck Family Task and the Wiltwyck Family Interaction Apperception Technique. These instruments were employed in the early research and exploratory phases of our work and reflect the status of our thinking at that time. Some of our findings were nevertheless consistent with our newer conceptualizations; presenting these data *after* Chapters 5 and 6 instead of before seemed necessary for reader understanding at the risk of creating some disjointedness in continuity.

REFERENCES

Ackerman, N. Emergence of family psychotherapy on the present scene. In M. I. Stein (Ed.), *Contemporary psychotherapy.* New York: The Free Press of Glencoe, 1961.

Bruner, J. S. The course of cognitive growth. *Amer. Psychologist,* 1964, 19, 1–15.

Haley, J. *Strategies of psychotherapy.* New York: Grune & Stratton, Inc., 1963.

Johnson, Adelaide M. Sanctions for superego lacunae of adolescents. Paper presented at the Chicago Psychoanalytic Society meetings, 1947.

Johnson, Adelaide M. Juvenile delinquency. In S. Arieti (Ed.), *American handbook of psychiatry.* New York: Basic Books, Inc., 1959, Vol. 1, pp. 840–856.

Johnson, Adelaide M., and Szurek, S. A. The genesis of antisocial acting out in children and adults. *Psychoanal. Quart.,* 1952, 21, 323–343.

Speck, R. V. Psychotherapy of the social network of a schizophrenic family. Paper presented at the American Psychological Association meetings, New York City, 1966.

CHAPTER *Family Assessment: The Wiltwyck Family Task and Family Interaction Apperception Technique*

The Wiltwyck Family Task

In order to elucidate some of the structural and dynamic features of our delinquent-producing families and to compare them with similar families that have not produced delinquent children, we developed a method of studying family members in interaction with one another while they discussed and answered a series of questions together. In this way we thought it would be possible to observe and analyze the overt behavior of the participants in a relatively "natural" yet structured situation which did not include authority figures such as observers or therapists. We also thought that any changes in family transactions as a result of therapy might be reflected in the Family Task situation in the final phase of our research. Our general procedure was similar to that used for direct observation of family interaction developed by Drechsler and Shapiro (1961), but with certain tasks, observations, and methods of scoring specifically designed to suit our particular needs.

Our rationale in employing this assessment procedure stemmed from the sorts of considerations already discussed in Chapter 2. The concrete "doing" of a task which does not involve a formal testing procedure (especially of the "paper and pencil" variety), and in which the participants can become completely submerged, has advantages for our population which have already been stressed.

Family Task Procedure

The room in which the Family Task was given was arranged for maximum viewing through a one-way mirror. Sofa and chairs were grouped in a semicircle facing the mirror; a small coffee table set in the middle of the circle of chairs held the refreshments which were offered to the family.

A block model was assembled on a table directly in front of the mirror.

The Task questions, which had been recorded, were ready for playback; the tape recorder rested on a table slightly outside the circle of chairs. (The Task questions were tape recorded to avoid giving centrality to the member of the family who had the best reading skills. In general, members of our families are retarded in reading skills, and some of the parents are functionally illiterate.)

The psychologist conducted the family into the room and gave instructions about the Task and the use of the tape recorder. The family were told that there were no right or wrong answers, and that they should all participate. It was suggested that any family member could operate the tape recorder.

After the instructions were given, the family were invited to help themselves to the refreshments whenever they felt like doing so, either before, during, or after the answering of the Task questions. Appendix C presents transcripts from pre-treatment recordings of responses to Tasks 1 and 3 of the Browns—an experimental research family.

Below is the list of "assignments" the families heard when the tape machine was switched on:

1. Suppose all of you had to work out a menu for dinner tonight and would all like to have your favorite foods for dinner, but you can only have one meat, two vegetables, one drink, and one dessert. Talk together about it, but you must decide on one meal you would all enjoy that has one meat, two vegetables, one drink, and one dessert. Remember, you must end up agreeing on just one meal that everyone would enjoy. Okay, turn off the machine and go ahead.

2. Here is something else for you to figure out together. In every

family different people have different ways about them. How about in your family: who's the most bossy, the biggest trouble-maker, the one who gets away with murder, the one who fights the most, the biggest crybaby? Now, suppose you talk about it together and decide who in your family is the most this way: which one is the most bossy, who is the biggest trouble-maker, which one gets away with murder, which one fights the most, and who is the biggest crybaby? Just talk about as many of these as you can remember. Now, turn off the machine and go ahead.

3. Now, in every family things happen that cause a fuss now and then. Discuss and talk together about an argument you had, a fight or argument at home that you can remember. Talk together about it, like what started it, who was in on it, and what went on, and also how it turned out in the end. See if you can remember what it was all about. Take your time. Turn off the machine and go ahead.

4. Let's make believe. Let's make believe that somebody gave the family $10 to spend together, but there's one thing: all of you must agree on how it should be spent, what you will do with it so everyone is satisfied. Talk it over and decide together how you would spend the $10 so that all of you agree on it. Turn off the machine and go ahead.

5. For this one, each of you tell about the things everyone does in the family: the things that please you the most and make you feel good, and also the things each one does that make you unhappy or mad. Everyone try to give his own ideas about this. You may turn off the machine and go ahead.

6. We have something we want you to build together. We have one made up for you to copy from. There are enough pieces for you to put it together. The model you will copy from is on the table. Use the pieces in the box next to it to build your copy from. You can work on the table. Remember, it's for the whole family to work on together. Okay, turn off the machine and go ahead.

This last and sixth instruction on the tape machine is the performance task, wherein the family is given the assignment of reassembling an asymmetric construction of wooden pieces. We used Creative Playthings Inc. Asymmetric Space Construction Kit A812 with 25 pieces for the whole family to reassemble. We now feel that a better procedure would be to divide the pieces of wood among the members of the group and then ask them to proceed with the construction of the model.

Two additional "implicit" tasks were employed:

7. *Task around gift selection*. When the above assignments had been carried out by the family members, the psychologist re-entered the room and after commenting about the constructed block model and the refreshments, offered the family a selection of three gifts from which they could choose only one. The psychologist then left the room, leaving the three gifts. These presents were selected specifically for each family and included a group game like Bingo or checkers; a game that only one child could play at a time; and another that was either for an older or a younger child, or a girl's or boy's game. The gifts cost approximately $1 to $1.50 each, and were selected on the basis of the family grouping.

8. *Task around nurturance*. Refreshments were offered to the family as a means of testing nurturance interaction under different conditions. One cupcake more and one bottle of soda and drinking cup less than the number of members present were provided. This situation made possible the observation of interaction around cooperation and competition with regard to the distribution of food.

The Family Task thus consisted of five discussion questions and a sixth—the only nonverbal task—which required the family members to copy a wooden construction model. Two additional "tasks" were implicit, stemming from the conditions of our over-all procedure (the gift and the refreshments).

The Family Task generally lasted about forty-five minutes. The entire Family Task session was tape recorded, and a verbatim transcript was subsequently typed. The family was observed throughout by two monitors via the one-way mirror. One monitor, listening to the discussion through earphones, identified and recorded the names of the speakers on a second channel of the tape. The other monitor, who could see the family but not hear what they were saying, dictated a running narrative-commentary on the nonverbal activity of the family members. Particular attention was paid to the spatial arrangement of the group, interactional activities (passing food, hitting), and individual activities (running around the room, reading a comic book). These were related whenever possible to the variables with which we were concerned. Subsequent to the Task session, family members were seen individually for the administration of our picture-story technique (FIAT), which will be described later in this chapter.

All family members over six were asked to participate in the Family Task procedure. The twelve experimental families and ten control families were assessed in the initial phase of our research (pre-therapy condition), and the experimental families were tested again after the termination of treatment (post-therapy condition).

Tables A and B in Appendix A present some information about our families including socioeconomic characteristics of the parents and number and age distributions of the children.[1]

Analysis of Responses to Tasks

Quantitative

All verbal statements made by family members to Task questions 1, 2, and 4 were classified according to a coding scheme which included 19 categories. These categories were designed to describe the verbal interactive behavior of the family members and are independent of the particular content of the task questions. Examples of the categories are leadership, behavior control, request for guidance, etc. The current report includes results based on the following variables:[2]

> Leadership
> Behavior Control
> Guidance
> Request for Leadership, Control, Guidance pooled
> Support for Leadership, Control, Guidance pooled
> Agreement
> Disagreement
> Disruptive

Other responses were classified as well, including number of verbalizations and the subgroup (e.g., mother, older child, etc.) to whom the verbalization was addressed. The above categories were selected on the

---

[1] Table A in Appendix A describes whether or not the fathers were in the home for the major portion of the treatment period. One father, who joined the family after treatment began, was not present for the Family Task pre-therapy condition but was available for the post-therapy procedure. Conversely, another father, who was seen with his family in the pre-condition, "dropped out" shortly after. He did not participate in the post-condition Family Task. All other fathers described as present and all mothers and children listed in Tables A and B were included in the pre-therapy Family Tasks. Five older children from three families and three younger children from two other families did not participate in the post-therapy Family Tasks.

[2] We remind the reader that our coding system was based on conceptualizations and implicit hypotheses at the time of initiation of our research and does not represent our approach as described in Chapters 5 and 6. A detailed manual for coding Family Task material is presented in Appendix C. Our discussion here will deal only with a limited number of variables, seen as most appropriate for our current purposes.

basis of their frequency of occurrence (at least 2 per cent of all responses scored or produced by subjects in at least 50 per cent of the families) and their pertinence to the areas in which we were interested.

These categories yielded quantifiable material which could be subjected to statistical treatment. A scorer reliability study of all the response categories in a sample of 401 responses disclosed 86 per cent agreement between two scorers. (One of these scorers, who was naive with respect to the theoretical concepts and expectations of the research, did the final scoring upon which our findings were based.) For the above categories, the percentage agreement between the two scorers was: Leadership—88 per cent; Behavior Control—85 per cent; Guidance—75 per cent; Request for Leadership, Control, Guidance pooled—87 per cent; Support for Leadership, Control, Guidance pooled—84 per cent; Agreement—87 per cent; Disagreement—89 per cent; and Disruptive—81 per cent.

Qualitative

This analysis addresses itself to the *content* of the five task questions and represents a "clinical" appreciation by one of the authors of the families' responses to each question separately. No reliability study was made of the qualitative "scoring," but an attempt was made to specify the criteria used for making the evaluations.[3] In the following discussion, material based on the qualitative scoring will be presented wherever applicable.

For our analysis of the data and discussion of findings, family members were divided into four subgroups: mothers, older children, younger children, and fathers. Within each family, responses made by all older children were pooled, and the same procedure was followed for younger children. Statistical treatment of the data was limited to the results obtained from the quantitative analysis. Since so few fathers were available, statistical comparisons involving fathers will not be reported. Fathers will be referred to in the qualitative discussion of our results, however.

Findings[4]

The discussion of our results is organized so as to complement the material presented in Chapter 5 concerning the structure and dynamics of

---

[3] See footnote 2.
[4] This section will report findings based on responses to the first five Task questions only.

the family systems with which we have worked. Thus, our findings are expressed in terms of communicational processes, affective variables, and one aspect of family structure—executive behavior. We are not making formal predictions here, but instead will present the results as empirical descriptions of the family's behaviors. When we had strong expectations which were or were not "confirmed," they will be mentioned. Thus, all conclusions must be considered as pilot findings; some of these strongly encourage further exploration of hypotheses in certain areas, while others point to the need for re-examination of our ideas and methodology with respect to the use of this instrument.

Comparisons between Experimental and Control Families (before Treatment)

COMMUNICATION

We have already described (in Chapter 5) our clinical impressions of the characteristic communication patterns of our families. Some of these patterns were also isolated from our analysis of the Family Task material.

Quantity of Verbalization was one of the initial formal characteristics to be examined. An "extremes" phenomenon appears. Experimental mothers and their older and younger children talked significantly *more* or *less* than their moderately talkative control counterparts (see Table 1).[5]

We were also interested in tracing whether the mother was used as a central pathway for verbal transactions in the Family Task. First, a measure of the degree to which the mother was a target for familial verbalizations, that is, how much she was talked to, was obtained as a simple percentage of the family's total communications. This score was then corrected for family size by calculating the average expected percentage (dividing the total number of family communications by the number of family members) and deriving the difference between this expected percentage and the actual percentage obtained. A significant result emerged (see Table 1), indicating that the experimental mothers were either talked to greatly in excess of other family members or relatively ignored in contrast to the control mothers. The latter were generally addressed more than other family members only to a moderate degree.

Correlations between (1) mother's verbalization score and the degree to

---

[5] For purposes of the present discussion, *tendency* refers to a finding with a p value greater than .10 and less than .20, 2 tails, obtained from the statistical analysis of the quantitative findings reported in the tables. The term *significant* refers to a finding achieving a p value of .10 or less, 2 tails.

TABLE 1

MEDIANS AND TOP AND BOTTOM QUARTILE FREQUENCIES
(COMBINED) OF EXPERIMENTAL AND CONTROL
FAMILIES ON FAMILY TASK VARIABLES
(Pre-Therapy Condition)[a]

Variable	Experimental (N—12)		Control (N—11)		p Value[b]
	Median	Frequency in quartiles	Median	Frequency in quartiles	
Mother—number of verbalizations	51.0	9	54.5	3	.04
Older children—number of verbalizations	78.0	8	82.0	4	.10
Younger children—number of verbalizations	56.5	9	57.5	3	.04
Mother as target for family's verbalizations—per cent above expected	+1.5	10	+4.0	2	.005
Mother's per cent Disruptive	5.0	5	14.5	6	$<.02$[c]
Older Children per cent Disruptive	11.5	9	11.3	2	.04
Younger Children per cent Disruptive	13.5	7	19.5	4	.22
Mother's per cent Leadership	28.0	7	24.0	4	no diff.
Mother's per cent Behavior Control	4.5	8	5.5	3	.10
Older Children per cent Leadership	10.0	5	14.0	7	no diff.
Older Children per cent Behavior Control	1.0	9	3.3	3	.07
Mother—per cent Agree minus per cent Disagree	11.0	6	11.5	6	no diff.
Older Children—per cent Agree minus per cent Disagree	24.6	6	21.7	5	no diff.
Younger Children—per cent Agree minus per cent Disagree	21.5	6	26.5	6	no diff.

[a] It should be noted that neither the medians nor quartile frequencies were actually employed in the statistical tests. They are presented so that the reader can see certain trends in our data.
[b] All p values are two-tailed values.
[c] Mann-Whitney U test. All other p values are based on Moses test of extreme reaction. (See Siegel, 1956, pp. 116–127, and 145–152.)

which she was a target and (2) between mother's behavior control score and her verbalization score were positive and significant for our experimental mothers' group, as shown in Table 2. Thus, these women seem to cluster in two extreme groups with respect to these variables. This seems to support our clinical view of these mothers as attempting to cope with their family groups by falling back on either engagement (enmeshment) or disengagement. These correlations were insignificant for the control mothers. The traits of talkativeness, being talked to, and using behavior control were unrelated.

TABLE 2

CORRELATION COEFFICIENTS BETWEEN PAIRS OF FAMILY TASK
VARIABLES IN EXPERIMENTAL AND CONTROL GROUPS
(Pre-Therapy Condition)

Variable	Experimental (N—12)	Control (N—10)	Coefficient Employed
Mother—number of verbalizations Mother as target for family's verbalizations—per cent above expected	+.68†	+.04	a
Mother's per cent Behavior Control Mother—number of verbalizations	+.51*	+.16	a
Mother's per cent Leadership[c] Older Children per cent Support[c]	0	+.70‡	b
Mother's per cent Leadership[c] Younger Children per cent Support[c]	—.18	+.70‡	b
Mother's per cent Leadership Older Children per cent Leadership	—.30	—.44	a
Mother's per cent Behavior Control Older Children per cent Behavior Control	+.51*	+.69†	a
Mother's Guidance Older Children's Guidance	+.36	+.57†	b

[a] Spearman rank correlation coefficient (Siegel, 1956, pp. 202–213).
[b] Contingency coefficient (*ibid.*, 196–202).
[c] Position above or below median for that group.
  * p value—.10
  † p value—.05
  ‡ p value—.01
All p values are two-tailed values.

Another formal characteristic of some interest was the degree of "noise" in the communications systems of the experimental families. We attempted to use the category "disruptive" to explore this quality in the Family Task transcripts. Not unexpectedly, the older experimental children were significantly "extreme," either showing very little disruptive behavior (disengaged?) or a great deal; the younger experimental children tended to fall into these clusters as well when they were compared with their moderately disruptive control counterparts (see Table 1).

We experienced surprise, however, when, contrary to our expectations, the control mothers were seen to exhibit significantly more disruptive responses (see Table 1). Since it was most difficult to account for this finding, further exploration of the data seemed in order. Inspection of the disruptive responses given by the mothers in the two groups suggests that those of the experimental mothers fell primarily in the leadership and behavior control categories, whereas those of the control mothers were primarily in the nonscorable category and appeared mostly toward the end of each task discussion. The experimental mothers may have been more highly involved in their task performance, seeing it as a prelude to family therapy, in contrast to the volunteer control mothers who felt freer to talk about other things. Also, it was our impression from inspection of the descriptions of the *nonverbal* behavior during the Family Task that much of the disruptive activity engaged in by the experimental families fell in this (nonverbal) area. Thus, some of the experimental mothers who were scored as least disruptive verbally were described as standing, pushing, slapping, taking off their shoes and cleaning them, fixing their hair while looking in the one-way mirror, and feeding their families—motor behaviors which tended to disrupt the ongoing discussion but which did not appear in the verbal transcripts. It is clear that more work in this area remains to be done to clarify and expand our definition of disruptive "noisy" behavior and to re-examine the experimental-control differences.

An attempt was made to study, qualitatively, the course and end product of one of the task questions to determine how effective and clear the discussion was and also to attempt to isolate those behaviors which tended to disrupt, distort, or prevent a successful task solution. For this purpose, the process and content of the responses to Task 3 (the family fight) were evaluated for clarity of the discussion. We scored for at least a minimal statement of what the conflict was about, who participated, how it ended, and whether some rough consensus was achieved among family members on these points.

"Conflict clarity" was judged to be adequate for eight of the ten control families, but only for four of the twelve experimental families.

Just determining the facts of the experimental families' conflicts presented great difficulty to the listener/reader who made the judgments. A complete story might be told as follows: "What about at the hospital—

the doctor." "The doctor?" "How did it end? . . . " "That's when I called the cops." One family could not agree whether a particular fight happened the day before or the week before. Another fight story was told twice by two family members with two different sets of facts and without any final reconciliation. "Butting in" by other family members only increased the confusion in a crescendo of blame and counterblame. The task question was misunderstood by two families: in one case, distorted by the father into "tell about your problems"; and in another case mixed up by the whole family with the preceding task question, "who is the trouble-maker?" In two other cases, the mothers were unaware of the particular fight their children were speaking about. Their requests for information went unheeded, and they ended up as uninformed as the judge reading the story.

Another factor contributing to lack of "conflict clarity" was the apparent meaninglessness and futility of communication, similar to that described by Wynne and Singer (1963), and more recently by Wild (1965). In four experimental families, for example, the mothers persistently denied that fights ever occurred in their families all the while their children were discussing family combats. The children in one family mentioned twelve different fights, but the mother rejected these answers, using constantly shifting, unpredictable criteria such as, "That was not an argument, that was a discussion"; or "Poopie wasn't home so that doesn't count"; or "That was so long ago." No wonder many of the story-telling participants gave up and went on, in relief, to the next task. In contrast, eight of the control families' stories were models of clarity, although the discussion was frequently sparse or heated. As for the two control families whose discussions were judged unclear, one initially presented a good story but left the resolution untold, and for the other the sequence of events was confused because of blaming and counterblaming. One control father tended to minimize the seriousness of the argument, which was otherwise clearly presented. There were no denials of conflict in any of the control families.

We also examined the different types of "messages" the family members sent when asked to describe what pleased and displeased them about each other (Task 5). Preliminary work on the qualitative scoring scheme suggested three types of interpersonal response to this question.

Type 1, Objective: The speaker focuses on some actions or behavior of the "other," and, whether it is expressed negatively or positively, presents an "objective" content-oriented opinion of him. For example, "I like him when he does his work, keeps out of trouble, plays with his brother, etc." It is assumed that guidance can grow from this type of response.

Type 2, Personal: The speaker focuses on the "other" mainly in relation to himself (the speaker). "I don't like him because he hits me." "I do like him because he helps me." Personal contact seems an integral part of the evaluation or perception of the other.

Type 3, Affect: This response conveys an affect message primarily, and tells more about the attitude of the speaker than about the characteristics of the other. The view of the other is global; the trait is identified with the whole person. "He's lovable," or "He always gets away with things," or "He blabs his mouth too much."

One interesting finding was that this task seemed to pose great difficulty for our experimental families, particularly the parents. Only in six of the twelve families did a parent give a spontaneous, appropriate response. In the others, the question was misunderstood or just not responded to by a mother or father. In three of the twelve experimental families no child responded to the question. A blatant example of misinterpretation of the task was provided by three members of one family, each presenting his own version—mother: "Tell what we do to make others happy"; older child: "Tell the arguments we have"; younger child: "What we (like to) do that makes us happy." In contrast, only in one control family did a parent fail to speak. One father in another family misunderstood the question ("Tell what we like and dislike"), but his wife answered appropriately. At least one child responded in every control family.

We can only speculate about the nature of the difficulty for the experimental families. Perhaps the question's affective arousal was too great for them to cope with effectively. Another possibility is that they have real problems in differentiating, formulating, and expressing in words their feelings about another family member.

When we examined the frequency of Type 1, 2, and 3 responses by parents who did respond appropriately, or at least scorably, we found that five of the six experimental parents and all of the nine control parents gave Type 1 (objective) responses. However, some difference appears between the groups when we look at Type 2 (personal) responses. Only one of the nine control parents gave such responses in contrast to parents in four of the six experimental families. Type 3 responses (affect) appeared only once in each group. (This does not mean that parents did not express aggressive feelings toward their children. In fact, one of the most aggressive remarks was made by a control mother, but neatly separated from her Type 1 (objective) response: "What makes me mad is when you don't empty the garbage, don't wash the dishes—that's what really makes me mad and I really can get mad and I feel like crushing you.")

For the children the situation was reversed. In almost all of the families (eight out of ten control, eight out of nine experimental) they gave Type 2 (personal) responses. However, the children in nine control families gave Type 1 answers as well, unlike the experimental group, in which only three sets of children responded at this level. A developmental hypothesis suggests itself: Type 2 responses are more primitive than Type 1, reflecting an egocentric level; Type 1 responses represent a more mature, objective level of verbalization. Type 1 responses may not, as yet, have become part of the verbal repertoire of the experimental children, while their parents may not have dropped Type 2 responses from theirs.

One additional point is that the children in seven families in each group used Type 3 responses (affect). For our control children, these are almost evenly divided between positive (affectionate) and negative (aggressive) expressions. The experimental children, however, used this category almost exclusively for negative expressions.

EXECUTIVE BEHAVIOR

Our analysis focused on three types of "executive" or managerial behavior: leadership, behavior control, and guidance. Leadership is a category devised to describe executive activities directed toward the performance of the task; it included calling on people, directing the discussion, summing up, etc. Behavior control and guidance were categories intended to describe verbalizations regulating the nontask behaviors of others in the group. Behavior control, as differentiated from guidance, refers to "presence-control" (discussed in Chapter 5). "Do this," or "Don't do that," are paradigms of this type of management. Guidance, however, carries instruction as to ways of behaving in the *future* and points out inappropriate aspects of the criticized behavior.

No differences were found between experimental and control mothers with respect to the categories of leadership (see Table 1) or guidance (see Table 3). However, if we look at the variable of behavior control (Table 1), an interesting finding emerges. The experimental mothers cluster significantly at the extremes; that is, some spend a good deal of their time controlling the behavior of their children, while the others hardly do so at all. The control mothers, however, form a more homogeneous group in their "moderate" use of this response. The situation seems to reflect our clinical impressions of the mothers previously described as caught up on the enmeshment-disengagement dimension (see Chapter 5). It is not clear here, however, whether in the task we are "catching" these mothers in one extreme position at a given point in time (from which they might vacillate to the opposite extreme) or whether these represent their habitual patterns of responding.

TABLE 3

PROPORTION OF EXPERIMENTAL AND CONTROL FAMILIES
MANIFESTING EXECUTIVE BEHAVIOR
IN THE FAMILY TASK
(Pre-Therapy Condition)

| Variables | Proportion of Families | | p Value[a] |
	Experimental	Control	
Mother's Guidance	6/12	7/10	no diff.
Older Children—Request Leadership, Behavior Control, Guidance	7/12	7/10	no diff.
Younger Children—Request Leadership, Behavior Control, Guidance (number above median)	4/12	6/10	no diff.
Children's Requests LCG answered more than 50 per cent of time	3/11[b]	7/9[b]	$<.05$
Parent answers Children's Requests LCG	4/11[b]	7/9[b]	$<.10$
Older Children Support Mother's LCG	5/12	7/10	no diff.
Younger Children Support Mother's LCG	3/12	7/10	$<.10$
Older Children's Guidance	4/12	3/10	no diff.

[a] Fisher exact probability test—two tails (Siegel, 1956, pp. 96–104).
[b] One family in each group contained children who never made Requests for Leadership, Behavior Control, or Guidance.

Up to this point we have described only the relative amounts of time spent by these mothers in such behaviors. How much the mothers lead must be examined in terms of what we can see of them as effective leaders who truly have an influence on the "led." A qualitative analysis was made of the *content* of the discussion of Tasks 1, 2, and 4—those questions which elicited the most diverse responses from different members of the group and which had to be organized into one family answer. A judgment was made of the actual impact of different people in the family group on the group decision. This might be independent of how many leadership responses were made. The following criteria were employed in this judgment:

(1) Who selected from among the answers (Task suggestions) by approval or disapproval and made the final decision if any.

(2) Who presented the final consensus or summarized the answer.

(3) To a lesser extent, how many of one's answers were incorporated in the final answer through one's *own* insistence or persuasion.

(4) Whether these above criteria were met consistently across the three task questions.

(5) The term "weak leader" was reserved for an individual who met some of the above criteria in a borderline way on only one or two questions; there might be no leader apparent for the remaining question(s), or the person might present only part of the final decision.

In the experimental group, parents were "weak leaders" in five of the families. Three other families were led by the mother with the assistance of an older child, two more with the assistance of a younger child, and in two, an older child was the exclusive "weak leader." In the control group, four families were led by the parent alone, five by a parent with the assistance of an older child, and one family by an older child alone. There were no "weak leaders."

Thus, in nine of the control families, a parent exerted strong or exclusive influence on the final answers to the three Task questions even though these parents might have spent relatively little time in leadership behavior. No assistance was requested from or delegated to a younger child. In the experimental group, however, only in five of the twelve families did a parent exert strong (but never exclusive) influence on the three Task answers, and in seven cases, the parents exerted only a partial ("weak") influence, or none at all.

From the families' responses to Tasks 3 (the family fight) and 5 (the things that please you the most . . . the things each does that make you unhappy . . .) it was possible to gain some idea as to the views of family members about the extent to which behavior control and guidance functions form part of the parental image.

Although the descriptions of the family fights or arguments varied greatly, both in elaborateness of detail and clarity of presentation (see foregoing discussion under *Communication*), it was possible to note whether or not behavior control and guidance were exerted during the course of the dispute to bring it to a resolution.

Few of the experimental families (four) described a parent as exerting any behavior control over the participants in the fight, whereas in eight of the control families parents were so described. Hardly any parent from either group was described as offering guidance during the dispute (only one control parent), but in slightly more than half of the control families (six) a parent offered such guidance retrospectively during the Task discussion. Only in three of the experimental Task discussions did this occur. The *quality* of guidance offered in the two groups must also be contrasted. One parent in the experimental group, a father, made a positive guidance statement, but confused and deflected the child's attention from it by ruminating over his own controlling behavior:

> "It's nice to hit people?" (Son: "With a ball?") "You wouldn't like nobody to hit you, right? . . . What did I do with the ball . . . Did I bust it—that was good or wrong?" (Son: "Right.") "No, it was wrong." (Son: " 'Cause I was hitting people with it.") "I admit I was wrong that time but I was right in some way."

He did somewhat better, however, in guiding another child on the same question:

> ". . . when you got something that belongs to you [a pet] you gotta take care."

The typical guidance offered by the three experimental parents met the minimal criteria but was of poor quality due to nonspecificity and vagueness, thus providing limited opportunities for learning:

> "There's a reason for this sitting down talking things over together and if you go out, one reason is missing."

> "Don't try to do that again because that's no good any more."

> "He got to learn that he have to do whatever is good for him because Mama or me won't be around."

In contrast, the control parents offered concrete advice, couching it in the form of rules that applied to particular situations.

> "You should keep your hands off of it [sibling's bike] . . . you can't do just what you want." (Son: ". . . have an argument.") "Not when you leave things alone that don't belong to you."

> "Yes, but the point is, in order to make it fair on everybody you should take a turn about going to get the paper . . . The boys take turns . . . so I don't see why you shouldn't . . . and so just

time yourself (not to be late for school)—ah—that you'll be able to get it."

(Daughter: ". . . the boys?") "They're good . . . They share everything . . . that's right, they do share everything . . . all their clothes."

Even the guidance offered by *children* in one control family compared favorably with that given by experimental parents.

"Yeah, but sometimes you know we might compromise (over watching this or that TV program) . . . you gonna compromise eventually." (Sibling: "So now we have a compromise because then we get togetherness.")

It was also noted that differences emerged in the area of implementation by the parent of his/her controlling behavior. The primary, almost exclusive mention of such parental implementation in five experimental families reflected a reliance on physical punishment and/or threats of such. This type of punishment was described by only two of the control families. Instead, the control families described a variety of other remedies ranging through the following: nonphysical punishments (four families); eliminating the source of the dispute, such as turning off the TV (four); distributing nurturance equally (two); and forced restitution of property (one). Such nonphysically punitive solutions were mentioned only by one experimental family.

Thus, the control parents were recalled as having intervened in the family dispute more frequently, and a variety of methods were described as used to enforce behavior control in a way seen as not physically threatening by the children.

An interesting highlight to these impressions is provided by examining the children's responses to the parents on Task 5, in which they told what pleases and displeases them about others in the family. The children did not talk about the parents in every family discussion, so we have relevant material from only eight of the experimental families and six of the control families. Based on these data, we find that the children in six of the experimental families described the parents as behavior controllers, none as guiders. In the control families, however, parents were described as behavior controllers in two families and guiders in two families. Because of overlap, parents in three families were seen as behavior controllers and/or guiders. To further point up the difference between groups, five of the six control parents were described as nurturant, while only two were so mentioned by the experimental children (one father, in particular, was described as a highly inappropriate nurturance-giver).

Thus, the predominant view given by the experimental children who did give responses concerning parents on this question was of parents as behavior controllers. This is in contrast to the control children's more widespread view of their parents as nurturant rather than controlling figures. If we recall the results previously described for the "fight" question, it is interesting to reflect upon the discrepancies. Although the parents of many of the experimental families were described by their children primarily around the theme of behavior control and punishment, these same parents were not seen or recalled as having used control or guidance in situations in which it would have been appropriately integrated into family life—namely, intrafamily conflict. Conversely, parents in most of the control families were presented as having exerted a controlling influence in the dispute discussed in Task 3, but behavior control did not spring to their children's minds as the major trait around which to focus their attitudes toward their parents when asked what they liked or disliked about them.

We may speculate whether the exaggerated and unpredictable control and the memory-invoking reliance on physical punishment used by our experimental parents is contributory to this picture. A further speculation comes to mind from the finding that fewer parents in the experimental group are seen as nurturant, in spite of our clinical impressions of the excessive and inappropriate nurturance displayed at times by the parents in this group. However, the parental use of nurturance as a socializing mechanism in lieu of effective control and guidance may be perceived by the children as just that—a placating and enforcing device used by inadequate parents in an attempt to cope with the children's behavior, rather than a true expression of concern for the children's needs or an expression of affection.

From parents' responses to Task 5 (what pleases and displeases them about others in their families), we were able to form some picture of their views of the behavior control-guidance relationship vis-à-vis their children. Three mothers and one father in the experimental group focused specifically on the child's acceptance or nonacceptance of the mother's behavior control in general. This issue was not raised in any of the control families. In six families in each group, the parents' approval or disapproval was expressed around the child's "behaving" or "not be-having" himself, a rough approximation of self-control. This response, however, in three of the experimental families only emerged upon *coaching* by a child in the family, rather than as a spontaneous remark by the parent. That is, the child would say, "What you like (or don't like) is when I (or we) . . ." to which the parent replied, "That's right, how did you know?" or "Yes, that's what I like." The children seemed to wish to present the parent as a behavior controller or guider even when this did not occur to the parents as a response. The children did not coach the parents in the six control families in which the "behave" response was given spontaneously.

One other important type of remark was made by control parents. In five families, the requirement that children perform household chores (wash dishes), accept a regular or routine responsibility (take care of one's room or clothes), or cooperate with the mother in such tasks was expressed by the parents as a basis for approval (four mothers, one father). This response was given in only one experimental family by a parent coached by a child as described above. Expectations by the control parents stated in such a specific form certainly make plain to the children what constitutes "good" behavior, carry directions for behavior over a long period of time, and seem based on a rationale of cooperation rather than a power struggle over obedience.

We were interested in the degree to which the children evoked the mother's role as an executive by requesting leadership, behavior control, and guidance from her; that is, asking her for advice and direction. These requests were pooled into one category (request for lcg). Further, we wished to explore the dynamic relationship between these requests and the responses which may or may not have been made to them. This may be described as following up the "vicissitudes" of requests for lcg. It was found that there was no difference between the experimental and control older or younger children in the degree to which they made such requests (see Table 3). A tally was made for each such request by a child to determine whether or not it was answered and further, who answered. Significant differences between the experimental and control groups were found for both of these variables (Table 3).

Children made such requests for lcg in eleven of the twelve experimental families and nine of the ten control families. In four of the experimental families, none of the children's requests were answered at all, and in four more families fewer than half of their requests received some attention. However, in the control group, replies were made in all the families, and only in two families were fewer than half of the children's requests replied to.

Since all of the requests were made to the parents or to the group at large, it is interesting to note the number of families in each group in which a parent replied to the children's requests for lcg. This occurred in only four of the eleven experimental families and in seven of the nine control families. (Of course, in four of the experimental families it must be remembered that no replies were given at all.)

Thus, although no significant difference emerged in the degree to which children asked for leadership, behavior control, or guidance between our groups, the control parents appeared to fulfill the executive role more responsively to requests by their children. It was noted that five of the seven experimental mothers who answered few or none of their children's requests nevertheless were among those who scored extremely high (upper 25 per cent) in giving leadership or behavior control responses. The children in these families, while bombarded by their mothers with leadership or behavior control directives, were apparently not able to elicit these upon request, when they, the children, felt they needed such help and direction. We might have described this behavior in the preceding section on *Communication*, for it appears to exemplify the characteristic of "nonhearing" or "nonlistening" of our experimental families described in Chapter 5.

Another aspect of the children's behavior which we viewed as reinforcing or upholding the mother's executive position was the category of supports leadership, behavior control, or guidance pooled as supports lcg. This category was scored for affirmative responses by the children following a leadership, behavior control, or guidance response by the mother, or when the mother's response was repeated or elaborated by a child. In the control group, significantly more younger children made such supporting responses, but no difference was found for the older children (see Table 3).

Clinical impressions from the task material suggested that when the mother was more active as a task leader in the experimental group, there was sometimes an overt or covert resistance on the part of the older children or even competition in this area. In other cases, when the mother was a "slacker" in this area, the children seemed to try to urge a higher level of performance. These impressions could not be tested directly.

However, it was possible to examine the relationship between mother's leadership and children's support of mother's leadership, behavior control, or guidance. In the control group, there were highly significant positive correlations between these variables for both older and younger children (Table 2). That is, the more leadership given by a mother, the more support responses were given by the children. This would seem reasonable if only on a logical basis, since support of lcg is a dependent response. A leadership, behavior control, or guidance response must be made before someone can support it. However, this is not necessarily the case, since in the experimental group, the correlations between these variables were insignificant or zero. Thus, there was no relationship between mother's leadership and the degree to which the children supported her executive role in the experimental group. This finding may reflect a solidarity and mutuality among the control mothers and children in the area of executive behavior. The mothers seemed responsive to the children's requests for direction, and the children seemed responsive to the mothers' leadership. Both of these "give and take" aspects are not apparent in the mother-child relationships in our experimental families.

In our early thinking we placed great emphasis on the role of the older siblings in these families who "took over" or were delegated executive responsibility for the younger siblings because of the inadequacies of the parents. Although this interest found methodological expression in our therapeutic maneuvers (the use of Stage 2 sessions), in which the children were seen and studied without their parents for part of the time, this practice, unfortunately, was not followed in the Family Task. Thus, the role of the older siblings in the absence of the parents cannot be described.

No differences between the experimental and control older children were found with respect to the amounts of leadership (see Table 1) and guidance (see Table 3) which they gave. However, for the variable behavior control, the experimental older children showed a pattern of responding similar to their mothers'. When compared to the control older children, the experimental older children were significantly extremely high or low in their use of behavior control (Table 1). Furthermore, significant positive correlations between mothers' and older children's behavior control scores were found for both experimental and control groups (Table 2). In the control group, a significant positive correlation was obtained for the coded variable of guidance as well (Table 2). These positive correlations suggest that the older children in both groups are learning to use control and guidance from their mothers. In our experimental group, undercontrolling or overcontrolling mothers may provide an extreme model, while mothers in the control group demonstrate moderate behavior control and the use of guidance as well to their maturing offspring.

AFFECTIVE RELATIONS BETWEEN FAMILY MEMBERS

The coded variables support (agree) and disagree were selected as pertinent, perhaps, to the area of affective transactions. (Aggressive and affectionate responses were too infrequently given to permit study.) The differences between support and disagree were obtained and treated as one score. In practically all cases, support surpassed disagree. None of the differences were significant or showed any trend (Table 1). Thus, we are unable to obtain much information from the coded variables in this area, and are required to rely primarily on the qualitative analysis.

Returning to Task 3 (the fight), we categorized the source or origin of the conflict as labeled by the story-tellers and whom they described as the participants.

It will be recalled from the preceding discussion that ten experimental families answered the question. They described, in all, twenty-one fights. Of these, thirteen were between siblings, reported as occurring in seven families. The other fights included one parent-child dispute, four parent-parent conflicts, and three between children and nonfamilial figures.

In eight of the families (including all seven in which sibling fights were reported), an aggressive act against a person was described as the initial event precipitating the conflict. In only one case was this nonphysical aggression. The typical opening followed the model: "It started when X hit Y." Noncooperation by a sibling and disputes over mother's nurturance and over property were also mentioned, all by one family. One parent-child fight was over nonacceptance of parental control, during which the child threatened physical aggression to the parent. The parental disputes were over nurturance distribution to the children, controlling each other, or obscure.

The ten control families described fourteen fights, of which eleven were between siblings and three between parent and child. None was described between parents, or with an outside figure. The sources of their disputes were primarily nonphysical; noncooperation of sibling (two); competition (two); competition over mother's nurturance (three); and dispute over property (three). One conflict only was described as originating with a physically aggressive act. The parent-child conflicts were over the child's nonfulfillment of the parents' demand that he perform a specific chore (two); or accept a family norm (one).

The outstanding feature in this analysis is the prevalence of physically aggressive acts mentioned by the experimental families as the precipitating event in a family dispute. We do not know whether this reflects a greater amount of physically aggressive interaction among the children in our experimental group or whether these acts were provoked by the same type of initial interactive events as those mentioned by the control families: noncooperation, property disputes, etc. If the latter is true, we may be seeing the experimental families' tendency to perceive all conflict behavior as necessarily physically aggressive and threatening and to focus only on the affectively charged components of a sequence of events, rather than on the "real content" of that which sets them in motion.

A similar pattern of response emerges if we examine the responses made by the children to Task 5, when they describe what they like and dislike about their siblings. The children in nine experimental families responded to this question, and in every case the thematic content of the responses included physical aggression. In contrast, only in four of the ten control families did the children present their siblings as aggressive. The primary thematic material for the control children emerged around cooperation such as sharing, play, etc., in eight families (in contrast to only four experimental families). Control children also focused on other liked or disliked attributes of their siblings such as cooperating with mother (three families), following family norms (three), and disputing over property (four). Cooperating with mother and following the norm were each mentioned once by a child in an experimental family.

Again, we seem to see in our control subjects the ability to focus on differentiated aspects of behavior around which affective attitudes may crystallize, whereas the experimental subjects tended to concentrate on primitive affect expression which follows or accompanies interpersonal transactions.

We will not comment further on the responses made by parents to children or children to parents, since this material was discussed in the preceding section on *Executive Behavior*. We wish to remind the reader, however, that the control children presented their parents as nurturant to a much greater extent than the experimental children did.

A final qualitative analysis was made of Task 4 (spending $10) to explore the types of positive activity which might unify the family, that is, around which they could integrate. Although a variety of activities were mentioned, three main categories appeared: (a) buying food (groceries) for all to eat; (b) some pleasurable, even frivolous object or activity; and (c) splitting up the cash, that is, no joint family object or activity. Some of the families presented more than one final answer, and their alternatives will also be considered.

Eight of the experimental families gave buying some food as an answer to the question. In six, this was the only activity around which they could get together, while the other two families mentioned splitting the cash as an alternative. One family suggested splitting the cash as their only solution. Three families described pleasurable joint activities (a party, a picnic), in one case as an alternative to splitting the money or buying food.

In contrast, only two control families resolved on food (one with the alternative of splitting the money). None settled for splitting the money alone. In six families pleasurable activities or objects (buy a new birdcage for the family pet, go to Coney Island together) were selected, with two families alternatively suggesting splitting the money. Thus, even though the same number of families suggested group or "unified" solutions to the question, the experimental families seemed to conceive of pleasurable or integrated family activity in terms of satisfaction of a primary need (food), whereas the control families verbalized a wider range of pleasurable experiences.

Summary of Experimental-Control Findings

COMMUNICATION

Experimental family members were extremely talkative or relatively silent compared to their control counterparts. Experimental children addressed their mothers excessively or relatively ignored them. A positive relationship was found between how much the experimental mothers talked and how frequently they were addressed. These findings were interpreted as reflecting the engagement-disengagement dimension described clinically for the experimental group. Whereas experimental children were extremely over- or underdisruptive, experimental mothers were less disruptive than the control mothers. It was suggested that the experimental family members might be disruptive in nonverbal ways. Qualitatively, experimental family members seemed to communicate with greater difficulty. They misunderstood, misinterpreted, and avoided task assignments, confused facts and issues, and denied their own and others' communications. Experimental parents expressed attitudes toward their children in a way seen as egocentric compared to the more objective verbalizations by the control parents. Control children were more able to express their attitudes in objective terms than were the experimental children.

EXECUTIVE BEHAVIOR

Experimental mothers were more extreme in their use of behavior control than control mothers. No quantitative differences were found for the categories of leadership and guidance. Qualitatively, more control parents appeared to be effective leaders in a family discussion, and more were described as exerting behavior control in family disputes. More control parents offered rules and concrete examples of acceptable or unacceptable behavior, thus making their expectations clear and perhaps providing a better learning experience. Control families recounted a variety of non-physical methods used by the parents to implement executive behavior, whereas experimental parents were more frequently described as resorting to physical punishment. Children's attitudes toward parents crystallized around themes of behavior control in the experimental families, while control children focused on parental nurturance. Children's requests for leadership, behavior control, and guidance received attention in more control families, and in more cases were responded to by the parents. Control children supported their mothers' executive behavior in proportion to the amount the mothers manifested.

AFFECT

No difference was found in amount of agreement-disagreement between groups. Themes of physical aggression were prominent in discussions of family disputes and attitudes toward siblings in the experimental group, whereas more control children focused on their siblings' cooperativeness or competitiveness. About the same number of families in each group conceptualized pleasurable, joint family activities, but for the experimental families these revolved primarily around eating, while the control families described a wider variety of shared family experiences.

Comparisons of Pre- and Post-Therapy Responses of Experimental Families

The interpretations of changes in Family Task transcripts in a comparison of pre- and post-therapy responses of the experimental families are somewhat ambiguous. First, since the control families were not tested twice, we cannot conclude that any changes in the experimental families' responses were necessarily due to their intervening therapeutic experiences (we cannot show that the control families did *not* change, or if they *did* change, how much). Second, there is a problem involving the shifting composition of our family groups (see footnote 1). Of the twelve experimental pre-therapy families, only six were the same in member composition when seen in the post-therapy condition. In one family, a father joined a "fatherless" family, and in another the father dropped out. In five families, a child or children were not available for the post-therapy Family Task session, although we never lost a complete subcategory (older children, younger children) for any family. Not only did this introduce problems of selective "drop-in" or "drop-out" of subjects, but also the shifting family composition may have affected the responses of the other family members with whom they had been interacting.

Thus, all statements about "change" in our experimental families must be considered most tentative, and only as potential indicators rather than as conclusive findings.

COMMUNICATION

No consistent differences were found for quantity of mothers' verbalization or the degree to which the mother was a target for the family's communications, either as to the central tendencies (medians) or the previously mentioned clustering of the mothers into "extreme" groups (see Table 4). Quantity of verbalization for older and younger children was not tested, since raw scores (rather than percentages) were used, and these were contaminated by the attrition of subjects in these subgroups. No changes were noted in number of disruptive responses given by mothers, older children, or younger children (Table 4). Thus, no changes in the formal coded communication variables were obtained in the pre- to post-therapy comparisons.

Qualitative analysis of responses to Task 3 (the fight) revealed that eight families (in contrast to four, pre-therapy) now told stories whose conflict clarity was judged adequate. The four in the post-condition who did not tell clear stories were among those who "failed" in the pre-condition as well. Denials of family fights still emerged for three families. One mother said, after the children told of fierce fighting and threatened attack with a chair, "Oh, you were just playing, that was no fight," and an older daughter chimed in, "That was a game, they mean a real fight." Another mother termed a physical aggression by one child upon another

TABLE 4

MEDIANS OF FAMILY TASK VARIABLES FOR EXPERIMENTAL GROUP IN PRE- AND POST-THERAPY CONDITIONS

Variable	Median Pre-therapy	Median Post-therapy	p Value[a]
Mother—number of verbalizations	51	41	no diff.
Mother as target for family's verbalizations —per cent above expected	+1.5	+3.0	no diff.
Mother's per cent Disruptive	5.0	5.0	no diff.
Older Children per cent Disruptive	11.5	10.5	no diff.
Younger Children per cent Disruptive	13.5	11.5	no diff.
Mother's per cent Leadership	28.0	21.5	.10
Mother's per cent Behavior Control	4.5	9.5	no diff.
Older Children per cent Request LCG	2.0	2.5	.10
Younger Children per cent Request LCG	3.5	3.5	no diff.
Older Children per cent Leadership	10.0	15.0	no diff.
Older Children per cent Behavior Control	1.0	1.0	no diff.
Mother—per cent Agree minus per cent Disagree	11.0	12.5	no diff.
Older Children—per cent Agree minus per cent Disagree	24.6	20.0	no diff.
Younger Children—per cent Agree minus per cent Disagree	21.5	17.5	no diff.

[a] Wilcoxin matched pairs signed-ranks test (see Siegel, 1956, pp. 75–83). All p values are two-tailed values.

"a mistake." In one family, a mother who in the pre-therapy task had been unaware of her children's fights was equally uncomprehending in the post-condition, and when she asked questions, the story-teller shifted his ground, saying, "No fights. Two years ago we had the last fight." The other sources of lack of conflict clarity were similar to those described previously. However, eight families told stories that were at least minimally clear as to facts and sequence, and achieved a reasonable family consensus.

Qualitative analysis of the types of responses given to Task 5 (what pleases and displeases . . . about other members of the family) revealed first, that parents and children in more families were able to respond to this question. In the pre-therapy condition, parents in six and children in three families did not respond. In the post condition, however, parents and children in only two families did not respond. Some misinterpretations of the question, such as "Tell who pleases you most" or "Tell what we like to do" still emerged, but to a lesser degree, thus facilitating more scorable responses.[6] The major shift in the types of responses given showed up in the parents' distributions. Parents in about the same number of families gave Type 1, objective responses (five out of six pre-, and seven out of ten, post-). Proportionally fewer parents in the post-condition gave Type 2, personal responses, however (four out of six, pre- and four out of ten, post-). Again, Type 3, affect responses were infrequent, given by only two parents.

The distribution of Type 1 and Type 2 responses given by the children remained essentially unchanged. Children in about the same number of families made Type 3, affect responses, but although they had used this type of response to convey exclusively negative (aggressive) affect in the pre-condition, they gave about an equal number of positive (affectionate) and negative ones in the post-condition.

EXECUTIVE BEHAVIOR

If we examine the coded variables for mother's executive behavior, the only significant change obtained was for leadership, which declined (Table 4). By inspection, there was a tendency for the extremely undercontrolling mothers to make more behavior control responses, but this did not emerge in the statistical analysis (Table 4). Guidance did not change in any consistent way (see Table 5).

When we turn to a qualitative examination to determine leadership effectiveness we find that four families were led (post-condition) by the parent alone, where before there were none. Two families were led by the parent with the assistance of an older child, one with the assistance of a younger child, and in five there was a "weak" parent alone. To sum up, a change occurred in seven families: in four due to the dropping out of the child's influence, and in three due to the increase in the parents' effectiveness. In five families the pattern remained essentially unchanged.

Turning to the qualitative analysis of Task 3 (the fight) to examine the executive role played by the parents, the main change seemed to be in the number of families reporting use of behavior control by the parents during the conflict. Parents in seven post-condition families made this response, compared to those in four pre-condition families. An increased number of guidance statements ascribed to parents during the course of

---

[6] One interesting and instructive example of the "training" children in the experimental families receive in the blurring of affect experience and expression, may be seen in the explanation given by a mother to a child during this question, "Unhappy and mad are the same thing."

TABLE 5

NUMBER OF EXPERIMENTAL FAMILIES CHANGING BETWEEN
PRE- AND POST-THERAPY CONDITIONS ON FAMILY
TASK VARIABLES THAT MEASURE OR DESCRIBE
EXECUTIVE BEHAVIOR

| Variable | Number of Families Showing Change (Out of 12) | | p Value[a] |
	Increased pre-post	Decreased pre-post	
Mother's Guidance	5	4	no diff.
Children's Requests LCG answered more than 50 per cent of the time	5	0	.06
Parent answers Children's Requests LCG	5	0	.06
Older Children Support Mother's LCG	5	1	.22
Younger Children Support Mother's LCG	5	0	.06
Older Children's Guidance	3	4	no diff.

[a] Binomial test (Siegel, 1956, pp. 36–42).

the dispute (no families, pre-condition; three families, post-condition) as well as given during the task discussion (three families, pre-condition; five families, post-condition) was also found.

Qualitatively, the guidance statements seemed to be of a higher order as well, for example:

"If someone takes something from you why can't you come and tell me instead of beating up on these kids?"

"This is not a way to talk to your mother, right? . . . If someone hears what you say to your mother what will they think about you, what about this fellow . . ."

"Don't go through nobody's pockets. You're not supposed to do that . . . that's what causes the fights . . . you all wind up fighting each other, hurting each other . . . and not speaking to each other, right?"

However, there was little change in the description of the type of implementation used by parents of their behavior control. About the same number of parents were described as relying on physical punishment, and only one parent was reported using nonphysical punishment, as before.

It is difficult to say much about the children's views of the parents as derived from the qualitative analysis of Task 5 (what you like and dislike, etc.), because responses were made in this category in only four families. One parent was described as controlling-punitive, two as aggressive, and two as nurturant. We cannot even speculate about these meager results.

Parents in nine families did talk about their children, so perhaps we can say more about this area. Only one parent complained of a child's nonacceptance of control. About the same number of parents focused on the children's "behaving" themselves as before, but only one of the responses was coached by a child. The others were spontaneous.

To return to the coded variables, if we look at the children's requests for leadership, behavior control, and guidance (lcg) from mother and their "vicissitudes," we see some changes. Older children in the same number of families as before (seven) made requests for lcg from their mothers, but those who did so made them to a significantly greater degree. No difference was obtained for the younger children (Table 4). In significantly more of the families in which such requests were made, at least half of the requests were replied to (Table 5). The number of cases where a parent replied to the requests also increased significantly (Table 5). The younger children supported mother's lcg responses in a significantly greater number of families, and the number of families in which the older children made these support responses tended to increase as well (Table 5).

Without wishing to draw strong conclusions about the foregoing findings, we will merely point out that the increased "responsiveness" of parents to children's requests for lcg and the increased "support" of the children for the parents' executive behavior tended to make them appear more similar to the control group.

No consistent differences were found for the coded variables relating to the executive behavior of the older children: leadership, behavior control (Table 4), and guidance (Table 5).

AFFECTIVE RELATIONS BETWEEN FAMILY MEMBERS

The coded scores Agree-minus-Disagree were not significantly different from pre- to post-conditions for mothers, older children, or younger children (see Table 4). Again we must look to the qualitative analyses for information in this area.

For Task 3 in the post-therapy condition, eleven families told of thirteen fights, with one family not giving any categorizable answer. This represented a considerable decrease in the number of fights reported.

Nine of the fights, reported by seven families (about the same as before), were between siblings. Two parent-child (two families) and two parent-parent (two families) fights were also described. None were mentioned involving outside figures.

Some decline in the number of families reporting an aggressive act as the precipitating event was noted. In the pre-therapy condition, eight of the ten families giving stories initiated them this way, while only five of the eleven families did so in the post-condition. Other sibling-sibling disputes mentioned were over nurturance distribution (one), nonacceptance of control by a sibling (one), and property (two). Parent-child disputes were over the child's nonacceptance of mother's control, and nonfulfillment of a chore. The parental fights were over controlling each other, in one case involving jealousy.

Qualitative analysis of the thematic content of like-dislike characteristics of the siblings, as seen in Task 5, revealed a minor trend toward a reduced emphasis on physical aggression. In the pre-condition, children in all nine families from which material was available described each other as aggressive, but children in only seven of the ten families in the post-condition did so. About the same number as before (few) included cooperation, property disputes, following of norms, and "behaving" as evaluative criteria.

Finally, the qualitative analysis of Task 4 material (how the family will spend $10) shows only a minor change, or no change. Six families elected to buy food (these six were among the eight which offered the same solution previously), two families chose to split up the cash, and four described pleasurable joint family activities (compared with three families in the pre-condition). Basically, the families still seemed unable to unify themselves, even in fantasy, around integrative family activities other than eating.

Summary of Changes from Pre-Therapy to Post-Therapy Condition

COMMUNICATION

No changes were found for the formal variables in this area (quantity of mother's verbalization, degree to which she was spoken to, or disruptive responses). Conflict clarity of the "fight" stories was judged improved for a number of families, although some parents still denied or were unaware of their family's conflicts. Parents and children in more families were able to express their attitudes about others in the family. Proportionally, the number of parents giving objective responses remained the same but fewer parents gave personal responses. The children's responses (primarily personal, few objective) remained relatively unchanged.

EXECUTIVE BEHAVIOR

In the post-therapy condition mothers spent less of their time in leadership activity, but the amount of behavior control and guidance remained essentially unchanged. Qualitatively, parents appeared to be more effective leaders in the task discussions in the post-therapy condition. Reports of family conflicts suggested that parents played a greater executive role with respect to behavior control and guidance than they had in the pre-therapy condition. Qualitative improvements in the expression of parental guidance were noted. However, parents were reported as relying as heavily on physical punishment and as little on other methods of implementing behavior control as before. Parents appeared more responsive to their children's requests for leadership, behavior control, and guidance, and the children showed increased support of the parents' executive behavior. No changes were seen in the executive behavior of the older children.

AFFECTIVE RELATIONS BETWEEN FAMILY MEMBERS

No differences were found for the coded score agree-disagree. Fewer fights were reported in the post-therapy condition, the majority between siblings, as before. Themes of aggressive acts declined considerably in the descriptions of family fights and, to a lesser extent, in the reported attitudes toward siblings. As in the pre-therapy condition, few families were able to conceptualize, even in fantasy, integrative family activities other than eating.

The Wiltwyck Family Interaction Apperception Technique (FIAT)

The Family Interaction Apperception Technique (FIAT) is a pictorial projective technique modeled after the Thematic Apperception Test (TAT). It was specifically designed to elicit projective material concerning interaction among family members along dimensions such as control, guidance, nurturance, aggression, etc. The FIAT is comprised of ten pictures depicting families in different activities. It is individually administered, appropriate for children as well as adults, and was especially developed for administration to subjects who do not necessarily come from a white, middle-class background (subjects for whom most projective instruments were developed).

Our instrument differs from the TAT in the following ways:

1. The scenes depict family interaction situations, primarily. Their content is narrower, concerning only those areas which were considered relevant to our study. (This does not imply, however, that all possible dimensions of the FIAT are tapped by the variables we employed.)

2. The instructions specifically call for stories about families and family interaction, thereby limiting and structuring the responses of the subjects.

3. The action in the stories is specific, the content of the pictures less ambiguous than the TAT's, and the drawings themselves are clearly structured.

4. The racial characteristics of the people in the drawings are deliberately indeterminate so that, hopefully, this instrument is appropriate for cross-racial administration and for several subcultural groups in our society.

The above considerations are relevant to the particular characteristics of our subject population. The families we studied consisted of Negroes, Puerto Ricans, and whites. It was important to present stimuli which could be responded to with equal interest by all these groups. Also, we wished to explore family interaction by giving the same instrument to all members of the family. The simplicity and concreteness of the situations portrayed were designed so that children as well as adults could respond to these pictorial stimuli. In addition, it has been found (see Chapter 2) that many people from educationally deprived backgrounds or from different cultures have difficulty responding to most of our standard projective tools because they involve contents and meanings which are unfamiliar to them. The family pictures we have constructed show scenes which are familiar, recognizable, and applicable to situations which the population under study might experience. In general, the development of this instrument took into consideration a number of problems faced by those using projective techniques with respect to eliciting maximum productivity from various populations (see Murstein, 1963; and Zubin, Eron, and Schumer, 1965).

The instrument was pretested with children and adults from a group of Wiltwyck (nonresearch) families. On the basis of this preliminary exploration, some of the drawings were altered to increase family interactions and to focus more specifically on areas relevant to the hypothesis being explored. Because there was more variability in the productivity of children under seven as well as some difficulty in maintaining their attention span and eliciting free verbalizations, it was decided to use a cut-off point of age seven for testing the children in this study. In general, pretesting this instrument disclosed it to be quite satisfactory for our purposes. The testing period of about thirty minutes seemed short enough to sustain the attention level of the children. There were no discernible discrepancies in the responsiveness of Negro, Puerto Rican, and white families to the physical characteristics of the people drawn—either in terms of racial or cultural allusions to the characters in the stories or by the rejection of any cards in the series. No differences in productivity were noted among these groups.

The Instrument

The final series of pictures were photographed from the original ink drawings of the artist.[7] They are comprised of ten 8″ x 10″ pictures to be administered in a fixed order. Card I was placed first because it depicted a fairly neutral, nonthreatening situation which introduced the idea of talking about a family in interactional terms and because it portrayed all members of a family. Appendix D presents the ten FIAT pictures. They depict the following scenes:

I   Family around dinner table, mother giving out cake.
II   Brothers (or father and sons) around television set.
III   Mother reclining on chair, brother and sister performing household chores, baby playing.
IV   Brothers (three) fighting or playing, parents in background looking on.
V   Mother holding baby, toddler at her knee, older children (three) talking to each other.
VI   Younger boy kneeling near wallet in street, older boy or father standing close by.
VII   Mother and another woman (teacher) standing with a boy in front of a school.
VIII   Brothers and sister (or parent and children) playing a game together.
IX   Man, woman, and boy in front of a store with broken window.
X   Children watching parents arguing.

[7] The authors wish to express their appreciation to Virginia Cantarella, the artist who drew these pictures. We also wish to acknowledge the important contribution of Dr. Shirley Elbert, who was a member of our research team, in the development of the Family Task and FIAT procedures and the FIAT coding system. Dr. Elbert also assumed a major share in the analysis of the FIAT data.

Administration and Subjects

The following instructions were used:

Children

> I have some pictures which show a family together doing differ-
> ent things which I'd like you to look at—you know, like on
> TV sometimes they have a story every week and at the end
> they show you one scene of the coming attractions, the story
> that's going to be on next week. That's to give you an idea of
> what the story will be about. Well, these pictures are like the
> one scene of the story and I would like you to tell me what you
> think the story is about—what's going on, what's happening in
> the story, and how it's going to turn out. For instance, what about
> this family scene? What is this story going to be about?

Adults

> I have some pictures about family life which I am going to show
> you. Each one shows a family scene and I would like you to tell
> me what is happening in this scene with the family, about each
> of the people in the picture, and how you think it will turn out.

The cards were handed to the subject one at a time and a verbatim
account of his stories was recorded by the test administrator. If the
subject did not understand the instructions or departed from the instructions to tell stories about families, the instructions were repeated. Other
questions by the tester were designed to clarify who was involved in
the interaction described or to encourage free verbalization.[8]

For a number of practical reasons, several therapists, social workers,
and psychologists—all associated with our research project—were trained
to administer the FIAT. Having more than one FIAT administrator was
also necessitated by considerations involving the research plan. For ex-

---

[8] After all stories were given, the examiners had the subjects choose the story they
liked the most and the story they liked the least, and give the reasons for their choices.
Data concerning this instruction are available, but not yet analyzed. Two FIAT protocols from a research family are presented in Appendix D. One is from Mrs. Martinez
and the other from her son, Rafael, ten years old at the time of testing. Rafael was
the Wiltwyck (index) child.

ample, the requirement that all family members be present for the Family Task procedure made them also available for FIAT administration on an individual basis in the same session, provided that enough examiners were trained to administer it. This was particularly important because some of the families were large and could stay only for limited amounts of time. In addition, all testing had to be completed in the experimental group prior to the scheduling of therapy sessions. Although several different examiners administered the FIAT, the *same* examiner was used for the pre- and post-testing for each member of the experimental families; only one examiner was used for the testing of all of the control families. The effect of interexaminer differences on the variance in our findings is not known.

The administration of the FIAT to the family members followed their participation in the Family Task. FIAT protocols were obtained twice from the experimental families (pre- and post-therapy conditions) but only once from the control families. As already noted, all subjects over the age of seven were asked to participate in the FIAT procedure. Tables A and B in Appendix A present some information about our families including socioeconomic characteristics of the parents, and number and age distributions of the children.[9]

Scoring System[10]

A system was devised to code the stories on the FIAT according to eight main variables: control, guidance, acceptance of responsibility, nurturance, affection, cooperation, aggression, and family harmony. The FIAT was designed to elicit information about these dimensions because of our early interest in family interaction in these areas. For example, it was felt that in the experimental families, the parents relinquished executive functioning either to older siblings or to outside authority figures (behavior control and guidance). It was also thought that many of their guidance and behavior control functions were ineffective and

---

[9] See footnote 1, page 302. A FIAT was not available for one experimental mother in the pre-treatment condition; her post-treatment FIAT was therefore omitted from the pre-post-treatment comparisons. Two older children and one younger child did not receive the FIAT in the post-treatment condition. Seven experimental and one control younger children between the ages of six and seven participated in the Family Task but not the FIAT due to the different minimal age criteria for the two procedures.
[10] A detailed manual for coding the FIAT is presented in Appendix D.

inappropriate. Another characteristic of these families, and in particular of their acting-out children placed in residential treatment, is the marked amount of aggression in their interactive behavior. Thus, the variable of aggression within the family unit was included for examination. Also expected was that family cohesiveness and rapport would be minimal in the experimental families. Variables tapping the latter aspect of interaction were cooperation, family harmony, and affection. These variables were coded from the activity and interactions described by the subject in his FIAT stories.

In order to explore the nature of intrafamily focus on these dimensions, each coded score included a reference to the interacting figures within the stories, designating them by their role terms: "parent"; "child (sibling)"; "outsider"; and "family." For example, a theme could be coded as "guidance: mother to child," or "behavior control: sibling to sibling."

The eight variables could be accompanied by various subcategories, though these might not always be present in all stories by all subjects. For example, a behavior control move might be coded, but the subcategory of effective behavior control would appear as a separately coded item only if the effectiveness of the behavior control move was clearly indicated in the subsequent verbalization of the story.

To check the reliability of the coding procedure, two independent scorers categorized 110 responses. They achieved an over-all agreement of 86 per cent. All the protocols were then arranged in a random order, and "blind" coding was done by one psychologist. The only identifying information on each protocol indicated whether the subject was a mother, father, boy, or girl. This constituted the final coding.

After all the protocols were coded, it was found that some of the subcategories of the variables and kinds of interactions (who to whom) yielded so few responses that it was not feasible to include these in the quantitative analysis. An arbitrary cut-off point of at least 25 responses in an interaction category was set for either a variable or its subcategory to be retained for analysis. The variables and interaction categories listed on the following page formed the basis of the quantitative analysis.

All scores subsequently referred to are percentages obtained as a ratio of the number of responses in a category or subcategory to the total number of coded responses for a given protocol. The subcategories for each variable are not independent categories. For example, ineffective control is also included within the over-all behavior control score. This

Variables	*Interactions*
Behavior Control	parent-child, sib-sib, outsider-family
effective control	parent-child, sib-sib
ineffective control	parent-child, sib-sib
inappropriate control	parent-child, sib-sib
control with punishment	parent-child
Guidance	parent-child, sib-sib
effective guidance	parent-child
Acceptance of Responsibility[11]	self
Nurturance	parent-child
Affection	parent-child
Cooperation	sib-sib, child-parent
Aggression	parent-parent, sib-sib
physical aggression	parent-parent, sib-sib
Family Harmony	

is an additional rating given if it can be ascertained from the story that the control move is ineffective. Furthermore, a behavior control score may have two additional subcategories at one time, for example, if a behavior control move is effective and accompanied by punishment.[12]

For the purpose of making the presentation of the FIAT results conceptually comparable to those of the Family Task and to complement the discussion in Chapter 5, the variables have been organized around the rubrics of "executive behavior" and "affective relationships." (We have no scored information from the FIAT relating to communicational processes.) Under each of these two headings, the description of results is further subdivided by the interaction categories. Thus we will first present the findings pertaining to executive behavior attributed to *parents* vis-à-vis children in the stories and then proceed to discuss executive behavior described for *siblings*.

The classes of subjects whose scores were included in the statistical tests and discussed in the following sections are: mothers; older children; and younger children. The fathers comprised too small a group to analyze separately.

---

[11] This variable was not included in the earliest formulations of our study, but was included prior to the coding of FIAT protocols to provide another means for exploring the lack of responsibility noted in acting-out behavior of children with delinquent syndromes. The definition of this variable assumes a self-recognition of misbehavior and internalized or self-guidance and behavior control as expressed through apology and/or some attempt to make restitution.

[12] The tendency score and the plus-minus notations for behavior control and guidance described in the coding instructions in Appendix D are omitted from the present analysis due to considerations of time and space in the case of the former, and insufficient information with respect to the latter.

Findings

Comparisons between Experimental and Control Families (before Treatment)

EXECUTIVE BEHAVIOR

All results discussed in this section will be found in Table 6. Our initial focus in this analysis was in the area of parental executive behavior as seen in the stories told by our subjects. For the dimension of parental behavior control and its subcategories (effective, ineffective, inappropriate, with punishment) let us first compare the results obtained from the experimental and control mothers.

TABLE 6

MEANS OF PERCENTAGE SCORES OF FIAT EXECUTIVE BEHAVIOR
VARIABLES IN EXPERIMENTAL AND CONTROL GROUPS
(Pre-Therapy Condition)

Variable	Mothers		Older Children		Younger Children	
	Exper.	Control	Exper.	Control	Exper.	Control
N	11	10	26	20	21	20
Parental Behavior in Stories						
Behavior Control	19.1	20.5	21.1	14.9†	18.7	17.5
Effective control	9.5	12.1	11.5	10.1	8.3	9.1
Ineffective control	5.4	4.0	4.1	1.4†	2.7	3.1
Inappropriate control	3.4	0ᵃ	3.5	.7‡	3.3	1.0†
Control with punishment	9.7	9.4	9.9	7.3	9.8	9.3
Guidance	4.5	4.7	5.4	7.0	3.6	4.6
Effective guidance	.3	3.4ᵇ	1.2	5.4‡	2.0	4.6†
Acceptance of responsibility	1.6	2.2	2.3	3.2	1.5	4.0‡
Sibling Behavior in Stories						
Behavior Control	10.0	7.4	10.2	7.5ᵇ	8.9	5.9ᵇ
Effective control	5.1	3.6	5.1	3.5	2.6	2.2
Ineffective control	3.4	2.0	4.7	2.4†	3.4	3.0
Inappropriate control	2.4	1.3	2.0	1.5	2.0	1.3
Guidance	1.5	.8	1.8	2.1	2.1	1.6
Acceptance of responsibility	1.3	1.9	1.6	1.9	1.1	2.9*
Outsider to Family						
Behavior Control	10.8	4.2†	6.6	6.1	8.5	2.3‡

* $p < .10$
† $p < .05$
‡ $p < .01$
All p values are two-tailed "t" test values.
ᵃ No responses were elicited in this category.
ᵇ "Tendency": p of .10 to .20.

As may be seen in Table 6, there were no significant differences[13] in the mothers' group for either the over-all amount of parental behavior control seen or any of the subcategories. None of the stories told by the control mothers, however, contained any instance of inappropriate parental behavior control while five told by the experimental mothers did describe such an event. Both the older and younger experimental children's groups ascribed a significantly greater amount of inappropriate behavior control to parents in their stories than did their control counterparts. The older experimental children saw significantly more ineffective parental behavior control as well. These findings for the older children are complex since, it may be recalled, the percentages within the subcategories are part of the total dimension score. Over-all parental behavior control scores were significantly greater for the older experimental children, which may contribute to the significant results for this group with respect to ineffective and inappropriate behavior control. For none of the groups—mother, older, or younger children—were there any differences with respect to effective behavior control or control with punishment. Unfortunately, for this latter subcategory we were unable to distinguish physical from nonphysical punishment—a distinction which proved of some interest in the Family Task material.

There was no difference between the mothers' groups with respect to the over-all amount of parental guidance expressed in the stories, but there was a tendency for control mothers to describe such parental guidance as effective to a greater extent than the experimental mothers. Similarly, the older and younger control children saw significantly more effective parental guidance in their stories than did the experimental children, although there were no differences for total guidance.

The variable of acceptance of responsibility has been included in this section as representative of internalized executive activity or self-regulation (see footnote 11). No differences were obtained for parental acceptance of responsibility as seen by the mothers or older children. However, the younger control children did portray parents as accepting responsibility for their own behavior significantly more than did the experimental children.

---

[13] All statistical findings reported in the FIAT tables are based on two-tailed "t" tests. We felt more confident in employing "t" tests with respect to FIAT data than with Family Task data because of the larger number of subjects involved in the former—*individual* rather than family data were examined. Note, also, that because of the large number of "t" tests applied and because not all of them were based on independent data, there may be a spuriously high number of significant findings.

To sum up, then, in the area of parental executive behavior the amount of parental behavior control and guidance per se as portrayed in the stories did not differ (except in one instance) from the experimental to the control group. However, qualitative features such as greater inappropriateness of behavior control in the experimentals' stories and greater effectiveness of guidance in the controls' stories did appear to be significant and consistent. These findings complement our impressions from the Family Task and clinical material that differences in parental executive behavior between our clinical population of families and others are not simply differences in quantity. Qualitative features such as inappropriateness, vacillation between extremes, and lack of effective impact seem to be the major distinguishing features.

In our clinical thinking we hypothesized that as a result of the relinquishment and delegation of executive authority by the experimental parents, two alternative sources of executive activity would increase in importance for the family. These were the sibling subgroup, and extrafamilial figures or agencies, such as school, law enforcement figures, social workers, etc.

Let us first turn to the area of sibling executive behavior (see Table 6). No differences emerged for any of the pertinent variables from the stories told by the mothers. Both older and younger experimental children showed, however, a tendency to portray siblings controlling siblings to a greater extent than did those in the control group. The older experimental children saw such sibling behavior control as ineffective to a significantly greater degree than did the older control children. No differences between groups were obtained for sibling guidance. We were unable to test for any subcategories of sibling guidance due to an insufficient number of responses. With respect to children's acceptance of responsibility within the stories, the only significant difference was obtained from the younger children's group. The control subjects in this category saw more sibling acceptance of responsibility than did the experimental subjects. Thus, our notion of greater sibling executive activity in the experimental families may be said to be only minimally indicated from the children's FIAT results. Furthermore, the only significant finding indicates that such activity (behavior control) is seen as ineffective. It may be recalled that little quantitative evidence was obtained from the Family Task material to suggest experimental-control differences in sibling executive activity, although the structure of the Family Task tended to preclude the occurrence of such behavior.

An additional effort in this area was to examine the role of the outsider as the regulator of family behavior. Only with regard to the variable of behavior control did a sufficient number of responses emerge. We see from Table 6 that the experimental mothers and experimental younger children (but not the older children) saw an outside figure controlling a family member significantly more than the controls, as we had anticipated.

It may be of interest to speculate on the finding that only the younger children's groups differed significantly with regard to the variables relating to acceptance of responsibility by both parents and children in their stories. Also, in contrast to the older children's groups, they differed with respect to amount of outsider's behavior control of family members. Perhaps the younger control children are more sensitive than their counterparts to these issues of internal-external (literally extrafamilial) behavior control due to recent or current socialization training.

AFFECTIVE RELATIONS BETWEEN FAMILY MEMBERS

All of the results discussed in this section are presented in Table 7. Let us first examine parental affective behavior. No differences were found

TABLE 7

MEANS OF PERCENTAGE SCORES OF FIAT AFFECTIVE RELATIONSHIP
VARIABLES IN EXPERIMENTAL AND CONTROL GROUPS
(Pre-Therapy Condition)

Variable		Mothers		Older Children		Younger Children	
		Exper.	Control	Exper.	Control	Exper.	Control
	N	11	10	26	20	21	20
Parental Behavior in Stories							
Nurturance to children		3.5	2.9	4.9	4.6	3.3	3.2
Affection to children		1.3	4.0	1.3	2.9*	1.1	2.8†
Aggression to parent		7.0	5.2ᵃ	3.6	5.2†	5.6	5.4
Physical aggression		3.4	2.8	1.7	2.0	3.4	.7†
Children's Behavior in Stories							
Cooperation with sib		6.1	10.1ᵃ	7.2	7.6	4.1	9.3‡
Cooperation with parent		4.0	5.2	3.6	5.8†	3.4	5.9*
Aggression to sib		9.0	7.6ᵃ	10.1	6.8*	11.2	6.2‡
Physical aggression		7.5	5.8	6.5	3.8†	7.2	5.7
Family Harmony		4.3	9.6‡	3.2	5.5*	3.0	6.7‡

* $p < .10$
† $p < .05$
‡ $p < .01$
All p values are two-tailed "t" test values.
ᵃ "Tendency": $p.$ of .10 to .20.

between groups with respect to the variable of parental nurturance of children. Unfortunately, an insufficient number of responses in the sub-category inappropriate nurturance (a variable which particularly interested us in the light of our clinical experience) precluded further breakdown of this variable. On the other hand, significantly more parental affection to children was described by both control children's groups, particularly the younger, but not by the mothers.[14]

With respect to the only variable relating to parent-parent relationships, aggression, the findings are mixed. For over-all aggression, the experimental mothers tended to see more interparental aggression, whereas experimental older children described significantly *less* interparental aggression. No difference was found between the younger children's groups. When physical aggression between parents is singled out, results for the mothers and older children show no differences, but the younger experimental children saw significantly more parental combat than did their control counterparts. We might speculate that the older experimental children were defensively "blocking out" responses about parental disputes which in reality apparently occur frequently in their families. After all, this group saw less interparental aggression in their stories than any of the other groups, including their own mothers. However, this "defensiveness" apparently does not operate for the younger experimental children with respect to the even more loaded area of interparental physical aggression. Clearly, this area requires greater exploration; we cannot satisfactorily explain the inconsistencies in the findings at present.

Instances of children's affective behavior in the stories fell along two dimensions. Under the heading of cooperation, we see first that the control younger children saw significantly more cooperation for both sibling to sibling and child to parent interaction categories than did the experimental younger children. The older control children also portrayed significantly more child-to-parent cooperation than their experimental counterparts but did not differ from them on the variable of intersibling cooperation. Conversely, the control mothers tended to see children as cooperating among themselves to a greater extent than did the experi-

---

[14] There are no variables relating to negative aspects of parental affect toward children such as aggression. These were generally subsumed under the category, control with punishment, or were too few to be included in the quantitative analysis. Conversely, an insufficient number of responses was obtained for positive affective variables such as affection in the parent-to-parent, or child-to-parent interaction categories. While it is tempting to speculate on these findings, they are probably due mostly to the structure of the FIAT cards themselves.

mental mothers, but these groups did not differ from each other with respect to child-to-parent cooperation.

We found that both younger and older experimental children portrayed more sibling-to-sibling aggression than did the control children, and the experimental mothers showed a tendency in the same direction. When physical aggression was examined alone, these differences between the mothers' groups and between the younger children's groups disappeared. However, the experimental older children still saw significantly more intersibling combat than did the controls.

In sum, the control children described parents as more affectionate to children but not any more nurturant than did the experimental children. These control children also saw children as more cooperative with parents in their stories than did the experimental children. Younger experimental children portrayed sibling relationships as less cooperative and more generally aggressive (but not more physically aggressive) than did the controls. The older experimental children portrayed sibling relationships as more aggressive generally, and as more physically aggressive than did the controls but not any less cooperative. The latter findings pertaining to sibling relationships seem to relate to the thematic emphasis on intersibling aggressiveness which was so pronounced in the experimental Family Task protocols, in contrast to the control families' focus on intersibling cooperation. Interparental aggression was inconsistently portrayed by the groups as the experimental mothers tended to see more parental aggression, the older experimental children significantly less parental aggression, and the younger experimental children significantly more interparental physical aggression.

The final variable in this series, family harmony, is distinctive, since it reflects an expressive or attitudinal quality attributed to intrafamilial activity rather than describing a particular act. We found consistent results across our generational groups. The three groups of control subjects each portrayed significantly more family harmony than did the experimental groups. This may complement the qualitative impression from the Family Task that the control families can at least describe a greater variety of pleasurable conjoint family experiences.

Comparisons of Pre- and Post-Therapy Responses of Experimental Families

As we turn to an examination of the results obtained from the pre- post-treatment comparisons of the FIAT responses, the reader is again reminded that we have no control for changes in scores that might be due to test-retest phenomena or to the simple passage of time. Thus, any conclusions about change must be considered tentative and suggestive only.

EXECUTIVE BEHAVIOR

All results to be discussed in this section are shown in Table 8. Under the heading Parental Behavior in Stories, we see that in the post-treatment condition the mothers and the older children described significantly less parental control than they did in their pre-treatment stories. With respect to the subcategories of the control variable, the mothers tended to see less inappropriate parental control in their post-stories, and the older children's stories show significant declines in both

TABLE 8

MEAN PERCENTAGE DIFFERENCES OF FIAT EXECUTIVE BEHAVIOR
VARIABLES IN PRE-TREATMENT AND POST-TREATMENT
EXPERIMENTAL GROUP

Variable	Mean Differences[a]		
	Mothers	Older Children	Younger Children
N	11	24	20
Parental Behavior in Stories			
Control	−4.3*	−4.2†	2.1
Effective control	−2.8	− .9	2.5
Ineffective control	−1.3	−1.8[b]	.2
Inappropriate control	−2.1[b]	−2.5†	−1.2
Control with punishment	−2.3	−2.7*	0
Guidance	2.3	− .1	0
Effective guidance	4.3†	2.1*	1.1
Acceptance of responsibility	.1	.6	−1.2
Sibling Behavior in Stories			
Control	−2.2[b]	−2.9†	−2.8[b]
Effective control	−1.5	− .6	.6
Ineffective control	0	−2.0†	−2.0[b]
Inappropriate control	.4	− .7	− .6
Guidance	2.7*	1.2*	− .7
Acceptance of responsibility	1.7[b]	1.7[b]	.7
Outsider to Family			
Control	−5.4†	−2.2*	−2.4[b]

* $p < .10$
† $p < .05$
All p values are two-tailed "t" test values.
[a] The minus signs indicate *lower* percentage scores for the post-treatment groups. Conversely, the absence of a sign indicates *higher* percentage scores for post-treatment groups.
[b] "Tendency": p of .10 to .20.

inappropriate parental control and control with punishment, as well as a tendency for ineffective parental control to diminish from the pre- to post-conditions. No changes were noted with respect to any of the control variables in the younger children's stories.

The amount of parental guidance did not vary from the pre- to post-conditions for any of the groups, but *effective* parental guidance appeared to a significantly greater extent in the post-condition stories told by the mothers and the older children. No changes were seen for any of the groups with respect to parental acceptance of responsibility.

Over all, the most consistent results (from at least two groups in the same direction) seem to indicate a decline in the amount of total parental control as well as inappropriate parental control and an increase in effective parental guidance. (These changes seemed to move the scores in the direction of the control group findings previously reported.) The older children's group showed the greatest number of changes in their portrayals of parental executive behavior, while the younger children's group showed none.

With respect to sibling executive behavior, similar differences were seen in the pre-post comparisons. Over-all sibling control of siblings declined significantly in the stories of the older children, and the results from the mother and younger children's groups tended to be in the same direction, from the pre- to post-conditions. Ineffective sibling control likewise was seen significantly less by the older children, and the younger children's results again tended in the same direction. The other subcategories of sibling control did not change.

Sibling guidance of siblings increased significantly from the pre- to post-condition in the stories of the mothers and older children, but the younger children's scores did not change. The mothers and older children tended to see children accepting responsibility for their own actions to a greater extent in the post-condition than they had previously.

Thus, the change in sibling executive behavior in the stories that emerge from the pre-post treatment comparisons (decline in control, increase in guidance) seem to parallel the changes in parental executive behavior described above (decrease in control, increase in effective guidance).

The final result of interest in this section pertains to the amount of outside, extrafamilial control of family members. Both mothers' and older children's groups saw significantly less outsider control in their post-treatment stories than they reported before and the younger children tended to see less as well.

AFFECTIVE RELATIONS BETWEEN FAMILY MEMBERS

All results pertaining to affective relationships are presented in Table 9. With respect to parental affective behavior, significantly more parental nurturance appeared in the post-treatment stories of the younger children than in their earlier stories. Parental affection to children tended to increase pre- to post- for both children's groups. The mothers' stories showed no changes with respect to these two variables. The mothers did see significantly less interparental aggression in their post-stories than they had seen previously, but no change was noted for parent-to-parent physical aggression. Neither of the children's groups changed with respect to the amount of interparental over-all aggression or physical aggression.

No changes in intersibling cooperation appeared for any of the groups. The mothers (but neither children's group) did portray children as cooperative with parents to a greater extent in their post- as compared with their pre-treatment stories. Intersibling aggression declined significantly

TABLE 9

MEAN PERCENTAGE DIFFERENCES OF FIAT AFFECTIVE VARIABLES
IN PRE-TREATMENT AND POST-TREATMENT
EXPERIMENTAL GROUP

Variable		Mean Differences[a]		
		Mothers	Older Children	Younger Children
	N	11	24	20
Parental Behavior in Stories				
Nurturant to children		1.1	−1.1	6.1*
Affection to children		.7	2.1[b]	4.9[b]
Aggression to parent		−1.9†	.4	− .4
Physical aggression		−1.7	− .5	− .1
Children's Behavior in Stories				
Cooperation with sibling		.2	1.7	1.8
Cooperation with parent		2.2*	.7	0
Aggression to sibling		−4.0†	−5.6‡	−4.4†
Physical aggression		−1.3	−1.0	.2
Family Harmony		.4	− .2	.8

* $p < .10$
† $p < .05$
‡ $p < .01$
All p values are two-tailed "t" test values.
[a] The minus signs indicate *lower* percentage scores for the post-treatment groups. Conversely, the absence of a sign indicates *higher* percentage scores for post-treatment groups.
[b] "Tendency": p of .10 to .20.

from pre- to post-conditions in the stories of all three groups, although these differences disappeared for the subcategory physical aggression. Family harmony did not change.

In sum, the findings suggest that the mothers portrayed more instances of children cooperating with parents, while the children tended to see more parental affection and significantly more parental nurturance in the post- than in the pre-treatment condition. While there were no changes with respect to sibling cooperation, intersibling aggression was seen significantly less often by *all* groups. The mothers alone described less interparental aggression.

Summary—FIAT

With respect to findings comparing the pre-treatment experimental families and the control families, some of our expectations were fulfilled, while others were controverted or unsupported. Absolute amounts of executive behavior did not distinguish the groups, but we had no specific hypotheses here. Some of the qualitative variables, such as inappropriate control, ineffective control, and effective guidance were good differentiators in the directions we had expected, whereas others, such as effective control and control with punishment, were not. The sibling subgroup hypothesis was not supported by the data, but the notion of the influence of outsider control upon our experimental families did appear to be a relevant factor in their stories. In the area of affective behavior, the variable of nurturance did not emerge as a differentiator; however, our main expectations referred to inappropriate nurturance about which we obtained insufficient information. Generally, our findings with regard to parental affection, children's cooperativeness, and intersibling aggression were in the directions we had expected. Mixed findings were obtained for interparental aggression, with one significant result (deriving from the older children) contrary to our expectations. Finally, the over-all affective category, family harmony, was shown to be less prominent in the experimental subjects' stories, as we had anticipated.

With respect to the pre- and post-treatment experimental comparisons, over-all control did decline in the subjects' stories pre- to post-, although we had not predicted this. Again, inappropriate control, effective guidance, and, to a lesser extent, ineffective control, stood out as the subcategories most consistently varying (in the expected directions) pre- to post-, with the other subcategories showing little or no change.

Changes in sibling executive behavior as portrayed in the stories paralleled changes seen for parental activity. Outsider control of family members was consistently seen less pre- to post-, as we had hoped. In the area of affective relationships, some expected changes in parental affection, interparental aggression, and child-to-parent cooperation did emerge, although these were not consistent across generational classes. All groups were consistent in portraying no change in intersibling cooperation, but they did show significantly less intersibling aggression from pre- to post-conditions. While we might conclude that many affective components of intrafamilial relationships were seen as "improved," this was not reflected in the findings pertaining to the variable family harmony, since scores here did not change.

Concluding Remarks

One final word should be said here about the effectiveness of the two instruments described in this chapter. Both have advantages and limitations which are inherent in their design (such as the structuring of the FIAT cards around the particular variables under study, or the nonresponse by family members to Task questions in the absence of an examiner), as well as those imposed by our methods of presentation and analysis.

The Family Task, as we have seen, was particularly useful in eliciting a rich and complex body of information about *family structure* and *family communication* systems. However, it was necessary to supplement the formal coding analysis with the qualitative analysis in order to do justice to the material. Similarly, since affective behavior occurred too infrequently during the course of the Task to make the coding of it feasible, a content analysis was required to elucidate the important material available concerning intersibling relationships in the areas of cooperation and aggression. The qualitative analysis now poses a new challenge to us—to establish it in its own right as a rigorously defined and reliably quantified set of measures. However, even with both kinds of analyses certain types of interactions were not available for study. Interparental activity was relatively absent, due perhaps to the presence of the children in the situation. Information with respect to positive affect such as nurturance or affection (for parent-to-child or child-to-parent categories) simply did not emerge within the current Family Task framework as readily as it did in the FIAT.

The FIAT seems to provide a wider range of information about affective relationships, although, as mentioned before (footnote 14, page 340), some gaps do appear when all affective variables, positive and negative, are surveyed for all interaction categories. Information about family structure and executive behavior is also readily obtained with this instrument. An additional advantage in the FIAT analysis system is that qualitative aspects of executive behavior, at least as described in the stories, are specifically defined and reliably scored. However, some of the dynamic interplay (i.e., nature of parental control when children require it, request it, reject it, etc.) is not as available through the current FIAT analysis system as it is through the Family Task. Our interest in communication processes within families grew at a time when the FIAT coding system was already completed. Thus, this important area was neglected in the FIAT analysis. However, the potential for further research is great. Stylistic differences in mode of expression in the storytelling, linguistic features, as well as an examination of dialogue in the stories, may provide a fruitful source of data for future exploration.[15]

The clinical use of the material gleaned from a reading and interpretation of Family Task and FIAT protocols for an individual family may provide as valuable a contribution to family study as the use of these instruments in research. The reader is referred to one such individual family study reported by Elbert, Rosman, Minuchin, and Guerney (1964) and to the protocols presented in Appendixes C and D. Finally, it is hoped that our descriptions and discussion of the Family Task and the FIAT will provide some impetus for continued clinical and research explorations of their effectiveness.

REFERENCES

Drechsler, R. J., and Shapiro, M. I. A procedure for direct observation of family interaction in a child guidance clinic. *Psychiat.*, 1961, 24, 163–170.

Elbert, Shirley, Rosman, Bernice, Minuchin, S., and Guerney, B. G., Jr. A method for the clinical study of family interaction. *Amer. J. Orthopsychiat.*, 1964, 34, 885–894.

Murstein, B. I. *Theory and research in projective techniques (emphasizing the TAT)*. New York: John Wiley and Sons, 1963.

---

[15] For example, one informal attempt by two of the authors to distinguish blindly between experimental and control mothers' FIATs on the basis of the types of guidance and control verbalizations used proved quite successful.

Siegel, S. *Nonparametric statistics for the behavioral sciences*. New York: McGraw-Hill Book Co., Inc., 1956.

Wild, Cynthia. Disturbed styles of thinking. *Arch. gen. Psychiat.*, 1965, **13**, 464–470.

Wynne, L. C., and Singer, Margaret T. Thought disorder and family relations of schizophrenics: II a classification of forms of thinking. *Arch. gen. Psychiat.*, 1963, **9**, 199–206.

Zubin, J., Eron, L., and Schumer, Florence. *An experimental approach to projective techniques*. New York: John Wiley and Sons, 1965.

CHAPTER **8** *Afterword*

*W*hat have we learned from our exploratory investigations in this very complex area? Have we confirmed our initial expectations and hypotheses? The next few pages consider these and a few related questions.

First, a word about our research families and the "success" of our therapy. Seven out of our twelve research families were judged to be clinically improved at the end of treatment. The designations "improvement" or "nonimprovement" were not operationally defined. We tended to pool the judgments of the therapists in making such designations. We found that the specific content of the implicit or explicit criteria we used varied according to the over-all goals of therapy for a particular family and that these, in turn, were of necessity determined by what the family was like, how the members interacted with one another, and the kinds of roles which were available to them. In general, an increased capacity to explore alternative ways of coping in areas of stress among family members, a move away from either extreme of the disengagement-enmeshment dimension, a greater range of affective experience and expression, an increase in acceptance of parental roles, a strengthening of the spouse subsystem, more effective control and guidance by the parent or parents, and a more flexible, differentiated sibling subsystem which did not rely on the "parental child" for its organization entered into our judgments. Not all criteria were used for all families, of course. But above all, the flexibility of the pathways and even subtle changes in the quality of the communication process in our families received our careful attention when we were faced with the difficult, global task of judging whether or not a family had changed at the end of treatment.

Second, a few thoughts about changes in our conceptualizations. Our first crude appraisals of how our families functioned were later modified, developing into a rather detailed formulation of the nature of the family system—its structure, communicational processes, and affective resources. Our simple concern, for example, with the relinquishment of executive functions on the part of the parents gave way to the realization that *some* families apparently functioned as if the parents (the mothers in particular) were *overly* concerned with executive functions. This led us to the further realization that actually there seemed to be an axis of disengagement-enmeshment along which our research families were oriented, mostly toward either extreme. We were able to appreciate the paucity of roles available within the families and the rigidity of those which were available, and we were able to better examine the problems of families without a stable male figure and of families which contained a grandmother, a mother, and the latter's children but which did not function in a three-generational manner. Further, we came to appreciate the importance of the communicational systems in our families—an emphasis which had not been present at the beginning of our research.

Third, our bias for active therapeutic interventions in family structures has been sufficiently stressed as not to warrant further detailed specification. But we might say here that the techniques of our interventions—at first the use of stages in the research phase of our work, and later the use of multiple and alternating roles of observer and participant, varying subgroup composition, task assignments, attention to communication processes, mood allocation, etc.—all grew out of our earlier explorations.

Underlying the development of our newer techniques is the fact that our conceptualizations of the family as a total system became less static. We gradually became more concerned with the family "in motion" as a set of relatively autonomous, yet interdependent dynamic subsystems; and we also became concerned with the ways in which these subsystems maintain their rigidity, keeping certain hierarchies intact while masking or inhibiting the emergence of new subgroups which might modify the nature and content of family transactions. We were brought to this emphasis, too, by the clinical observation that new subsystems seem to emerge and to become stabilized only after the exploration and "loosening" of prominent and prevailing subsystems have been achieved.

This glimpse of a certain "order" in the unraveling and modification of the family's organization drew our attention to the basic significance of the power that group composition has to arrange the process of participation. That is, we realized more fully the technical significance of manipulating such fundamental aspects of structure as subgroup composition—who happens to be present interchanging around what problem area at what moment—and began to use such manipulation for therapeutic advantage. We employed this "power" to facilitate the appearance or disappearance of certain transactional processes, role definitions, and specific intrapsychic effects. The emphasis in Chapter 6 on the modification of the formats of family pathways by using interventions such as nonverbal distributional maneuvers, stages, and strategic compositional changes attests to this change in our thinking.

Fourth, our children's particular patterns of antisocial behavior seem to be imbued with the stylistic characteristics required for coping within their own families. The characteristics learned within the family carry over into their reactions to experiences outside the family, so that the coping devices available to them are largely limited to variations of the search for sheer excitement with siblings or their substitutes (peers) and the constant organization of the adult into controlling and aggressive positions.

We are particularly impressed with the intensity of our families' implicit training, which results in the curtailment of the children's ability to judge accurately the impact and implications of their behavior on others and themselves. As a result of this deficiency, the children are equipped neither to meet a culture with demands different from those of their families nor to use the ensuing clash with that different culture to refashion their coping patterns.

Therefore, our particular emphasis has been not on the intrapersonal dynamics of the delinquent act, which have been explored thoroughly by many authors,[1] but on the family culture which organizes the child's dominant style of coping. This style clashes with the differently defined rules and boundaries within large sectors of the extrafamilial world, where the child's behavior and its resultants are labeled "delinquent."

Finally, a few thoughts about our quantitative methods. Many of our results have confirmed our expectations. Moreover, when the FIAT and Family Task overlapped (in type of analysis), the results tended to be in the same direction. In addition, our experiences with these instruments have taught us a number of lessons for future research. For example, with all of our instruments we perhaps would stress in what we are looking for and in our specific measurements the so-called formal, stylistic variables such as the methods and means of communication, the pathways of communication, and the *manner*, the *form* of a message rather than its content. The capacity of the Family Task in this area has already been demonstrated.

For explorations of affective variables, the FIAT has proved to be especially useful, we might add. On the other hand, the Family Task was particularly helpful in highlighting aspects of executive behavior and communication processes. And the Verbal Behavior Analysis (see Appendix B) tended to reflect, par excellence, the nature of the therapy sessions themselves—the centrality of the therapists and the mothers, for example, and the directive nature of the therapy.

A More Differentiated View of Disorganized, Disadvantaged Families: Profiles

Our experiences with large numbers of disorganized, disadvantaged families yielded certain observations concerning distinguishing patterns or profiles (forms) of family structure which differentiated among these families in a surprisingly consistent fashion despite an array of differences in personality organization of individuals in families falling into the same family category. Thus, we have been able to distinguish the following patterns, which we have roughly labeled: the disengaged family; the enmeshed family; the family with the peripheral male; the family with nonevolved parents; and the family with juvenile parents. These formulations represent

---

[1] For example, Aichorn (see Fleischmann, Kramer, and Ross, 1964), Fenichel (1945), Friedlander (1949), Johnson (1959), and Johnson and Szurek (1952). Other approaches are sociological in nature, for example, Cohen (1955), Merton (1938, 1959), and Sutherland and Cressey (1960).

only the beginnings of our thinking. Undoubtedly other patterns exist; moreover, the criteria by which we differentiate these family forms are only roughly delineated—clearcut, sharply drawn distinguishing "signs" will hopefully emerge as a result of future empirical research. We offer our tentative conceptualizations with the foregoing goal in mind—as suggestive of hypotheses open to empirical investigation rather than as a definitive, "closed" conceptual framework.

The degree to which a particular family fits into one of these gross profiles can often be ascertained by the clinician in early phases of contact with the family—often before he knows individual family members in depth. Such diagnostic impressions can frequently be of considerable aid to the clinician, for they help him stress or minimize certain conflictual areas in his attempts to facilitate the emergence of certain roles or potentialize hidden stresses and strains so that new conflict resolutions and system modifications can be achieved. As already noted, the profiles which we will be describing do not constitute a set of rigorously drawn diagnostic entities—they simply reflect the structural forms most familiar in our sample and which have been helpful to our therapists in the development of strategies and techniques of entry into the family system.

When we make a "diagnosis" of a family system, we are stating where it stands at a specific point in its development from our particular angle of observation—the vantage point of the therapist. Through therapy the family profile can change, calling for a "moving" diagnosis and appropriate shifts in therapeutic interventions. Needless to say, natural processes in the life of a family may also produce changes; for instance, the absence or death of a grandmother in the "nonevolved parents" profile can yield a family form in which the center of the system becomes the "disengaged mother."

The Profiles

The next sections present "sketches" of the family profiles we have thus far delineated. We begin with a description of two types of families— the disengaged and the enmeshed—types that are clinically related (see Chapter 5). These clinical impressions, as well as the analysis of our data, pointed to a clustering of many of our families along the axis of disengagement-enmeshment. Although some of the families seem to waver at different moments between the two poles of this axis, others are seemingly "frozen" in a predominant way of organizing their interactions along this dimension. Those families that are thus "frozen" on either pole of this axis are generally organized around the mother and the children, with the father or other adult members more likely to be absent from the family system, though we have occasionally seen "intact" families with these organizations. These two groups of families, at either extreme, are characterized by an allocation or distribution of functioning among family members which lacks differentiation. We could say that they are simple, primitive, or poorly developed family systems with few specialized functions.

One further word: "disengagement" is not equivalent to passivity; and "enmeshment" is not necessarily equivalent to activity or acting-out. Both profiles essentially describe the characteristic channels and ways of establishing contact among family members rather than the ways of behaving of the individual family members.

The Disengaged Family

Observing this family, one gets the general impression that the actions of its members do not lead to vivid repercussions. Reactions from the others come very slowly and seem to fall into a vacuum. The over-all impression is one of an atomistic field; family members have long moments in which they move as in isolated orbits, unrelated to each other. They act as parts of a system so loosely interlocked that it challenges the clinician's notions that a change in one part of a system will be followed by a complementary change in other parts.

Delay of responses and lack of contact are prevalent modes of interaction in this group. The mother's functioning is characterized by disengagement, lack of response, and apathy. The children's predominant interactions vary. There are situations in which the children and their mother are involved in parallel play or in activities devoid of any contact among them; at other moments the children activate themselves in ways that are seemingly designed to activate their mother into making a relating response. But even when there is an increase in acting-out, the activities of the children do not seem to be related to a need for contacting others. One notices little attentiveness from member to member and few attempts to engage in reciprocal interplay.

The disconnected quality of the relationship among family members in this profile is a feature more distinguishing than the immobility and passivity of the mother. The mother in this group feels overwhelmed, has a derogatory self-image, experiences herself as exploited, and almost invariably presents psychosomatic complaints and depressive features along with her slow pace of response. Though these qualities in the mother seem originally to have been central in the organization of this system, by now, when she is removed, the sibling subsystem usually retains its loosely interlocked quality.

This family form impressed us at the beginning of our exploration by the marked inability of the mother to establish control and guidance over the children. At that time, we thought of the relinquishment of executive functions by the mother as a central hypothesis. The vacuum in the family system created by the lack of parental functioning is filled by the attempted assumption of executive functions on the part of the parental child or children.

SOCIAL CONTACT

A prominent feature of disengaged families is the isolation of the mother, who seems unable to contact the external world and to draw on extrafamilial sources of support. In the most extreme forms of this profile one must look beyond the chronicity of incompetence in mothering to a family history usually lacking in anchorage points such as stable work patterns and stable relationships to a male, friends, or other social groups. The mother is alone. Though the family may have contacted many social agencies, the mother's relationship to them is characterized by extreme passivity and dependency. The degree of incompetence in these families tends to push well-intentioned social welfare agents to "take over" in an attempt to reorganize the family structure and the family life. Often one of the first signs of modification in this family system is the mother's increasing ability to "manipulate" or use social agencies.

Most social welfare programs are designed to require a degree of autonomy, organization, and self-initiation that is simply not available to families in this profile. As a group, therefore, disengaged families are seldom contacted or "reached." Even if they are, however, they soon become dropouts from community programs.

THERAPEUTIC STRATEGY

Interweaving the loose parts by improving the foundations for dialogue between mother and children and the means for regulating it becomes a major goal. The therapist aims at providing to all members some sense of "re-echoing"—some evidence of contributions to the interpersonal field and of interpersonal causality. By organizing different situations, he demonstrates repeatedly the phenomenon of complementarity or reciprocity, which the family has difficulty experiencing.

In initial phases of therapy with this group we have found it helpful for the therapist to take over guiding and nurturance functions to increase the mother's dependency on him. By using this technique, the therapist assumes the adult role in the family group and frees the parental child or children from functioning in the parental role. He acts as a supporter of the mother and as a source of teaching competent ways of parenting. In families at the extreme end of the continuum there is, generally, no stable male figure or there is a series of peripheral males who "pass through" the family; male roles are seldom crystallized or stabilized within the family system. (If the man can stabilize his role within the system, the possibility of change is that much increased.)

In working with the children, it is important to actualize the parental child's experience of discomfort. We try to orient the mother to discourage the children's taking over some of her functions and to encourage their dependency on her.

In extreme cases, when the mother's degree of disengagement is so severe that the possibility of the parental child's learning to depend on her is almost absent, we work through the pathways of the sibling subsystem as they exist; that is, with the "stronger" parental child or children hierarchically and tyrannically related to the rest of the siblings. Separate sessions with the siblings are then observed and eventually joined by the mother so that she can learn from the therapist how to guide the parental child into new, more helpful ways of exercising power and pre-eminence over his siblings. Almost unavoidably, however, the parental child must be removed from the sibling subsystem for individual sessions. In these sessions the therapist can teach him to rely on an adult (himself), changing the child's concept of dependency by using it to teach him ways other than raw power through which he may maintain his sense of competence.

In these families the mother experiences herself as a bad mother, or as "mean" whenever she is in the position of control; therapeutic strategy lies in the possibility of relabeling control and guidance as an aspect of "good" mothering. We find in many of these mothers that the inability to take on the controlling role is a dynamic expression of rebellion against their own parents, whom they may have experienced as extremely controlling and restrictive. Therapy is focused upon increasing the mother's competence. This often begins in the child-rearing area, where she needs to learn how not to delay her reactions to the children. She is helped to intervene on time and effectively in order to avoid explosive and erratic interventions later. Gradually, the testing of competence is moved from child-rearing functions toward extrafamilial areas. The use of auxiliary services (homemakers, Y.M.C.A., P.T.A. groups, guidance counselors, etc.) that we employ in general with this population is indispensable in working with families falling into this profile.

THERAPEUTIC PITFALLS

One of the most common pitfalls in working with such families is the therapist's premature insistence that the mothers learn to control and guide their children. This was the most frequent mistake we made in our initial work with this group of families. If the therapist does not monitor his own tempo and intensity—that is, if he pushes too hard—the mother begins to feel rushed beyond her pace. Intermediate experiences of parity with the therapist are necessary before the therapist can attempt to move the mother into a competent role with the children. (See examples in Chapter 6 of the therapist in the room with the children while the mother observes.)

Another common pitfall is that the therapists, in their attempts to relieve the mother from her incompetent functioning, may take over so completely that they push the mother aside instead of serving as models for her to learn from.

In those extreme cases where the aim is mainly to keep the pathways among the siblings intact while changing the specifics of their interactions, there are many possible pitfalls. Since the therapist attempts not only to mobilize the parental child's dependency on him but also to transfer some of this dependency to a more equipped and guiding mother, problems in coordinating growth easily appear. The mother may not learn fast enough, or the therapist may encourage the child's dependency relationship to him while failing to transfer aspects of his training or guiding role to the mother. In this situation, even if the parental child gains the ability to be a "good older brother," his gains are seldom sufficient, and they often fail to become autonomous of his mother's influence. His frequent breakdowns from the role of "good older brother" to the old role of bully leave the sibling subsystem intact as crucial ground for negative personality formation; that is, the weaker children continue most of their socialization in the complementation of the parental child. They further entrench his position through their rebellious enslavement while they are themselves learning to be bullies.

TREATMENT OUTCOME—RESEARCH FAMILIES[2]

In our research sample, we had three families falling into this profile: the Jones, Romano, and Wainright families. Mr. Jones was in jail at the time of the project, returning to the family only after therapy was terminated. The Romano family had no stable male figure. All three of these families were considered clinically nonimproved. Hindsight tells us that this was due to our lack of understanding of this profile's dynamics; experience with this group in our practice today shows that they are amenable to therapeutic intervention.

The Enmeshed Family

This family system is characterized by a "tight interlocking" of its members. Their quality of connectedness is such that attempts on the part of one member to change elicit fast complementary resistance on the part of others.

In this profile a quality of immediate reactivity seems to be the predominant characteristic. But while the mother's operations seem to be "frozen" in continuous engagement or enmeshment, the children's responses can range from immediate response to the mother with a quality of escalation in their interactions and an increase of noise and static in the field of communication to engaged or disengaged passivity.

We are impressed by the constant engagement maneuvers in these families, most of which reflect or are in response to controlling operations on the part of the mother. These include fast interchanges around her controlling responses and the children's rebellious activities. The family members use each other as triggers for immediate reactivity.

Again, the clinical fact that one is dealing with an over-all system quality is demonstrated when the mother is removed and the sibling subgroup retains its tightly interlocked quality. While in the previous family group the mothers do not respond or else delay their reactions to the children, in this profile the mother's response is immediate. The recurrence of power conflicts and the runaway quality of escalation and counterescalation on the part of family members typify this family. Usually in such families there is virtually no possibility of developing any language of affection and concern. Almost all interchanges, whether positive or not, are simply variations of power maneuvers.

---

[2] The Garibaldi family is not accounted for here because three of its members were diagnosed as paranoid (see Appendix A). This extreme degree of pathology made treatment of this family by our methods impossible.

In the disengaged family the mother becomes anxious when she assumes control and guidance. In the enmeshed family profile any evidence of loss of control over her children makes the mother anxious. The predominant fear is that of becoming helpless, rather than of becoming "mean." The organizing tendency in the enmeshed family involves constant attempts by the mother to move away from a helpless role or stance. She has an overwhelming need for a continued hold on the children. These families usually do not include an adult male, but if there is one, his power is clearly restricted and controlled by the woman.

SOCIAL CONTACT

Families in this profile usually possess skills in connecting with and using extrafamilial resources; but there is a differential orientation to "authoritarian" and "nurturing" institutions. The relationship to authoritarian institutions, such as the police, courts, truant officers, and sometimes the guidance counselor, can be viewed as an extension of the authoritarian orientation of the family. Consistent with the powerlessness and lack of identification that these families have with society, the "nurturing" social institutions, such as the Department of Welfare, hospitals, and clinics, are seen as resources that can be exploited and manipulated. These two sets of community facilities are perceived as "tough" antagonists (authoritarian agencies) and depriving "suckers" (nurturing agencies).

THERAPEUTIC STRATEGY

In this profile the therapist must focus on decelerating the basic tempo and intensity of reverberations within the field. If the family's tempo does not decelerate, responses by one member continue to merge with the counterresponses of others, and the experience of the distinctness of one's own actions and the feeling of responsibility for one's actions are blurred. The therapist aims at regulating interactions to allow for responses sufficiently spaced and softened in tone to lay a groundwork for a minimal sense of separation from which autonomy and a sense of responsibility may develop. These operations are expected to diminish the tendency for fast externalization.

Helping these mothers relinquish control in order to let the children develop without a need to rebel constantly is impossible to attack frontally. Any relinquishment of control, any softening of her engagement operations, produces an overwhelming increase in the mother's anxiety and is seen by her as evidence that the children are "taking over." Many of our therapeutic operations are aimed to help the mother focus on her feelings of being "burdened" rather than of being "robbed" of power, and to change her perception of the children from one of being rebellious to one of being overdependent on her.

In order to achieve these changes in self-perception and in perception of the children, certain mediating experiences are required. We usually hold a number of therapy sessions in the early phases of therapy with the mother and a co-therapist behind the one-way mirror observing the other therapist work with the siblings. With this technique the mother's power operations are neutralized; she does not need to and cannot respond with immediate control. This increases her chances of learning to differentiate nuances in her children's behavior. With this "distancing" technique, the mother becomes more accessible as a person, for she is less involved in conflicts in the mother-child sphere. In this enmeshed profile, the therapeutic strategy that revolves around introducing various subsystems for the purpose of separating and disembedding and for directly manipulating proximity and distance among the family members has proven useful.

THERAPEUTIC PITFALLS

A common pitfall in working with these families stems from the fact that many of the mothers look relatively competent; the therapist supports their enmeshment by capitalizing on their centrality instead of potentializing their ability to disengage. Another problem in working with this group is that the speed of affective responses and the predominance of power operations as a way of solving conflicts may induct the therapist into useless power struggles. Such power struggles are not limited to the therapist as change agent; they can also develop in the family's relationships to outside agencies. Many representatives of social agencies present themselves to these families as primarily linked to their reference source —the social agency—not as an intimate person who wants to help the family. This crystallizes the sense of separation, anonymity, and powerlessness that these families have in relation to society and its established institutions. This is unfortunate, because enmeshed families seem to have a certain openness to interventions from extrafamilial sources which can become an important avenue to change.

TREATMENT OUTCOME—RESEARCH FAMILIES

In our project we had four enmeshed families: the Smiths, the McCallisters, the La Salles, and the Montgomerys. The Montgomery family did not change; the others were considered clinically improved at the end of treatment.

The Family with the Peripheral Male

At the extremes of the disengaged-enmeshed continuum the possibility of a male's participation in the family system is somewhat remote. In the middle range of this dimension, however, the family unit is more complex, permitting the possibility of heterosexual models at the adult level.

In our population the center of power generally tends to be the mother. When a male plays a role in the family system, the organization of the system will vary according to the specific nature of the male-female subsystem. If the wife's role tends toward the disengagement position, participation of the male in the family becomes more possible; when she moves toward the enmeshed type of responsiveness, then her involvement with the children and her strong need to function as a mother push the man toward increased peripherality.

In general, we feel that the family has more possibility for change as the complexity of its system increases. When a man participates in the family in the role of an adult male, he adds differentiation and specialization to the family's manner of approaching life; therefore, the possibility of mobilizing resources for change within the family increases.

It is interesting to contrast the peripherality of the male in our disadvantaged families with a particular type of male peripherality which we find in some lower middle-class groups. In our population the male's peripherality seems relatively fixed and clearly visible, apparently accepted by him as well as by his family. Resistance to acknowledging the male's peripherality seems to be more characteristic of the middle-class "peripheral male profile," in which the man assumes a role that is a mixture of incompetent male and small tyrant. In the latter profile, the man's attempts to be "in" the family make him an intrusive nuisance in the perception of the other family members; he tries to mitigate his exclusion by intrusive and ineffective attempts to be "in" the family, but he is rejected. In the low socioeconomic group, however, the man's acceptance of family exclusion is accompanied by a movement of the center of his life to a realm outside of the family. In effect, he participates actively in the process of excluding himself.

In both groups, the male's peripherality is complemented by an alliance between mother and children in which the man is seen as responsible for the family unhappiness; the mother's problems and incompetence are frequently obscured by the projection of all family problems onto the man's incompetence.

The characteristics of interaction among family members in this profile have already been described in Chapter 5. Some of these include: the lack of communication among spouses as husband and wife with the consequent overuse of parental channels for transactions which belong in an underdeveloped husband-wife sphere; the centrality of the mother and the creation of a mother-children subsystem which excludes the man, who complements it by anchoring himself outside the family; and at a higher level of family integration, the dislodgement of one son from the mother-children subsystem. In the latter instance, we have a more clearly delineated and intense triadic conflict—the mother, son, and father situation which characterizes the Oedipal Complex (see Garcia family, Chapter 3).

SOCIAL CONTACT

Generally in this profile the mother is the main center of contact with social agencies, especially those having to do with the children (school, P.T.A. meetings, hospitals, the courts, etc.); she may relate to formal institutions—joining a church group or some other organized setting that helps her feel a sense of belonging to outer society. This is seldom so for the man, who relates to informal, nonorganized peer groups with which he exchanges primarily at the level of pleasurable activities.

THERAPEUTIC STRATEGY

It makes a difference in therapeutic strategy whether problems of families in this profile are placed in a framework of the peripheral male or the strong mother. Consider the following: the problem is one of a dominant mother who has a strong controlling relationship with her children and pushes the husband aside. The main task becomes one of helping her change her behavior so that the male finds he is more included in the family. Though valid, the essence of this formulation gives centrality to the mother, yielding a strategy of intervention that reinforces her centrality and keeps the man peripheral. What is likely to happen under this strategy is that though the therapist may, in content, consider or talk about the man as important, the target of intervention is the mother; her behavioral output remains significantly higher than the father's.

Our emphasis is to promote the opposite. The target of the therapist's communications should be the man, and the therapist's interventions should facilitate his increased participation from the beginning. It should be clear by now that this should be done both in structural as well as content interventions. The therapist usually needs to concentrate on delineating a spouse subsystem, trying to resolve some of the unfocused problems of mutuality as spouses. The father-children area of functioning becomes, then, more accessible to exploration. The beginning of treatment requires focusing on these two subsystems through sessions with the total family and isolated sessions with the spouses and father and children. The latter sessions could be observed by the mother to help her develop an increased recognition of the husband as father. This strategy seems successful with families that include a peripheral man and a mother who tends toward the "disengaged" position.

When the mother's relationship with her children tends toward the enmeshed type, the possible effectiveness of this strategy lessens. It seems that in this situation the self-definition of the mother is exclusively in the area of mothering; generally, the possibility of mobilizing some husband-wife interactions can emerge only after the mother and children achieve a moderate level of disengagement. While this process is going on, individual sessions with the man and his observing a family subgroup comprised of the mother and children can be utilized to enhance his sense of participation in the family.

THERAPEUTIC PITFALLS

One of the most common therapeutic pitfalls is that the therapist's attempts to use the mother to reach the man only reinforce her centrality in the family structure. This can begin at the point of initial contact, when the mother is chosen to assemble the family, and it can move to subtler levels when the therapists are unsuccessful in their attempts to make the man central.

Another common pitfall at the social agency level is that work with families in this profile seems to be handicapped by the organization of most clinics and their philosophy of work. Most clinics are oriented toward the mother as if she were the only crucial influence in the life of the children. This orientation organizes most services wittingly or unwittingly into disregard of the man and his vital role in the formation and repair of the family system. Clinic hours and staffing patterns (many females) in most service organizations also militate against the strategy which we have indicated. By accident or design, then, most social agencies are in collusion to keep the man peripheral.

TREATMENT OUTCOME—RESEARCH FAMILIES

In our sample we had four families that could be included in this category. They were the Martinez, Brown, Garcia, and Lewis families. The first two had mothers who tended toward the disengaged position, while the other two tended toward the enmeshed position. All four were considered clinically improved after treatment.

In the foregoing profiles our discussion centered mostly on the quality of relatedness (disengaged or enmeshed) and the structural configuration this quality of relatedness upholds. In the next two profiles, however, we are concerned with the arrested development of the personalities of the adult members of the family and the way in which they reinforce each other's lack of development.

The Family with Nonevolved Parents

Families in this profile have already been described in Chapter 5 in the section *The Nonexistent Grandmother*. We will therefore limit ourselves here only to a brief description of the dominant features of such families.

In this type of family the grandmother is allocated executive power, while the mother and grandchildren function as one vaguely differentiated subgroup. The mother assumes the role of an older sibling, with a consequent impairment of a three-generation family. When this profile includes a man, the emergence of spouse functions is relatively rare because of the arrested development of the role of wife-mother—the role of *daughter* is rigidly maintained.

SOCIAL CONTACT

Usually the mother is brought into contact with the social agency because of some situation with the school authorities or the courts involving her children. She equates such authorities with her way of experiencing her own mother; in other words, some kind of older, "punitive," rigid authority has pushed her into this move.

THERAPEUTIC STRATEGY

Usually this family is composed of a grandmother, a young mother, and the latter's children. With these families we work with the enmeshed subsystem of grandmother and daughter separately, and with the children and mother separately, while the grandmother observes them through the one-way mirror with a co-therapist. We eventually alternate groupings, with the mother as an observer of the grandmother's new attempts to uphold her daughter's control in interaction with the children. In certain cases, when the pervasiveness of the mother-daughter transaction is frozen and does not permit direct contact with the mother, we work through the grandmother as the stronger member of the system; but we are aware that by doing so we are not changing the nature of the family's interaction. In a sense, we are maintaining the pathological system. This operation, which consists of keeping the direction of the pathways intact while attempting to change the content of the interaction, has proven in our experience to be a difficult strategy.

When there is a husband in this constellation, the therapist focuses on strengthening the husband-wife subsystem, trying to use this particular arena to help "daughter-mother" evolve as a wife. Insofar as she gains differentiation of herself as an adult and changes her self-perception from younger daughter to adult daughter, the whole system begins to change.

Other types of sessions are comprised of the total family, including the grandmother. The therapist confronts the mother and grandmother around the areas of child rearing, while at the same time promoting *in situ* the husband as a supporter and helper of his wife in the process of differentiating herself from her mother.

THERAPEUTIC PITFALLS

Often the social agency may completely miss this family profile because the mother comes in without the grandmother and can appear as a competent center of power. Also, working through the grandmother to help the daughter grow up may only crystallize the family organization that already exists.

TREATMENT OUTCOME—RESEARCH FAMILIES

There were no research families that fell into this profile, but if we consider one segment of the Montgomery family, composed of Mrs. Montgomery, Phyllis, and her baby, we could include this group in this classification. As already noted, the Montgomerys were not considered to be clinically improved after treatment. Our experimentation with this profile is still very new—too new to form judgments about outcome after treatment.

The Family with Juvenile Parents

In this profile the parents are involved in a complementary system of avoidance of adult roles. Both parents are dynamically related to peer reference groups primarily. The functions of spouses and parents are secondary to the dynamic importance of their relationship to peer systems outside of the family. Because the parents as people have remained frozen in their individual development in a pre-adolescent stage in which the significance of peer relationships is paramount, the appearance of such complex functions as mutuality and responsibility that are requirements of the complex roles of parents and spouses is blocked.

This couple may go through crisis after crisis talking about their impending separation and marital break-up, but actually there has never been a true marriage.

The adult female sees herself as a "fickle" girl. In many cases she is promiscuous, rejects motherly functions, and centers her activity and justification of herself on being "an attractive woman" and in some cases an effective provider. The male is dependent on her and frequently assumes an attitude of defiance against the authority of organized institutions. In their interaction, the woman assumes predominance. Although she exerts managerial functions, she is insufficiently related to child care functions. The male sometimes assumes some of these rejected nurturing functions. His acceptance of the maternal role seems to be a compensation for his sense of incompetence as a provider or as a husband. His resentment of his wife is manifested by his pleasurable activities outside of the realm of the family in his life with his peers. The wife clusters her husband with the children in a subsystem of burdensome dependents; she rejects the spouse and maternal roles and feels unfairly saddled with the job of caring for incompetent people. This sense of rightful indignation becomes her justification for promiscuous activities. Families in this profile usually function in twosomes: husband-wife; father-child; and mother-child.

For the children the consequences are divided loyalties and frequently confused sex role identity. The lack of generational boundaries in these families pushes the children into the roles of mediators in the parental strife.

Because of the immature level of arrest of the adult members in this type of family, a bantering, light quality seems to prevail in their interactions during sessions; as a result, the seriousness of their conflicts and the possibility of delineating conflict-resolutions are minimized.

This profile, it might be noted, seems to be a product of the more stable lower-class culture. The implicit rules for regulating communicational flow and the clarity of content which most of our families lack seem to be better developed in adults from this population than in the members of most of our disengaged, enmeshed, or nonevolved families. Therefore, the clinician may feel more at home with these "juvenile" adults than he does with members of other types of disadvantaged families.

SOCIAL CONTACT

As already noted, the informal peer group is the most important social structure for people in this profile. The husband and wife each turns to his or her own group; they do not have social contacts as a family. When these people deal with formal agencies such as the school and courts, the wife is the spokesman for the family.

THERAPEUTIC STRATEGY

Families in this profile should be treated, if possible, by co-therapists of each sex with the male therapist assuming pre-eminence in directing the therapeutic sessions. At first he should direct most of his attention to the male, couching his participation in "peer language." The female therapist should do the same with the mother.

Then, drawing on his own capacity to be adolescent, the male therapist tries to engage the man as a "chum"; at the same time, he must serve as a model of effective confrontation of the wife. The female therapist encourages the wife to take over some of the maternal role functions and to confront her husband with his attempts to rob her of the pleasure of maternal caretaking, as well as with his escape into irresponsible peer activity.

Often the therapists have to drop their "chum" approach and move into frankly parental roles—becoming serious and almost "preachy" to impress on the couple the seriousness of what is happening and of what they are doing to each other. Their usual narrow affective range and the disqualifying nature of their bantering mood must be challenged.

Sessions should also be conducted with the mother and the children with the father observing and learning that when he curtails his own mothering functions, he is not "out," but is actively helping his wife become a mother.

Individual sessions, or second stages in which the female co-therapist sees the wife and the male therapist sees the man, seem useful. The aim here is to negotiate certain sex-appropriate functions which seem to require isolated development before they can emerge in the interactional field of husband and wife.

THERAPEUTIC PITFALLS

In many situations, especially at the beginning of therapy, the man in this family seems to appeal rather strongly to the therapists because of his warmth and concern toward the children. If the therapist responds by an alliance with him, one may see the eventual appearance of seductive maneuvers on the part of the wife toward the male therapist. The husband may then become a victim of a hidden alliance between the male therapist and his wife. Another common pitfall in work with such families is that sometimes the co-therapists mirror the image of the couple

—the male therapist siding with the man and the female therapist with the woman.

TREATMENT OUTCOME—RESEARCH FAMILIES

As with families with nonevolved parents, our experimentation with this profile is still in the beginning phases. None of our research families fell into this profile.

In describing these profiles we have the biased orientation of therapists concerned with introducing change. With this orientation we see families as small groups of interacting members in patterned transactions. The possibilities of growth and change in the family system are intimately related to the degree of interlocking and the flexibility of the system: the availability of alternative pathways; the possibility of shifts from dyadic to triadic groupings or vice-versa; a repertoire of different themes and moods; diversity of role allocation to specific family members, etc.

The stereotyped interaction in our families can be expressed as a result of paucity and rigidity of interpersonal transactional patterns and also, on a higher level of abstraction, as frozen development of the family as a total system—the system is "at rest" as a relatively simple social "organism" with a concomitant lack of specialization and differentiation in the component functions of its members. The therapist's strategies of intervention are designed to introduce an appropriate level of tension and complexity necessary for the emergence of new forms of approaching and resolving interpersonal conflicts. The emergence of such new forms implies changes in the functions of family members, and with these functional changes come gradual or sometimes simultaneous intrapsychic changes.

We have described the therapist's manipulation of family patterns and the use of himself as an integral part of the family-therapist system, but we again remind the reader that at certain moments in therapy this procedure is insufficient. In such situations the therapist should search the social periphery of the family for "significant others" to build a "relevant unit of intervention."

Interaction between Family and Social Systems

Our emphasis up to now has been on ways in which the family functions within its own system. Nevertheless, we are deeply aware that we cannot limit ourselves entirely to intrafamilial functioning when working with the disadvantaged population. The relationship between the larger social system and the family system, as a matter of fact, merits detailed investigation. This is particularly urgent in the light of the ever-increasing interest in and development of large-scale poverty intervention programs. For a massive effort is currently in progress—supported in large part by government funds under the aegis of the Federal Economic Opportunity Act of 1964 which made $800 million available—to make an inroad into poverty and the psychological, social, and health deficits which are its chronic companions. (In 1965, $1.7 billion was appropriated for the war on poverty by Congress.) As a result of this impetus, the war on poverty and the evolution toward the "great society" are currently being translated into a variety of federal, state, and local community programs.

There is growing concern over using the power of the poor with respect to strategies and implementations in various anti-poverty programs. The mobilization and utilization of resources within a deprived community itself are thought to be powerful weapons for smashing into the overriding effects of poverty.[3]

However, the alienated, the apathetic, and the anomic—in sum, the members of the kinds of families with whom we have been working— are not that easily reached or recruited, for obvious reasons. The recruitment and enlistment of people from deprived communities into community action programs often tap the more educated and more "aware" members of that community—those possessing the linguistic, cognitive, and communicational skills required to participate in such efforts.

Evaluation of large-scale intervention programs, such as the exploration of youth-study programs (Herman and Sadofsky, 1966), points to the following: first, the group contacted is a self-selected one, and, as a result, a large part of the target population is never reached; second, there is a shrinkage of the contacted group in the initial period of recruitment, selection, and intake; and third, large groups drop out during the period of training and later on in the period of job development and placement.

Gordon (1965), along similar lines, cited the failure of two government-sponsored agencies in a program designed to counsel underemployed and unemployed selective service rejectees and presented considerable evidence to implement his statement. He stated:

---

[3] For example, Sexton (1965)—political and social action; self-help; Clark (1965)— political strength, power, and unity; action for social change; and Alinsky (1965) —"Poverty means not only lacking money but also lacking power" (p. 47). These authors feel that self-help and action programs are necessary to break through and change the culture of poverty.

. . . the irony of it is that the subculture of chronically unemployed youth has evolved to the point at which even the
availability of work is insufficient by itself to end the unemployment. Making jobs available to people who have little interest
in work, little belief in its rewards, and no skills, produces the
paradox of continued unemployment together with labor short-
age. We are thus in the unfortunate position of sitting on a
powder keg and not knowing how to defuse it (p. 334).

Failures of some of these large-scale intervention programs, thus, might
in part be accounted for by the difficulties involved in negotiating through
the massive resistance to change in the cultural styles of populations who
would presumably be the beneficiaries of such interventions.

While it is clear, then, that large-scale intervention programs at the
societal level alone would reach only a segment of the low socioeconomic
population, it seems equally clear that reliance on psychotherapy (individual, group, or family) alone, besides reaching only a pitifully small
number of families, could not alter the larger sources of social pathology
which perpetuate and foster the disorganization of groups and individuals.
The need has become increasingly evident: the development of large-
scale interventive programs requires an integration of the social scientist's
knowledge about social structure and social processes with knowledge
derived from intensive clinical work with a small number of people. The
questions are no longer, "can we introduce change by just working within
the family system?" or "can intervention at the societal level alone modify
the ecological unbalance in these families?" The false dichotomy implied
by such questions and the need for multiple levels of intervention have
been acknowledged. The coordination of work within the family with
community approaches now raises a new set of questions: How can the
use of multiple levels of intervention be made coherently functional?
What patterns of linkage and feedback between specific intrafamilial and
extrafamilial influences must first be differentiated?

Questions such as those raised by Moynihan (1965a) concerning the
impact of unemployment on family structure in Negro American families
exemplify the kinds of issues that require a multi-level, integrated (societal
and familial) approach. This author pinpointed this particular issue thus:

Obviously, the most pressing question for American social policy
is whether the essential first step for resolving the problem of
the Negro American is to provide such a measure of full employ-

ment of Negro workers that the impact of unemployment on family structure is removed. The assumption would be that only then will the wide and increasing range and level of social services available to the Negro American have their full effect, and only then will there be a Negro population that not only has equal opportunities in the American economy, but is equal to those opportunities.

This, of course, is not an inconsiderable assumption. No one knows whether it is justified or not. The relation between economic phenomena, such as employment, and social phenomena, such as family structure, has hardly begun to be traced in the United States (pp. 764–765).

Later, he stated:

A more sophisticated but not less pressing question is whether the impact of economic disadvantage on the Negro community has gone on so long that genuine structural damage has occurred, so that a reversal in the course of economic events will no longer produce the expected response in social areas (p. 766).

He made similar points in his well-publicized report (Moynihan, 1965b), which has been criticized by some social scientists and by a larger group of civil rights activists for its alleged emphasis on a middle-class family model as a necessary ingredient for healthy child development, especially for the process of male identification in the Negro boy. Nonetheless, the questions he raised remain unanswered and point to a significant area of exploration.

The reciprocal relations among child, family, and society should indeed become the target of significant exploration if our aim is to develop differentiated, interventive programs.

Focusing on exploration of and intervention in disadvantaged families located at the extreme of social and psychological disorganization may be one way to search for answers to the above as well as related problems. An understanding of family systems in this group, because of these families' simultaneous and multiple needs, can be of considerable help in the development of differentiated, large-scale intervention programs.

The family system is at a crossroads between society and the individual, transmitting social rules and regulations to the growing child and providing blueprints for his cognitive and emotional development. Investigations of family organization can provide vantage points from which to understand how social phenomena are incorporated into the intrapsychic life of the individual—the relationship, specifically, between the subculture of poverty and the person who is poor.

For example, at the intrafamilial level, we observe a hierarchical power organization among members of the multi-problem family that seems meaningfully related to the child's sense of powerlessness and his reliance on externalization. Is this phenomenon related to Alinksy's concept of powerlessness in decision-making by the poor? Is there a relationship between the undifferentiated communicational style at the family level, the inhibition of cognitive exploration in the child and his reliance on the adult as problem-solver, and at the social level, the undifferentiated mapping of the world by the poor, who are surrounded and trapped by institutions designed by and for the middle classes?

Clearly, whatever our point of focus as investigators may be, we need to understand how our level of intervention relates to other levels. How and in what situations should we direct our interventions at the level of the individual, the family, or society? Would intervention at one level affect the others? Are some points of entry more effective than others?

These questions are even more pressing when we consider certain reciprocities between societal structure and family systems. In certain sections of Puerto Rico, for example, the community exerts some supervisory pressures on the children—pressures which fade away in *El Barrio* in New York City; these missing community influences must be supplied by the family, and involve an increase of control on the parental level and restrictions in the social geography of the children.

In the early fifties the state of Israel's policy of open immigration and active recruitment of Jews from the Diaspora resulted in a massive immigration of African and Asiatic Jews who were collectively called the "oriental immigrant." Of course the patterns of acculturation to the host society varied among the different groups. Relevant to this discussion is the differential appearance of symptoms of stress in the Moroccan and Yemenite groups.[4]

The low socioeconomic Moroccan families, while adhering in form to a patriarchal organization—a vestige of the biblical tradition—had been living in the urban ghettos of Casablanca and Marrakesh in a state of

---

[4] The senior author was Director of Psychiatric Service in Youth Immigration (Aliath Hanoar) in Israel for 1952 to 1954.

transition and disorganization. The stresses of acculturation to Israel were manifested almost upon their arrival. There was an immediate and significant increase of juvenile delinquency in the Moroccan youth and a great lack of social adaptation. Many Moroccan children responded to the relaxed structure of Israeli schools and the benevolent, casual teacher-pupil relationships with an increase in acting-out that made an impact all over the nation and succeeded in causing many teachers to assume more distant and hierarchical modalities of teaching and in making contact with their pupils.

Adaptation of the Yemenite child to the Israeli culture, on the other hand, seems to have been mediated by the support of a family organization which, for reasons still to be explored, was strong enough to allow the children to go through a slower process of acculturation and exposure to problems.

Intergenerational conflicts and the clash of cultures within the family appeared in the Yemenite group years later, with a concomitant increase in juvenile delinquency. Apparently this time lag between immigration and the appearance of the resulting social stresses was the result of the cohesiveness of the Yemenites' family organization, which acted as a buffer in the acculturation process.

Another example of this particular aspect of the reciprocity of family and society is provided by the Chinese-Americans. Sollenberger (1966), in a study of Chinatown, New York City, suggested that the strong influence of the family and the development in the child of a sense of responsibility toward the family are responsible for the lack of juvenile delinquency in this group. It would seem that these inner controls are externally supported by the community. An informant reported a saying: "As you walk around the streets of Chinatown, you have a hundred cousins watching you." Here the family and the community are fused. Where the New York City Puerto Rican family needs to take over the control institutions that were carried by the community in Puerto Rico, the New York Chinese community succeeds in utilizing the community as an extension of the family.[5]

This beneficial phenomenon of extrafamilial support of the family's socialization of children is very different from the phenomenon found in disengaged and enmeshed families, who tend to lose their offspring to

---

[5] Interestingly, a study by Wang (1966) suggests to us that intergenerational conflicts similar to those of the Yemenite group are beginning to appear in second- and third-generation Chinese-Americans in San Francisco.

the extrafamilial community. Adults in these families, through their patterns of interaction with their offspring (see Chapter 5), "release" the children to their siblings, and the sibling subgroup, though unguided, becomes a very powerful element in the socialization process. These intrafamilial patterns of extreme anchorage among siblings condition the children to anchor among extrafamilial "siblings." They find a substitute for their family in the street-corner gang, and their own family may lose its influence to a surprising extent.

In this situation we have an instance in which the neighborhood is in phase with the family pattern. However, every therapist who works with our population is familiar with numerous instances in which patterns of change within the family are out of phase with patterns of change in the neighborhood. Consider, for instance, the plight of a family attempting to change certain internal patterns while it is living in the midst of a rapidly deteriorating urban neighborhood which seems to require them to retain these patterns. A mother's attempts to modify her hierarchical and punitive relationship with her adolescent daughters may be defeated by the social phenomena outside her door. When her daughters satisfy their understandable heterosexual curiosity by continually glancing out the front door to see if any boys are passing, she is compelled to adopt her old punitive role: "Sure, I want to change. I don't want to yell at them for that, but how can I *not* tell them to stop looking out? The winos are taking over that corner, and pimps are beginning to come around. The girls have got to stay in."

Whatever elements of rationalization her statement may contain, they cannot obscure the force of her argument. The reality of events and people outside her door force her to hold on to and maintain an unwanted intrafamilial pattern.

Or consider the negative and insidious interaction of unemployment and an underdelineated spouse subsystem, in which the couple expects almost no separate consideration as "wife" or "husband." The chronic lack of jobs and training for the male can make his role as "provider" all-important and can diminish the value of his other roles—husband, father, human being. We see cases where any attempt he makes to fill the latter roles are considered insignificant; "reliability" and "earning power" become so overvalued as rare commodities that concern with any other qualities becomes virtually nonexistent. A bright, sensitive mother of eight children, six of whom were conceived in a previous relationship, states about her current man, "I know my man now is not so smart. He is like one of the children, but I don't care if he is so good husbanding me or if he is a father, so long as he don't mess with the kids. But look at this pantry [pointing to shelves well stocked with canned foods]!"

These and other situations point to the importance of little-understood mechanisms through which different family systems regulate their interactions with extrafamilial sources. Large-scale intervention programmers, on the one hand, need to consider the ways in which family systems can support or impede the success of such programs; clinicians, on the other hand, must perforce be aware of how their work within the family system is related to the social structures that may support or hinder their therapeutic interventions.

For the researcher with a broad sociopsychological, intergenerational perspective, the foregoing situations highlight the need to study, in addition to the transmission of the culture of poverty, the evolvement and transmission of mechanisms for resisting or modifying the effects of that culture. Explorations of the interaction between external supports provided by the community and the internal events of the family may disclose the limits of the social environment within which the family is able to gradually modify its behavior—changes which can eventually be incorporated by the children, constituting the strength and hope of the second generation.

A cross-sectional investigation like ours cannot explain the processes by which the external environment of the past managed to be essentially protective—shielding the family's boundaries sufficiently to facilitate its internal work, the growth of stable patterns of interaction—but at the same time sufficiently challenging to encourage the development of that flexibility within and between members which seems characteristic of families that cope effectively. Sound preventive programs await our ability to render explicit a set of interactive experiences between the family and its social environment, distinguishable in nature, kind, and duration, through which the ability to use internal and external resources is developed by earlier generations and transmitted to the members of future families.

We believe that our disengaged families would not support or potentialize the resources of many current large-scale intervention programs. They are seldom reached by these programs, and when they are, they tend to become dropouts. People as isolated and nonparticipant as the members of these families would be too threatened by the need to learn the first rudiments of competence in programs which require them to deal, and implicitly or explicitly compete, with other people. Disengaged family members seem to need an initial sense of change and competence. This can be derived more easily from participation within their own families than from participation in a group of more competent adults. It is in the minute details of the failures and the successes of family interchanges and family chores that disengaged family members can begin to gain new, more positive perceptions of self and the surrounding world. With this group of families, the use of extrafamilial resources must be closely monitored. To produce change often entails the sustained use of homemakers to offer direct training in how to cope with such issues as budget, cooking, and housecleaning; the creative use of teachers and guidance counselors; and the gradual expansion of the mother's and children's contact with certain formal, but benign institutions (e.g., school, Y.M.C.A., church, and civil rights groups). To increase a sense of mastery and competence in these family members, the everyday functions of mothering can never be neglected; gradually increased participation in community agencies with small group programs in sewing, baking, etc., is often essential.

In the enmeshed family, large-scale intervention programs designed to increase working skills and train people for successful competition in the labor market may succeed in helping the male to become a reliable wage-earner without changing his peripheral position within the family. The increased competence of the male in the extrafamilial system does not penetrate the semiporous membrane of the family system easily.

Various patterns of family structure and family experiences may result in differing reactions to youth programs offering job training. We feel, for example, that youngsters from disengaged families would display prolonged difficulties in learning and in developing meaningful involvement during the initial period of training. They would tend to drop out in this early period; yet, if they managed to negotiate this phase, they would continue on to lasting gains. The youngsters from enmeshed families, however, might display an opposite pattern, showing quick and active involvement during the initial periods, only to evince rebellious and negativistic responses later which would result in discarding their fast gains.

Attempts by some societies to modify the course of their development by means of abrupt cultural discontinuities, thus ignoring the ties of the young to their families, always arouse healthy controversy. Out of such controversy we can expect that today's large-scale programs, to the extent that they rely on a "curriculum" which generally ignores the hidden "family curriculum" to which the young are exposed, will have to regain a new focus—one which attempts to understand the cultural clash which emerges when the formats of training developed by reformers and the formats of training employed by families converge, and one which attempts to develop techniques for organizing manageable continuity and interfacilitation between the two formats.

"Headstart" may do well to examine the ways in which the family does or does not provide supportive systems to potentialize the efforts involved in such an educational program. It could be that school and family send a set of contradictory messages which are more manageable for children from certain families than for children from other families. Large-scale educational programs may need to intervene not only at the level of having the parents participate in the facilities of the school,[6] but also at the level of increasing the teacher's sensitivity to characteristic patterns of intrafamilial life in the disadvantaged population. The boundaries between intrafamilial and extrafamilial systems can, after all, become opened or closed both ways.[7] To open them both ways, the reactions of the change-agents interacting with the poor must be as earnestly studied as the reactions of the poor themselves. Our unprecise knowledge of family patterns might then resolve into more identifiable and precise knowledge of the patterns through which resources in the social system interlock or not with the needs of particular families.

A well-differentiated, successful, large-scale application of social services

---

[6] Exploration of methods for educating parents into becoming sustainers of the educational processes of the school has been conducted, for instance, in the lower east side of New York City by Pamela Chamberlain. She taught a large number of parents how to play games with their children during the summer—games that tend to develop an ability to focus attention and to relate in exploratory ways. Such skills are helpful for children's work in the classroom.

[7] A. B. Wilson (1966) has indicated the possible tendencies of the schools to atrophy the motoric learning style of these children; he noted that schools can place such a premium on discipline and on "obedient" and "rote" learning that they may fail to discover and accommodate to the children's particular ways of learning. Clark (1965) has also emphasized similar problems in the school system. Teachers may assume such a low intellectual-emotional baseline in these children that they may in effect crystallize their defects, while explaining their own shortcomings in terms of unmodifiable levels of motivation and functioning in the children. Some of our own current pilot work is relevant here. Groups of teachers are invited by family and therapists to join in observation and discussion of parent-children interaction. The interaction occurs around specific tasks which require from the parents the establishing of controls and the encouraging of learning; teachers are encouraged to study differences and similarities between parental styles and their own, with the ensuing crossings of information between teachers and parents being the focus of therapeutic assistance.

which meets the needs of multi-problem families will one day be a reality. Across and within cultures, across and within socioeconomic levels, diverse natural experiments in family forms all manage somehow to salvage, if not enhance, what is uniquely flexible, purposeful, and human. Versions of the sound and functioning person are constantly fashioned even within the confining possibilities of dire poverty. Even here capable forms of the family emerge, providing as yet unstudied models of mental health which cope quite effectively with the world of the poor which they share with our subjects. So striking is the variety of family forms through which personality comes forth unimpaired, that when such experiments fail, the event cannot be considered less than tragic.

REFERENCES

Alinsky, S. D. The war on poverty—political pornography. *J. soc. issues*, 1965, 21, 41–47.

Clark, K. *Dark ghetto: dilemmas of social power*. New York: Harper & Row, 1965.

Cohen, A. K. *Delinquent boys: the culture of the gang*. Glencoe, Ill.: The Free Press, 1955.

Fenichel, O. *The psychoanalytic theory of neurosis*. New York: W. W. Norton and Co., 1945.

Fleischmann, O., Kramer, P., and Ross, Helen (Eds.). *August Aichord. Delinquency and child guidance: selected papers*. New York: International Universities Press, 1964.

Friedlander, Kate. Latent delinquency and ego development. In K. R. Eissler (Ed.), *Searchlights on delinquency*. New York: International Universities Press, 1949. Pp. 205–215.

Gordon, J. E. Project CAUSE, the federal anti-poverty program, and some implications of subprofessional training. *Amer. Psychologist*, 1965, 20, 334–343.

Herman, M., and Sadofsky, S. *Youth-work programs: problems of planning and operation*. New York: New York University Press, 1966.

Johnson, Adelaide M. Juvenile delinquency. In S. Arieti (Ed.), *American handbook of psychiatry*. New York: Basic Books, Inc., 1959. Vol. I. Pp. 840–856.

Johnson, Adelaide M., and Szurek, S. A. The genesis of antisocial acting out in children and adults. *Psychoanal. Quart.*, 1952, 21, 323–343.

Merton, R. K. Social structure and anomie. *Amer. soc. Rev.*, 1938, 3, 672–682.

Merton, R. K. *Social theory and social structure*. Glencoe, Ill.: The Free Press, 1959.

Moynihan, D. P. Employment, income, and the ordeal of the Negro family. *Daedalus*, 1965, 94, 745–770. (a)

Moynihan, D. P. *The Negro family: the case for national action.* Washington, D.C.: Office of Policy Planning and Research, United States Department of Labor, 1965. (b)

Sexton, Patricia C. *Spanish Harlem: anatomy of poverty.* New York: Harper & Row, 1965.

Sollenberger, R. T. Why no juvenile delinquency? Paper presented at the American Psychological Association meetings, New York City, 1966.

Sutherland, E. H., and Cressey, D. R. *Principles of criminology.* 6th ed.; Chicago: J. B. Lippincott Co., 1960.

Wang, R. P. A study of alcoholism in Chinatown. *Psychiat. spectator,* 1966, 3, 4–5.

Wilson, A. B. Discussion of: A project to teach learning skills to disturbed, delinquent children, paper presented by S. Minuchin, Pamela Chamberlain, and P. Graubard, American Orthopsychiatric Association meetings, San Francisco, 1966.

APPENDIX  Twelve Families[1]

Our explorations and research eventually focused on twelve families, each with a Wiltwyck child. Although our book goes considerably beyond these families, we can think of no better introduction to the kinds of families with which we are concerned than to briefly describe these twelve.

THE JONESES

Mrs. Jones, 29, is the fourth oldest of seven siblings: six half-sisters and brothers from the same father, but not the same mother. Originally from North Carolina, she came to New York when she was 14 and has a seventh-grade education. Mr. Jones, like Mrs. Jones, is a Negro and a Baptist, and is said to have married Mrs. Jones at one time, but then deserted. He is the father of all the Jones children except Nathaniel. All seven children were born out of wedlock.

The family's income is from the New York City Department of Wel-

---

[1] The brief summaries below represent the status of the experimental families at the time of first testing for the research. Our research spanned a period of several years during which time some of these family circumstances changed. Ages reported, for example, differ according to the time period being discussed. All names are fictitious.

fare. They share an apartment, which occupies two floors, with three other families. The Joneses have two rooms, one of which is the kitchen. There are two double beds, one single cot, and a crib. Nathaniel, 10, Tom, 8, Lionel 7, and Keith, 5, share a double bed; Margaret, 11, Sally, 13, and Paul, 4, share the other double bed. Mrs. Jones sleeps alone on the cot. Sally had lived with her maternal grandmother until she was 11 years old. She has run away from home, and Tom is a serious behavior problem in school.

Nathaniel is the Wiltwyck child. The Bureau of Child Guidance of the New York City Board of Education referred him to Jacobi Hospital because of his poor adjustment in school, and because he had beaten, stabbed, and tried to set fire to his younger siblings. He was an out-patient in the Department of Pediatric Psychiatry there for a few months, and was then admitted to the psychiatric ward, where he remained for an additional seven months. He was then discharged with the diagnosis of behavior disorder.

THE ROMANOS

Mrs. Romano, 38, and her husband, 39, both Catholics of Italian descent, were born in New York City. Each has a ninth-grade education. Mrs. Romano was described at intake by a Wiltwyck psychiatrist as a pseudo-neurotic schizophrenic. She related to her husband (when he was at home) as a daughter to a father, and was generally an extremely infantile person. Mr. Romano was serving a prison term for the second time because of parole violation during most of the time the family was being seen for therapy; he joined the group toward the end of therapy, however. The Romanos live in a five-room apartment and are supported by public welfare funds.

There are two girls in the family, 14 and 8 years of age. The five boys range in age from 16 to 6. Roger, the Wiltwyck child, is 9 years old. He had been referred to Wiltwyck by the court because of excessive truancy, beyond the control of his parents. The other delinquent child is Victor, 16, who previously had been in a state training school.

THE LEWISES

Mr. and Mrs. Lewis are both Negro Protestants. Mrs. Lewis was born in Pennsylvania and grew up on Long Island. She is an only child who was raised by her grandmother's sister, and after the latter's death, by her grandmother. She received three years of high-school education. Mr. Lewis, born in Virginia, was also raised by a grandmother, as were two younger sisters, until he was 12 years old, when he went to live with his mother in New York City. He does not recall how many years of schooling he had. He is an assistant truck driver and is a responsible worker, having been employed at the same place for a number of years. He is a heavy drinker on weekends, however, and often leaves the family for a number of days at a time.

The Lewises live in a five-room apartment in a housing project. There are three girls in the family ranging from 9 to 17 years of age, and four boys ranging from 6 to 12 years of age. Leonard, the Wiltwyck child, 11, was referred to Wiltwyck by the court after being apprehended while breaking into a warehouse with a group of children. Bertha, 17, has a two-year-old out-of-wedlock child. Dorothy, 15, has been caught stealing and is generally antisocial. Keith has also been involved in stealing episodes, and is a chronic truant and trouble-maker in school.

THE LA SALLES[2]

Mrs. La Salle, 40, a Protestant, West Indian Negro, is an obviously intelligent woman with a high school education. Mr. La Salle, also a West Indian Negro, is in a Federal prison. He has been in four different prisons. Once, in a moment of rage, he shot at but missed his father-in-law. Mrs. La Salle's father, who lives with the family, is senile and neurologically impaired. The family lives in a four-room apartment on funds from public welfare. There are three boys in the family, Meredith, 12, at a New York State training school; George, 8; and the Wiltwyck child, Tim, 10, who was referred to Wiltwyck for breaking into a synagogue with a group of boys and setting it afire.

THE MARTINEZES

Mrs. Martinez, 34, is a depressed woman with chronic psychosomatic complaints and symptoms. She was born in Puerto Rico, and has been living in New York City for 14 years. She had nine years of schooling, and is a Catholic. Mr. Martinez, 36, also grew up in Puerto Rico, and is a veteran of the Korean war. He is a chronic alcoholic who was once hospitalized for delirium tremens. He frequently leaves the family for days at a time during binges. Nevertheless, he is a steady and reliable factory worker. The family lives in a brownstone tenement apartment with two bedrooms, separated by a curtain.

There are four children in the family, a girl of 9, and three boys: Rafael, the Wiltwyck child, 10, Arturo, 8, and a little boy of 2. Rafael was referred to Wiltwyck after suspension from school for uncontrollably

---

[2] Chapter 4 presents in greater detail the family background of the La Salles, along with excerpts from transcripts of family treatment sessions with them.

aggressive behavior. As a member of a gang, he stole in his neighborhood. Arturo, the other delinquent child, has stolen and is a chronic truant from school.

THE BROWNS

Mrs. Brown, 33, is a Negro Protestant woman. Her mother died when she was 3, and her father when she was 11. She was raised by an older sister who then brought her to New York City from South Carolina. She has two half-sisters on her father's side, one of whom she has never seen. She married Mr. Brown when she was 14, but her sister had the marriage annulled. She left school at 17, was committed to a state training school as a wayward minor, was released, and then institutionalized again. The oldest daughter, Barbara, was born at this time. Mrs. Brown is now living with Mr. Beach, age 44, as man and wife. Mr. Beach has three children and is waiting for a divorce, after which he plans to marry Mrs. Brown. He works as a maintenance man in housing projects when asthmatic attacks do not disable him. They live in a five-room apartment, and Mrs. Brown is supported by public welfare.

The children in the family are: Barbara, 15, Doris, 12, Anne, 2, Martin, 10, James, 8, and Dennis, 1. Mrs. Brown stated that although she wanted her first three children, after that she "wished that all the rest were miscarriages." She knows little about Barbara's father, but went with the father of Martin and Doris for eight years. It is uncertain how long she has sustained her relationship with Mr. Brown, but he is the father of Anne and Dennis.

Martin was referred to Wiltwyck by the Bureau of Child Guidance to have a diagnostic work-up after suspension from school for aggressive and disruptive behavior. He has also stolen. Doris has been placed on probation for severely beating and injuring another child. James was a serious behavior problem in school and has been suspended. Barbara is a chronic truant.

THE SMITHS

Mrs. Smith, 32, was born in New York City and spent most of her life there except for two periods in North Carolina. She is a high-school graduate. Mr. Smith, 32, is also a native New Yorker. Both are Negro. Mr. Smith is a Protestant, and Mrs. Smith is a very religious Jehovah's Witness. She has periods of depression and alcoholism. Mr. Smith was himself institutionalized at Wiltwyck as a child. He was recently released from prison after serving a term for robbery, and divorced Mrs. Smith upon his release.

The family lives in five and a half rooms, and Mrs. Smith receives support from public welfare. There are five boys in the family ranging from 8 to 13 years of age, and three girls ranging from 1 to 6 years old.

The Wiltwyck child is Lewis, 10. He is at Wiltwyck because of a history of stealing and vandalism; with another boy on one occasion he destroyed $1,000 worth of school property. All of the children have been involved in stealing, sometimes alone and often together. All have difficulties in school.

THE GARCIAS[3]

The Garcias are both Puerto Rican. Mr. Garcia, 42, is a Catholic, and Mrs. Garcia, 35, is of the Pentacostal faith. Her religion plays a very important role in her life. The youngest of six children, she was sent, along with a sister, to be raised by a foster mother when she was one year old. She received a sixth-grade education.

Mrs. Garcia married Mr. Garcia when she was 13 years old, but left him after several years to come to New York City with their baby, Felipe, now 14 years old. Mr. Garcia followed her, but soon deserted the family for several years, returning to "stay" some time ago. He has an eighth-grade education, and is steadily employed as a factory worker. They live in three and a half rooms in a housing project in Manhattan, and their household included a piano, purchased on installments. Spanish is spoken at home, but their English is fairly fluent.

Felipe is institutionalized in a state training school. Juan, age 10, is the Wiltwyck child; he was referred by the court to Wiltwyck after he was suspended from school. He has been a severe behavior problem in school, a chronic truant, and had been involved in stealing episodes.

THE MCCALLISTERS

Mrs. McCallister, 29, was born in Georgia. She is subject to mood swings from depression and suicidal thoughts to periods of great elation and manic activity. Mr. McCallister, 33, had a third-grade education and a record of delinquency as a child. He is a chronic traffic offender and has been taken to court for nonsupport. He goes on heavy alcoholic binges during which he becomes physically aggressive to his wife and children. After the first few therapy sessions, Mr. McCallister separated from Mrs. McCallister and was no longer part of the nuclear family.

The McCallisters, both Negro Protestants, were married in Georgia when Mrs. McCallister was 13 years old. They have been in New York

---

[3] Chapter 3 presents the Garcias and excerpts from transcripts of their family treatment sessions.

City for about 11 years. There are four girls in the family, ranging from 4 to 14 years, and four boys, ranging from 2 to 11 years. The members of this family live in a six-room apartment, and are supported by public welfare funds.

Daniel, 11, is the Wiltwyck child, and was referred to Wiltwyck because of a history of truancy, and appearances in Children's Court for turning in a false fire alarm, and for stealing. Margaret, 14, is promiscuous. Bonnie, 13, is a transvestite and acts out homosexually. Herbert, 8, is a chronic truant.

THE WAINRIGHTS

Mrs. Wainright, 27, came to New York from North Carolina when she was 11 years old. She is a Negro, Methodist, and has an eighth-grade education. She married, bore Robert, now age 12, and then separated from her husband. She soon entered a common-law marriage which dissolved about two years after the birth of Ted.

Mrs. Wainright is a depressed person with psychosomatic complaints, prolonged episodes of drunkenness, and periods of withdrawal during which she stays in her room without leaving her bed and is "nursed" by the children. The family receives welfare assistance, and lives in a one-and-a-half-room apartment in which two boys share a bed. Ted, 10, came to Wiltwyck from the courts because of truancy and acting out. Robert is a discipline and guidance problem in school, having been reported for extreme insolence and fighting.

THE MONTGOMERYS[4]

Mrs. Montgomery, age 38, a Negro Protestant, was born in North Carolina, the second of seven children. Her mother died when she was 10 years old. After a year of college, she left North Carolina to have an out-of-wedlock child who is still in North Carolina with Mrs. Montgomery's sister. In 1940, she came to New York City, but returned to North Carolina to work as a nurse; during the next five years she had two more illegitimate children by a Mr. H. She then came back to New York City where, since 1946, she has been living with Mr. Montgomery.

Mrs. Montgomery had been diagnosed as schizoid by the Manhattan Court Clinic six years ago. Mr. Montgomery, age 45, is ill and unable to work. He had lived with Mrs. Montgomery for 10 years, although they were not legally married. Several years ago, he was ordered out of the

---

[4] The Montgomerys are presented in Chapter 3 along with excerpts from their family treatment sessions.

household by the court for sexually molesting Mrs. Montgomery's oldest daughter. Mrs. Montgomery is supported by public welfare funds.

The two girls in the family are 17 and 16 years old. Each has an illegitimate child, and the younger girl is pregnant again. There are five boys in the family, ranging from 9 to 14 years; all were fathered by Mr. Montgomery.

Richard, 10, was referred to Wiltwyck because he was impossible to control in school and was suspended for deliberately manhandling another child in front of his teacher; outside of school he was constantly fighting, and cursing other children and adults. Another boy had been institutionalized since the age of 5 at Letchworth Village, a state training school. Henry, 13, is institutionalized at Warwick for stealing. Michael, 11, is in a "600" school.[5] Thomas, 9 years old, is said to be doing well in school.

THE GARIBALDIS

Mrs. Garibaldi, 38, a Caucasian Episcopalian of German descent, is a native New Yorker with an eighth-grade education. During pre-adolescence and adolescence she was sexually involved with her father. She ran away from home and was institutionalized in a home for wayward girls. Her psychiatric diagnosis at the time of the children's referral was ambulatory schizophrenia. Two of her brothers were institutionalized at Wiltwyck.

Mr. Garibaldi, 45, a Catholic, was born in New York and is of Italian extraction. He was reared in an orphanage until he was 16. A high-school graduate, he is employed as a house painter for eight months of the year and is a steady and reliable worker. The family lives in a five-room apartment in a low-income housing project. His psychiatric diagnosis when the children were referred was paranoid personality.

Mrs. Garibaldi has had extramarital affairs. When her husband accuses her of infidelity, as he frequently does, she obliges by having another affair. The oldest boy in the family was fathered by another man and born prior to the marriage. Anthony, the third child, also has a different father.

There are eight children in this family, ranging in age from 3 to 20 years. Rudolph, 20, has completed a vocational high-school course and is now studying for a general diploma. A 16-year-old boy, Daniel, is institutionalized at Letchworth Village. Anthony, 13, Frank, 11, and Angelo,

---

[5] See footnote 8, Chapter 3.

9, who was diagnosed as a childhood schizophrenic, are all at Wiltwyck because of stealing and truancy. A 7-year-old boy and two girls, 4 and 3 years old, comprise the rest of the eight children in this family, but at the beginning of treatment they were referred by the court to a children's shelter because of parental neglect.

TABLE A

DESCRIPTIVE DATA FOR EXPERIMENTAL AND CONTROL FAMILIES

Family	Father-Figure in Home?	Mother's Religion	Mother's Ethnic Background	Mother's Education in Years	Source of Income
Experimental (N = 12)					
Jones	No	Baptist	Negro	7	DPW
Romano	No	Catholic	Italian	9	DPW
Lewis	Yes	Protestant	Negro	11	Mr. L./DPW
La Salle	No	Protestant	Negro	12 (HS)	DPW
Martinez	Yes	Catholic	Puerto Rican	9	Mr. M.
Brown	Yes	Protestant	Negro	9	DPW
Smith	No	Jehovah's Witness	Negro	12 (HS)	DPW
Garcia	Yes	Pentacostal	Puerto Rican	6	Mr. G.
McCallister	No	Protestant	Negro	?	DPW
Wainright	No	Methodist	Negro	8	DPW
Montgomery	No	Protestant	Negro	13	DPW
Garibaldi	Yes	Episcopalian	German	8	Mr. G./DPW
Mean				9.4	
Control (N = 10)					
Alberto	Yes	Catholic	Puerto Rican	8	Mr. A.
Holt	No	Catholic	Negro	9	DPW
Chevalier	No	Protestant	Negro	10	DPW
Grant	Yes	Protestant	Negro	11	Mr. G./DPW
Masters	No	?	Negro	7	DPW
McKale	No	Protestant	Negro	8	DPW
Merdock	No	Protestant	Negro	10	DPW
Perez	Yes	?	Puerto Rican	8	Mr. P.
Price	No	?	Negro	8	DPW
Richards	No	Protestant	Negro	12 (HS)	DPW
Mean				9.1	

NOTE: Mr. Romano had been in prison, but was released; he was available for the last month of treatment. When religious denomination was available, it is specified. Religious affiliation was not available for some control mothers. DPW = New York City Department of Public Welfare. Mr. McCallister was available only for the first few therapy sessions.

TABLE B

CHILDREN OF THE EXPERIMENTAL AND CONTROL FAMILIES

Family	No. of Children in Family	Participating Children			
		Younger		*Older*	
		N	Mean Age	N	Mean Age
Experimental					
Jones	7	3	8–4	2	12–2
Romano	7	4	8–6	3	13–10
Lewis	7	2	9–10	3	13–0
La Salle	3	2	8–2	1	13–1
Martinez	4	1	8–1	2	9–7
Brown	6	2	9–2	2	13–4
Smith	8	3	8–1	3	12–5
Garcia	2	1	10–9	1	14–0
McCallister	8	3	9–8	2	13–8
Wainright	2	1	10–5	1	12–6
Montgomery	7	3	11–4	3	15–8
Garibaldi	8	2	9–7	2	13–0
Mean (N = 12)	5.75 (N = 69)	2.3 (N = 27)	9–4	2.1 (N = 25)	13–0
Control					
Alberto	5	2	11–6	2	14–6
Holt	2	1	15–0	1	16–0
Chevalier	8	3	9–8	3	14–4
Grant	8	3	11–4	2	15–5
Masters	6	2	11–0	2	16–6
McKale	5	2	10–6	2	15–0
Merdock	4	2	9–0	2	14–0
Perez	5	1	8–0	1	9–0
Price	3	1	12–0	2	14–5
Richards	6	3	9–4	3	13–0
Mean (N = 10)	5.2 (N = 52)	2 (N = 20)	10–8	2 (N = 20)	14–2

NOTE: Table includes children in various institutions, but not children living with another family on a permanent basis. Age is available to the nearest month for each experimental child and to the past whole year for each control child. Age is at time of first therapy session for experimental children and at time of initial testing for control children. The designation of younger or older is based on the distribution within a given family because it was decided very early in the project that family position and role provided a more relevant basis for differentiation than chronological age. The children within the family were therefore split according to their age relative to one another. When there was only one child, or an uneven number of children, age was taken into consideration, with the children under 12 being assigned to the younger group and the children over 12 being assigned to the older group. In the experimental group there were 4 girls and 23 boys in the younger group and 11 girls and 14 boys in the older group. In the control group, there were 7 girls and 13 boys in the younger group and 11 girls and 9 boys in the older group.

Selected Family Therapy Sessions:
A Verbal Behavior Analysis

PART I   Method and Findings

As a supplement to the clinical description of ongoing processes in the therapy sessions in the research phase, it seemed desirable to analyze certain aspects of the therapy sessions by objectively coding the verbal behavior of the participants. Note, this verbal behavior analysis reflects our conceptualizations and therapeutic maneuvers at the time of our research and not the techniques and conceptualizations we are currently employing (see Chapter 6).

A systematic analysis was felt to be desirable for several reasons. First, because the theoretical biases of the therapists may induce them to perceive therapeutic events selectively. An objective, quantitative description of the events that occur in therapy, however, can perhaps reveal important aspects of a process that might otherwise be missed. Second, the process of developing a reliable system of coding forces the investigator to define his variables much more clearly than he is otherwise wont to do. Finally, an objective coding system can be reliably communicated to and utilized by others, allowing for independent verification and for comparative studies using different populations or treatment techniques.

There was no intent to draw firm conclusions from the data thus obtained, and statistical treatment beyond simple description was not employed. We hoped, rather, to describe quantitatively the kind and extent of verbal interaction that took place along certain relevant dimensions and to search for any tendencies for such interactions to change from early to late phases of therapy.

In devising the particular system used in the present study, a number of methods for analyzing verbal interactions in individual psychotherapy settings were considered. These included: a detailed procedure described by Lennard and Bernstein (1960); a technique developed by Strupp (1957) for assessing therapist-behavior along dimensions such as depth, dynamic focus, and initiative; and another for categorizing therapist-behavior in terms such as restatement of content, interpretation, and reflection of feeling, and client responses in terms of such categories as dependency, guardedness, and resistance (Ashby, Ford, Guerney, and Guerney, 1957). Coding systems for assessing verbal behavior in group settings were also reviewed. These included several developed by Gorlow, Hoch, and Telschow (1952), Bales (1950), and Leary (1957).

As our thinking developed, we decided to focus primarily on the ways in which our family members and subgroups within the families tended to respond to one another and to the therapist (along dimensions which seemed maximally relevant to the dynamics of the family and its problems) rather than on technical aspects of our therapeutic interventions. As a result, we decided not to use the coding systems based on therapeutic techniques but instead to use the Leary (1957) and Bales (1950) systems as jumping-off points for devising our own procedures. The development of our coding system was also, in part, guided by our decision to work with variables similar to those employed in our analysis of the FIAT and Family Task (see Chapter 7).

Rules of coding and definitions of categories were developed, according to which each statement of the therapist or family member could be placed under one or more of twenty-six major categories, some of which contained subcategories. A *statement* was defined as "everything a person says between the remarks of two speakers." The coding was done from the typescripts of therapy sessions in a manner which specified for each statement the *category* or *categories* in which it fell, the *speaker, addressee* (the person to whom the remark was addressed), and when appropriate, the target (the person who was the subject of the remark).[1] A therapist had assisted the typist in identifying the voices of the participants.

---

[1] For practical reasons the target data were not tabulated or analyzed.

The sixth and twenty-eighth sessions were chosen for analysis so that both an early and a late phase of the therapy could be represented by sessions which were not too close to the first or last session. Presumably, these would be representative of a typical session of that phase but not be subject to the uniqueness of beginning or ending sessions. A session immediately following or preceding these sessions was substituted in a few instances when poor recording of a session prevented its use. To narrow the scope of the coding task to practical limits, only alternate pages of a session were coded. Definitions of these coding categories are presented in Part II of this Appendix.

A study of coder reliability of the categories utilized as judges three college students who had spent approximately thirty hours in training and practice separately and together. (They were also the coders in the actual study.) In neither the reliability study nor the coding of all the data did the coders know which transcripts came from the early sessions or the late ones, nor did they know any of the expectations we may have had concerning findings.

The arbitrarily chosen interview used in the reliability study contained 929 responses. There was no agreement on 77 responses (8 per cent). Two out of three judges agreed on 345 responses (37 per cent). There was complete agreement on 507 responses (55 per cent). Thus, at least two out of the three judges agreed 92 per cent of the time. In general, the reliability of the categories seemed sufficiently high to justify their use in an exploratory investigation.

The reliability study and the coding were based on the twenty-six categories. At a later stage of data analysis, however, computer analysis required that the number of categories be reduced to thirteen. This was achieved by combining certain categories according to similarity of meaning and grouping the remaining categories, most of these having appeared very infrequently, into an "other" category.

The categories were grouped as follows:[2]

1. Exchange of information (categories 1, 2, 3, and 4 neutral)
2. Expresses positive feelings (category 4 positive)
3. Expresses negative feelings (category 4 negative)
4. Harmonious responses (categories 6 and 7)
5. Requests control, guidance, or suggestion (categories 8 and 11)

---

[2] Reference to the original categories as presented in Part II of this Appendix will provide the reader with the operational definition of each of these thirteen categories.

6. Control with neutral or positive responses (categories 9 neutral and 9 positive)
7. Control with negative response (category 9 negative)
8. Guidance (category 12)
9. Does not give information (category 13)
10. Disagreement (category 15)
11. Aggression (category 16)
12. Describes lack of role fulfillment (category 23)
13. Other (remaining categories)

All codings were tabulated for the following speaker and addressee person-categories: therapist, mother, father, younger children, older children, and total family. The number of responses falling into each of the thirteen categories was determined for each of the person-categories. In addition to a frequency count, the percentage of each person's total responses falling into a given category was similarly determined. This was done for each family separately and for all families combined. The analysis was conducted separately for those stages in which the family was seen as a unit (Stages 1 and 3) and when parents and children were separated (Stage 2). Our major analysis was of the family stage (material from Stages 1 and 3).

All the subjects in our twelve experimental families were included in the verbal analysis of the therapy sessions. One of the unavoidable difficulties in interpreting the data obtained is that not all family members included in our over-all research were always present in the particular session chosen for analysis, and the family composition in the early session was not always the same as in the late session. Also, it should be noted that there was no attempt to control for the uneven number of responses contributed by the families: some families contributed more to the over-all findings than others. In our analysis, however, we checked the over-all percentage findings against a consideration of the actual numbers of families that did in fact show these patterns suggested by the percentage findings.

Pathways of Interpersonal Interaction (Who Talks to Whom) in Family Stages (1 and 3)

The transcripts used in the analysis of the early phase of therapy contain 3,459 responses while those from the later phase contain 4,355 responses. Although it is possible that the increase in number of responses from the early to the later sessions may be due to artifacts rather than to variables intrinsic to the therapeutic process, it is equally plausible to assume that the therapeutic process encouraged greater verbal interaction and discouraged the recourse to paraverbal channels of communication so characteristic of this population. In any event, the validity of either of these alternative explanations cannot be ascertained.

Table C shows who was making verbal responses to whom. The data are presented in the form of percentages as well as frequency of responses for ease of interpretation. For example, at the upper left of the table we see that in the early therapy sample therapists made 180 responses to another therapist and 692 responses to mothers, constituting 10 per cent and 39 per cent respectively of all therapist responses. Looking at the over-all number of responses (last column), it is quite clear that the therapist took a very active role in the sessions, making about as many responses as did all the members of the family combined. The mothers were the next most active participants, even when allowances are made for the fact that fewer fathers were present in the sessions. If a similar adjustment (according to numbers present) is made in viewing the responses of fathers in comparison to children, the father emerges as the next most active participant. Initially, the older children participated more actively than the younger, but their ranking is reversed in the sample from the late sessions, which suggests that the younger children took a much more active role as therapy progressed. The centrality of the therapist and the mother in these sessions, as empirically suggested by this verbal behavior analysis, has already been discussed in the preceding chapters together with the implications of this centrality in terms of the therapeutic process.

It appears from the summary data—even when allowances are made for numbers—that the mother was more frequently responded to by the therapist than the father. But inspection of the family-by-family data reveals that when both mother and father were present together they were responded to by the therapist about equally. The predominance of responses to the mother, then, came only from those sessions in which the father was not present; this finding would probably not have emerged had more fathers been present.

In absolute terms, the children were receiving more verbal attention from the therapists than the parents; but on a per-person basis, of course, the parents were the central object of the therapists' attention.

The most striking finding about the nature of verbal interaction in the

TABLE C

INTERPERSONAL VERBAL INTERACTION IN STAGES 1 AND 3, EARLY AND LATE PHASES OF THERAPY

Phase of Therapy	Speaker	N	Responses	Addressee						
				Therapist	Mothers	Fathers	Younger Children	Older Children	(Total Family)	Total by Row
	Therapist		number	180	692	108	308	500	(1,608)	1,788
			%	10	39	6	17	28	(90)	100[a]
	Mother	12	number	629	0	3	50	55	(108)	737
			%	85	0	0	7	7	(14)	99
E A R L Y	Father	6	number	105	7	0	12	16	(35)	140
			%	75	5	0	9	11	(25)	100
	Younger Children	21	number	245	33	7	3	27	(70)	315
			%	78	10	2	1	9	(22)	100
	Older Children	22	number	370	54	8	21	26	(109)	479
			%	77	11	2	4	5	(22)	99
	Total Family	61	number	(1,349)	(94)	(18)	(86)	(124)	(322)	(1,671)
			%	(81)	(6)	(1)	(5)	(7)	(19)	(100)
	Total		number	1,529	786	126	394	624	(1,930)	3,459
			%	44	23	4	11	18	(56)	100
	Therapist		number	190	553	295	572	411	(1,831)	2,021
			%	9	27	15	28	20	(90)	99
	Mother	11	number	490	1	15	170	155	(341)	831
			%	59	0	2	20	19	(41)	100
L A T E	Father	6	number	268	11	1	20	22	(54)	322
			%	83	3	0	6	7	(16)	99
	Younger Children	19	number	419	135	12	47	51	(245)	664
			%	63	20	2	7	8	(37)	100
	Older Children	20	number	293	124	11	63	26	(224)	517
			%	57	24	2	12	5	(43)	100
	Total Family	56	number	(1,470)	(271)	(39)	(300)	(254)	(864)	(2,334)
			%	(63)	(12)	(2)	(13)	(11)	(38)	(101)
	Total		number	1,660	824	334	872	665	(2,695)	4,355
			%	38	19	8	20	15	(62)	100

[a] Percentages are reported to the nearest whole number in this and the other tables in this Appendix. Percentage totals are not always 100 because of this rounding

therapy is the extent to which the therapists serve as the center of the communicational process. Initially, all family members directed about 80 per cent of their responses to the therapist. From inspection of the individual family data, it was found that in every one of the early sessions the therapist received more responses from the family than did all family members combined. Also, there was very little parent-parent interaction, this finding confirming our picture of a poorly integrated spouse sub-system. In nine of eleven sessions, when both parents were present, they addressed more remarks to their children than to each other.

Clearly, then, the nature of our therapy in the research phase was such that the therapists served as the focal point of communications; in addition, the interaction pattern that the therapist had available to work with, or fostered, was primarily parent-child interaction, even when both parents were present in the family stage. These empirical findings once more confirm some of the material we have discussed in Chapters 5 and 6.

A comparison of the late with the early samples (percentages) shows that although the therapists still remained central, there was an obvious shift away from therapist-centered communication to more direct inter-action among family members in the later sample. This was confirmed in the individual family data. It was found there that only three families increased the percentage of responses to the therapist, while eight increased the percentage of responses to other family members (one family remaining unchanged). The only sessions (three) in which family members directed more remarks to each other than to the therapist occurred in the late sample. Actually, as may be seen in Table C, this shift was not true for the fathers but was limited to an increase in the mother-child interaction and child-child interaction (particularly the younger children interacting more with each other and with the older children). This, too, was consistent with the findings when the data were inspected family by family. The shift from the therapists to other family members may well be a reflection of therapeutic interventions in the course of therapy —language as a vehicle of communication among the family members may have been used more frequently in the later phases of therapy; and a reduction in the centrality of the therapist may have been taking place.

Content of Interpersonal Interaction in Family Stages (1 and 3)

Exchange of Information

Tables D and E show by number and percentage the types of responses made by the therapists and family members during the family stages in the early and late phases of therapy. Most striking is the pre-emption of the field by one type of response: the exchange of factual information and neutral feeling. Therapists and family members alike devoted about 70 per cent of their statements to this sort of interchange both early and late in therapy.

This particular category reflects, in our opinion, the tremendous effort the therapists and family members made to obtain even a consensual description of what the family's problems were; that is, the effort toward maintaining a coherent conversational pattern and toward obtaining any focus on a family problem accounts for the prepotency of this category. The exchange of factual information, which comprised the vast majority of the responses in this category, was really the vehicle for establishing focus and providing a basis for mutual understanding. The pervasiveness of this category reflected the need for incessant repetition of communicational stimuli to register the stimuli in the family's perception as well as the family's need to be given a shared groundwork of meaning around a problem through constant feedback from the therapist. The families seldom had a description of a problem to present as such. Much of such informational exchange interaction was necessary just to search for and focus vague complaints into what could be described as a "problem." When the ability to communicate is in *itself* a primary problem, it takes much longer to pattern the communication field in a way that permits shared meanings and understandings.[3]

An interesting comparison could be made of the distribution of our subjects' responses and that found in a group of middle-class families. Would there be such a disproportionately high frequency of responses falling into this category in the latter group? Our interpretations suggest this would not be the case.

The predominance of this category also reflects the constant and multiple interruptions (especially from the children) and the misunderstandings brought about by the frequency of confusing verbal and nonverbal

---

[3] The use of tasks is a therapeutic innovation designed to reduce this problem (see Chapter 6).

TABLE D

CONTENT OF INTERPERSONAL VERBAL INTERACTION IN STAGES 1 AND 3, EARLY PHASE OF THERAPY

Speaker	Responses	Information	Positive Feelings	Negative Feelings	Harmony	Requests Control, Guidance, Suggestion	Control	Ineffective Control	Guidance	Does Not Give Information	Disagree	Aggression	Describes Lack Role Fulfillment	Other	Totals[a]
Therapist	number	1,409	37	58	36	8	84	3	91	1	76	10	35	19	1,867
	%	75	2	3	2	0	4	0	5	0	4	1	2	1	99
Mother	number	520	25	41	11	2	13	5	4	16	46	26	10	24	743
	%	70	3	6	1	0	2	1	1	2	6	3	1	3	99
Father	number	69	9	5	2	1	3	0	3	2	13	11	4	19	141
	%	49	6	4	1	1	2	0	2	2	9	8	3	13	99
Younger Children	number	216	7	8	0	4	5	1	1	21	34	15	0	9	321
	%	67	2	2	0	1	2	0	0	7	11	5	0	3	100
Older Children	number	324	13	17	2	0	5	0	0	22	61	24	11	14	493
	%	66	3	3	0	0	1	0	0	4	12	5	2	3	99
Total Family	number	(1,129)	(54)	(71)	(15)	(7)	(26)	(6)	(8)	(61)	(154)	(76)	(25)	(67)	(1,699)
	%	(66)	(3)	(4)	(1)	(0)	(2)	(0)	(0)	(4)	(9)	(4)	(1)	(4)	(98)
Total	number	2,538	91	129	51	15	110	9	99	62	230	86	60	86	3,566
	%	71	3	4	1	0	4	0	3	2	6	2	2	—	98
Rank Order of Frequency of R[b]		1	6	3	10	11	4	12	5	8	2	7	9	—	—

[a] Number totals slightly exceed those in Table C because responses to people other than therapist and family are included here. This outside group consisted almost exclusively of social workers attending the session.

[b] "Other" responses were not included in ranking information.

TABLE E

CONTENT OF INTERPERSONAL VERBAL INTERACTION IN STAGES 1 AND 3, LATE PHASE OF THERAPY

Speaker	Responses	Information	Positive Feelings	Negative Feelings	Harmony	Requests Control, Guidance, Suggestion	Control	Ineffective Control	Guidance	Does Not Give Information	Disagree	Aggression	Describes Lack Role Fulfillment	Other	Totals[a]
Therapist	number	1,547	33	28	112	2	90	3	124	1	121	13	11	15	2,100
	%	74	2	1	5	0	4		6	0	6	1	1	1	101
Mother	number	551	25	12	26	1	69	1	8	16	86	36	2	13	846
	%	65	3	1	3	0	8	0	1	2	10	4	0	2	99
Father	number	230	30	4	10	2	9	1	5	1	19	1	1	14	327
	%	70	9	1	3	1	3	0	2	0	6	0	0	4	99
Younger Children	number	401	10	20	5	8	19	0	0	41	94	63	3	6	670
	%	60	1	3	1	1	3	0	0	6	14	9	0	1	99
Older Children	number	372	8	10	7	5	21	2	0	27	61	24	0	3	540
	%	69	1	2	1	1	4	0	0	5	11	4	0	1	99
Total Family	number	(1,554)	(73)	(46)	(48)	(16)	(118)	(4)	(13)	(85)	(260)	(124)	(6)	(36)	(2,383)
	%	(65)	(2)	(2)	(2)	(1)	(5)	(0)	(1)	(4)	(11)	(5)	(0)	(2)	(101)
Total	number	3,101	106	74	160	18	208	7	137	86	381	137	17	51	4,483
	%	69	2	2	4	0	5	0	3	2	8	3	0	1	99
Rank Order of Frequency of R[b]		1	7	9	4	10	3	12	5.5	8	2	5.5	11	—	—

[a] Number totals slightly exceed those in Table C because responses to people other than therapist and family are included here. This outside group consisted almost exclusively of social workers attending the session.

[b] "Other" responses were not included in ranking information.

communications occurring in the sessions. It was often necessary for the therapist, for example, to try to get back to the starting point to establish a base from which to proceed with meaningful communication. The questioning around specific factual information also reflected a great need to separate the relevant issues from the irrelevant or less useful ones being brought in by family members, particularly by the children, who would frequently make comments of uncertain relevance to the issue being discussed. To establish whether or not such comments were relevant, and if so in what way, frequently called for a whole series of questions and answers between the therapist and the new participant. The preceding chapters have already discussed many aspects of this process, and Chapters 3 and 4 especially have provided concrete illustrations from the transcripts themselves of the tortuous interchanges among the participants in the sessions to establish a baseline of communication. The reader should keep in mind that the general predominance of exchange of factual information and the reasons underlying it best characterize our families and provide the context in which the other categories must be evaluated.

Excluding the "other" category leaves about 28 per cent of the statements to be distributed across ten categories. This amounts to 2,333 responses over the early and late interview samples combined, or an average of only about 20 responses per category per family. It is worth bearing in mind that when percentage shifts occur when dealing with such small numbers, such shifts may sometimes be more a reflection of the over-all increase in responses than a true shift because the distribution of a given category may vary partly as a function of the total number of responses. Because of such considerations, we will note only those categories of response that were most frequent and which therefore presumably present the most reliable basis for discussion. Even so, it is obvious that any comments based on our figures are highly tentative and that even if those figures are reliable, any changes that are noted can still not be regarded —in the absence of controls and outside criteria—as representing generalized change or as necessarily attributable to the therapy itself. Nevertheless, it does seem worthwhile to attempt to describe the picture that emerges, faint though it may be.

Disagreement Responses

From Tables D and E we see that the category used most frequently after the information category, considering therapist and family members combined, is the category of disagreement. Although this type of response was relatively high for the therapist as a percentage of his own responses, it was really outstanding as far as the family members were concerned. In absolute terms as well as relative to their own general participation, the children contributed more disagreement responses than did their parents. The therapists disagreed more than the parents in absolute terms, but less when considered in proportion to general participation.

Control

Tables D and E show that the next most frequent type of response category was a control response not detectably ineffective on the person upon whom the control was attempted. As may be seen in these tables, the therapist was consistent from early to late sessions in devoting 4 per cent of his responses to control. The family used control responses infrequently, relative to other responses early in therapy, but later attempted verbal control relatively more frequently. Originally, the mothers made by far the most control responses, although as a percentage of all responses, they used this category of response no more than the other family members. In the late phase, mothers were attempting more verbal control than any other family member, from a percentage as well as an absolute point of view.

Other Responses

Following disagreement and control responses in frequency were a group of response categories containing about 200 responses each. These categories were guidance, family harmony, positive feelings, aggression, and negative feelings.[4] We will discuss these data only on a broad basis, mentioning only the most salient figures from the data summarized in Tables D and E and from the data showing the who-to-whom analysis.[5] The reader should bear in mind that these figures represent data summed for twelve families and therefore may mask wide individual differences among families or reflect frequencies in only a *few* of the families.

We must remind the reader also of our discussion in Chapter 5, which highlights the paraverbal, physical, and motor styles of communication of our family members. Attempts to control the other person, for example,

---

[4] Three other categories, describing lack of role fulfillment, obviously ineffective control, and asking for control or guidance contained so few responses that results pertaining to them will not be discussed here.
[5] Who-to-whom breakdowns will not be presented here in tabular form because of space limitations.

whether effective or ineffective, are frequently nonverbal. The limitations and restrictions in our sample's resources are manifested particularly in the expression of affect. Obviously, many transactions, particularly those of control and affect, are rather elusive to the tape recorder and transcript!

Initially, the mother stood almost alone as the recipient of guidance responses. Apparently, other family members were drawn into the guidance process on a more equal basis as therapy progressed. This may be a reflection of a tendency for therapists to concentrate on helping the mother toward her parenting function in the early phase of therapy, trying to guide her in this direction. Later, as the mother's communication with the children increased, the therapist was more willing to assume a guiding role toward the children. It is also possible that, as therapy progressed, the therapist became more a part of the family system; that is, he became more like an auxiliary parent. The therapists may also have felt that the children were more receptive to guidance later in the therapy.

There were very few guidance responses directed from one family member to another. One would expect attempts at guidance from one family member to another to be a frequent mode of response in the family therapy situation. Its absence confirms the clinical impression that parents in these families either ignore their children's behavior or respond very strongly to immediate pressures without being oriented toward training them and influencing their future behavior. A comparative study of this variable comparing these families with nondelinquent families of the same social class would be highly interesting.

Positive feelings were expressed more frequently by the family than by the therapist. Neither the therapist nor the family as a whole changed in expression of positive feeling from the early to the late sessions in the percentage of their responses that represented positive feelings.

Harmony responses (agreement, cooperation, and affection responses), however, were made about twice as frequently by therapists as by members of the family, from an absolute as well as a percentage point of view. Both therapists' and families' harmony responses rose in the later phase of therapy. Each of the family member groups shared in this rise. This, of course, may be due to the desire of family members to present a good picture of themselves as therapy neared an end. Also relevant, however, is the observation that as therapy progressed, the therapists became somewhat incorporated into the family system and developed genuine affectional ties toward the family members; and whereas in the beginning the therapist was concerned primarily with helping the parent with the parenting function, later he became concerned with expanding the perception of positive factors and attributes among the family members.

As can be seen from Tables D and E, aggressive responses came mostly from the family. The highest number of aggressive responses in the early phase of therapy came from the mother, followed closely by the older children, and then by the younger children. In this phase, as a percentage of their total responses, the fathers were most aggressive. In terms of proportion of responses for the families as a whole, there was little change in aggression responses from the early to the late phase of therapy. But late in therapy the fathers' aggressive responses dropped to only 1 response in 327; whereas the younger children became the most aggressive—proportionately to their participation as well as in absolute terms.[6]

Responses categorized as negative feelings were also made more frequently by family members than by therapists. Both therapists' and families' negative feeling responses dropped noticeably from the early to the late phase of therapy. Unlike the rise in family harmony, this change was not distributed among all family members. The percentage of children's responses of this nature remained about the same, while the mothers' and fathers' proportional expression of negative feeling declined sharply.

Relative Hierarchies of Response in Family Stages (1 and 3)

The family-stage data were also analyzed from a different point of view, considering only the family members. The following questions were asked: what similarities and differences exist in modes of response among family members, and what changes in such response hierarchies occur in the late as compared to the early sessions? To answer these questions, the types of response used by mothers, fathers, and older and younger children were ranked according to frequency for early and late therapy sessions and compared across family members and between sessions.

---

[6] Another category, refusal to give information, is somewhat related to this group of "negative" responses. This category contained only 148 responses (2 per cent of all responses), and all but two came from family members. Thus, such responses were more frequently made by the family than negative feeling, harmony, or control and guidance responses, and they constitute 4 per cent of the families' responses early in therapy. Neither the family as a whole nor different subgroups responded differently in the later sample, and in both instances it was obviously the children who were the ones most likely to evade giving information or reporting their feelings when they were asked to do so. Of the children's 111 evasive responses, all but 14 were vis-à-vis the therapist.

Although the rank of each variable is of course dependent upon the movement or lack of it in the other variables, it was felt that this method would be useful for detecting relatively large differences in response tendencies. In singling out a difference as being noteworthy, we used a difference of 3 points in rank order (out of a total of 12 possible ranks) as the cutoff point. Although such a cutoff is arbitrary, a shift of this magnitude seemed large enough to omit minor fluctuations, yet not so high as to exclude from consideration differences that might be genuine. The resulting observations must be treated cautiously, particularly with respect to those categories containing few responses, and they do not bring new data into the picture. But these observations do present another focus or mode of analysis which serves to summarize the data from a family-member point of view.

Table F presents such rankings, as well as the percentages of total responses they represent. The findings here can be summarized as follows: Initially, the mothers seemed to differ most from the rest of the family in reporting negative feelings and perhaps also in giving more harmonious responses. The fathers seemed to differ most in being less likely to refuse to give information, being more likely to describe lack of role fulfillment in the family, and being more likely to offer guidance. The younger children differed most in their greater tendency to refuse to give information, to ask for control, guidance, and suggestions, and in not giving harmonious responses or responses that describe lack of role fulfillment. The older children also were initially prone to refuse to provide information, but otherwise they were not very different from the general picture presented by the parents.

Later in therapy, the mother was relatively *less* prone to report negative feelings than the rest of the family. She also stands out with respect to a relative willingness to give control responses and not to ask for control, guidance, or suggestions. The fathers, later in therapy, remained relatively less likely to refuse to give information and relatively high in guidance responses; they were by then also singularly low in aggression. The younger children, later in therapy, differed most from the parents, again, in refusing to give information and in giving less guidance and harmonious responses than the parents. A similar picture is presented by the older children.

To summarize the *change* findings from the point of view of hierarchy of categories, using the same criterion of a three-rank shift, we find control rising in the case of the mothers and the older children; harmony

TABLE F

RANKS AND PERCENTAGES OF FAMILY MEMBERS' RESPONSES, STAGES 1 AND 3, EARLY AND LATE PHASES OF THERAPY

Response Category	Mothers				Fathers				Younger Children				Older Children			
	Early		Late		Early		Late		Early		Late		Early		Late	
	Rank	%	Rank	%	Rank	%	Rank	%	Rank	%	Rank	%	Rank	%	Rank	%
Information	1	70.0	1	65.0	1	49.0	1	70.0	1	67.0	1	60.0	1	66.0	1	69.0
Disagreement	2	6.2	2	10.0	2	9.2	3	5.8	2	11.0	2	14.0	2	12.0	2	11.0
Negative Feelings	3	5.5	8	1.4	5	3.5	7	1.2	5	2.5	5	3.0	5	3.4	6	1.8
Aggression	4	3.5	4	4.2	3	7.8	10.5	.30	4	4.7	3	9.4	3	4.9	4	4.4
Positive Feelings	5	3.4	6	3.0	4	6.4	2	30.0	6	2.2	7	1.5	6	2.6	7	1.5
Refusal to Give Information	6	2.2	7	1.9	9.5	1.4	10.5	.30	3	6.5	4	6.1	4	4.5	3	5.0
Control	7	1.8	3	8.1	7.5	2.1	5	2.7	7	1.6	6	2.8	8	1.0	5	3.9
Harmony	8	1.5	5	3.1	9.5	1.4	4	3.0	11.5	0	9	.75	9	.40	8	1.2
Lack Role Fulfillment	9	1.3	10	.24	6	2.8	10.5	.30	11.5	0	10	.45	7	2.2	11.5	0
Ineffective Control	10	.71	11.5	.12	12	0	10.5	.30	9.5	.31	11.5	0	11	0	10	.37
Guidance	11	.54	9	.94	7.5	2.1	6	1.5	9.5	.31	11.5	0	11	0	11.5	0
Requests Control, Guidance, or Suggestion	12	.27	11.5	.12	11	.71	8	.61	8	1.2	8	1.2	11	0	9	9.2

responses rising in the mothers' and fathers' response hierarchy; complaint about lack of role fulfillment falling in the hierarchies of the fathers and the older children; negative feelings declining in the mothers' response hierarchy; and aggressive remarks declining in the fathers' response hierarchy.

Pathways and Content of Interpersonal Interaction in Subgroup Stage (Stage 2)

Tables G, H, and I summarize data with respect to our analysis of Stage 2 sessions. These data can be easily compared to those in the tables we have previously presented. Such a comparison shows that there is a striking resemblance in the patterns of response in the stage in which family subgroups were separated from each other and the stages in which they were together. In terms of both pathways of verbal interaction and content, then, our Stage 2 analysis yielded the same sorts of trends already discussed when Stage 1 and Stage 3 findings were presented.

For example, in terms of the most prominent response categories, the information exchange category still heads the list in both early and late phases of therapy and again accounts for roughly 70 per cent of the responses. Disagreement responses retain the same rank (second) in Stage 2, early and late in therapy, that they had in the family stage, and the family members again contributed about twice as many disagreement responses as did the therapists. The who-to-whom analysis showed the same pattern of high disagreement in parent-parent and child-child interaction that was observed in the family stage.

Our Method of Analysis—A Backward Look

The area of primary concern in the traditional psychotherapeutic methods deals with organization of affect, insight into intrapsychic organization of experience, patterns of interpersonal transactions, etc., and not with ways of establishing effective communication among participants. Although we did not feel bound by traditional measures of verbal behavior in psychotherapy, nevertheless we overestimated the frequency of occurrence of many of the verbal response categories we used on the basis of our experiences with other types of patients and families. We also did not anticipate the extent to which we would rely on what we found to be a useful therapeutic technique with these families: interventive measures aimed toward establishing and promulgating effective means and tech-

TABLE G

INTERPERSONAL VERBAL INTERACTION IN STAGE 2, EARLY AND LATE PHASES OF THERAPY

Phase of Therapy	Speaker	N	Responses	Therapist	Mothers	Fathers	Younger Children	Older Children	(Total Family)	Total by Row
	Therapist		number	59	462	43	346	353	(1,204)	1,263
			%	5	37	3	27	28	(95)	100
	Mother	12	number	483		27			(27)	510
			%	94		5			(5)	99
E A R L Y	Father	6	number	43	19				(19)	62
			%	69	31				(31)	100
	Younger Children	21	number	277			24	53	(77)	354
			%	78			7	15	(22)	100
	Older Children	22	number	281			62	74	(136)	417
			%	67			15	18	(33)	100
	Total Family	61	number	(1,084)	(19)	(27)	(86)	(127)	(259)	(1,343)
			%	(81)	(1)	(2)	(6)	(9)	(18)	(99)
	Total		number	1,143	481	70	432	480	(1,463)	2,606
			%	44	18	3	17	18	(56)	100
	Therapist		number	25	256	181	317	350	(1,104)	1,129
			%	2	23	16	28	31	(98)	100
	Mother	11	number	240		47			(47)	287
			%	83		16			(16)	99
L A T E	Father	6	number	174	40				(40)	214
			%	81	19				(19)	100
	Younger Children	19	number	297			67	101	(168)	465
			%	64			14	22	(36)	100
	Older Children	20	number	299			95	30	(125)	424
			%	70			22	7	(29)	99
	Total Family	56	number	(1,010)	(40)	(47)	(162)	(131)	(380)	(1,390)
			%	(73)	(3)	(3)	(12)	(9)	(27)	(100)
	Total		number	1,035	296	228	479	481	(1,484)	2,519
			%	41	12	9	19	19	(59)	100

TABLE H

CONTENT OF INTERPERSONAL VERBAL INTERACTION IN STAGE 2, EARLY PHASE OF THERAPY

Speaker	Responses	Information	Positive Feelings	Negative Feelings	Harmony	Requests Control, Guidance, Suggestion	Control	Ineffective Control	Guidance	Does Not Give Information	Disagree	Aggression	Describes Lack Role Fulfillment	Other	Totals[a]
Therapist	number	982	21	21	27	3	71	2	56	0	71	8	15	14	1,291
	%	76	2	2	2	0	5	0	4	0	5	1	1	1	99
Mother	number	328	57	39	7	1	5	0	1	9	33	14	6	16	516
	%	64	11	8	1	0	1	0	0	2	6	3	1	3	100
Father	number	35	2	6	1	0	1	0	0	2	9	4	4	3	65
	%	54	3	9	2	0	1	0	0	0	14	6	6	5	101
Younger Children	number	207	15	7	0	2	4	0	0	32	42	30	2	15	356
	%	58	4	2	0	1	1	0	0	9	12	8	1	4	100
Older Children	number	202	19	30	0	1	5	7	0	32	70	39	9	10	425
	%	48	4	7	0	0	1	2	0	8	16	9	2	2	99
Total Family[b]	number	(772)	(93)	(82)	(9)	(4)	(15)	(7)	(1)	(73)	(154)	(87)	(21)	(44)	(1,362)
	%	(57)	(7)	(6)	(1)	(0)	(1)	(1)	(0)	(5)	(11)	(6)	(2)	(3)	(100)
Total	number	1,754	114	103	36	7	86	9	57	73	225	95	36	58	2,653
	%	66	4	4	1	0	3	0	2	3	8	4	1	2	98
Rank Order of Frequency of R[c]		1	3	4	9.5	12	5	11	8	7	2	6	9.5	—	—

[a] Number totals slightly exceed those in Table F because responses to people other than therapist and family are included here. This outside group consisted almost exclusively of social workers attending the session.

[b] Data of separate sessions combined for purposes of comparability to Stages 1 and 3.

[c] "Other" responses were not included in ranking information.

TABLE 1

CONTENT OF INTERPERSONAL VERBAL INTERACTION IN STAGE 2, LATE PHASE OF THERAPY

Speaker	Responses	Information	Positive Feelings	Negative Feelings	Harmony	Requests Control, Guidance, Suggestion	Control	Ineffective Control	Guidance	Does Not Give Information	Disagree	Aggression	Describes Lack Role Fulfillment	Other	Totals[a]
Therapist	number	847	25	28	36	5	85	5	51	0	60	11	7	5	1,165
	%	73	2	2	3	0	7	0	4	0	5	1	1	0	98
Mother	number	197	13	10	7	0	4	1	1	11	19	20	0	7	290
	%	68	4	3	2	0	1	0	0	4	7	7	0	2	98
Father	number	124	20	9	0	0	2	0	1	5	35	8	4	8	216
	%	57	9	4	0	0	1	0	0	2	16	4	2	4	99
Younger Children	number	313	3	5	2	6	24	3	4	19	60	31	0	4	474
	%	66	1	1	0	1	5	1	1	4	13	7	0	1	101
Older Children	number	308	5	4	0	1	13	1	1	27	38	35	3	3	439
	%	70	1	1	0	0	3	0	0	6	9	8	1	1	100
Total Family[b]	number	(942)	(41)	(28)	(9)	(7)	(43)	(5)	(7)	(62)	(152)	(94)	(7)	(22)	(1,419)
	%	(66)	(3)	(2)	(1)	(0)	(3)	(0)	(0)	(4)	(11)	(7)	(0)	(2)	(99)
Total	number	1,789	66	56	45	12	128	10	58	62	212	105	14	27	2,584
	%	69	3	2	2	0	5	0	2	2	8	4	1	1	99
Rank Order of Frequency of R[c]		1	3	8	9	11	3	12	7	6	2	4	10	—	—

[a] Number totals slightly exceed those in Table F because responses to people other than therapist and family are included here. This outside group consisted almost exclusively of social workers attending the session.

[b] Data of separate sessions combined for purposes of comparability to Stages 1 and 3.

[c] "Other" responses were not included in ranking information.

niques of communication. To review some of the characteristics of the communication of our family members as qualitatively observed:

1. They tend to pay selective attention to relationship messages at the expense of content messages.
2. They tend not to listen to each other.
3. They often do not carry a subject matter to a logical conclusion.
4. They transact many operations through *paraverbal* channels. They often do not finish their phrases, interrupt one another, and (especially the children) substitute motor activity and noise for language in their transactions.

Some of our therapeutic techniques (see Chapter 6) became focused on helping the families develop the capacity for establishing meaningful dialogue and conversation. This meant persistent attention to such matters as encouraging the family members to listen to one another, not to interrupt, to direct their remarks toward one another rather than to the therapist, and to continue discussions on a given theme rather than jumping to other topics.

In addition, the therapists had to constantly direct attention to reducing the noise level and motility of the children. Because of our population's restricted cognitive and language skills as well as their concrete, non-introspective orientation, therapy sessions were frequently directive, informational, and concrete. This heavy concentration on teaching the family members how to communicate, along with the concrete, restricted nature of the family members' dialogue and the directive nature of our therapeutic approach, was reflected in the predominance of our first verbal category: exchange of information. Had the extremely high frequency of responses in this category been anticipated, we might have modified our research plans to allow for the coding of more sessions, making it possible for the less frequently used categories to accumulate more responses, thus permitting increased confidence in the findings.

However, in any repetition of our study with this particular population, in addition to exploring content we would pay more specific attention to the nature of the communication process itself and the changes that might take place in this area. We would be interested in exploring such questions as: Does A respond to B around the same content? How long does conversation remain focused on the same area? Do interruptions with change of theme decrease? Have the pathways of communication changed, indicating a change in family structure? Has the flexibility of pathway interactions increased? And so forth. Other workers in family research have reached similar conclusions with regard to appropriate family research strategies.

In summary, then, the foregoing pages show some verbal response patterns which correspond with clinical impressions. For example, the special need for the therapist in these families to serve in a central position in opening and maintaining communication seems to be reflected in the pattern of response rates; and the tendency of parents to respond either strongly or not at all and seldom with an orientation toward teaching or influencing future behavior seems to be reflected in the strength of disagreement and control responses vis-à-vis the near absence of guidance responses. At least one strong clinical impression—the ineffectiveness of parental control—was not reflected in the data, probably because of the limitations inherent in coding from tapes. With respect to suggestions for future research, the data suggest that certain variables, particularly guidance and the variables related to guidance, would be highly useful in comparative studies with similar families not containing delinquent children. We also concluded that variables having to do with the process and adequacy of the communication system itself in addition to many of the content variables employed here would be significant dimensions in future research.

REFERENCES

Ashby, J. D., Ford, D. H., Guerney, B. G., Jr., and Guerney, Louise. Effects on clients of a reflective and a leading type of psychotherapy. *Psychol. Monogr.*, 1957, **71**, No. 24.

Bales, R. F. *Interaction process analysis: a method for the study of small groups.* Cambridge, Mass.: Addison-Wesley Press, Inc., 1950.

Gorlow, L., Hoch, E. L., and Telschow, E. F. *The nature of non–directive group psychotherapy.* New York: Bureau of Publications, Teachers College, Columbia University, 1952.

Leary, T. *Interpersonal diagnosis of personality.* New York: The Ronald Press Co., 1957.

Lennard, H. L., and Bernstein, A. *The anatomy of psychotherapy.* New York: Columbia University Press, 1960.

Strupp, H. H. A multidimensional system for analyzing psychotherapeutic techniques. *Psychiat.*, 1957, **20**, 293–306.

PART II   Definitions of Initial Coding Categories Employed in Verbal Behavior Analysis

General Instructions

A "statement" is defined as everything a person says between the re-marks of two speakers.

All categorizations, with the exception of "aggressive theme," should be followed by the designation of the probable addressee of the statement —i.e., the person toward whom the statement is directed—as inferred from a person named, the subject of the sentence, the preceding person, or the following person speaking. If choice between the last two is ar-bitrary, choose the latter. Addressees are to be designated by "fam" for family; "Mo" and "Fa" for mother and father; therapist's initial for therapist; the distinguishing initials of the children.

The addressee of an answer to a question is the questioner; the ad-dressee of a request for information is the person specified in the request or the person replying if no one is specified.

When the subject under discussion is different from the person ad-dressed, this is to be indicated in a separate column, labeled "Target."

When the target is not a family member, the following categories may be used: "outsider(s)" for particular nonfamily members; "fate" for religion, superstition targets; "Wilt" for Wiltwyck and its representatives other than the therapist; "law" for police courts; "ppl" for unspecified persons; "Au" for other representatives of the culture, authority, in-groups, etc.; and "Soc" for the society or world at large.

Nonverbal replies that are readily translated into verbal replies (e.g., head-shaking or shrugging) are coded, except when a corresponding verbal reply is given simultaneously.

After every five pages, reread those pages for content or themes that may have been missed in the statement-by-statement coding, and add any such coding in the marginal column.

Statements that describe events or feelings as they occur outside the ses-sion are to be coded for all categories except "Requests Information, Clarification, or Opinion"; "Gives Information, Clarification, or Opinion"; "Requires Information, Clarification of Feeling"; "Gives Information, Clarification of Feeling"; "Doesn't Give Information"; "Transcript"; and "Uncodable."

Such classifications will be made only when the speaker is referring

to an event which is descriptive of a family member or familial relationships, as seen, or an event which has clearly taken place in recent weeks.
These codings are entered in a separate column. The initial person described is followed by the code and, where appropriate, the initials of the
target. A session coding is always made in addition to such coding, even
if it is only "Gives Information, Clarification, or Opinion."

1. *Requests Information, Clarification, or Opinion*

A request for information of a factual nature; or for clarification or
elaboration of what someone has said; or for an opinion about something.
(Requests for Opinions may sometimes fall under the Asking for Guidance definition, and if so, should be classified there.)

Rhetorical questions are not categorized here: i.e., to qualify, a question
must come reasonably near the end of the speaker's statement so that it
is clear that an answer is expected.

2. *Gives Information, Clarification, or Opinion*

A response supplying information, or clarifying or elaborating upon a
previous statement of one's own or someone else's, or giving an opinion
that does not obviously serve a guidance function. A simple acceptance,
restatement, or reflection of another person's opinion (without a question
mark) belongs here. With a question mark, it belongs in "Requests Information or Opinion." A restatement or clarification of a specific, labeled
feeling (without a question mark) belongs under "Expresses or Clarifies
Feeling." With a question mark, it belongs in "Requests Information
About Feeling."

When a person is asked to repeat (e.g., "huh?") and does so, score
here rather than by content.

This category is not used if the content of the statement as a whole
can be placed in any other category. This applies whether or not a new
and different topic is being introduced.

3. *Requests Information, Clarification, Opinion about Feeling*

Asking someone to describe how he or someone else in the immediate
family feels or felt about something or the circumstances and reasons for
feeling certain ways.

Do not be misled by the word "feel," which is often used instead of
"think." (E.g., "Do you feel things have been any different lately?", and
in answer, "Yes, I feel they have," would be classified as "Request for

Information or Opinion" and "Gives Information or Opinion," respectively.) The distinction is based on the content under discussion: i.e., whether it involves a thought or a feeling. If the content of the discussion and the question are not clear and the word "feel" is used, classify here. If both thought and feeling are inquired about in the same statement, classify only here. This applies even if the feeling in question is not that of the person addressed.

When in doubt between "Requests Clarification or Information about Feeling" and "Requests Information or Clarification or Opinion," use the latter.

4. *Expresses or Clarifies Feeling*

Speaker supplies information which includes *mentioning* a *specific* feeling (emotion) past or present of his own or somebody in the immediate family, or agrees to having a feeling suggested by someone else, or supplies information about reasons or circumstances connected with a feeling. (Indicate person whose feeling is labeled.) Terminology need not be precise (e.g., "felt great," "felt rotten," "bugged" would qualify). "Wish," "want," and "like" are considered feelings if they apply to persons; "nice time" and "good time" are not. A denial of self or other feeling a certain way is not categorized here. (E.g., "It didn't bother me," "I didn't care," or "I didn't want" would be classified under "Gives Information or Clarification." So would physical pain or other physical states such as tiredness or sleepiness.) No judgment is attempted as to whether the person is reporting the truth or covering up.

Do not be misled by the presence of the word "feel," which is often used as a synonym for "think." If you can substitute "think" for "feel" without changing the meaningfulness of the statement, classify under "Gives Information, Clarification, Opinion."

When in doubt between "Clarification of Feeling" and "Requests Information about Feeling," apply the following rule: when a question mark is included, use the latter; when it is not, use the former category.

If the feeling can be unambiguously described as pleasant or positive, add a +; if it is unambiguously unpleasant or negative, add a —. Calm to excited is an ambiguous dimension in this respect.

5a. Request for Nurturance

A statement asking for gratification as defined below.

5b. Nurturance

A response which promotes the gratification of financial or physical (but nonsexual) needs or desires of another or reflects a willingness to physically help another meet social standards. Examples: "Do you want some water?"; "Come sit on my lap"; "Let me fix your shirt"; "Yes, I'll give you a nickel"; "Here's a tissue." Control responses ("Fix your shirt" or "Go out and get a drink") should not be classified as nurturance responses, regardless of the content.

Protection from danger of any kind is also included here.

6. Agreement and Cooperation

Active agreement and support of another person's views, opinions, plans, etc.

A perfunctory "yes," "sure," "very good," which is then followed by a separate theme of one's own does *not* qualify, nor does an unelaborated single "yes" to indicate simple acceptance of the view stated, or one of a factual or recognition nature: e.g., "Yes (that's correct)," or "Oh yeah (it did happen last week)."

Accepting the point of view of another person who has just disagreed with the speaker, without counterargument in the same statement, is classified here.

Agreement or cooperative statements are not to be classed as an interruption.

7. Affection

A response which praises, approves of some specific behavior of another individual, or enhances his esteem. A statement showing the desire to be in the presence of another person is included. May also apply to nonfamily, institution, etc.

Code response following same rules as a (4) response.

8. Requests Control

A request for permission to do something or not to do something. Examples: "Can I . . . ?" "Do I have to . . . ?"

9. *Control + (Directing)*

A response telling or ordering a person to do something or giving somebody permission to do something.

10. *Control — (Forbidding)*

A response telling a person not to do something or refusing permission. The control responses refer to the immediate situation only.

In "Control + or —" there is an imperative quality to the statement. A "Let's now" type of statement should be classified as Control; a "Maybe we should now . . ." type of statement is classified as an opinion. A "Go ahead (continue talking)" type of reply is not considered control, but rather "Request for Information or Clarification."

Includes "will you . . ." "please . . ." and similar statements.

11. *Requests Guidance or Suggestions*

Asking someone for advice, instruction, information, suggestion, or opinion to serve as a guide for thinking or behavior.

12. *Guidance*

Attempting to influence the behavior of another person. Such responses contain an explicit or implicit reference to the future or other occasions than the immediate one. The response may take on a generalized form. Pointing out cause-and-effect relationships between the individual's future behavior and possible future consequences or statements telling what the norm or cultural expectation is are included in this category. So is the teaching of skills or methods.

13. *Does Not Give Information*

The subject does not answer a question about his feelings, thoughts, or opinions except through an "I don't know" type of response or by throwing the question back at the questioner in one way or another, including answering another question than the one asked. This category does *not* apply to such answers when the question being answered asks for purely factual information, which the person might really not know.

14. *Interruption*[7]

Typists should be instructed to use a consistent set of typed symbols for various kinds of interruptions. For example, " . . . " for pauses or for

---

[7] This category was abandoned because of technical difficulties which occurred in the transcription of the tapes.

the trailing off of speech of one person followed by the speech of another; "?????" for words not understood; "————" for clear interruptions. Speaking into a pause (e.g., an "Uh") is not considered an interruption. "Yes," or "hm, hmms" should not be considered interruptions even if they occur in the middle of another person's statement.

An interruption should always be followed by another category, even if it is "Uncodable" or "Gives Information or Opinion."

Acceptance of what someone else says is not classified as an interruption under any circumstances.

15. Disagreement

A response showing a difference of view, opinion, etc., from that of another person. E.g., "No . . ." "But . . ." "I don't think so," etc. Or a response expressing a different viewpoint, explanation, etc., from the preceding person's or correcting another person's statement. Or a refusal to cooperate, incredulity, "fighting" (nonphysical), "arguing."

The target of the disagreement is the person disagreed with rather than the person spoken to, who is the addressee.

16. Aggression

Responses which (a) verbally derogate an individual(s) or institution, and (b) accuse, blame, scold, etc.

In the case of blame, the event for which the person is being blamed may have taken place outside the session and/or a long time ago, but it still qualifies as aggression during the session.

The target of an aggressive coding is the person or institution toward whom the blame, threat, etc., is directed whether or not this is the person being addressed.

Antisocial acts (stealing, etc.) are classified here when committed by a family member.

17. Aggressive Theme

These are responses in which aggressive acts—broadly defined to include verbal derogation and antisocial behavior of any sort (e.g., stealing) —are discussed but are not classifiable under "Aggression" for the session.

This category is different from the others in that there is no concern over the speaker or people involved or over whether they are in the family. The coding is done in a separate column.

When a (17) is coded, scan ahead to see where the theme ends. Count each statement from the beginning to the end of the theme, and enter the number after the (17) in a circle. If more than a page, multiply number of pages by average number of responses per page, which has been computed (based on a 20-page sample) at 15.

This coding is also used when a (4—) coding pertains to anger or aggression.

18. Transcript

Not enough information in typed statement to permit coding, due to unclear transcript. Statements should be coded whenever there is enough content to do so, even though some portions of the statement may be missing. This category is not used when a categorization is made of any other portion of the statement.

If a statement is complete, but cannot be classified because the prior statement (e.g., a question) was not completely transcribed, classify here, and not under "Uncodable."

If it is not a full sentence (except an imperative one), code here.

19. Uncodable

Use when an entire statement cannot be placed in any other category, but only if the transcript is not the reason.

Include interrupted statements that do not have enough content to be coded.

Code here if cannot tell at all to whom person is speaking (i.e., if cannot be attributed to person before or after).

20. Sibling Influence +

21. Sibling Influence —

A clear-cut indication that a sibling of a child has exerted or is exerting positive or negative influence on a sibling with respect to behavior in an interpersonal or societal context.

22. Lack of Knowledge by Parents of Children's Activities

Parental lack of knowledge must be clear-cut, not just inferred; this includes parental acknowledgment of being absent from the home overnight or more or just not knowing about the child's activities.

23. Lack of Role Fulfillment

This category is differentiated from (16)—aggression—in that it is not a generalized criticism of the person or a name-calling or personal disparagement so much as it is a criticism of a specific behavior or a comment indicating that the person is not properly fulfilling his role (obligations) as society defines this role.

24. *Acceptance of Responsibility for One's Behavior*

Includes acceptance of responsibility for wrongdoing, of blame when this is *more than a passive acceptance*, or acceptance after prolonged argument and much pressure. Examples of passive acceptance are, "Yeah," "OK," "If you say so," "Have it your own way." Restitution and apologies are included here.

25. *Punishment of Children*

Threatening or carrying out punishment for behavior. When forbidding a certain act is for purposes of punishment, code here rather than in (10).

26. *Expresses Wish, Desire, or Need*

Includes "wish," "want," and "like" applying to needs and desires.

Transcript from a Pre-Treatment Family Task Session with the Browns—an Experimental Family

Mrs. Brown, Barbara, 15, Doris, 12, Martin, 10, and James, 8, were present during the Family Task session. Doris is nicknamed "Dummy," and Martin, "Chimpy." Chimpy was the Wiltwyck child. Their responses to two of the Task questions only are presented below.

TASK I.   AGREE ON A MENU FOR DINNER

James: I would like . . . some ice cream and cake.

   (*All talk at once.*)

Mrs. B.: Do something with some sense to it sometime.

Martin: We could split the meat up, cut the dessert in half, split up the vegetables.

Mrs. B.: You didn't get the question . . .

Doris: She said you would have to agree on one meat, two vegetables, one dessert, and one drink.

Barbara: I would like to have some nice fried chicken. Would you like that?

Martin: Mom, I would rather have some . . .

   . . .

Martin: What about the vegetables?

James: . . . I would like to have some bacon.

Mrs. B.: You would think of something silly, anyhow, James. Wait a minute.

Barbara: Know what I'd like to have?
   (*All talk at once.*)

Martin: Hey, you said already.

Doris: Franks and beans.

Barbara: Shut up, you're making me . . .

James: I would like to have some red rice. (*Voices: No!*)

Mrs. B.: Don't turn it on 'cause we ain't even agreed on what we'd like to have.

James: I would like to have red rice and chicken.

Doris: Ain't even say nothing about no red rice.

Mrs. B.: She said the meat . . . meat.

Martin: I'd rather have the vegetables.

Mrs. B.: Wait a minute . . . one meat, two vegetables . . .

Barbara: What she say . . . one meat, one vegetable.

Martin: Two vegetables.

Doris: One dessert and one drink. (*Barbara, Martin, and Doris said above simultaneously.*)

James: I would like to have red rice and chicken.

Doris: A soda. And a nice cold soda.

James: I would like to have a nice root beer soda.

Doris: We got to all agree to one thing.

Martin: Okay, Ma?

Mrs. B.: That's right.

Doris: Agree too.

Barbara: All agreed.

Mrs. B.: Nobody said anything about dessert.

James: Chicken. I'd rather have chicken.

Barbara: Everybody have soda.

Doris: Red rice . . .

Martin: Red rice and . . .

Mrs. B.: And which the vegetables?

Doris: Ah . . .

James: Cabbage.

Martin: And . . . vegetable . . . ah . . . tomatoes.

Barbara: Green peas.

Martin: I'd rather have carrots.

James: Tomatoes and . . .

Barbara: Yeah, and green peas.

Doris: I'm going to turn it on now.

   (*Recorded instruction is heard as Martin imitates its voice.*)

TASK III.   DISCUSS A FAMILY FIGHT OR ARGUMENT

Doris: Daddy . . .

James: Daddy is the biggest fighter . . . Barbara, Barbara.

Doris: Daddy's the one who fight . . .

James: Daddy almost kicked me on the . . .

Barbara: Dummy's draining the bottle, Mama. (*Referring to refreshment.*)

Mrs. B.: . . . James and Dummy are always fighting.

Martin: Dummy's draining the bottle.

Mrs. B.: You and James always having a fight.

Doris: I told her . . . and she's going to order a hero sandwich.

Mrs. B.: Give me one of them.

Barbara: Do you want a hero sandwich? Order it if you want to.

Mrs. B.: Come on, we're supposed to be answering the question. Never mind . . .

Martin: James and Chimpy.

   (*Many voices over each other.*)

Doris: You're not in the fight, Chimpy.

Barbara: She looks for trouble.

Mrs. B.: Now you're starting to act silly.

Doris: Chimpy keeps bother me.

Mrs. B.: You too, Chimpy.

Barbara: Dummy, she looks for trouble.

Doris: I never looked for trouble in my life.

Martin: What's the third question?

Mrs. B.: Nobody answered, did they?

Barbara: Dummy, she's going to answer. She's the one who's the trouble-maker. Don't turn it on yet. (*Tape machine.*)

Martin: If you turn it on that makes the fourth time.

Doris: So, start the question on there.

Mrs. B.: Hey, son. Come here, James.

James: Huh?

Mrs. B.: Come over here, leave that alone.

James: Okay.

Barbara: Dummy's the biggest trouble-maker.

Mrs. B.: . . . No she isn't.

Barbara: . . . Maybe that's why they've got that over there . . .

Martin: I hope they have seconds.

Mrs. B.: Now you know . . .

Barbara: . . .

   (*Recorded instruction is heard.*)

Coding System for the Family Task

Analysis 1—Quantitative

1. *Leadership*
2. *Behavior Control*
3. *Behavior Guidance*
4. *Task Suggestion*
5. *Agreement*
6. *Disagreement*
7. *Request*
8. *Aggression*
9. *Affection*
10. *Defends*
11. *Indirect Control*
12. *I don't know or refusal to answer*
13. *Inaudible*
14. *Unscorable*
15. *Disruptive*
16. *Rational Reason*
17. *Aggressive Tone*
18. *Affectionate Tone*

General Instructions

When the scoring notation instructions specify that a preceding response is to be included, it does not have to be literally the preceding response, but the one the examiner judged to be the preceding response in terms of meaningful communication.

If one speech contains several scorable responses, the scores should be bracketed together to facilitate later counts on the number of speeches made.

Although these categories may be used to analyze all five Task questions, we found it most efficient and reliable to score only Task questions 1, 2, and 4. Task Questions 3 and 5 were analyzed qualitatively only.

1. Leadership

Calls on people to answer, directs people to answer, or calls for opinion, suggestions, or answers.

Makes summaries of the answers, asks people if they agree to a certain answer, takes a consensus, etc.

Telling someone to turn on the tape recorder if the purpose (as far as can be judged) is to proceed to the next question or to indicate that everyone is finished with a question, or questioning whether one or all individuals have finished or have answered.

Stating what an answer is, a decision rather than a suggestion or an opinion.

Sometimes, hopefully rarely, a leadership response (making a summary or decision) may also include support for a particular Task suggestion (agreement) and some difficulty ensues as to decision. Score both and bracket. However, agreement with a Task suggestion usually is indicated as a personal choice by the speaker, while the summary may come at the end of the group discussion and is not arbitrary or distorted toward personal choice. It is scored after no one has offered further contrary opinions or after the group has agreed on the item.

Leadership also includes defining the Task, explaining what the question is, what the people are supposed to do, what the "examiner" said or wants, and giving information about the content of the Task.

Scoring notation: *who (1) whom*
    who   is making the response
    (1)   the category number
    whom   if this is specified by name or obvious from context that the (1) is directed to a particular individual rather than the group

(For our purposes, we also noted whether this response category was competitive with someone else's leadership. In addition, we noted whether the leadership response was successful and accepted or not and whether the leadership was ever incomplete, incorrect, or misleading in interpreting the Task. These additional scorings are optional, depending on whether the examiner is interested in this information.)

2. Behavior Control

Control of behavior during Task but not about Task per se. Do not score if control is expressed about some outside situation under discussion (control expressed now about some event that is described in the story of the family argument). This category should be used for ongoing behavior.

Examples of the responses to be scored here are: "sit down," "wait till he's finished," "you may go get a drink." Also, "you turn on the tape recorder," if meant to tell the children whose turn it is to avoid conflicts, etc., rather than to suggest going from one question to another.

Scoring notation: *who (2) whom*
  who   speaker who is controlling
  (2)   the category number
  whom   person controlled

(For our purposes we noted whether the control was morally wrong, challenged the test situation, etc. We also noted whether the control was preceded by a request for control or disruptive behavior and whether it was accepted if this was possible to determine.)

3. Behavior Guidance

Similar to Control except that Guidance Behavior:

(a) Contains an explicit or implicit reference to the future or other occasions than the immediate one.

(b) The statement may take a generalized form, such as stating a principle rather than making a concrete point.

(a) and (b) include pointing out cause-and-effect relations between the object's behavior and consequences or normative statements.

(c) Teaching of skills and methods.

Examples: "Don't do that *again*." "Speak louder so that everyone can hear what you're saying." "It's not polite to interrupt all the time."

Scoring notation: (similar notation as for Behavior Control) *who (3) whom*

(Same additional points noted for Guidance as for Behavior Control)

4. Task Suggestion

Responses answering the Task question. Score separately on Task questions 1, 2, and 4, for each particular suggestion given.

Task 1. If the subject suggests a meat and two vegetables in one speech, this is scored as three Task suggestions (bracketed together as in the general instructions).

Task 2. Giving a label to someone (bossiest, etc.). Each label is one Task suggestion.

Task 4. If the subject offers several suggestions in one speech about spending the money (example: "we should buy everyone some clothes and divide up the money that's left"), this is scored as two or more Task suggestions (bracketed together).

The Task suggestion score is given only for each *new* suggestion. Subsequent repetitions of the suggestion, disagreement, or support of it are scored differently.

Scoring notation: *who (4) content of suggestion* (to facilitate qualitative scoring later)

who	speaker
(4)	the category number

5. Agreement

A repetition of what someone else has said implying agreement or support (rather than questioning it), actually specifying agreement, or minor elaborations of someone else's remark.

Example: "I want raspberry Jello" after someone has suggested "Jello."

This can be scored for any preceding response, thus agreeing with someone else's Task suggestion, Leadership, Guidance, etc.

Scoring notation: *who (5) whom*

who	speaker
(5)	the category number
whom	self or other—then note the response supported

Examples: Mother (5) Father, Father (2) Daughter
      (Mother agrees with father's behavior control of daughter.)
        Mother (5) Daughter, Daughter (4)
      (Mother supports daughter's Task suggestion.)

6. *Disagreement*

The person has to particularly disagree with a response, not just give an alternative response. Disagreement can also be scored for any response as for Agreement and the notation is similar.

> Scoring notation: *who (6) whom, response disagreed with*
> *who – whom*

> Example: Mother (6) Daughter, Daughter (4)
> (Mother disagrees with daughter's Task suggestion.)

On Task 2, if an individual disagrees with a response label attached to another and does not give an alternative, this is counted as defense of that person, and *not* as a disagreement.

Example: "Joe is not a crybaby."

A denial of a label applied to one's self is never counted as disagreement.

Example: "I am not a crybaby."

A disagreement on this Task *is* scored if a simple denial of the label as appropriate for one person because it applied to someone else is the response.

Example: "Joe isn't the crybaby, Mary is."

7. *Request*

7–1 *Request for Leadership*

> Examples: "What does the question say or mean; what are we supposed to do?" "Who should speak next?"

7–2 *Request for Behavior Control*

> Examples: "May I have a cupcake?" "May I have a turn at the tape recorder?"

7–3 *Request for Guidance*

> Example: "Why must we take these tests?"

Scoring notation: *who (7) of whom*

who	speaker
(7), (1)	the category number
(7), (2)	
(7), (3)	

(We have noted whether the question was answered, by whom, if incorrect or incomplete, and if "morally" wrong.)

8. *Aggression*

A personal attack or derogation.

Do not score for nonderogatory criticism of behavior which can be scored behavior control (see Behavior Control).

Do not score for correct labels in Task 2, only for additional idiosyncratic labels, cracks, remarks, etc.

Scoring notation: *who (8) whom*

who	speaker
(8)	the category number
to whom	or about what

9. *Affection: praise, enhancing esteem, etc.*

Score only positive remarks, not defense of someone. If the two occur together, score both bracketed together.

Examples: "That's an excellent suggestion" (affection and agreement); "You're a good boy."

Scoring notation: Similar notation as for Aggression *who (9) whom*

10. *Defends*

(a) A rebuttal made to an aggressive response to self or about another person.

Example: (To) "Joe is stupid." "No, he isn't."

(b) Any disagreement with a labeling of self by someone else on Task 2.

Example: "*I am not the crybaby.*"

Or, if the label is repeated questioningly.

Example: "Joe is the crybaby." "*Joe is the crybaby?*" (tone of voice doubtful).

(c) A disagreement with a labeling of someone by someone else on Task 2 if no alternative Task suggestion is given.

Example: "Joe is the crybaby." "*No, he never cries.*"

Scoring notation: *who (10) whom*

who	speaker
(10)	the category number
whom	self or other

(We noted what response elicited the defense, for example: Mother (10) Joe was preceded by Mary (8) Joe.)

11. Indirect Control

Speaking for someone else, saying this is his opinion.

Attributing one's own opinion to someone else.

Supposedly repeating someone's speech but distorting it to such an extent that it means something else.

Telling someone what the content of his answer should be.

Controlling, guiding, being aggressive to someone but saying someone else is doing it.

Scoring notation: *who (11) whom*

Followed by the notation indicating the kind of response attributed, and to whom attributed if necessary.

Examples: "Your answer should be such and such."
          Mother (11) Daughter, Mother (4)
          "Father says your answer should be such and such."
          Mother (11) Daughter, Mother (4)
          attributed to Father
          "You mean you think he's stupid" (mother to daughter about father)
          Mother (11) Daughter, Mother (8) Father

12. I don't know or refusal to answer

Scoring notation: *who (12) whom*

13. Inaudible

Scoring notation: *who (13)*

14. Unscorable

Scoring notation: *who (14)*

Remarks which do not fit into any other category, repeating one's remark when asked because others didn't hear it, meaningless noises, etc.

15. Disruptive

Any scoring category can be accompanied by a disruptive score as long as it deflects or impedes the Task, disturbs or deflects the flow of others' communications, etc. Disruptive scores must always accompany another score, even if it be the unscorable category (14) for noises, etc.

Examples: Someone is giving Task suggestions and someone else breaks in with leadership responses to hurry them up or not permit them to speak. Scored as a leadership response, but score number (1) is immediately followed by a (15) to indicate disruptive. Joe (1)–(15) Mary.

Someone is talking to someone in answer to the Task. The recipient not listening or calling for temporary halt, but simultaneously controlling someone else's behavior. Scored as behavior control but followed immediately by (15). Joe (2)–(15) Mary.

Giving an inappropriate Task suggestion or yelling it in an annoying, interrupting way. Scored (4)–(15).

Funny noises, or irrelevant remarks. Scored (14)–(15).

16. Giving an Objective Reason

Categories (5) and (6) can be accompanied by this category when the speaker gives an objective, nonpersonal, nonaffective reason for his agreement or disagreement. For example: "Carrots should be included—they're good for your eyes." "Let's not have potatoes and spaghetti—too much starch isn't good."

17. Aggressive Tone

These scores are judgments of extremes in the affective tone of the voice.

18. Affectionate Tone

Examples: "All right, you can have your jelly" (said in a very exasperated tone of voice) is scored Mother (1)–(17) Willy.

"Why don't you have the extra cupcake?" (said in a very loving, giving way) is scored Joe (14)–(18) Mother.

Analysis 2—Qualitative

Scoring for Tasks I, II, and IV—Menu, the Bossiest, etc., and Spending $10

1. List for each person every task suggestion he made and star winning items—how many suggestions each one gave and how many adopted in the final answer.
2. List final answer (if settled) and state for each item who made the suggestion, and who supported and who rejected it. If someone shifted from support to rejection or vice versa, note the direction of the shift. If one of the supporters is a person who gave a suggestion in the same category (meat, vegetable, etc.), note this.
3. Follow vicissitudes of suggestions made which were not included

in final answer (rejected? by whom? ignored? withdrawn by suggester?).

Evaluation of the above:

4. Major roles or styles of each individual (who made many suggestions? who spends more time supporting? rejecting? nonparticipants? ignored isolates? etc.)
5. Power organization
   a. alliances between particular people—parents vs. children; one parent with one or more children; no strong clusters; parents neutral with children split, etc.
   b. compromises effected—how? cooperative; mutual give-and-take; competitive, etc.
   c. who makes final decisions, if anyone? who presents summary— attitude of the group toward decision.
6. Mode of discussion and decision-making
   a. self-initiative in discussion; being called on; going in turn; chaos and disorder; many interruptions or irrelevant points brought in which disrupt the Task.
   b. any guidance given about how Task should be performed, over and above interpretation of the Task question, which reveals family attitudes or ideology.
   c. consensus for final decision or one decision-maker who lays down the law? voting? agreement that a particular person shall answer for all?
7. Task efficiency
   a. is it clear that one answer has been agreed upon for the whole family, or is the reader left hanging with many separate answers? do the subjects seem to feel that they have agreed on an answer? have completed a question? agreed to disagree, or what?
   b. did the family get off the track and perform incorrectly because of incorrect leadership? incorrect perception of task? or do they refuse to do the task?

ADDITIONAL FOR TASK II

8. Is blame spread out or concentrated on one individual?
9. Anyone not included? Do parents include themselves? Do children label parents? Are labels reserved exclusively for the children?
10. Is aggression aroused by this question? Counterblaming?
11. Assignment of labels to self.
12. Self-defense: denials of labels or defense of others.

ADDITIONAL FOR TASK IV
8. Content of money solution
   a. money split up or spent for family unit.
   b. pleasurable, frivolous, luxury content, or is money used for necessity; grim, desperate quality to answer.
   c. do parents use the money for children exclusively? for themselves; for all in the family? nurturant use of money?

Scoring for Task III   The Family Fight

There may be several arguments described—follow each separately.
1. Family structure of argument (marital fight, parent-child, sibling conflict).
2. Family members' functioning—follow each step in the conflict and label with our variables in sequence as if it were a FIAT story—the roles assumed by family members, coalitions, etc.
3. Assignment of cause (intrafamilial, one person's fault, outside agent, cannot be determined).
4. Attitudes expressed during and about the fight story. Is there a consensus? Denial of family conflict, minimizing of aggression or of particular people's behavior, defending, storyteller's view of self and others.
5. Resolution of fight—some family harmony or resolution achieved; or breakdown of family relations, no resolution.
6. If resolved—nature of resolution (siblings cooperated, father successfully exerted control, etc.). Any control, guidance, aggression, punishment offered during task as additional comments on family conflict?
7. Are there any inappropriate behaviors with respect to roles adopted, attitudes expressed either in fight story or task behavior during this task?

Scoring for Task V—What Pleases You and Displeases You Most about Other Family Members

All responses to this task receive a two-part score. The first part of the score is a label describing what the speaker is doing, and the second part of the score is a label characterizing the person spoken about.

WHAT THE SPEAKER IS DOING

Type 1. *Objective*

The remark is behavioral—a description of another person's action which is not described as done to the speaker and not presented as an enduring characteristic or personality trait of the other.

Type 2. *Personal*

The behavior of the person referred to by the speaker is described specifically as something done to the speaker.

Type 3. *Affect*

The speaker describes characteristics of the person spoken about as if they were enduring personality traits.

SPEAKER'S PERCEPTION OF THE PERSON SPOKEN ABOUT

The following fifteen categories are used to designate how the person spoken about is seen by the speaker:

1. Aggressive or nonaggressive
2. Affectionate or nonaffectionate
3. Nurturant or nonnurturant
4. Requires nurturance
5. Accepts or does not accept nurturance, affection
6. Cooperative or noncooperative
7. Competitive or noncompetitive
8. Controlling or noncontrolling
9. Needs control or guidance
10. Guiding or nonguiding
11. Accepts or does not accept control or guidance
12. Accepts or does not accept responsibility
13. Delinquent
14. Other (crazy, reasonable, gets good marks, etc.)
15. Formal role (sister, mother, etc.)—used primarily in conjunction with Type 3, above

EXAMPLES OF SCORING

"I like it when she cooks a good meal."

Type 1   Objective
3. nurturant

"I like him when he brings home good marks."

Type 1   Objective
14. other

"I don't like it when he hits me."

Type 2   Personal
1. aggressive

"I like him because he helps me with my
problems."
   Type 2 Personal
   3. nurturant

"I like him because he is lovable."
   Type 3 Affect
   14. other

"I don't like him because he always hurts everybody—he
just likes to hurt."
   Type 3 Affect
   1. aggressive

In addition, all statements in Task V are scored $+$, $-$, or $\times$, indicating
that the speaker's view of the other person is positive, negative, or neutral.
(A "like" statement which refers only to the absence of a bad trait is
scored as negative.) The analysis and scoring of Task V include the
following sets of scores:

1. Number of Type 1, Type 2, and Type 3 responses.
2. Number of responses categorized under each of the fifteen variables
   describing the person spoken about.
3. Number of $+$, $-$, and $\times$ remarks.
4. Compatibility and complementarity between two speakers' perceptions of each other, according to the foregoing fifteen categories
   (e.g., mother—children; sibling—sibling, etc.).
5. Was the task incomplete because not every person described every
   other?
6. Was the task not performed correctly because of misunderstood
   task question, incorrect leadership?

APPENDIX **D** Wiltwyck Family
Interaction Apperception Technique—
The FIAT Cards

I   II

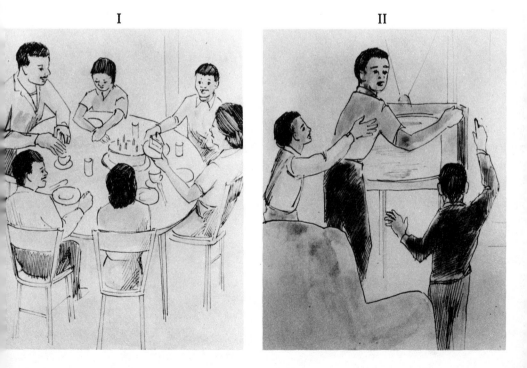

III

IV

V

VI

VII VIII

IX X

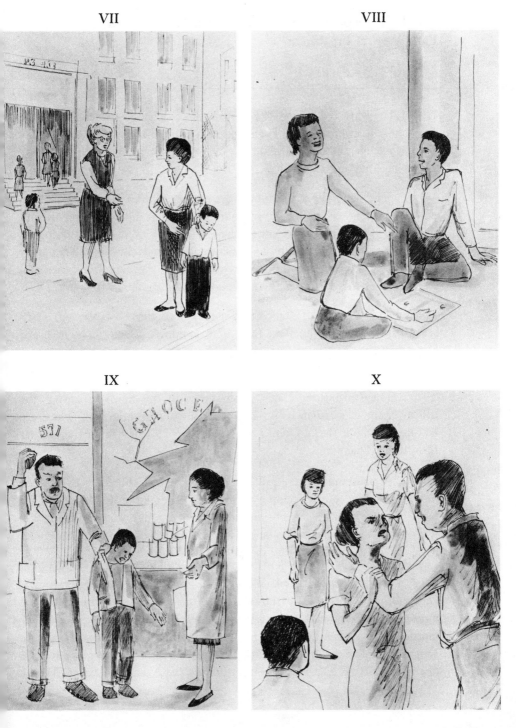

FIAT Protocol from Mrs. Martinez, a Mother in an Experimental Family—Pre-Treatment

I   This is a happy birthday. The party is for the child, for the children. They have cut the cake. They will have fun.

II   They are watching TV. One wants to change the channel. The other boy doesn't want it changed. The other boy will stand up. He tries to change the channel. The big boy will not let him. This big boy will win. They are all brothers.

III   The daughter is working—the mother is tired. The little baby is playing. The other boy is playing with something. The daughter doesn't feel well. The daughter is angry that she has to work. The mother is sick or tired. The mother knows how the daughter feels. No, the daughter will not say anything. The mother will look at the daughter's face and see the anger there . . . daughter is angry because she has to work.

IV   (*Long pause.*) I don't know if they are fighting or playing. They are playing. The mother and father are looking, only looking. (?) (*E:* What happens if they are fighting?) The mother and father should . . . would separate the children.

V   These are three boys, a big girl and the mother feeding the baby. There is another baby. I don't know how they feel. They are talking . . . about the mother. They are saying . . . they think the mother feels tired. That's all.

VI   A man and a boy. (?) Maybe it is a pocketbook. It is his (*the standing figure*). He is seeing . . . the boy will take it. He wants to see what the boy will do. Maybe he will take it or give it to the man. He will give it to the man. Maybe the man will give him some money. (*E:* If he takes the money?) The man will call a cop.

VII   (*Long pause.*) Looks like trouble. Two kids . . . maybe fighting. One mother wants to say something to the other (*mother*). She (*the figure to the left*) said, "I am sorry," to the other mother. The other mother (*figure holding the child*) doesn't say nothing. She got a bad face (*angry*). I think this boy (*the one being held*) started the fight. He feels like it is his fault. She will take him home (*the boy being held*). Maybe she will talk to him about what happened. (*E:* What will happen?) (*No response.*) If she doesn't believe him . . . maybe she will punish him.

VIII   This is mother, sister, or brother. One boy is playing on the floor. The other two are talking. The girl is laughing. The girl laughs because the boy lost the game. The boy feels bad (*kneeling figure*).

IX   This is father, mother, and son. The boy took something from the store. The father . . . maybe this as a storekeeper and a lady. The lady looks like the mother. He is going to take the boy to the cop. It is in his hand what was taken. She is talking to the boy. She said, "What happened, why did you do it?" The boy said, "I am sorry." Yes, he did it. The man will give him to the mother. The mother will take him home. She will give him a good spanking.

X   Oh, they are fighting. The mother and father are fighting about the children. The children . . . they are looking. The children don't like to see the fight. They won't do anything. Looks like the mother started it. They will talk. They will stop themselves.

FIAT Protocol from Rafael Martinez, Age 10, Wiltwyck Child —Pre-Treatment

I   This is a story about eatin' . . . (*Silence.*) (*E:* What do you see?) People are passing cake to this boy and he is happy, and the girl is sad. (*E:* What's she sad about?) She didn't get any cake on her plate. This other man is happy because he sees cake. The other man is happy too and the boy because of the cake. They are happy about the same thing. (*E:* What happens next?) Everybody is waiting for cake and all the brothers are happy. Everybody is happy except for one girl. She didn't get any cake. (*E:* Anything else?) Na, that's all.

II   This guy is putting on his own channel. This guy is the oldest one and he is saying I want another channel. And this guy wants another one. The boy says he put on his own channel because he is older. Everybody is raising their hand. This boy (*on the right*) is sad. (*E:* Why is he sad?) Because he can't have what he wants. The older boy is telling the other boy to get out of here. (*E:* Who gets to watch the channel he wants?) The older boy. (*E:* Anything else?) That's all.

III   I don't see no story in this one . . . (*Silence*). This boy is putting the dishes away. Mother is tired. She hears all that noise with the baby.

(*E*: Is this a girl or boy?) (*He points to the figure that is ironing.*) She's cleaning up for Mama. I think it's a girl. Mother is lying down resting, with all that noise around her. The baby is laughing and yelling. This boy (*boy putting dishes away*) is kind of sad. Mother feels sad. This boy don't look too happy, and the girl is sad. The baby is fine. He's playing. This boy is sad. (*E*: Why is the boy sad?) I don't know.

IV   First of all it looks like this boy (*in the middle*) wants to go outside. The little one next to the big one is holding him. They like each other and the other two (*bigger boys*) don't. Maybe the two boys who is trying to stop him don't got no clothes and they want him to stay in too. Mother and father are trying to find out what's going on. The boys feel sad. (*E*: Why sad?) They don't want to leave each other.

V   Mother don't look too good. She's taking the bottle and giving it to the baby. The other boy sitting on the floor is hitting mother on the dress. (*E*: Why?) I don't know. He's just hitting her. The other boy is sitting with his feet on the cover laughing with the girls. The boy (*behind the chair*) is sad. I mean mother is sad. The girl comes in and they are happy. (*E*: You mean the girl makes them happy?) Yeah. (*E*: What happens next?) I don't know what happens next . . . (*Silence*).

VI   I see the boy walking down the street with the other boy. That's his big brother. The big boy stuck his hands straight out and he sees the other boy bending on his knees. They know each other. (*E*: Remember these are pictures about families.) Yes, they are two brothers. The guy on his knees sees a pocketbook and he wants to keep it. He feels sad. The big guy, he took it and he gave it to a lady, I think. The lady said, "Give me it." (*E*: How did little boy feel?) He didn't feel nothing. No. He feel sad.

VII   These are boys going to school. This lady said to the other lady, "What's my boy doing down there and all this jazz?" The boy is looking down and she say this boy is playing hookey and he don't want to go to school. The lady don't look so happy and the boy looks sad. The mother is looking sad. (*E*: Why is he playing hookey?) He hate school. (*E*: Why?) I don't know. He don't want to go to school. He feels sad and his mother feel sad.

VIII   The boy is making a funny mouth and the lady in front of him is laughing. The other boy is moving the checkers. I don't know how the other boy is feeling. They're all happy. The little boy wins the checker game. She's laughing because the big boy lost and the little boy won.

IX   (*Rafael looks at the card and begins to laugh heartily.*) (*E:* What do you see here?) The boy went robbing. A dirty guy goes around breaking windows. He's coppin' things. He shot the big rock in the window. The man took the rock and said, "You fool! Look what you did!" The boy's mother came down. She says, "Look what you did. Now I have to pay for the window." The man feels sad, and the man feels mad, and the lady is in between! A little mad, a little happy, and a little sad.

X   This big boy in front . . . is drunk, come from a place, is messing around with his mother. Mother looks sad. They all look sad. The boy is having trouble and the mother's having trouble. The others are looking and can't get in other people's business. (*E:* What are they fighting about?) The boy is drunk. (*E:* What happened then?) He goes to bed, when he gets up the next morning he will feel better. Looks like that other girl is saying something to him. Maybe she is telling him to go to bed. This boy down here (*lower corner*). He don't know what's going on.

Coding System for the Wiltwyck Family Interaction Apperception Technique

1. *Nurturance*
2. *Behavior Control*
3. *Guidance*
4. *Aggression*
5. *Cooperation*
6. *Affection*
7. *Family Harmony*
8. *Acceptance of Responsibility*

General Instructions

Scores of each individual's FIAT are to be listed on a coding sheet and each card (from which the score is elicited) should be noted. There are ten FIAT cards from which stories have been gathered.

A given story may have no scorable responses, one response, or several responses. If there are several responses, they are coded separately but with the notation that the same card is involved.

"Tendency" Scores

The eight variables listed above may be scored as nurturance tendency, control tendency, etc. These do not involve action or overt behavior in the story, but concern thoughts, desires, or wishes for any of the variables to be scored. An arrow plus the category is used to indicate "tendency." These may be given a special weighting in the final scoring system. Example: mother wishes the children would help her clean the house.

"Who to Whom" Scores

Do not score for interactions unless at least one family member is involved in the action. For example, most interactions involve two or more family members, e.g., mother to children, sibling to sibling, and some involve one family member with an outside person, such as mother to teacher, or grocer to boy. However, if the interaction is between two outside people, it is not to be scored, e.g., grocer to policeman.

1. Nurturance

a. For cards I and VII, do not score nurturance if either (I) "mother is handing out cake," or (VII) "mother, etc., is feeding the baby." These are considered descriptive statements—responses structured by the formal qualities of the picture. If additional comments clarify or extend this initial statement more clearly, then nurturance may be scored.

b. The concept of protection is scorable as nurturance. For example, if a child is in danger or a mother protects him from being hit, this is scored as nurturance.

c. If someone gives a child money, gifts, presents, this is scored as nurturance.

d. Nurturance to self is scorable. Examples: a mother makes herself a birthday party; or a little baby crawls to the refrigerator to get his own milk.

e. Nurturance is scored appropriate or inappropriate. Example: mother protects child from punishment by father even though he has done something bad. (inap.)

2. *Behavior Control*

a. This is scored control from doing something (—), which is inhibitory in nature, or control to do something (+) which is facilitating. All control scores must be coded either — or +. Examples: (—) father stops the children from fighting; (+) mother sends the girl to the grocery store.

b. When possible, control interactions are scored effective or ineffective in terms of ongoing action of the story. Examples: (effective) father tells the boys to stop making noise, and they quiet down; (inef.) mother asks the children to help, but they pay no attention.

c. If control moves are accompanied by physical or nonphysical punishment, these are scored. Examples: (phys. pun.) mother tells them to stop fighting and gives them a spanking; (nonphys.) mother takes the boy home from school, scolds him, and makes him stay in. Both physical and nonphysical punishment may be scored if both are part of the same control act.

d. Physical punishment (by parents) accompanying control moves is not scored as aggression unless it is overly punitive or the wording indicates excessive severity. For example, a spanking is quite different from being smashed in the face with a fist. The latter is scored as control and aggression. The former is scored as control accompanied by physical punishment.

e. If aggression is accompanied by control or vice versa, it is to be coded twice, as aggression and then control. In most cases, aggression is a sibling or a spouse interaction rather than a parent-child interaction, but there may be exceptions, as described above.

f. Control moves can also be scored appropriate-inappropriate. If one sibling, for example, controls his brothers as to what to watch on TV because he is bigger and stronger, this is control, inap.

3. *Guidance*

a. Scoring categories are similar to those used for control, that is, (—), (+), effective, ineffective; appropriate, inappropriate; physical punishment, nonphysical punishment. All guidance is scored (—) or (+) and other scores are to be made whenever the information is available.

b. For clarification, guidance influences not only the immediate behavior but alludes to past or future references to such action.

c. Guidance can also involve a general principle of behavior. Example: "Take the wallet back to the owner. You wouldn't want someone to keep your money if you lost it."

d. A "model" is scored as guidance. Example: If a member of the family acts in such a way in the presence of another member as to indicate he is setting a guiding example by his own behavior (probably social) or if an action is made with an accompanying guidance principle expressed as explanation for the behavior (without it necessarily being *explicit*), this is scored guidance.

e. Delinquent guidance, that is, guidance toward antisocial behavior or morally reprehensible conduct is scored inappropriate guidance.

4. *Aggression*

This is to be differentiated primarily in terms of physical versus nonphysical aggression.

Anger, shown or expressed, is scored as nonphysical aggression, whereas if it is felt or thought, it is scored as a tendency to anger.

5. *Cooperation*

a. Cooperation implies a mutuality of activity among two or more members of the family or between members of the family and the outside environment in connection with a similar end or goal.

b. The definition also includes the concept of two or more family members playing together, e.g., a game, in a cooperative manner.

c. Voting procedures to decide matters among the family members is scored as cooperation.

d. Helpfulness, volunteering of assistance by one family member to another or others, is seen as a collaborative effort and is considered cooperation.

e. Cooperation for delinquent or antisocial activities or goals is scored as inappropriate cooperation.

6. *Affection*

Affection is scored when there is positive affect, action, or verbalization from one family member to another.

7. *Family Harmony*

Family harmony is scored when a familial feeling or action is elicited in the story which focuses on the happiness, pleasure, or "togetherness" of the family as a unit; anything that binds the family together in a positive way. If the action is explicit, an example would be a mother who plays with the children to give them a sense of security as a family. A tendency score will be made if there is a wish or desire for such unity.

Example: the children wish the parents would not fight so the family could be happy.

8. *Acceptance of Responsibility*

a. This is not an interaction score, but involves the person to whom it applies.

b. It is defined as the acknowledgment of one's actions, e.g., accepting responsibility for a transgression, inappropriate behavior, delinquent activity, etc. It is overtly expressed through verbal apology or acted upon through restitution, repair, etc. It is scored when a person accepts such responsibility for his own behavior or for the behavior (as described) of others.

c. A tendency score will be made when overt apology or restitution is not indicated, but when the person describes feelings of shame, guilt, feeling sorry for what he has done, etc., without any specific verbalization of apology or restitution being made.

Recapitulation of the Scoring Accompaniments of the Eight Variables

1. Nurturance—appropriate, inappropriate
2. Control—(—), (+), effective, ineffective, appropriate, inappropriate, physical punishment, nonphysical punishment
3. Guidance—(—), (+), effective, ineffective, appropriate, inappropriate, physical punishment, nonphysical punishment
4. Aggression—physical, nonphysical
5. Cooperation—appropriate, inappropriate
6. Affection
7. Family Harmony
8. Acceptance of Responsibility

Psychotic and/or Resistant Records

If such records are encountered (not codable) they will be omitted from the scoring system or scored separately with a modified coding system.

Index

abstraction, 200, 216, 246, 248

accommodation, 145, 180, 181, 284, 285–286, 288n., 289, 294

Ackerman, N., 265

acting-out, 7, 18, 26, 36, 95, 207, 217, 228, 229, 240, 258, 259, 260, 266, 289, 334, 354, 373

action orientation, 6, 24, 27, 30, 37, 133, 180, 189, 190, 195, 215, 246, 247, 266

activation, 97, 203, 204, 354

addiction, 6, 22, 23, 25, 127–128, 139, 204, 226

adult, 4, 31, 96, 127, 129, 169, 198, 200, 214, 226, 235, 255, 264, 267, 351, 356, 361, 365, 372; see also people, child's orientation toward

affect, 4, 30, 35, 61, 98, 99, 108, 124, 176, 189, 193, 195, 198, 200, 201, 206, 208, 209, 210, 215, 230, 236, 237, 242, 245, 252, 253, 263, 266, 267, 271, 274–284, 286, 289, 290, 293–294, 304, 309–310, 319–320, 322, 327, 329, 335, 339, 344, 345, 347, 350, 360, 367

affective valences, 278–279

agencies, 6, 18, 19, 21, 36, 37, 38, 46, 47, 92, 93–95, 119, 137, 139, 212, 217, 224, 225, 226, 273, 290, 338, 355, 357, 359, 360, 362, 363, 364, 365, 367, 376, 382–388

aggression, 3, 4, 28n., 30, 47, 96, 114–127, 128, 136, 154, 157, 159, 160, 165, 173, 180–181, 183, 189, 193, 196, 204, 206, 208, 209, 210–211, 213, 216, 217, 220, 223, 226, 228, 229, 235, 238, 240, 248, 256–257, 258, 264, 267, 268, 274, 275, 281, 282, 290, 310, 319, 320, 322, 323,

325, 328, 329, 351; see also Verbal Behavior Analysis; Wiltwyck Family Interaction Apperception Technique

alcoholism, 6, 22, 25, 46, 121–122, 127–128, 135, 139, 204, 207, 209, 212, 217n., 374, 384, 386

Alinsky, S. D., 369n., 372

alliance, 59, 69, 75, 135, 136, 218, 223, 233, 239, 255, 263, 361, 367–368

animal behavior, 221n.

anxiety, 10, 158–159, 160–161, 165, 174, 180, 209, 211, 216, 217, 229, 238, 267, 284, 292, 359

apathy, 22, 274, 354

Arabic families, 24

Aronson, H., 36

articulation, see verbalization

Ashby, J. D., 392

aspiration, 23, 28n., 30, 62n.

assessment, qualitative, 9, 303, 311–312, 323–329, 346

assessment, quantitative, 8, 9, 10, 13, 16–18, 20, 31, 42, 298–347, 352, 391–450

assistance to family, 13n., 20, 37n., 290

attack, 63, 98, 110, 210, 221, 236, 263, 266, 277, 281

attention, 30, 31, 59, 189, 190, 195, 197, 198, 216, 250, 271, 278, 284, 288, 289, 294, 330

Auerswald, E., 192n.

authority, 11, 32, 36, 60, 110, 111, 114, 122, 132–133, 162, 169, 173, 180–181, 183, 190, 204, 215, 238, 255, 267, 270, 281, 298, 359, 364, 366, 413; see also delegation

autism, 97

autonomy, 11, 95, 170, 180, 186, 188, 189, 190, 213, 222, 230, 232, 238, 255, 260, 273, 280, 290, 351, 355, 357, 359

Bales, R. F., 17, 232n., 392
bantering, 274, 275, 366, 367; see also teasing
behavior, nonverbal, 15, 42, 43, 45–46, 85, 222, 260, 301, 307, 321
behavior, overt, 17, 298
behavior, verbal, 17, 42, 141n., 222
Beker, J., 33
Bernstein, A., 392
Bernstein, B., 30, 35, 195, 199
bias, therapeutic, 15–16, 48, 98n., 105, 245, 270, 291–296, 350, 352, 368, 391
blame, 252, 264, 308
boundaries, 160, 220
boundaries, intergenerational, 74, 218, 230–232, 350, 364–365, 366
brain injury, 227, 260
Brancusi family, 223–224
Bredemeier, H. C., 35
Brown, B., 32
Brown, C., frontispiece, 21n.
Brown family, 299, 363, 384, 388–389, 421–424
Bruner, J. S., 246n.
bully, 95, 119, 204, 357

Cantarella, Virginia, 331n.
caseworker, 13, 14, 15, 45n., 142–143
causality, interpersonal, 176, 178–179, 190, 201, 215, 216, 222, 247, 250, 272, 351, 355
centrality, 203, 204, 211, 227, 234, 256, 257, 258–259, 260, 269, 270, 280, 287, 290, 299, 304, 323, 352, 355, 360, 362, 363, 395, 397, 412
Chamberlain, Pamela, 377n.
change, indications of, 44, 77, 78, 82, 85, 86, 87, 91–92, 93, 140, 154, 170, 179–188, 190, 249, 251, 282–283, 323–329, 349–350, 355
change, production of, 8, 9, 30, 42, 136, 170, 173, 243–297 passim
child-rearing, see socialization
child's viewpoint, 26, 180, 242, 279
children, number of, see overcrowding in family

Chinese-American families, 373
civil rights, 21, 371, 376
Clark, K., 23, 369fn, 377n.
class, 24, 25, 31, 32, 33, 34, 164, 192–193; see also specific listings: e.g., middle-class
coalition, see alliance
coding, 17, 298, 302n., 303, 304, 333, 334, 391–450; see also Verbal Behavior Analysis; Wiltwyck Family Interaction Apperception Technique; Wiltwyck Family Task
cognition, 30, 31, 60, 113, 125, 154, 167, 170, 184, 187, 188, 190, 195, 198, 199, 200n., 201, 206n., 210, 211, 213, 214, 216, 222, 230, 242, 246, 248, 252, 253, 266, 267, 282, 369, 371, 372, 411
Cohen, A. K., 352n.
Cohen, J., 24, 25n.
communication, 11, 15, 16, 24, 25, 26, 30, 36, 60, 73, 93, 96–105, 111, 113, 116, 124, 126, 136, 140, 141, 144, 145, 146, 161, 170, 171, 174, 175, 179, 180, 181, 182–183, 185, 186, 187, 189, 190, 193, 195, 196, 198–217, 219, 220, 227, 229, 242, 245, 246, 247, 248, 249, 250, 251, 252, 257, 259, 263, 269, 274, 285, 287, 289, 290, 291, 304, 317, 321–322, 323, 329, 346, 350, 352, 355, 358, 362, 369, 372, 391–412
communication, paraverbal, 30, 140, 147, 189, 198, 200, 203, 206, 268, 395, 402–403, 411; see also behavior, nonverbal
communication, rules of, 145, 170, 185–186, 199, 200, 201, 202, 242, 249, 250, 251, 366
communicational modality, 246–247, 248, 249; see also language
community, 5, 22, 28, 38, 110, 114, 166–168, 355, 372
competence, 28n., 189, 196, 198, 212, 247, 251, 252, 257, 258, 294–295, 355, 356, 357, 360, 361, 366, 375–376
compositional maneuvers, 218, 245, 248, 254, 255, 261, 262, 268, 271–272, 279, 280, 282, 293, 296, 350, 351
conceptualization, 16, 24, 30, 31, 36, 176, 199, 246
concern, see nurturance

concreteness, 27, 37, 57, 111, 128*n.*, 161, 173, ʹ174, 208, 227, 246

conflict resolution, 4, 14, 15, 16, 48, 50, 56, 59, 62, 63, 65, 69, 76, 77, 79, 82, 83–85, 87–88, 98, 126, 136, 170, 184, 186–187, 189, 195, 200, 201, 204, 216, 220, 223, 240, 247, 248, 250, 258, 261, 263, 265, 266, 268, 269, 270, 276, 285, 291, 293, 294, 296, 315, 349, 353, 360, 366, 368

confusion, 96, 103, 104, 112, 135, 145, 164, 198, 217, 219, 222, 235, 282

contact, 97, 99–100, 102–103, 145, 148, 154–155, 159, 166, 180, 189, 194, 196, 202, 209, 210–211, 212, 221, 249, 260, 268, 273, 290, 354, 373

content, *see* messages

contract, implicit, 62, 63, 65

control, 10, 11, 111, 114, 135, 139, 142, 144, 148, 150, 155, 158, 160, 164, 168–169, 180, 181, 189, 194, 195, 201, 203, 204, 205, 207, 210, 211, 215, 216, 217, 219, 222, 223, 227, 228, 229, 234, 249, 253, 254, 255, 259, 260, 265, 266, 267, 268, 275, 280, 282, 285, 289, 319, 327, 328, 347, 350, 351, 355, 356, 357, 358, 359, 360, 362, 364, 372; *see also* Verbal Behavior Analysis; Wiltwyck Family Interaction Apperception Technique: Wiltwyck Family Task

control families, 7, 8, 10, 12, 17, 18, 19, 20, 301, 304, 305, 306, 307, 308, 310–323, 333, 336–341, 347*n.*

coping, 5, 11, 14, 127, 154, 159, 161, 164, 176, 180, 184, 193, 198, 202, 205, 216, 217, 222, 223, 235, 242, 251, 252, 261, 290, 293, 306, 349, 351, 352

cotherapy, 7, 245, 267, 281, 287–288, 360, 364, 367, 368

Cottrell, L. S., Jr., 38

courts, *see* agencies

Creative Playthings, Inc., 300

Cressey, D. R., 352*n.*

crime, *see* delinquency

cue, *see* communication, rules of; communication, paraverbal ̄

cultural deprivation, 27, 29

culture of poverty, 22–24, 27, 28, 29, 237, 272, 273, 375

danger, 23, 133, 159, 165–166, 209

defense, 47, 63, 102, 113, 133, 220, 223, 227, 229, 266, 267, 348

delegation, 11, 105, 111, 219, 318, 333, 338, 350, 355

delinquency, 6, 13, 18, 20, 25, 47, 57–60, 61, 62, 63, 71, 93, 95, 114–127, 136, 139, 177, 190, 209, 217*n.*, 223, 239, 241, 273, 298, 351, 352, 373, 381–388

dependence, 6, 20, 135, 139, 212, 259, 263, 273, 290, 355, 356, 357, 360, 366

depression, 105, 139, 180, 203, 207, 212, 240, 274, 276, 279, 355

detachment, *see* disengagement

Deutsch, M., 29, 30, 31, 32, 197, 199

differentiation, 26, 105, 189, 195, 198, 199, 210, 211, 212, 216, 218, 220–221, 227, 229, 231, 237, 242, 246, 247, 251, 253, 254, 267, 271, 272, 278, 279, 293, 309, 320, 350, 354, 359, 361, 364, 365, 368

disadvantaged, *see* research population

discharge, 26, 195, 228, 258, 263, 266, 271

disease, 23, 25, 34, 94, 95, 103, 217*n.*

disengagement, 43, 97, 98*n.*, 105, 202, 203, 206, 211, 213, 214, 215, 216, 217, 273, 291, 306, 311, 321, 349, 350, 352, 353, 354–358, 359, 360, 361, 363, 364, 366, 376; *see also* Jones family; Romano family; Wainright family

dislocation, 283–284

disruption, 126, 136, 139, 141, 142–144, 145, 148, 154, 158, 164, 170, 179, 185, 186, 189, 190, 201–205, 210, 246, 248, 249, 250, 257, 269; *see also* noise; Wiltwyck Family Task

distance, 98, 249, 269, 288, 296, 360

dominance, 48, 50, 53, 56, 59, 79, 91–92, 248, 263, 274, 362, 366

Drechsler, R. J., 298

drunks, *see* alcoholism

eating, 6, 22, 26, 96, 130, 193–194, 208, 299, 301, 307, 321, 322, 328, 329

education, 21, 24, 25, 29, 30, 31, 32, 33, 36, 103, 145, 161–164, 168–170, 180–181, 190, 202, 212, 214, 216, 229, 248, 251, 257, 258, 260, 263, 330, 373, 377; *see also* agencies

education of family members, *see specific listings, e.g.,* Montgomery family

Education, New York City Board of, 18, 47, 95n., 382

effectance, see identity, sense of

Elbert, Shirley, 331n., 347

Eliasoph, E., 33

empathy, 30, 63, 65, 264

employment, 19, 23, 25, 27, 38, 47, 164, 228, 233, 257, 366, 369–370, 371, 374–375, 376

enaction, 246

enactive coding, 246n., 247, 248

engagement, see contact; enmeshment

English language, 16, 47

English low socioeconomic population, 198

enmeshment, 105, 144, 165, 203, 206, 211, 213, 215, 217, 221, 237, 266–267, 272, 285, 291, 306, 311, 321, 349, 350, 352, 353, 354, 358–360, 361, 363, 364, 366, 376; see also La Salle family; McCallister family; Montgomery family; Smith family

enrichment, 29, 30

Eron, L., 32, 33, 330

espiritistas, 240–241

ethnic background, 19, 20, 22, 23, 24, 52–53, 149, 236–237, 381–388; see also specific listings: e.g., Italian-American family

evangelical churches, see religion

excitement, 4, 6, 24, 30, 112, 118, 127, 133, 204, 351

executive function, 10, 11, 74, 105, 108, 109, 114, 136, 189, 217, 219, 223, 226, 227, 229, 277, 304, 310, 316, 317, 318, 322, 325, 327, 329, 335–338, 342, 346, 350, 355, 364

expectation, 30, 36, 43, 44, 149, 168–169, 170, 175, 190, 197, 253, 270, 283, 290, 304, 322, 345

experience, 4, 5, 59, 171, 193, 209, 220, 246n., 254, 255, 258, 265, 266, 269, 270, 271, 279, 350

experimental families, 7, 8, 10, 12, 13, 17, 18, 19, 20, 301, 302, 304, 305, 307–329, 333, 336–347, 349–365, 391–450 passim

exploration, 14, 73, 97–98, 154–155, 170, 173, 179–183, 186–190, 204–206, 213, 216, 220, 223, 247, 251, 257, 266, 270, 281, 282, 294, 296, 349, 351, 372

extended family, 101n., 128, 135, 194, 229, 230–232, 242, 272, 288

externalization, 59, 70, 198, 209, 237–238, 241, 254, 272, 359, 372

family composition, 19, 20, 24, 197, 262, 323, 389

family cooperation, 119, 180, 181, 223, 241, 256, 257, 270, 316, 319; see also Wiltwyck Family Interaction Apperception Technique

family dynamics, 5, 9, 11, 12, 13, 15, 20, 38, 43, 74, 190, 245, 253, 257, 263, 270, 273, 280, 298, 303, 351, 358

family income, 19, 22n., 25, 233, 234, 381–388

family interaction, 15, 17, 30, 44, 45, 61, 63, 65, 81, 86, 92, 93, 95–97, 102, 114, 116, 136, 140, 149, 152, 153, 156, 160, 170, 180–181, 186, 189, 198–206, 211–222, 224, 226, 228, 237, 245, 248, 249, 254, 255, 259, 260–269, 271, 274, 278, 281, 292, 296, 298, 301, 330, 349, 350–351, 354–368, 372, 374, 375, 376–377, 391–450 passim

Family Interaction Apperception Technique, see Wiltwyck Family Interaction Apperception Technique

family, nuclear, 46, 218

family profiles, 352–368; see also disengagement; enmeshment; juvenile parents; non-evolved parents; peripheral male

family and society, 368–378; see also outside world

family structure, 9, 12, 20, 27, 30, 38, 43, 44, 45, 50, 79, 91–92, 190, 192, 195, 196, 206, 216, 218–242, 245, 254, 255, 256, 258, 259, 262–263, 265, 285, 287, 292–293, 298, 303, 346, 347, 350–353, 355, 364, 411

family structure, frozen, see rigidity

Family Task, see Wiltwyck Family Task

family tasks, see tasks, interpersonal

family and therapist, 17, 43, 48, 50, 56, 66, 99, 105, 108, 165, 173, 221, 254, 255,

264n., 266, 267, 269, 270–272, 281, 284, 285, 288, 289, 290–294, 352, 355–357, 359–360, 362–363, 391–412 *passim*
family therapy, 7, 8, 10, 15, 38, 145, 269
fantasy, 26, 86, 133, 160, 236, 240, 328, 329
father, child's relationship to, 23, 232–233, 238, 240, 263–264, 276–277, 280, 303, 308, 309, 313, 315, 366–367
  Mr. Garcia, 47, 57–60, 70, 76, 79, 80, 81, 82–84, 92, 256–257
  Mr. La Salle, 137–138, 189
  Mr. Montgomery, 102, 116, 135, 136
father figure, 10, 19, 20, 388
favorite, 95, 117, 237
Fenichel, O., 352n.
Ferman, L. A., 21n.
figure-ground, 29, 30
Fink, M., 34
Fleischmann, O., 352n.
flexibility, 184, 193, 242, 262, 269, 276, 285, 292, 350, 368, 375, 411
focus, 14, 58, 170, 181, 183, 188, 189, 193, 246, 249, 250, 251, 263, 267
food, *see* eating
Ford, D. H., 392
free association, *see* psychotherapy, traditional
freezing, *see* rigidity
Freud, 35
Friedlander, Kate, 352n.
frustration tolerance, *see* reward

gangs, *see* peers
Gans, H., 24, 27, 28, 35
Garcia family, 38, 42, 44–94, 105–106, 192, 254, 256–257, 286, 293, 362, 363, 385, 388–389
  Felipe, 193
Garibaldi family, 358n., 387–389
Garota family, 224–225
Geismar, L. L., 38
ghetto, *see* slums
Glasser, P., 232n.
global, *see* nondifferentiation
goals, therapeutic, 11, 13, 35, 37n., 45, 92, 136, 170, 179, 190, 255, 272, 291–296, 349
Goldfarb, Jean, 37
Gordon, J. E., 35, 36, 369

Gorlow, L., 392
government programs, 5, 21, 22, 369, 370, 371, 375
grandmother, *see* nonexistent grandmother
gratification, *see* reward
Greek-American family, 223n.
Guerney, B. G. Jr., 347, 392
Guerney, Louise, 392
guidance, 10, 11, 135, 152, 180, 189, 194, 217n., 222, 223, 224, 229, 235, 249, 265, 280, 309, 350, 355, 356, 357, 359; *see also* Verbal Behavior Analysis; Wiltwyck Family Interaction Apperception Technique; Wiltwyck Family Task
guilt, 60, 105, 132, 136, 205, 229

Haase, W., 32,
Haber, A., 21n.
Haley, J., 203n., 253n.
hard-core, *see* research population
Harlem, 21n., 23, 94
Harrington, M., 22, 23
Headstart, 377
helplessness, 11, 60, 106, 108–114, 148, 204, 208, 212, 215, 219, 240, 253, 259, 263, 267, 268, 359
Henry, Charlotte S., 38
here-and-now, 36, 43, 66, 86, 91, 113, 135, 208, 214, 234, 271, 288, 293–294
Herman, M., 369
Hess, R. D., 194
Higher Horizons, 30
Hoch, E. L., 392
hollering, 98–101, 251
Hollingshead, A. B., 34, 36
homeostasis, *see* rigidity
homosexuality, 6, 96, 239, 276, 386
hostility, 47, 114, 183, 184, 263
housing, public, 19n., 23, 140n.
Hunt, R. G., 34
Hunter, D. R., 35
husband, *see* spouse subsystem

iconic coding, 246n., 248
identity, sense of, 4, 6, 26, 133, 180, 183, 193, 194, 196–198, 201, 205, 209, 210, 212, 217n., 218, 220–223, 239, 260, 263, 363, 365, 366

illegitimacy, *see* motherhood, unwed
impulse, 26, 159*n*., 195, 215, 228, 266, 271, 281
individual therapy, 5, 10, 13, 35, 36, 145, 153, 284, 356, 363, 367
induction, 104, 165, 190, 258, 259, 275, 284, 285, 360
infantilism, 139, 165, 180, 228
inhibition, 194, 195, 260
inroads, 8, 9, 15, 20, 22, 35, 37, 43, 44, 45, 93, 100, 145, 175, 178, 190, 191, 244–245, 247, 248, 249, 250, 251, 252, 254, 259, 260, 261, 350, 355–356, 359–360, 362–363, 364, 367, 368, 369, 371, 372, 411
interaction, intensity of, 4, 140
interaction, tempo of, 4, 194, 198, 206, 215, 216, 220, 247, 266, 267, 271, 275, 276, 289, 357, 358, 359, 360
interaction of therapists, *see* cotherapy
interlocking, 354–360, 368
internalization, 194, 211, 217, 241, 255, 269
Interpersonal Rating Form, 16*n*.
interpretation, 224–225, 245, 248, 252, 258, 270, 296
intrapsychism, *see* psychotherapy, traditional
introspection, 16, 30, 36, 186, 248, 265, 266, 269, 271, 411
involvement, *see* contact
isolation, 24, 47, 53, 68–74, 97, 166–168, 228, 233, 241, 257, 263, 264, 273, 277, 354, 355, 367, 375
Israel, 24, 200*n*., 372–373
Italian-American family, 24, 27, 242; *see also* Brancusi family; Garibaldi family; Garota family; Menotti family; Romano family

Jackson, D., 203*n*.
Jaffe, J., 285*n*.
Jefferson family, 233–234
Jimmy, 3, 4, 192, 193
John, Vera, 30, 31, 32
Johnson, Adelaide M., 258*n*., 352*n*.
joint, *see* mutuality
Jones family, 234, 358, 381–382, 388–389
juvenile parents, 352, 365–368

Kagan, J., 195
Kahn, R. L., 34
King, C. H., 192*n*.
Kohn, M. L., 28
Kornbluh, Joyce L., 21*n*.
Kornhauser, A., 34
Kramer, P., 352*n*.
Kreuger, D. B., 34

labeling, 63, 65, 95, 170, 175, 176, 182, 184, 200*n*., 218, 251, 252, 253, 269, 279, 282, 284, 352, 356
Langner, T. S., 34
language, 26, 28*n*., 30, 31, 32, 36, 96*n*., 98, 99, 139, 190, 195, 198–200, 206*n*., 218, 257, 270, 278, 281, 285, 286, 358, 367, 369, 411
language, "physical," 247, 248
La Salle family, 38, 44, 45, 47, 137–190, 192, 232, 233, 250*n*., 254, 255, 286, 360, 383, 388–389
    George, 193, 209
    Mrs. La Salle, 209, 235, 273
La Sorte, M. A., 38
leadership, 79, 136, 180, 218, 254, 269; *See also* Wiltwyck Family Task
Leary, T., 17, 392
Lemkau, P. W., 34
Lennard, H. L., 392
Levine, Rachael A., 37
Lewis, H., 25
Lewis, O., 24
Lewis family, 233, 363, 382–383, 388–389
literacy, 16, 31, 97, 227, 299
love, *see* nurturance
low socioeconomic population, *see* research population
lower class, *see* working class
loyalty, 28*n*., 120–121, 228, 366

McCallister family, 210–211, 226–229, 287, 360, 385, 388–389
McMahon, J. T., 35
machismo, *see* masculinity
magical thinking, 27*n*., 135, 173, 288
males, *see* father, child's relationship to; masculine identity; masculinity; peripheral male
Malone, C. A., 25
marriage, 23, 24, 46, 50–57, 61–74, 75–

76, 82–83, 86–91, 95, 140*n.*, 229, 233, 234, 366; *see also* spouse subsystem
Martinez family, 206–209, 276–277, 287, 332*n.*, 363, 383–384, 388–389, 440–443
masculine identity, 23, 234–236, 257, 371
masculinity, 23, 235, 236, 238, 299
measurement techniques, *see* assessment
Menotti family, 257–258
mental illness, 25, 33, 34
Merton, R. K., 352*n.*
messages, content, 73, 96, 102, 103, 198–202, 204–206, 226, 246, 249, 250, 411
messages, implicit, 96, 103–104
messages, relationship, 99, 102, 198, 199, 201, 202, 205, 218, 220, 246, 249, 250, 308–309, 411
Mexican families, 24
Michael, S. T., 34
middle-class, 6, 22, 23, 25, 28*n.*, 29, 30, 33–37, 195, 198, 199, 201, 216, 219, 222, 241, 329, 361, 371, 372
migration, 23, 372–373
Miller, S. M., 24*n.*, 34
minority groups, 6, 13, 20, 22, 23; *see also* specific listings
Minuchin, S., 192*n.*, 347
Mishler, E. G., 34
mistrust, 47, 53, 60, 61–65, 80, 84, 85, 87, 88, 96, 114, 127, 132, 140, 165, 168, 190, 214, 264
model, 247, 276, 277, 295–296, 367
money, 23, 47, 61–65, 70, 86–88, 102, 114–127, 129–131, 133–135, 204, 208, 220, 234, 237, 300, 321, 328
monitor, 15, 45, 275, 276, 282, 286, 293, 295, 301, 376
monsters, fear of, 146, 152, 174
Montalvo, B., 192*n.*
Montgomery family, 38, 42, 44, 45, 47*n.*, 92–136, 192, 213, 234, 237, 252, 286, 360, 365, 386, 388–389
  Phyllis, 202, 231–232, 251
  Mrs. Montgomery, 231–232
  Richard, 193
mood, 43, 97, 98, 194, 206, 210, 220, 274, 275, 277, 278, 280, 282, 283, 286, 291, 350, 368
Morocean families, 372–373
Moss, H. A., 195
mother, child's relationship to, 4, 10,

203, 204–205, 207–219, 223, 229, 230–232, 234–236, 304–347 *passim*, 350, 374, 394–412 *passim*; *see also* specific families and profiles
motherhood, concept of, 10, 105, 151–152, 212, 214, 226, 227, 252, 356, 358
motherhood, unwed, 18, 94, 95, 101, 106–108, 140*n.*, 205, 223, 230, 233, 387
motility, 26, 27*n.*, 30, 31, 36, 37, 43, 140, 169, 195, 204, 228, 307, 367*n.*, 402, 411
motivation, 28*n.*, 31, 32, 57, 197, 230*n.*, 269, 377*n.*
Moynihan, D. P., 370–371
multi-problem, *see* research population
Murstein, B. I., 330
mutuality, 14, 62, 64–66, 69, 72, 74–82, 86, 89, 187, 220, 235, 264, 318, 321, 322, 328, 329, 341, 362, 365

Navarre, Elizabeth, 232*n.*
Negro, 6, 23, 32, 33, 95*n.*, 139, 196, 232–233, 236, 237, 242, 277, 330, 370–371; *see also* Brown family; Jones family; La Salle family; Lewis family; McCallister family; Montgomery family; Parrington family; Peters family; Smith family; Wainright family
neutrality, 56, 65, 281
New York City, 5, 6, 18, 46, 94, 133, 139, 172*n.*, 224*n.*, 372, 373, 382, 383, 384, 385–387
noise, 30, 43, 101, 136, 140, 142–144, 179, 199, 201, 202, 203, 246, 249, 250, 267, 268, 269, 286, 289, 306, 307, 358, 411
nondifferentiation, 26, 114, 116, 124, 154–155, 165, 169, 170*n.*, 179, 182, 189, 195, 198, 199, 205, 206,. 208, 209, 210, 212, 213, 216, 217, 220, 262, 271, 293, 309, 313, 325*n.*, 372
nonevolved parents, 352, 353, 364–368
nonexistent grandmother, 196, 230–232, 248, 259, 350, 364; *see also* La Salle family; Montgomery family
nonverbal, *see* behavior, nonverbal; communication
nuances, 193, 198, 208, 236, 246, 252, 279, 281, 286, 360
nurturance, 10, 28*n.*, 135, 136, 154–155, 165, 180, 189, 196, 201, 206, 208–211, 213, 217, 220, 223, 227, 229, 251, 280,

nurturance, (*cont'd*)
285, 301, 314, 315, 319, 320, 327, 328, 356, 359, 366; *see also* Wiltwyck Family Interaction Apperception Technique

obedience, 155, 170, 187, 231, 233, 234, 238, 257, 278, 316, 367*n*.; *see also* respeto
object constancy, 27*n*., 195, 196, 214
object, focus on, 57, 58, 59, 60, 125, 126, 127
observation, clinical, 15, 16, 17, 42, 245, 288, 298, 350
observation, intrafamily, 248, 262, 264–268, 270–272, 279, 281, 296, 356, 357, 360, 363, 364, 367
observation, self, 195–198, 265–266, 268–269, 271–272
Oedipal situation, 28*n*., 219, 240, 256, 362
one-to-one, *see* individual therapy
one-way mirror, 13*n*., 15, 204, 248, 261, 262, 266, 267, 269, 271, 281, 288, 299, 307, 360
Opler, M. K., 34
oscillation, 283, 284
outside world, 23, 32, 93, 103, 114, 120–122, 127–128, 132, 135, 140, 162, 164, 165–168, 170, 172, 173, 180, 190, 193, 198, 204, 212, 214, 216, 222, 223, 225, 228, 240, 242, 251, 272, 294, 338–339, 346, 351, 352, 355, 357, 359, 360, 368–377, 413
Overall, Betty, 36
overburdened, feeling of being, 11, 105, 108, 138–139, 148, 189, 194, 214–215, 217, 227, 228, 253, 354, 359, 366
overcrowding in family, 20, 22, 24, 27*n*., 30, 95*n*., 197, 200
Overton, Alice, 38

paramour, *see* peripheral male
paranoia, 62, 163, 358*n*., 387
parental child, 11, 162, 190, 219, 223, 226–228, 350, 355, 356, 357
Parrington family, 275–276, 280–283, 293
Parsons, T., 218–219, 232*n*.
Pasamanick, B., 34

passivity, 193, 227, 248, 354, 355, 358
Paterson, Floyd House, *see* Wiltwyck School for Boys
pathology, 9, 11, 19, 22, 23, 27, 33, 36, 44, 255, 259
pathway, 91, 203, 256–262, 264, 274, 283*n*., 291, 293, 294, 304, 350, 351, 352, 356, 357, 364, 368, 394–397, 407–409, 411
patriarchy, 236, 238, 372
Pavenstedt, Eleanor, 25, 26, 213*n*.
Pearl, A., 25*n*.
pecking order, 96*n*., 165; *see also* ranking
peer culture, 24, 28*n*., 73, 96*n*., 139, 180, 217*n*., 221*n*., 222–229, 233, 239, 374
peers, 11, 114, 244, 266, 267, 351, 362, 365, 366, 367
people, child's orientation toward, 26, 27*n*,. 194–195, 201, 203, 211, 213–214, 215, 216, 217, 372
perception, 5, 14, 16, 48, 111, 140, 148, 169, 173, 175, 184, 252, 262, 267, 268, 270, 276, 281, 283
sensory, 29–31
peripheral male, 10, 19, 27, 53, 70–72, 91–92, 94, 129–130, 138, 189, 196, 212, 219, 224, 230, 232–236, 239, 260–261, 280, 350, 352, 354, 356, 358, 359, 361–363, 376; *see also* Brown family; Garcia family; Lewis family; Martinez family
Peter, 3, 4, 192, 193
Peters family, 226
Pettigrew, T., 23, 232*n*.
play, 26, 28*n*., 29, 30, 229, 367*n*.
Pollack, M., 34
poverty, 6, 7, 13, 20, 21–38, 198
power, 11, 95, 96, 98, 99, 103, 104, 108, 136, 194, 198, 200, 201, 204, 211, 218, 223, 234, 240, 259, 260, 264, 267, 270, 272, 275, 276, 278, 280, 282, 284, 290, 316, 356, 358, 359, 360, 361, 372, 374; *see also* ranking
power of the poor, 24, 369, 372
predictability, 11, 26, 169, 193–194, 196, 198, 207, 211, 216, 223
primitive, 44, 165, 171, 200*n*., 209, 226, 248, 310, 354
problem solving, *see* conflict resolution
profiles, *see* family profiles

projection, 4, 120, 153, 258, 272, 329, 361; *see also* tests, projective
proximity, 155–158, 165, 179, 189, 190, 216, 229, 236, 250, 266, 286, 287, 289, 291, 296, 360
psychotherapy, traditional, 6, 9, 35, 36, 37, 38, 205, 214, 220, 238, 241, 258, 277, 279, 284, 351, 370, 407
Puerto Rican families, 6, 95*n.*, 139, 196, 207, 233, 236, 237–242, 272, 286, 330, 372, 373; *see also* Garcia family; Martinez family
punishment, 11, 26, 28*n.*, 104, 109, 139, 154, 189, 314, 315, 322, 326, 329, 335, 337, 340*n.*

quantification, *see* assessment, quantitative

Rabinowitz, Clara, 192*n.*
race, 22, 24, 32, 33, 329, 330; *see also* specific listings
ranking, 96, 103, 136, 165, 200, 201, 202, 204, 223, 269
reading, *see* literacy
reality, 6, 28*n.*, 31, 127, 146, 159, 165, 174, 176, 187, 188, 196, 198, 204, 205, 214, 225, 226, 252, 253, 274, 286, 290
rebellion, 60, 92, 95*n.*, 232, 235, 236, 253, 257, 263, 267, 356, 357, 358, 359, 360, 376
recording, 13*n.*, 14, 15, 43, 299, 301, 332; *see also* assessment, quantitative
Redlich, F. C., 34, 36
Reiff, R., 38
reinforcement, *see* support
relationship, *see* messages, relationship
religion, 22, 38, 55, 57, 68, 69, 71–74, 205, 240–241, 277, 381–388, 413
relinquishment, *see* delegation
Rennie, T. A. C., 34
rescue squad, 226–229
research families, *see* control families; experimental families
research families, selection of, 18–20
research population, 6, 13, 15, 16, 17, 20, 22, 23, 25, 26, 27, 28, 35, 36, 37, 38, 45, 48, 62*n.*, 168, 169, 190, 197, 198, 199, 200, 215, 242, 244, 245, 254, 266,

271, 277, 291, 330, 352, 361, 369, 370, 371, 373, 375, 376–378
Resnick, D., 33
resources, indigenous, 240–242
respeto, 49, 238, 257
response, affect, 309, 310, 322, 325
response, objective, 308–309, 310, 322, 325, 329
response, personal, 309, 310, 322, 325, 329
response time, 195
responsibility, 60, 62, 63, 71, 102, 108, 113, 120, 123, 124, 205, 213, 222, 227, 234, 235, 240, 241, 359, 365–367; *see also* Wiltwyck Family Interaction Apperception Technique
reward, 24, 26, 30, 197–198, 205, 223, 250, 268, 278, 370
Riessman, F., 25*n.*, 30*n.*, 32, 33, 37, 38
rigidity, 24, 206, 232, 255, 258, 259, 261, 268, 273, 274, 281, 285, 287, 291, 292, 294, 350, 351, 353–354, 358, 364, 365, 368
Roberts, D. W., 34
role organization, 24, 53, 94–95, 214, 218, 219, 220–221, 223, 226, 228, 230–231, 235, 237, 254, 255, 258, 259, 262, 265, 266, 268, 272, 280, 285, 287, 292, 295, 299–300, 349, 350, 351, 353, 356, 361, 364, 365, 367, 368, 374–375; *see also* specific listings
role playing, 33, 37
Romano family, 358, 382, 388–389
Rorschach Technique, 32–33
Rosman, Bernice, 347
Ross, Helen, 352
routine, 27*n.*, 28; *see also* predictability
routinization, *see* rigidity
Ruhig, T., 37
rules, *see* communication; internalization

Sadofsky, S., 369
scapegoat, 76, 94, 95, 114, 135, 180, 183, 226, 237, 255, 257, 258
Scheidlinger, S., 37
schizophrenia, 47, 382, 386, 387, 388
Schnachtel, E. G., 196
school, *see* education
Schumer, Florence, 32, 33, 330
scoring, *see* coding

Scott, J. P., 221n.
Scribner, Sylvia, 38
self-definition, see identity, sense of
self-esteem, 23, 197, 212, 221, 252, 267, 289
self-help, see power of the poor
self-image, 105, 106, 110, 149, 151, 152, 153, 189, 239, 240, 255, 263, 354
self-reliance, 6, 111, 131, 159
Semler, I. J., 32
sex, 18, 24, 47, 51–52, 65–68, 70, 89–91, 92, 94, 96, 156, 204, 217n., 218, 220, 233, 237, 238, 241, 263, 366, 367, 374, 386, 387
Sexton, Patricia C., 23, 369n.
Shapiro, M. I., 298
sharing, see mutuality
Shipman, Virginia C., 194
sibling subsystem, 11, 24, 44, 47n., 93, 121, 136, 140, 156, 157, 171, 173, 180, 184, 190, 196, 200, 204, 217n., 219, 221–229, 232, 254, 255, 267, 269, 281, 350, 356, 357, 358
Siegel, I. E., 195
Siegel, N. H., 34
Siegel, S., 305n., 306, 324, 326
signal, see communication
significant others, 101n., 128, 240, 272, 273
Singer, Margaret T., 308
skills: communicational, 65, 170, 190
employment, 31, 164, 376
slums, 4, 6, 22, 23, 24, 26, 27, 28, 95n., 127, 128, 139, 165–166, 170n., 192, 193, 204, 235, 238, 241, 372, 374
Smilansky, Sarah, 200n.
Smith family, 205, 213, 253, 267, 360, 384, 388–389
social network, 272–274
social status, 25n., 33
social worker talk, 247
socialization, 5, 9, 11, 23, 57, 59–60, 61, 77–81, 83–85, 92, 115, 117–118, 122, 126–127, 135, 136, 155, 162, 163, 168, 175, 189, 190, 194, 195, 206, 207, 208, 209–217, 219, 221, 222–224, 227, 229, 230, 232n., 233, 235, 242, 315, 325n., 339, 351–352, 357, 371, 373, 374
Sollenberger, R. T., 373
Spanish Harlem, 23

Spanish language, 13, 237; see also Garcia family
Speck, R. V., 274n.
Spiegel, J. P., 36, 223n.
spiritualists, see espiritistas
splits, 255, 263
spouse subsystem, 44, 47, 48–57, 60–71, 76, 77, 82, 83, 86–91, 92, 106, 196, 204, 219–221, 254, 258, 264, 268, 270, 277, 293, 350, 362, 365, 374
Srole, L., 34
stable poor, 6, 20, 22, 23, 25, 26, 27, 28, 167–168, 242, 355, 366
stages, 13–14, 15, 45, 254, 255, 350, 351, 404–407
stealing, 57–60, 76, 95, 96, 102, 114–127, 133, 134, 139, 204, 205, 212, 213, 224, 226, 233, 252, 266, 278, 383
stereotyping, 4, 5, 139, 193, 206, 237, 262, 282, 285, 291, 292, 295, 368
stimuli, 4, 193, 194, 197, 209, 216, 271, 289, 330
stimulus deprivation, 29, 199
streets, see slums
strengths of the poor, see culture of poverty
Strupp, H. H., 392
subgrouping, 7, 14, 203, 218, 262–263, 271, 272–273, 274, 277, 279, 302–329, 335–346, 351, 364, 368, 374, 395–412
subsystems, family, 14, 15, 228, 271, 292–293, 351, 360, 363; see also specific listings
suction, 44, 74, 103, 116, 120, 121, 136, 189, 250, 255–256, 258–259, 285, 287–288, 289, 290
Sullivan, H. S., 192, 221
superstition, 151, 413
support, 36, 37n., 182–184, 187, 190, 197, 223, 241, 248, 255, 259, 260, 264, 268, 270, 272, 273, 356, 365, 373, 377
suspicion, see mistrust
Sutherland, E. H., 352n.
symbolic coding, 246n., 247, 285
symbolism, 4, 86, 186, 216, 246
symmetric escalation, 203n.
Szurek, S. A., 258n., 352n.

tasks, interpersonal, 16, 17, 42, 241, 245, 248, 261–265, 268–271, 279, 294, 350

task orientation, 31
teasing, 158–159, 164, 180, 209, 210, 239, 276, 290
teaching, therapeutic, 249, 250, 251, 252, 270, 294, 296, 356, 367
Telschow, E. F., 392
tempo, *see* interaction, tempo of
testing, 9, 30, 31–33; *see also specific listings*
tests, intelligence, 9, 32
tests, objective, 31, 33
tests, projective, 8, 16, 17, 31, 32, 33, 42; *see also* Wiltwyck Family Interaction Apperception Technique
Thematic Apperception Test, 17, 33, 329–330
Thompson, 33
themes, 61, 82, 96, 97, 102, 114, 200, 201, 202, 204, 206, 218, 223, 237, 249, 251, 252, 253, 257, 260, 279, 281, 288, 289, 320, 368, 411
therapist, third, *see* cotherapy
therapists, 13–15, 42, 45*n.*, 97, 245
therapist's experiences, 289–291
time, 27*n.*, 30, 31, 32, 33, 170, 171, 183, 248, 284, 293, 357
Tinker, Katherine H., 38
training, *see* skills; socialization
transcription, 15, 45
truancy, 47, 95, 104–105, 139, 205, 226, 258, 382, 384, 386, 388
trust, *see* mistrust

units, *see* subgrouping
unstable poor, *see* research population

value systems, 11, 14, 30, 36, 108
Verbal Behavior Analysis, 8, 10, 12, 17, 203*n.*, 252, 391–420
　variables, coding, 414–420
　　aggression, 394, 399–400, 402, 404, 405, 406, 409, 410
　　control with negative response, 394, 399–400, 406, 409, 410
　　control with neutral or positive response, 394, 399, 400, 402, 404*n.*, 405, 406, 409, 410, 412
　　describes lack of role fulfillment, 394, 399, 400, 406, 409, 410

disagreement, 394, 399, 400, 401–402, 406, 407, 409, 410, 412
does not give information, 394, 399, 400, 404*n.*, 405, 406, 409, 410
exchange of information, 393, 398–401, 406, 407, 409, 410, 411
expresses negative feelings, 12, 393, 399, 400, 402, 403, 405, 406, 409, 410
expresses positive feelings, 12, 393, 399, 400, 402, 403, 406, 409, 410
guidance, 10, 11, 394, 399, 400, 402, 403, 404*n.*, 405, 406, 409, 410, 412
harmonious responses, 12, 393, 399, 400, 402, 403, 404*n.*, 405, 406, 409, 410
other, 394, 399, 400, 409, 410
requests control, guidance, or suggestion, 393, 399, 400, 405, 406, 409, 410
verbalization, 14, 16, 30, 32, 33, 36, 52, 55, 85, 91, 109, 152, 180, 189, 193, 199, 200, 201, 206, 207, 209, 221, 227, 229, 235, 246, 247, 250, 258, 259, 266, 268, 271, 293, 302, 304, 306, 309, 310, 323, 324, 329, 330, 332
violence, 3, 4, 128, 138, 174, 207, 228, 229, 233, 234, 235, 237
Visotsky, H. M., 35, 36

Wainright family, 358, 386, 388–389
waiting lists, 36, 37*n.*
Wang, R. P., 373*n.*
weak leader, 312, 325
Wechsler Intelligence Scale for Children Intelligence Quotient, 32, 47
welfare, 20, 21, 94, 127, 130, 133, 135, 137
Welfare, New York City Department of, 19, 20, 225, 234*n.*, 381–388
West Indies, *see* La Salle family
White, R. W., 195, 197
wife, *see* spouse subsystem
Wild, Cynthia, 308
Wilson, A. B., 377*n.*
Wilson family, 248, 259
Wiltwyck Family Interaction Apperception Technique, 8, 12, 16, 17, 33, 296, 298, 301, 329–347, 352, 392 436–443
　variables, coding, 443–450

Wiltwyck Family Interaction Apperception Technique (*cont'd*)
  affection, 12, 333, 334, 335, 339, 340, 344
  aggression, 12, 329, 333, 334, 335, 339, 340*n.*, 341, 344, 345, 346
    control, 10, 11, 12, 329, 333, 335, 336, 337, 338, 339, 342, 345
    cooperation, 333, 334, 335, 339, 340, 341, 344, 346
    family harmony, 333, 334, 335, 339, 341, 344, 345, 346
    guidance, 10, 329, 333, 335, 336–338, 342, 345
    nurturance, 329, 333, 335, 339, 340, 344, 345
    responsibility, acceptance of, 12, 333, 335, 336, 337, 342
Wiltwyck Family Task, 8, 17, 33, 203*n.*, 296, 298, 299–329, 333, 338, 341, 346–347, 352, 392, 421–424
  conflict clarity, 307–308, 323, 324, 329
  variables, coding, 424–435
    agreement, 302, 303, 305, 322, 324, 327, 329
    behavior control, 302, 303, 305, 306, 307, 310, 312, 313, 314, 315, 316, 318–319, 322, 324, 325, 327, 329

    disagreement, 12, 302, 303, 305, 319, 322, 324, 327, 329
    disruptive, 12, 302, 303, 305, 306, 307, 321, 323, 324, 329
    guidance, 302, 303, 306, 310, 312, 313, 314, 316, 319, 322, 325, 326, 327, 329
    leadership, 12, 302, 303, 305, 306, 307, 310, 318, 322, 324, 325, 327, 329
    request for leadership, control, guidance, 302, 303, 306, 311, 316, 317, 322, 324, 325, 326, 327, 329
    support for leadership, control, guidance, 302, 303, 311, 317, 318, 319, 322, 325, 327, 329
Wiltwyck School for Boys, 3, 5, 8, 9, 13, 18, 21*n.*, 45*n.*, 46*n.*, 47, 86, 94, 95, 137, 139, 147, 166, 171, 172, 173, 208, 210, 224, 229, 330, 332, 381–388, 413
Wolff, P. H., 195
working class, 6, 24, 25, 28, 31, 32, 33, 36, 219; *see also* stable poor
Wynne, L. C., 308

Yemenite families, 24, 372–373

Zubin, J., 32, 33, 330